The Crosscultural, Language, and Academic Development Handbook

SECOND EDITION

The Crosscultural, Language, and Academic Development Handbook

A Complete K–12 Reference Guide

Lynne T. Díaz-Rico
California State University, San Bernardino

Kathryn Z. Weed
California State University, San Bernardino

Allyn and Bacon

Boston ■ London ■ Toronto ■ Sydney ■ Tokyo ■ Singapore

Series Editor: *Aurora Martinez-Ramos*
Editorial Assistant: *Beth Slater*
Executive Marketing Managers: *Amy Cronin/Stephen Smith*
Manufacturing Buyer: *Julie McNeill*
Production Coordinator: *Pat Torelli Publishing Services*
Cover Designer: *Suzanne Harbison*
Editorial-Production Service: *Lynda Griffiths,* TKM Productions
Electronic Composition: *TKM Productions*

Copyright © 2002, 1995 by Allyn & Bacon
A Pearson Education Company
75 Arlington Street
Boston, MA 02116

Internet: www.ablongman.com

Library of Congress Cataloging-in-Publication Data

Díaz-Rico, Lynne T.
   The crosscultural, language, and academic development handbook : a complete K-12 reference guide / Lynne T. Díaz-Rico, Kathryn Z. Weed. --2nd ed.
      p. cm.
   Includes bibliographical references (p.) and indexes.
   ISBN 0-205-33685-X
   1. English language--Study and teaching (Higher)--Foreign speakers--Handbooks, manuals, etc. 2. Multicultural education--United States--Handbooks, manuals, etc. 3. Language and education--United States--Handbooks, manuals, etc. 4. Education, Bilingual--United States--Handbooks, manuals, etc. I. Weed, Kathryn Z. II. Title.

PE1128.A2 D45 2001
428'.007'173--dc21   2001034095

Printed in the United States of America

10   9   8   7   6   05   04   03

*To Phillip, with deepest thanks, for his wisdom, love, and understanding;
to Eva, Daniel, and Voltaire, for their companionship and humor;
and to my friends, students, and colleagues who study, struggle, and
learn alongside me.*

*To Steve, Diana, and Timothy for their continuing love and support, and to
my friends, students, and colleagues in Dakar, Senegal, and Hermosillo,
Sonora, Mexico—insightful English (and other language) learners all.*

CONTENTS

PART FOUR   Language Planning and Special Populations

11 The Role of Educators in Language Planning and Policy   266

12   English Learners and Special Education   284

ACKNOWLEDGMENTS

This book could not have been written without the help and support of numerous individuals. The teachers and students with whom we have worked have given us insights and examples, and our colleagues have shared their experiences and expertise. In addition to those who gave so much of their time, expertise, and support to our first edition, we also thank those who have made this second edition a reality. We owe a tremendous debt to the California Commission on Teacher Credentialing under the leadership of Priscilla Walton and to the Bilingual Crosscultural Advisory Committee for their work in designing California's CLAD credential. Lynne thanks the teacher education and TESOL masters' students at CSUSB who have enriched her understanding of the teaching/learning process as it relates to second language learners. Thanks also go to the second language students, teacher education students, and EFL teachers Kathy worked with at the Ecole Normale Supérieure in Dakar, Senegal, and at the University of Sonora in Hermosillo, Mexico, who provided further insights into the realities of second language acquisition and second language teaching.

We are grateful also to Yvette Verdugo Figueroa, head of the foreign language department of the University of Sonora, for her critique of Chapter 6 and to Sofia Cota, coordinator of the B.A. program in English Language Teaching at the University of Sonora, for her insights into Chapter 4. In addition, we extend our gratitude to the following reviewers for their helpful comments: Melissa Aronson, California State University, Stanislaus; Lu Chang, College of Notre Dame; Judy Cortes, California State University, Monterey Bay; and Stephanie Jacobson, Chapman University, San Diego Campus.

To all those who have provided linguistic and cultural support not only to English learners but also to those who have struggled to acquire a second language and adapt to a new culture, we salute you. To the researchers and authors who provided valuable insights into this process, our deepest thanks for your pioneering efforts. Finally, we thank the editors at Allyn and Bacon for their efforts in producing this *Handbook*.

ABOUT THE AUTHORS

Lynne T. Díaz-Rico is professor of education, California State University, San Bernardino (CSUSB). Dr. Díaz-Rico obtained the doctoral degree in English as a Second Language at InterAmerican University in Puerto Rico and has taught students at all levels from kindergarten to high school. At CSUSB, Dr. Díaz-Rico is coordinator of the Masters in Education, Teaching English to Speakers of Other Language Option program. She is actively involved in teacher education and gives presentations at numerous professional conferences on such subjects as intercultural education, computer-assisted language instruction, and cultural diversity. Her current research interests are in the areas of language use in complex, particularly crosscultural, contexts.

Kathryn Z. Weed is associate professor of education at California State University San Bernardino. Prior to completing her Ph.D. in Education at Claremont Graduate University, Dr. Weed spent 15 years as an EFL and ESL teacher. In 1997, she was a Fulbright Scholar to the Ecole Normale Supérieure in Dakar, Senegal. From 1999 to 2001, she taught at the University of Sonora in Hermosillo, Mexico, and worked with CSUSB student teachers at a local bilingual elementary school. Dr. Weed continues her research and publications in language acquisition in schools and language-enhancing teaching practices.

INTRODUCTION

The presence of many linguistic and ethnic minority students in the United States has challenged educators to rethink basic assumptions about schooling. School models and methods based on the notions that students share the same cultural background, speak the same language, and have the same academic preparation are no longer sufficient to meet the needs of today's students. The urgent need to provide a high-quality education for students in the United States whose native language is not English calls for increased expertise on the part of classroom teachers, administrators, and community leaders.

In the past, schools were designed to educate specialists (those students who were capable of completing graduate study); professionals (those students who completed college study and obtained white-collar employment); and blue-collar workers who may or may not have graduated from high school. Those who could not succeed in school generally could find a place in society, although not always with secure employment. For the most part, those students who found professional or specialist positions in society represented a similar cultural background—that of the White middle class. Schools reflected the values and habits of this class; little wonder, then, that students with this background were the most successful.

Today's students come from diverse cultural backgrounds. They, like their traditional predecessors, aspire to economic and social success and view schools as the means to accomplish their dreams. But are schools accommodating them? The cultural patterns of schools and classrooms may not ensure that all students have equal opportunity to succeed. Culture is a part of the educational process that has been invisible but that can no longer remain so. Through an understanding of the influence of culture, educators can avoid inadvertently advantaging those students who share the dominant culture, while neglecting those students whose cultures differ from the mainstream. Culture includes more than the habits and beliefs of students and teachers; the school itself is a culture in which the physical environment, daily routines, and interactions advantage some and alienate others. Educators now need a foundation of cultural awareness in order to adapt schools to the needs of multicultural students.

Similarly, schools in the United States were generally designed to educate students whose native language was English. Students whose home language was other than English were expected to succeed without special language assistance. This sink-or-swim approach functioned in a simple manner: Those with the ability to understand English "swam," and those who could not "sank." Luckily, those with poor English skills could often find adequate employment without advanced schooling. In today's complex society, however, those without schooling often are offered employment at barely minimum wage, and jobs at the high end of the technological scale are well beyond their grasp.

In the sink-or-swim approach, there was general naiveté about the role of language in learning and a lack of understanding about language acquisition pro-

1

cesses. The principal belief in the approach was that exposure to English was the means to learn it. More was better (the more exposure to the English language, the more rapid students' advancement). If schools recognized a need for English language instruction, such instruction took on a compensatory quality. Students without English language skills were deemed deficient, and remediation was prescribed. English as a second language (ESL) was considered a remedial curriculum—one that often emphasized grammatical accuracy, correct spelling, and flawless pronunciation. However, many language minority students did not find success in public school despite many years of instruction in English.

Language acquisition research findings now stress the importance of language in providing a cognitive foundation for instruction—a foundation that must be laid properly. Language and academic development is better approached through a respect for, and incorporation of, a student's primary language. Moreover, an emphasis on grammar, spelling, and accurate pronunciation is secondary to the primary purpose of language instruction: to teach students to communicate and to function in society. To help students attain their goals, educators now need a foundation of language acquisition and development principles and knowledge of language development methodology in order to adapt instruction to the needs of multilingual students.

One exciting advance in teaching methodology in classes with English learners is the increased use of Specially Designed Academic Instruction in English (SDAIE). Rather than relying heavily on lectures to transmit information, teachers are using cooperative learning, audiovisual media, multicultural sources, various grouping strategies within and across grades, and other instructional techniques that help motivate students to learn English as they learn academic content. Although schools with large numbers of immigrants from specific language groups are able to schedule classes in academic subjects using the students' home language, schools with a linguistically diverse student body can offer special "sheltered" sections of academic subjects in which English skills and academic content are developed simultaneously. Teachers who use SDAIE techniques find that mainstream students benefit as well. Many of the instructional modifications designed to benefit English learners may, in fact, improve the learning for all students.

Crosscultural, Language, and Academic Development: A Model for Teacher Preparation

Much has been written that serves as general and specific information about the effect of culture on schooling, second language acquisition, and ways to help English learners achieve access to the core curriculum. In order to synthesize this wealth of information, a means of organizing this knowledge is needed. The central elements that tie together culture, language, and academic achievement in the context of education are the learning that takes place, the instruction that promotes learning, and the policies that govern schooling. Figure I.1 combines these elements to illustrate their influence and interdependence on one another.

In the figure, *learning* occupies the central area. Learning is subdivided into *domains* and *factors*. The three domains are culture, language, and academic content. The factors are the language acquisition processes, psychological and sociolinguistic influences, and the structure of the language being learned. Within the cultural context, all learning is affected by instruction and policies. Understanding the nature and interdependence of the domains and factors helps teachers to meet the needs of individual learners. Learning is discussed in Part One.

Instruction is the second major area that organizes knowledge about teaching English learners. This term refers to both the *curriculum* and the *methods* employed in classrooms. Curricular content is determined at various levels (state, district, school, classroom) and is interpreted differently by teachers and students (the "taught" curriculum and the "received" curriculum). This book provides examples of curricular content in the context of second language acquisition but does not attempt an exhaustive presentation. Methods are the manner in which curriculum is taught. Current understanding about language acquisition has revolutionized traditional language methodology. Methods for English language learners fall into three categories: English language instruction, specially designed academic instruction in English (also known as sheltered instruction), and primary language instruction within bilingual education models. These are covered in Part Two.

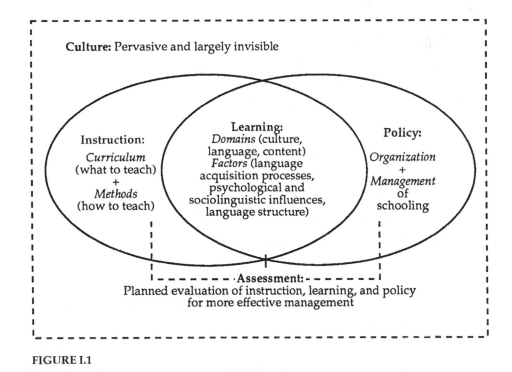

FIGURE I.1

Assessment practices are influenced by instruction and policymaking, and assessment, in turn, affects learning. Assessment of students is the way to determine if curricular content is appropriate and teaching methods are successful. Through assessment, one can ascertain what learning has taken place. The placement of students as a function of assessment influences the organization and management of schooling; thus, assessment involves not only issues of instruction and learning but also policy. Assessment is also covered in Part Two.

The third area, *policy*, denotes the *organization* and *management* of schooling, elements that affect the operation of schools. Policy can be top down, driven by national or state agendas. Conversely, policy can be bottom up, as an outgrowth of teachers' daily plans. Because the policies affecting schooling can be better understood with a background on the influence and importance of culture, policy for English learners is discussed in Part Four.

Culture permeates the activities of learning, instruction, and policymaking. Fundamental insights into the nature of culture, the influence of culture on schools, a brief history of cultural and immigration policies in the United States, and the means for learning about cultures and culturally appropriate pedagogy are provided in Part Three.

Chapter 12 discusses policies and practices in the relationship between English language development (ELD) services and special education. The chapter addresses effective curriculum, teaching methods, assessment, organization, and management of instruction.

Teachers can be resources within their schools and districts on matters pertaining to English language and academic development for their multicultural and multilinguistic students. A framework that organizes crosscultural, language, and academic development in terms of learning, instruction, and policy contributes to teachers' abilities to describe, communicate, and teach others about this field.

Overview

This book brings together theories and resources in promoting crosscultural awareness, language development, and academic progress. Part One offers insights from classic and contemporary research in language acquisition and development (Chapter 1), particularly in the context of the classroom. A focus on psychological factors in language learning encourages the recognition that language learners are individuals; attention to sociocultural factors extends this understanding to acknowledge that individuals sharing similar cultural patterns may learn in similar ways (Chapter 2). Chapter 3 introduces language structure and functions.

Part Two examines English language development (ELD) methods (Chapter 4) and models of schooling for language instruction and academic development (Chapters 5 and 6). The key role of assessment in determining academic progress is discussed in the context of curriculum design (Chapter 7).

Part Three contains a broad look at culture, exploring how culture influences every aspect of life, including schooling (Chapter 8), and offering a historical background on cultural diversity and its treatment in the United States (Chapter 9). Specific insights for classroom teachers on the use and understanding of culture are available in Chapter 10.

Language policies and specific program models constitute Part Four. Rather than summarizing the policy "big picture"—at the national or state level—Chapter 11 begins with the role of the classroom teacher in daily policymaking, and proceeds from that level to a more comprehensive overview. Chapter 12 contains a description of the issues surrounding identification and referral of English learners to special school services.

Care has been taken to use acceptable terminology to denote various racial and ethnic groups. The terms *Hispanic* and *Hispanic American* denote those whose ancestors originated in Spain or Spanish America. Although some dislike this term, it is probably preferable to any alternative (Hernández, 1993). *European American* is used in preference to *White* or *Anglo* to denote those whose ancestral background is European. *African American* is similarly used to refer to those whose ancestors came from Africa. Other ethnic group labels follow a similar logic. In some cases, data are cited that classify groups according to other labels; in these cases, the labels used in the citation are preserved.

In addition to the changes in terminology for racial and ethnic groups, terminology for students learning English has undergone change. Over the years, these students have been called *language minority, limited-English proficient (LEP), non-English-proficient (NEP), English-as-a-second language (ESL) learners, English language learners (ELL),* and *learners of English as a new language.* In this book the term *English learner* is used to designate students who are learning English as an additional language, and classrooms and programs that promote English learners' language and academic learning are designated as *English language development (ELD).*

Burgeoning information in the areas of culture and linguistic/academic development has made the second edition of *The Crosscultural, Language, and Academic Development Handbook* a difficult yet useful synthesis. The result, we believe, is a readable text that brings into focus the challenges and possibilities in educating new Americans. We hope this *Handbook* will be beneficial in the process of teacher preparation and school restructuring. Principles and practices that promote crosscultural understanding are relevant for all. Knowledge about second language acquisition helps not only those working with English learners but also anyone in the teaching field. Studying language acquisition involves processes and principles that are appropriate across the curriculum. Principles of specially designed academic instruction are, in reality, principles that constitute good teaching.

No handbook about teaching is ever vital enough to reflect the actual experience of the classroom, replete with challenges and triumphs for teachers as well as students. The reward for educators in the skillful use of this *Handbook* will be the success of students, and students' success is the ultimate measure of the worth of this work.

Second Language Acquisition and Learning

Theory and Practice

Without communication the world would be so dark. Life would be boring. It is through language that we find a way into people's hearts, their lives, and their culture. Through language we explore into the secrets of other cultures.

I was born in Afghanistan. . . . I came to the United States when I was sixteen years old. This was my new home and yet, because I could not speak any English, I was a stranger to my new home. How I wished to express my gratitude to people who helped my family and me, but all I could do was to give them an empty look and a confused smile. I was living among the people and yet I was not one of them. I thought everybody was cold and unfriendly. Sometimes I got angry and wanted to scream at the whole world.

Slowly the ice broke. I started learning English. New windows started opening. The once cold and unfriendly became warm and caring. My family and I found a way into the hearts of the people.

—Ahmad Shukoor, grade 12, in Shukoor, 1991, p. 34

Language is largely responsible for the human ability to form a society. Schools, as an institution within a society, perform an important role in socializing students and helping them gain the knowledge and skills they need for success. Schools help students to acquire the roles and identities within the larger culture and to maintain social relationships. In the majority of schools of the United States, the English language is the dominant vehicle for expression. Students who enter school must develop a high level of English proficiency, and teachers are challenged to develop English skills during the K–12 period of schooling. With the influx of large numbers of students who speak languages other than English, schools are seeking teachers who not only can help students develop literacy, but also can teach the fundamentals of speaking and listening to those students.

The challenge is obvious, the prospect exciting. Teachers have the opportunity to guide and inspire English learners in new ways; to learn about their students, their lives and cultures, their dreams and expectations; and to expand their own teaching repertoire. By knowing about language acquisition and use, teachers (particularly those who are monolingual) can come to recognize and use communication strategies that help break down barriers. Collaboration and cooperation with students, parents, and community members enrich the lives of all. Classrooms become lively and productive places.

To begin the teacher's introduction to the study of language, this chapter presents an overview of historical and contemporary theories of teaching and learning that will help the teacher place issues of English language development within an orienting framework.

Historical Theories of Language Development

Humans have been describing and analyzing language for over 2,300 years. As early as the fourth century B.C., Greek philosophers were debating the nature of language. Early theory held that words were the natural and logical representations of ideas and objects, rather than arbitrarily chosen symbols. The early Greeks identified two classes of words, one that identified the action performed in a sentence and one that identified the person or thing that performs the action. In about the second century B.C., Dionysius Thrax identified eight different word classes. His book, *The Art of Grammar*, became a model for both Greek and Latin grammars. Latin was the model for grammar throughout the Middle Ages. When grammarians finally began writing grammars for vernacular languages, they generally copied the Latin grammars, using the same terminology and the same word classes (Kitzhaber et al., 1970).

Prescriptive Grammar

Grammarians who believed there were certain "correct" forms when using a language proceeded to write prescriptive grammars. Using Latin grammar as a model, English grammarians not only ignored the syntactic differences between Latin and English but also tried to force English to fit the Latin description. Moreover, in copying from the Latin, they limited themselves to using classical grammar to prescribe how language should be used. No effort was made to describe the nature of language or how people use it (Kitzhaber et al., 1970).

This approach to language led to the grammar-translation method of instruction, in which learners memorized long lists of vocabulary words, verb forms, and noun declensions. The chief activity in class was to translate written texts. Teachers were not expected to speak the language, but merely to have a thorough knowledge of grammatical rules.

Descriptive Linguistics

In the eighteenth and nineteenth centuries, scholars began to notice similarities that existed among some ancient languages. Studying written documents of earlier forms of languages, they traced the origin of words and sounds and attempted to show particular changes languages had undergone over time and the historical relationships among various languages. These linguists analyzed the sound units of a language, showed how these units were organized, and described the structure of sentences. The descriptive linguists developed a method for identifying the speech sounds of languages, for analyzing words into morphemes, and for analyzing the forms of sentences. They did not concern themselves with describing the meaning of sentences or how they relate to each other.

Diagramming sentences became an important pedagogical tool based on the language descriptions. Teachers began the analysis of sentences by dividing sentences into two parts, or constituents, each of which could be further subdivided, until the entire sentence had been analyzed. Knowledge of the structure of one language was believed to transfer to a second language. Furthermore, it was believed that a thorough understanding of the phonetic basis of the first language could help to contrast the phonemic constituents of the target language. Knowing about the structure of the first and second language was an important part of the teacher's role, so that the second language could be explained in terms of the first.

Behaviorist Theory

Although behaviorism is not strictly a linguistic theory, its vast influence on learning theory has affected second language teaching. Behaviorists claim that the mind is a "blank slate"; a learner must be filled with content during the course of teaching. Strict principles of timing, repetition, and reward led to classroom methodology that incorporated extensive drill and practice of language components—from sounds to complex sentences.

The audiolingual method of language learning is based on behavioral principles. Oral language practice is believed to be the primary means to language learning. Teachers provide constant oral pattern drills that are based on specific grammatical forms; for example, a complete lesson can be centered around the tag question (It's cold today, *isn't it?*). Meaning is not specifically addressed, only the appropriate form.

Current Theories of Language Development

Starting in the mid-twentieth century, several important new theories have shaped current understanding of language acquisition and development. The prevailing belief, promulgated in B. F. Skinner's book *Verbal Behavior* (1957), held that language is learned through constant verbal input shaped by reinforcement. This notion was refuted by Noam Chomsky (1959) in an incisive review of Skinner's book. Chomsky asserted that if language were learned solely by reinforcement, native speakers would find it impossible to understand sentences that they had never before heard. He claimed that language is not learned solely through a process of memorizing and repeating, but that the mind contains an active language processor, the language acquisition device (LAD), that generates rules through the unconscious acquisition of grammar. Hymes (1961) directed attention away from the purely descriptive linguistic approach or structural analysis of language toward the idea of communicative competence: that the *use* of language in the social setting is important in language performance. Halliday (1975) elaborated on the role of social relations in language by stating that the social structure is an essential element in linguistic interaction. Current theories of language have thus moved away from the merely linguistic components of a language to the more inclusive realm of language in use—which includes its social, political, and psychological domains.

Along with the previously mentioned broadening of concepts about the nature of language, language teaching itself is being shaped by several important ideas. First, the shift toward a cognitive paradigm means that *learning* has taken precedence over *teaching*. What the student learns is the important outcome of the teaching/learning process, not what the teacher does. Second, teaching/learning is maximized when it is compatible with the processes that take place naturally within the brain. Third, thematic integration now often unites teaching objectives across content areas as well as unifies the language processes of reading, writing, speaking, listening, thinking, and acting. These changes in thinking about language learning began in the late 1950s with the birth of the cognitive perspective and information-processing theories of learning. Chomsky's work on transformational grammar was an important impetus.

Transformational Grammar

Transformational grammarians, following Chomsky's lead, assume that language consists of a set of rules that human beings unconsciously know and use. They believe that human beings, once exposed to the language(s) of their environment, use their innate ability to understand and produce sentences they have never before heard because the mind has the capacity to internalize and construct these rules. According to this view, human beings do not need prior experience with a particular sentence in order to produce or understand it. The rules help native speakers distinguish whether a group of words forms a sentence in their language. The goal of transformational grammar is to understand and describe these internalized rules.

In the early 1970s, some grammar texts created for the use of classroom teachers included the use of transformational grammar to explain language structures. Much research has been published about children's acquisition of language using the transformational paradigm. Although this paradigm never became a second language teaching methodology per se, much of Krashen's Monitor Model can be traced to Chomsky's influence.

Krashen's Monitor Model

Krashen (1981, 1982) has proposed a theory of second language acquisition that provides a framework for understanding the processes by which adults learn second languages. Krashen's theory includes five hypotheses: the *acquisition-learning hypothesis,* which distinguishes acquisition (which leads to fluency) from learning (which involves knowledge of language rules); the *natural order hypothesis,* which asserts that language rules are acquired in a predictable order; the *monitor hypothesis,* which postulates a device for attaining accuracy; the *input hypothesis,* which claims that languages are acquired in only one way—by comprehending messages; and the *affective filter hypothesis,* which describes the mental and emotional blocks that can prevent language acquirers from fully comprehending input. Briefly, Krashen's theory states that people acquire second language structures in a predictable order only if they obtain comprehensible input, and if their affective filters are low enough to allow input into the system. A *monitor* edits language usage. Although the Monitor Model has been extensively criticized, it has nonetheless provided the theoretical base for the Natural Approach, which has had an extensive impact in changing the nature of second language instruction in the United States.

The Acquisition-Learning Hypothesis.   This hypothesis defines *acquisition* and *learning* as two separate processes in the mastering of a second language. Learning is "knowing about" a language. It is the formal knowledge one has of a second language. Formal teaching promotes learning by providing the learner with explicit knowledge about the rules of a language. Acquisition, on the other hand, is an unconscious process that occurs when language is used for real communication. Formal teaching of grammatical rules is not a part of acquisition (Krashen, 1981, 1982, 1985). Acquirers gain a "feel" for the correctness of their own utterances but cannot state any specific rules as to why such utterances are "correct."

Krashen distinguishes the role each process plays, but considers acquisition more important. He turns to child language acquisition studies to strengthen his point. "Research in child language acquisition suggests quite strongly that teaching [the rules of a language] . . . does not facilitate acquisition. Error correction in particular does not seem to help" (Krashen & Terrell, 1983, p. 27).

As with any theory, this one too has its detractors. Some find the distinction between learning and acquisition vague or difficult to prove (Af Trampe, 1994; Ellis, 1986). Others find it misleading (McLaughlin, 1990) and still others criticize its assumption that the processes of first and second language acquisition are the same (Dunlop, 1994).

Despite these criticisms, for the classroom teacher, Krashen's distinction between acquisition and learning is important in that teachers acknowledge the fact that students will produce some language unself-consciously and will need rules and help for others. Thus, when children chat with one another as they stroke the classroom pet rabbit or recreate meiosis with modeling, they are learning language; and the alert teacher, hearing their discussions, will emphasize specific troublesome spots in subsequent language lessons. In this way, students learn language while actively engaged in other pursuits, and the teacher is able to use the students' errors as an impetus to improving their language.

The Natural Order Hypothesis.   This hypothesis draws on studies done in first and second language acquisition of children. According to this hypothesis, certain rules of the language tend to be acquired before others. Following first language acquisition work done by Brown (1973), second language researchers have discovered that there appears to be a natural order of acquisition of English morphemes for child second language learners also. The order is slightly different from the first language order, but there are similarities.

Here is an example of the developmental sequence for the structure of negation:

1. Negative marker outside the sentence
   Not a teddy bear.   (L1 acquisition)
   Not like it now.   (L2 acquisition)
2. Negative marker between the subject and verb
   He no bite you.   (L1 acquisition)
   I no like this one.   (L2 acquisition)
3. Negative marker in correct position
   I don't like this one. (Dulay, Burt, & Krashen, 1982, p. 124)

This example demonstrates that children acquire correct usage of grammatical structures in their first language (L1) gradually, and so do children acquiring a second language (L2).

Again, critics argue that there is insufficient evidence for the natural order hypothesis, claiming there is too much variability in the learners' contexts to support the notion of a predictable order of acquisition (Ellis, 1994; McLaughlin, 1987). For the classroom teacher, however, the importance of this hypothesis is the fact that learners go through a process to achieve full control of a structure and that language learners seem to find order by seeking patterns from the input they see and hear. A teacher cannot expect perfect formation of a grammatical structure even after intensive drilling.

The Monitor Hypothesis.   This hypothesis states explicitly the relationship between acquisition and learning: Acquisition initiates an utterance and is responsible for fluency; learning serves to develop a monitor, an editor (Krashen, 1981, 1982). The monitor is an error-detecting mechanism; it scans utterances for accuracy in order to make corrections. An individual initiates an utterance and that individual's monitor edits—that is, confirms or repairs—the utterance either prior to or after attempted communication. However, the monitor cannot always be used. In a situation involving rapid verbal exchange, an individual may have little time to be concerned with grammatical correctness.

The monitor hypothesis, however, is not without flaws. The monitor is impossible to observe or distinguish during its use (Shannon, 1994). Krashen's claim that children are more successful language learners because they are not burdened by the monitor is disputed by McLaughlin (1987), who argues that adolescents are more successful learners than are children. Thus, for many theorists, the usefulness of the monitor as a construct is disputed.

Despite these objections, however, Krashen, through his monitor construct, has changed the orientation that previously drove language instruction. The notion that language learning, the conscious knowledge of rules, leads to language acquisition has been replaced by the realization that a "natural" language-rich environment facilitates acquisition. Additional mediation can be provided for students in the form of specific suggestions or explicit grammatical hints, but these specific lessons are interspersed throughout a general communicative environment.

The Input Hypothesis. The input hypothesis claims that language is acquired in an "amazingly simple way—when we understand messages" (Krashen, 1985, p. vii). Language is acquired, not by focusing on form, but by understanding messages. But what kind of messages? Contrary to popular belief, simply immersing a learner in a second language is not sufficient. Imagine, for example, listening to Finnish on the radio. Unless the listener had some knowledge of that language beforehand, there would be no way to understand words or even topics. Language must contain what Krashen calls "comprehensible" input.

Comprehensible input has generally been assumed to contain elements characteristic of "caretaker" speech, the speech directed to young children by their primary caregivers. This caretaker speech (which includes shorter sentences; more intelligible, well-formed utterances; less subordination; and more restricted vocabulary and range of topics) focuses on communication. It is not meant to teach language. Topics often center about the here and now. Simpler structures roughly tuned to the child's ability are used, and speech is slower.

However, caretaker speech is not a universal phenomenon. Other languages and cultures use context, world knowledge, and extralinguistic information to help in comprehensibility. The African American children studied by Heath (1983b) received a large amount of exposure to language. The Samoan children in Ochs's study (1982) heard conversations that focused on the immediate past (accusations), the immediate present, and an immediate future (directives). Guatemalan children studied by Harkness (1971) benefited by a variety of input sources. Thus, simplified language may not be the central criterion in making language comprehensible; rather, the focus on the message and its relevance for the language learner within the environment appear to be more critical.

To conceptualize the input hypothesis, Krashen introduced the expression $i + 1$, where i stands for the current level of the acquirer's competence and 1 is the next structure due to be acquired in the natural order. Input needs to contain structures at the $i + 1$ level in order for the acquirer to proceed. However, research in first and second language acquisition, including that of caretaker speech, indicates that such speech is not what Krashen calls "finely tuned"—that is, including only structures at the $i + 1$ level.

Critics have pointed out that there is in fact no way of measuring the $i + 1$ level. Therefore, it is impossible to tell what "comprehensible input" really means. As Marton (1994) points out, Krashen's emphasis on comprehensible input ignores the active role of the learner in communicating and negotiating useful and understandable language.

For the classroom teacher, the relevance of this hypothesis lies in its emphasis on "comprehensible." Teachers' general training prepares them to help students understand. When working with English learners, teachers need to use a variety of techniques and modalities, including visual and kinesthetic, to ensure their speech is comprehensible.

The Affective Filter Hypothesis.   This hypothesis relates to emotional variables, including anxiety, motivation, and self-confidence. These are crucial because they can block input from reaching the language acquisition device (LAD). If the affective filter blocks some of the comprehensible input, less input enters the learner's LAD, and thus less language is learned. A positive affective context increases the input. These emotional variables are discussed in Chapter 2. Like others of Krashen's hypotheses, the affective filter is virtually impossible to define operationally. Larsen-Freeman and Long (1991) contend that the affective filter is useful only as a metaphor. Most teachers understand that a nonthreatening and encouraging environment promotes learning. Moskowitz's (1978) *Caring and Sharing in the Foreign Language Classroom* offers techniques designed to relax students, increase the enjoyment of learning, raise self-esteem, and blend self-awareness with an increase in proficiency in the target language.

Communicative Competence

Since Hymes (1972) introduced the term *communicative competence,* the notion of what is involved in knowing a language has expanded. Communicative competence is the aspect of language users' competence, their knowledge of the language, that enables them to "convey and interpret messages and to negotiate meanings interpersonally within specific contexts" (Brown, 1987). Language is a form of communication that occurs in social interaction. It is used for a purpose, such as persuading, commanding, and establishing social relationships. Knowing a language is no longer seen as merely knowing grammatical forms. Instead, the competent speaker is recognized as one who knows when, where, and how to use language appropriately.

Canale (1983) identifies four components of communicative competence: grammatical competence, sociolinguistic competence, discourse competence, and strategic competence.

Grammatical Competence.   This component involves knowing the language code: vocabulary, word formation and meaning, sentence formation, pronunciation, and spelling. This type of competence focuses on the skills and knowledge necessary to speak and write accurately. Although an emphasis on fluency and vocabulary acquisition rather than on grammatical accuracy is preferable in the early stages of language learning, there is no question that grammatical competence becomes increasingly important to the English learner in more advanced stages of proficiency.

Sociolinguistic Competence.   This involves knowing how to produce and understand language in different sociolinguistic contexts, taking into consideration such factors as the status of participants, the purposes of the interaction, and the norms or conventions of interaction. The appropriateness of an utterance refers to both meaning and form. One of the tasks of kindergarten and first-grade teachers is to help children use both appropriate forms and appropriate meanings when interacting in the classroom. Unfortunately, in language classrooms, emphasis has been placed on grammatical competence over sociolinguistic competence. This emphasis gives the mistaken impression that grammatical correctness is more important than sociolinguistic competence.

Discourse Competence.   This involves the ability to combine and connect utterances (spoken) and sentences (written) into a meaningful whole. Discourse ranges from a simple spoken conversation to long written texts. An example of discourse competence can be seen in the following conversation between two kindergarten boys, one a native English speaker and the other an English learner:

> ANDREW: Can I play?
>
> ROLANDO: No.
>
> ANDREW: There are only 3 people here.
>
> ROLANDO: Kevin went to the bathroom.
>
> ANDREW: Can I take his place 'til he comes back?
>
> ROLANDO: You're not playing.

Rolando was able to respond appropriately (though not kindly) to Andrew's request and to add information about his decision at the proper moment. This conversation shows that Rolando has discourse competence. We have all experienced situations in which a speaker has spoken both grammatically correctly and at the proper time, but the utterance has left us mystified. "Where did that come from?" we ask. Such a disconnected utterance shows a lack of discourse competence.

Strategic Competence.   Strategic competence involves the manipulation of language in order to meet communicative goals. It involves both verbal and nonverbal behaviors. Canale (1983) notes that speakers employ this competence for two main reasons: to compensate for breakdowns in communication (as when a speaker forgets or does not know a term and is forced to paraphrase or gesture to get the idea across) and to enhance the effectiveness of communication (as when a speaker raises or lowers the voice for effect).

Use of this competence occurred when one of the authors (Weed) was taking an oral Spanish exam. The tester asked her to read a poem and then explain it. Everything but the main word, the subject of the poem, was clear. So Weed decided to use the word *it* throughout her explanation, figuring (rightly) that by starting off positively, the tester would rate her more highly than if she admitted up front she didn't know that particular word. Weed used strategic competence in this situation to achieve a more satisfying outcome—a higher score on the test.

Building on Strategies for Communicative Competence. Chesterfield and Chesterfield (1985) found a natural order of strategies in students' development of a second language. These incorporate sociolinguistic, discourse, and strategic factors. Teachers who are aware of this order can recognize the strategies and use them to build on students' developing competence. These strategies, in their order of development, include the following:

- *Repetition:* Imitating a word or structure used by another
- *Memorization:* Recalling by rote songs, rhymes, or sequences
- *Formulaic expressions:* Using words or phrases that function as units, such as greetings ("Hi! How are you?")
- *Verbal attention getters:* Using language to initiate interaction ("Hey!" "I think . . .")
- *Answering in unison:* Responding with others
- *Talking to self:* Engaging in subvocal or internal monologue
- *Elaboration:* Providing information beyond that which is necessary
- *Anticipatory answers:* Responding to an anticipated question, or completing another's phrase or statement
- *Monitoring:* Correcting one's own errors in vocabulary, style, or grammar
- *Appeal for assistance:* Asking another for help
- *Request for clarification:* Asking the speaker to explain or repeat
- *Role play:* Interacting with another by taking on roles

Weed (1989) found evidence of almost all of these strategies among English learners in kindergarten. For example, the earliest strategy, repetition, occurred while three kindergarten girls were working puzzles together. Upon noticing that one of the girls had new shoes, the English speaker started chanting, "Pretty shoes, Daniella, pretty shoes." One of the Spanish-speaking girls picked up the chant and repeated, "Pretty shoes." A spontaneous role play, a later strategy, occurred in the same kindergarten class. Ms. Anderson, the teacher, had to use the phone, which was situated by the playhouse area. "Excuse me, children, I have to use the phone," she said. Jimmy, a Vietnamese speaker, picked up the play phone and watched the teacher's actions. After a pause, he said, "Hello, hello, anybody home?" He then left, but another boy picked up the phone and called, "Jimmy, it's your mom." "Where, where," called Jimmy as he ran to the phone. "Hi, mom," he said as he spoke into the instrument.

Teachers can specifically plan to increase students' skills in discourse, sociolinguistic, and strategic competence by building experiences into the curriculum that involve students in solving problems, exploring areas of interest, and designing projects. Students carry over knowledge of how to communicate from experiences in their first language. This knowledge can be tapped as they develop specific forms and usage in English.

> In a high school economics class, Mr. Godfried often demonstrated consumer economics to the students by having them role play. In the fifth-period class, several students were recent immigrants who had been placed in this class as a graduation requirement despite their limited English. Mr. Godfried's job became more complicated than in the past; he had to teach not only economics but also basic communication skills in English. The process of opening a checking account was not difficult for Takeo, a Japanese student, who had had a checking account as a student in Japan. But, Vasalli, a immigrant from Byelorussia, found the task mystifying. He had had limited experience with consumerism in general and no experience with the concept of a checking account. What he did have, however, was a general knowledge of how to interact with an official. Through the role plays, Mr. Godfried was able to help the students use their background knowledge to conduct appropriate verbal interactions in the banking situation and use their communication experience to expand their content knowledge.

The Social Context for Language Learning

Examining the social contexts in which learning takes place expands language teaching and learning from a strictly communicative endeavor to one that includes the analysis of social and cultural interaction. The Russian psychologist Lev Vygotsky emphasized the role played by social interaction in the development of language and thought. According to Vygotsky (1978), teaching must be matched in some manner with the student's developmental level, taking into consideration the student's "zone of proximal development." Vygotsky defines this zone as "the distance between the actual developmental level as determined by independent problem solving and the level of potential development . . . under adult guidance or in collaboration with more capable peers" (p. 86).

Second language learners profit most from language that is slightly more complex than they can themselves easily understand—the notion of Krashen's $i + 1$. In this way, they are challenged to acquire more complex vocabulary and structures. Using peer conversation as a means for enriching a student's exposure to language maximizes the opportunity for a student to hear and enjoy English; mixing more skilled with less skilled speakers supplies more advanced language models to English learners. These nontraditional contexts of instruction play as critical a role in language development as does the actual language exchanged.

The teacher who is aware of the social uses of language provides a classroom environment where students engage in communicative pair or group tasks. These can include practicing a Reader's Theater with other students in order to perform for their class or school; developing interview questions in order to survey local opinion on a timely topic; and planning an exhibition of art or written work in which to invite parents or other students.

Discourse Theory

Discourse theorists (Brown & Yule, 1983; Fox, 1987; Hatch, 1992) have analyzed conversation to understand how meaning is negotiated. According to them, face-to-face interaction is a key to second language acquisition. By holding conversations (discourse), nonnative speakers acquire commonly occurring formulas and grammar as they attend to the various features in the input they obtain. Through their own speech, their *output*, they also affect both the quantity and the quality of the language they receive. The more learners talk, the more other people will talk to them. The more they converse, the more opportunity they have to initiate and expand topics, signal comprehension breakdowns, and try out new formulas and expressions.

In constructing discourse, second language learners use four kinds of knowledge: knowledge about the second language, competence in their native language, ability to use the functions of language, and their general world knowledge. The language they produce is an *interlanguage*, an intermediate system that learners create as they attempt to achieve native-like competence. Selinker's interlanguage hypothesis (1972, 1991) asserts that "non-native speaking students do not learn to produce second languages; what they do is to create and develop interlanguages in particular contexts" (1991, p. 23). Through a variety of discourse opportunities, learners sort out the ways language is used and gradually achieve proficiency.

Based on this understanding of the active role of the language learner, teachers need to provide many opportunities for nonnative speakers of English to interact with native speakers in a variety of situations. ESL program models that confine English learners to certain tracks or special classrooms, without incorporating specific opportunities for native/nonnative speaker interaction, do a disservice to English learners. *Bridge to Communication,* an ESL program published by Santillana (1992), encourages native/nonnative speaker interaction by asking students to interview others briefly on topics such as "My favorite sport" (Middle Level B, p. 7) and "Most popular tool" (Middle Level B, p. 21). The responses from the interviews are tallied and form the basis for subsequent class discussion in conjunction with a thematic unit. Teachers can also incorporate opportunities for nonnative English-speaking students to interact with native English speakers during school hours through cross-age or peer interactions.

Meaning-Centered vs. "Commonsense" Approaches to Language Acquisition

Top-Down Approaches.   Researchers (Goodman, 1986; Smith, 1983) looking at children learning to read in naturalistic settings noticed that they go through similar developmental processes in learning to read as in learning to speak. That is, children actively seek meaning. They work to make sense of text. They combine text clues with their own prior knowledge to construct meanings. The theory called *whole language* arose from these notions of the centrality of meaning, of the interaction and interdependence of language modes (speaking, listening, reading, writing) and language subsystems (phonological, syntactic, semantic, pragmatic). Whole language, a philosophy of reading instruction, complimented many of the findings of studies in first and second language acquisition.

Meaning-centered systems of language acquisition (also called *top-down* systems—see Weaver, 1988) support the view of language as espoused by Halliday—that language is a complex system for creating meanings through socially shared conventions (Halliday, 1978). It is complex in that language is made up of *interdependent* and *inseparable* systems and in that it is *predictable*. There is an organizing structure of each subsystem and for the language system as a whole (Edelsky, Altwerger, & Flores, 1991). The notion of *meaning making* implies that learners are generating hypotheses from and actively constructing interpretations about the input they receive, be it oral or written. Language is *social* in that it occurs within a community of users who attach agreed-upon meaning to their experiences.

Meaning-centered language advocates view the learning of language as the process that occurs when language is used for specific purposes. Language is learned not from drills and worksheets but, rather, from the active process of seeking meaning, through learners exchanging information while doing a science project or researching aspects of their local history. It is best achieved through direct engagement and experience when the learners' purposes and intentions are central. Meaning-centered approaches encourage language development and literacy across a wide variety of academic contexts. This view of language and literacy underlies a "constructivist" perspective. Constructivist-oriented classrooms tend to be those in which students' lives and experiences are valued, and where children explore the multiple functions of literacy, reading and writing to satisfy their own needs and goals. Skills and strategy lessons emerge from students' needs.

Bottom-Up Approaches. Phonics, as well as approaches compatible with a traditional "linguistics" view of language, is derived from what Weaver (1988) calls "commonsense" views of language. Advocates of *bottom-up* approaches are concerned that learners connect the individual sounds of language with its written form as soon as possible, leading to the ability to decode whole words. Once words are identified, meaning will take care of itself. Instruction in "decoding" the sound-symbol relationship includes a set of rules for sounding out words. This approach is often intertwined with the sight-word approach, in which students commit to memory a stock of basic words that do not follow the sound-symbol "rules."

The linguistics approach (so named because it was advocated originally by Leonard Bloomfield, the founder of the field of structural linguistics) advocates exposing students to regularly spelled words from which to unconsciously infer common spelling/sound patterns. Basal (controlled-vocabulary) readers are used to present simplified language, and teachers are encouraged to "preteach" vocabulary words that appear in reading passages. The underlying similarity in linguistics approaches is the emphasis on skills for identifying words and sentence patterns, rather than on strategies for creating meaning from text.

Further research and observation of children learning to read indicates that, in fact, readers use both top-down strategies and bottom-up skills as they read. Current reading instruction now favors a balanced approach (see Tompkins, 1997, particularly Chapter 1, for further discussion; also see ERIC Digest, 1999). Perhaps because the stakes have been large—the fortunes of publishers of reading textbooks have risen and fallen on sales of materials that reflect acceptable theories—the field of reading instruction has been characterized by pendulum swings between contrasting theories of language acquisition. Theories of second language acquisition have naturally been coupled with those that affect first language learning.

Contributions of Semiotics

The previous theories have attempted to explain second language acquisition in linguistic, psycholinguistic, or sociolinguistic terms. *Semiotics* is a discipline that studies the ways in which humans use signs to make meaning. According to semiotic theory, there are three kinds of signs: symbols, icons, and indexes. Symbols are signs in which there is an arbitrary relationship between the object and its sign; the word *table* is arbitrarily linked to the object "table," for example. Icons are signs that resemble what they stand for, such as a drawing of a table. Indexes are signs that indicate a fact or condition; for instance, thunder clouds indicate rain. Importantly, signs are organized into systems of objects and behaviors. Thus, the way chairs are arranged in a classroom and the manner in which students are expected to respond to the teacher are both signs signaling meaning. Semioticians explore the ways people utilize signs to make meaning and then compare them. They strive to make the implicit explicit—to formalize what people do of which they are not aware.

Semiotics provides a perspective for examining human development—that humans are constantly deriving meaning from experience. By adopting this perspective, teachers accept that students are learning from the experiences provided to them; that they are learning not just the content of a specific lesson, but the entire context in which the lesson is embedded. And, through the interplay of multiple meaning systems, wise teachers provide and accept various ways through which students demonstrate their knowledge. Using themselves, students, other teachers, the community, and culturally authentic materials (phone books, voicemail messages, advertising brochures, music videos, etc.), teachers along with students examine ways of knowing by, for example, producing music, creating collages, writing up observations, and generally engaging in a variety of purposeful cross-media activities.

Semiotics has become increasingly important within the last decade as visual information, rather than primarily text, has become more available and salient in the lives of students. Sophisticated computer art, animation, and graphics programs available via the Internet have opened up a language of two-dimensional shape and color that supplements, if not replaces, text as a source of information and experience for many young people. For a brief explanation about semiotics, see

ERIC Digest (1991); for those interested in knowing more about this field, try Chandler (2001).

Contributions of Research about the Brain

Almost all the foregoing theories have left to speculation the involvement of the brain in learning language. Neurofunctional theories attempt to explain the connection between language function and neuroanatomy—to identify, if possible, which areas of the brain are responsible for language functioning. Functional and clinical studies (Asher & Garcia, 1969; Krashen, Long, & Scarcella, 1979; Lenneberg, 1967) have focused on specific aspects of language acquisition: age differences, neural maturation, and the like. Although previous language learning theories acknowledge the role of the brain in learning, several contemporary educators have specialized in developing learning methods that take into consideration brain processing.

According to research (Caine & Caine, 1994; Hart, 1975, 1983; Nummela & Rosengren, 1986), learning is the brain's primary function. Many aspects of the brain help to process reality simultaneously, using thoughts, emotions, imagination, and the senses to understand and interact with the environment. This rich reaction can be tapped in heretofore unrealized ways to facilitate language acquisition. Table 1.1 lists principles of brain-based learning and provides teachers with a way to apply knowledge about the brain to language teaching. For further information about brain-based learning, *Making Connections* by Caine and Caine (1994) is a

TABLE 1.1   Principles and Implications for Brain-Based Instruction

Principle	Implications for Instruction
1. The brain can perform multiple processes simultaneously.	Learning experiences can be multimodal. As students perform experiments, develop a play from the text of a story, or take on complex projects, many facets of the brain are involved.
2. Learning engages the entire physiology.	Stress management, nutrition, exercise, relaxation, and natural rhythms and timing should be taken into consideration during teaching and learning.
3. The search for meaning is innate.	Language learning should involve a focus on meaning—language used in the context of interesting activities provides a situated, meaningful experience.
4. The brain is designed to perceive and generate patterns.	The ideal teaching process presents information in a way that allows brains to extract patterns and create meaning rather than react passively.
5. Emotions are crucial to memory.	Instruction should support the students' backgrounds and languages. Interaction should be marked by mutual respect and acceptance.

(continued)

TABLE 1.1   Continued

Principle	Implications for Instruction
6. The brain processes parts and wholes simultaneously.	Language skills, such as vocabulary and grammar, are best learned in authentic language environments (solving a problem, debating an issue, exploring) in which *parts* (specific language skills) are learned together with *wholes* (problems to be solved).
7. Learning involves both focused attention and peripheral perception.	Music, art, and other rich environmental stimuli can enhance and influence the natural acquisition of language. Subtle signals from the teacher (processed peripherally by students) communicate enthusiasm and interest.
8. Learning always involves conscious and unconscious processes.	Students need opportunities to review what they learn so they can reflect, take charge, and develop personal meaning. This encourages and gives shape to unconscious learning.
9. There are at least two types of memory: spatial memory and rote learning systems.	Teaching techniques that focus on the memorization of language bits—words and grammar points—use the rote learning system. Teaching that actively involves the learner in novel experiences taps into the spatial system.
10. Learning occurs best when facts and skills are embedded in natural, spatial memory.	Discrete language skills can be learned when they are embedded in real-life activities (demonstrations, field trips, performances, stories, drama, visual imagery).
11. Learning is enhanced by challenge and inhibited by threat.	Teachers need to create an atmosphere of acceptance. Learners are taken from the point where they are at present to the next level of competence through a balance of support and challenge.
12. Each brain is unique.	Teaching should be multifaceted. English learners can express their understanding through visual, tactile, emotional, and auditory means.

highly readable and insightful text as is Jensen Learning Corporation's *Brain Based Learning: Truth or Deception* (2001).

Theories of second language acquisition provide the rationale and framework for the daily activities of instruction. An excellent general background reading is Durkin's *Language Issues: Readings for Teachers* (1995), which provides articles about first as well as second language acquisition, achieving grammatical competence, and developing literacy. Teachers who are aware of the basic principles of contemporary language acquisition and learning are better equipped to plan instruction and explain their practices to peers, parents, students, and administrators.

Although the teacher's role is valuable as students learn a second language, the actual language learned is the responsibility of the learner. Research on cognitive processes shows that the learner constructs language using rules internalized during problem solving or authentic communication. The shift from *what the teacher does* to *what the learner does* is a characteristic of contemporary thinking about learning in general and language acquisition specifically, and has wide implications for teaching English learners.

CHAPTER

2 Second Language Acquisition Factors

Psychological and Sociocultural

I believe the single most important strategy for a teacher to practice is to be a good listener. By this I mean genuinely listen to the children. If a child comes to speak, face him, put down the work you are doing and give him your whole attention. . . . In this way children see themselves as valued members of the special community of the classroom. . . .

When they do speak, it is important to listen to the meanings. I remember the following exchange between Jack and a teacher.

"We went to Nagi on Saturday, Sir."

"How far away is Nagi, Jack?"

"Four drums, Sir."

(The journey in a dinghy driven by an outboard motor would take four drums of petrol.)

What it really comes down to is that we must have respect for the children themselves. . . . With respect comes confidence. With confidence comes a willingness to take risks. With risk taking comes learning.

—Louise Carothers, teacher of Torres Strait Island children, in Murray, 1989

Language cannot be learned in a vacuum. It involves interaction with others. Psychological and sociocultural factors play important roles in a learner's success in acquiring and using a second language (see Figure I.1). Each learner is simultaneously an individual and a member of a group. As an individual, a person carries character traits that enable him or her to function in specific ways and deal with situations in a unique style. As a member of a group, a person learns characteristic ways of behaving and, largely unconsciously, adopts rules for interaction and takes on roles appropriate for effective functioning in that group. These individual (psychological) and group (sociocultural) factors influence second language acquisition as much as does the nature of the target language. Both psychological and sociocultural factors are examined in this chapter in light of their implications in language development classrooms.

Psychological Factors

Psychological factors are traits specific to individuals that enable them to acquire a second language. Learners use the assets of their personalities to absorb the ambiance of the culture, to process the language they hear, and to create meaningful responses. Psychological factors can be divided into two categories: *affective/emotional* and *cognitive* (although it is often difficult to separate neatly affective and cognitive processes in language learning). Learners bring emotions to learning, such as positive or negative attitudes. As they learn, the sense of mastery of a language creates an affective/emotional response: enjoyment, pride, competence. The work of mastering a second language can be considered cognitive. Teachers can help students be aware of those psychological factors that further their language learning and can work with students to ensure that these factors promote rather than impede their learning.

Affective/Emotional Factors

The affective domain, the emotional side of human behavior, is the means through which individuals become aware of their environment, respond to it with feeling, and act as though their feelings make a difference. This emotional dimension helps determine how language acquisition and communication take place. Some affective factors within this domain pertain specifically to individuals' feelings about themselves, whereas other factors pertain to their ability to interact with others. Those affective factors that are discussed here are self-esteem, motivation, anxiety, attitudes, and other related factors.

Self-Esteem. A large part of one's feelings revolve around how one feels about oneself, one's self-esteem. According to Schumann (1978b), there are three aspects of self-esteem: *global* (overall assessment of one's worth); *specific* (self-evaluation in various life situations such as work and social interactions and in individual characteristics such as personality and intelligence); and *task* (self-valuation in particular tasks). High self-esteem may *cause* language success or *result from* language success. Research is lacking about the influence of global, specific, or task self-esteem in any particular situation. Many teachers, however, intuitively recognize that self-esteem issues play important roles in their classrooms and encourage students to feel proud of their successes and abilities. Global self-esteem enhancement, such as efforts to empower students with positive images of self, family, and culture, may facilitate language learning. Teachers also strive to ensure that learners feel good about specific aspects of their language learning (speaking, writing) or about their success on a particular task.

Anita Alvarez was a Spanish-speaking first-grade student at the beginning stages of English language acquisition. She was shy and retiring, and Mrs. Figueroa noticed that she seldom took advantage of opportunities to chat with her peers. Anita seemed physically well developed for her age and had good sensory motor abilities. She was particularly adept at building three-dimensional models following printed diagrams. When Mrs. Figueroa observed that Mary, another student in the class, had a lot of difficulty in constructing objects, Anita was teamed with Mary, and, with Anita's help, Mary completed her project successfully. Noting this success, Mrs. Figueroa "assigned competence" to Anita by publicly praising her to the class and referring students to her for help. This boosted Anita's feelings of worth—her "task" self-esteem—and the effects transferred to academic areas. Mrs. Figueroa was pleased to see that, subsequently, Anita talked more with other students and seemed to acquire English at a faster rate.

Moskowitz's *Caring and Sharing in the Foreign Language Classroom* (1978) offers many activities that enhance self-esteem. "Me Power" is an activity that asks students to imagine they are going to give a speech before a large group of people. The assignment is to write a brief description of their accomplishments for the person who is to introduce them. Another activity, "Success Story," asks students to describe an incident in which they achieved a victory or reached a goal. A third activity, "Ageless," asks students to think positively about their age and other ages by answering eight questions, such as "What do you like about being your present age?" and "What did you like about being younger?"

Siccone (1995) offers several activities that encourage students to be proud of their identities and to share them with others. "The Name Game" asks students to introduce themselves by first name, adding a word that describes how they are feeling that day—using a word that begins with the same letter as the first name (English learners may wish to think about this and prepare in advance; the teacher may provide an alphabetized list of adjectives). Each subsequent person repeats what the others have said in sequence. Another activity, "Name Interviews," lets students work in partners to use a teacher-provided questionnaire. This includes such questions as, "What do you like about your name? Who named you? Were you named for someone? Are there members of your family who have the same name?" and more. A useful overall guide to self-esteem activities is Canfield and Wells's *100 Ways to Enhance Self-Concept in the Classroom* (1976). In these and other sources, a theory of humanistic education is elaborated and suggestions are given for building a climate of acceptance, trust, and low anxiety to increase language learning.

Related to self-esteem is the concept of *inhibition*, a term that suggests defensiveness against new experiences and feelings. Guiora, Beit-Hallami, Brannon, Dull, and Schovel (1972) refer to a "language ego" that either defends against or facilitates verbal input and expression. One recent language teaching methodology in particular (see Suggestopedia, Chapter 4) focuses on a reduction of inhibitions so that students can communicate more freely. Emphasizing fluency over accuracy in the first stages of language learning may help students feel less inhibited.

A *tolerance for ambiguity* is also related to self-esteem, particularly in the area of task esteem. Such tolerance may help learners react in language situations where the topic and purpose of the conversation, as well as the appropriate response, are unclear. Rather than reacting with avoidance or dislike, a person with a high tolerance for ambiguity may be able to listen more attentively and perform more efficiently.

The ability to *take risks*, to "gamble," may facilitate second language acquisition. Intuitively, educators believe that those who are willing to guess at meaning when it is not clear and to be relatively unconcerned with creating errors will progress in language skills more rapidly than their more inhibited colleagues. As Brown (2000) points out, however, students who make random guesses and blurt out meaningless phrases have not been as successful. It appears that moderate risk takers stand the best chance at language development.

Motivation.   Motivation has been defined as the impulse, emotion, or desire that causes one to act in a certain way. Humans need to be active—to acquire knowledge, explore, manipulate, and enhance the ego. They strive to meet their basic needs, to achieve an identity within a group, and to learn about their world. Various individual, sociocultural, and instructional factors impact motivation. Gardner and Lambert (1972) have postulated two types of motivation in learning a second language: *instrumental* motivation, the need to acquire a language for a specific purpose such as reading technical material or getting a job; and *integrative* motivation, the desire to become a member of the culture of the second language group. Research suggests that these differences are not mutually exclusive; most situations involve a mixture of both types.

As with any of the affective factors, motivation is hard to identify and study. Research has demonstrated that motivation is a key to learning, but actually defining and detailing the components of motivation have not been done. Generally, in classrooms, teachers organize their instruction on the basis of one of two subconscious notions about motivation—that it is a trait or a state. As a *trait*, motivation is seen as being relatively consistent and persistent and is attributed to various groups—parents, communities, or cultures. The stereotype of the overachieving Asian student may be one example wherein student success is attributed to a trait of motivation. Students are motivated to learn English by such incentives as the desire to please—or not to shame— their families or by the drive to bring honor to their communities. As a *state,* motivation is viewed as a more temporary condition that can be influenced by the use of highly interesting materials or activities, or by contingencies of reward or punishment (Tharp, 1989b). The belief that motivation is a trait may be a disincentive for teachers to alter the curriculum for those students whose interest or achievement flags. The belief that motivation is a state may be a motivator for teachers to exert themselves to involve learners actively.

Counihan (1998) has developed a true/false questionaire that helps students understand what type of learner they are. The responses are grouped by motivation. He reports that this website activity, "What Type of Student Are You?" generates a lot of discussion.

Anxiety.   Anxiety when learning a second language can be seen as similar to general feelings of tension that students experience in the classroom. Almost everyone feels some anxiety when learning, and having to perform in a new language compounds anxious feelings. Anxiety about learning language resembles communication anxiety—that is, feelings of self-consciousness, desire to be perfect when speaking, and fear of making mistakes. In some ways, however, anxiety in a second language is more than simply communication anxiety; using a foreign language can threaten a person's sense of self because speakers know they cannot represent themselves fully in a new language or understand others readily (Horwitz, Horwitz, & Cope, 1991).

Because anxiety can cause learners to feel defensive and can block effective learning, several language educators have developed methodologies that make the learning environment as comfortable as possible and reduce tension and nervousness (e.g., see Gattegno's Silent Way and Lozanov's Suggestopedia in Chapter 4). Scovel (1991) comments that these methods have not been proved to reduce anxiety directly, but insofar as they are effective it is probably because "language teachers have known all along that students learn better in a supportive, nonthreatening environment" (p. 23). Crookall and Oxford (1991) suggest that the classroom become a place of warmth and friendliness, where risk taking is rewarded and encouraged, and peer work, small group work, games, and simulations are featured. In such contexts, student-to-student communication is increased.

Classroom techniques can teach students to confront anxiety directly (Crookall & Oxford, 1991). Specific activities explicitly train students to recognize their anxiety. "Agony Column" allows students to write a letter to an imaginary Ann Landers, relating a particular difficulty they have in language learning and asking for advice. Students working in groups read and discuss the letters, offer advice, and return the letters to their originators for follow-up discussion. "Mistakes Panel" is an activity in which students collect mistakes over a number of classes and, in groups, assess the errors. They then rate the errors on a scale of 1 to 3 for such qualities as amusement, originality, and intelligibility; and they tally points to reward the "winning" mistake. Again, class discussion follows. "Anxious Photos" features a series of photos of people in a wide range of communicative contexts, such as a restaurant, a post office, a family visit, and a classroom. Student groups arrange the photos in sets according to their own criteria, which reflect their judgments about the anxieties provoked in these situations. Students discuss in pairs their reasons for the photo sets that they created, and why anxiety is aroused in each context.

Koch and Terrell (1991) suggest several types of activities that allow all students to participate with little apprehension. Performing interviews in pairs makes students feel most comfortable because it gives them the opportunity to get to know a classmate. "Preference ranking" enables students to voice their opinions without using complex language. Beginning students tend to feel more comfort in activities that require sensorimotor involvement (see Total Physical Response, Chapter 4) and with hands-on tasks such as working with maps or playing games like Simon Says. These are simple activities that do not require complex production or a verbal response in English.

Woolfolk (1998) offers guidelines for dealing with excessive student anxiety. Teachers should monitor activities to ensure that students are receiving no undue pressure; ensure that students in competitive tasks have a reasonable chance to succeed; and avoid situations in which anxious students have to perform in front of large groups. When using a novel format or starting a new type of task, teachers should make sure students are given examples or models of how the task is done. Occasional take-home tests lower unnecessary time pressures for performance. Teaching test-taking skills explicitly and providing study guides give a boost to students who may need extra help to prepare academically. A variety of assignments distribute the opportunity to earn points toward grades over different types of schoolwork. If students are low in energy in class, teachers may wish to increase arousal by giving them a brief chance to be physically active, by introducing stimuli that whet their curiosity or surprise them. In this way, students can be energized without becoming overly anxious.

Attitudes of the Learner.   Attitudes play a critical role in learning English. Attitudes toward self, toward language (one's own and English), toward English-speaking people (particularly peers), and toward the teacher and the classroom environment affect students (Richard-Amato, 1996). One's *attitude toward the self* involves cognition about one's ability in general, ability to learn language, and self-esteem and its related emotions. These cognitions and feelings are seldom explicit and may be slow to change.

Attitudes toward language and those who speak it are largely a result of experience and the influence of people in the immediate environment, such as peers and parents. Negative reactions are often the result of negative stereotypes or the experience of discrimination or racism. Peñalosa (1980) points out that if English learners are made to feel inferior because of accent or language status, they may have a defensive reaction against English and English speakers. Students may also experience ambivalent feelings about their primary language. In some families, parents use English at the expense of the primary language in the hope of influencing children to learn English more rapidly. This can cause problems within the family and create a backlash against English or English speakers. Other students who acquire English at the expense of their primary language may be considered traitors by their peers or families.

Attitudes toward the teacher and the classroom environment play an important role in school success in general and English acquisition in particular. Families may promote positive attitudes toward school, thus influencing their child's success. However, Ogbu (1978) states that parents who have experienced discrimination and negative experiences at school may subconsciously mirror these same attitudes, adding to their children's ambivalent attitudes toward education. Students may emphasize cultural behaviors that help them differentiate themselves from the dominant culture and cling to language behavior that characterizes their group as opposed to the language group represented by the school. Some theorists have postulated that students' refusal to learn what schools teach can be seen as a form of political resistance, which promotes misbehavior, vandalism, and poor relationships with teachers (Nieto, 2000). Moskowitz (1978) offers techniques that can alter attitudes from hostile or apathetic to positive.

Other Affective Factors.   In addition to those affective factors discussed in this section, other affective factors involve the connection of oneself to others. *Empathy* is the capacity to be aware of another's feeling and to share it. When learning a second language, listeners must understand the intentions and emotions of a speaker and attempt to comprehend the message. Although some research has shown empathy to be predictive of success in language learning, it is difficult to know if empathy can be learned or taught. Using a methodology such as Community Language Learning has provided students with increased opportunities to share with and belong to their group and has led to significant language gains (Curran, 1982). *Extroversion* can be seen as the need to receive ego enhancement from other people. Some stereotypes exist that connect extroverted behavior with a lack of inhibition or an increased communicative ability. However, Brown (2000) points out that the definition of extroversion may vary considerably from one culture to another. Some students are more willing to speak out and to participate in class; this could be a personality factor or a cultural trait. Although the extrovert may be perceived as a person who takes more risks with language, an introverted or more reserved person may show more intuitive understanding or empathy with others.

Cognitive Factors

The cognitive perspective helps educators to understand language learners as people who are active processors of information. Learners seek out information to solve problems, reorganize what they already know to achieve new learning, and actively choose, pay attention, ignore, and make many other responses as they pursue goals (Wittrock, 1978). Students enter school knowing how to learn—from those around them and from personal experience. Students' primary languages, for the most part, are well developed before they enter school. For all children, however, not only for English learners, the language used in schools is different to some degree from their home language. Language is used in school in expanded ways: to create meaning from print, to encode ideas into print, to analyze and compare information, and to respond to classroom discussion. All of these activities involve cognitive factors. Students learn in many different ways using a variety of strategies and styles. The general cognitive processes that all individuals use to learn language are explored in this section, followed by a brief overview of individual learning styles. Finally, various types of bilingualism and their related cognitive effects are discussed.

Cognitive Academic Language Proficiency.   Cummins (1979b, 1980) has posited two different yet related language skills: Basic Interpersonal Communication Skills (BICS) and Cognitive Academic Language Proficiency (CALP). BICS involves those language skills and functions that allow students in school to communicate in everyday social contexts that are similar to those of the home: to perform classroom chores, chat with peers, or consume instructional media as they do television shows at home. However, the language required for success in school is vastly more complex than that required at home. During the elementary school years, and then even more so throughout middle and high school, students need to master much more than everyday English in order to have access to the school curriculum. Successful educators are aware that children not only need to continue to develop and fine-tune their interpersonal skills but they also need to acquire a completely new kind of scholastic language to succeed in school. Students who may appear to be fluent enough in English to survive in an all-English classroom may in fact have significant gaps in the development of academic aspects of English. Conversational skills have been found to approach native-like levels within two years of exposure to English, but five or more years may be required for minority students to match native speakers in CALP (Collier, 1987; Cummins, 1981a; Hakuta, Butler, & Witt, 2000).

Cummins (1984) calls BICS *context embedded* because participants can provide feedback to one another, the situation itself provides cues that further understanding, and factors apart from the linguistic code can furnish meaning. In contrast, CALP, as the name implies, is the language needed to perform school tasks successfully. Such tasks generally are more abstract and decontextualized. Students must rely primarily on language to attain meaning. Cummins calls CALP *context-reduced* communication because there are few concrete cues to aid students in comprehension. Successful educators are aware that students need skills in both language domains.

Both BICS and CALP are clearly more than words. BICS involves the totality of communication that takes place between two or more people in their everyday activities. Some exchanges with people involve no words at all; for instance, a nod of the head while passing in the hallway at work may serve the same communicative purpose as a greeting. CALP, on the other hand, is more difficult to define. Beyond words, it also involves systematic thought processes. It provides the human brain with necessary tools to systematically categorize, compare, analyze, and accommodate new experiences. One cannot separate words from knowledge or learning; it is not possible to say that one understands a topic but does not understand the terminology. CALP represents the cognitive toolbox, entire systems of thought as well as the language to encode and decode this thought. Without the acquisition of the CALP—that is, not only specific terminology but also the clarity of thought provided by the classification and organization inherent in academic language and thought processes—students are incapable of acquiring the in-depth knowledge that characterizes the well-educated individual in a complex modern society.

Cognitive Academic Language Proficiency requires a complex growth in many linguistic areas simultaneously. This growth is highly dependent on the assistance of teachers because, for the most part, CALP is learned exclusively in school. The complexity of CALP can be captured by examination of the five Cs: conceptualization, complexity, context, culture, and communication (see Table 2.1).

TABLE 2.1   Components of Cognitive/Academic Language Proficiency

Component	Explanation
Communication (see California State Department of Education, 1999a)	Reading: Increases speed; uses context cues to guess vocabulary meaning; masters a variety of genres in fiction (poetry, short story) and nonfiction (encyclopedias, magazines, Internet sources); knows how to "read the world" (interprets comics, print advertising, road signs)
	Listening: Follows verbal instructions; interprets nuances of intonation (e.g., in cases of teacher disciplinary warnings); solicits and profits from help of peers
	Speaking: Gives oral presentations, answers correctly in class, and reads aloud smoothly
	Writing: Uses conventions such as spelling, punctuation, report formats
Conceptualization	Concepts become abstract, and are expressed in longer words with more general meaning (*rain* becomes *precipitation*)
	Concepts fit into larger theories (precipitation cycle)
	Concepts fit into hierarchies (rain → precipitation cycle → weather systems → climate)
	Concepts are finely differentiated from similar concepts (*sleet* from *hail*, *typhoons* from *hurricanes*)
	Conceptual relations become important (opposites, subsets, causality, correlation)
Critical thinking	Uses graphic organizers to represent the structure of thought (comparison charts, Venn diagrams, time lines, "spider" charts)
	Uses textual structures (outlines, paragraphing, titles, main idea)
	Uses symbolic representation (math operators [<, >, +, =]; proofreading marks, grade indications [10/20 points, etc.])
	Reads between the lines (inference)
	Employs many other kinds of critical thinking
	Plans activities; monitors progress; evaluates results; employs self-knowledge (metacognition)
	Increases variety and efficiency in use of learning strategies
Context	Nonverbal: Uses appropriate gestures (and is able to refrain from inappropriate); interprets nonverbal signs accurately
	Formality: Behaves formally when required to do so
	Participation structures: fits in smoothly to classroom and schoolwide groups and procedures
Culture	Draws on experience in mainstream culture (background knowledge)
	Uses social class markers, such as "manners"
	Moves smoothly between home and school
	Marshals and controls parental support for school achievement
	Deploys primary language resources when required
	Maintains uninterrupted primary culture profile ("fits in" to neighborhood social structures)
	Develops and sustains supportive peer interactions

Many of the skills that are a part of CALP are refinements of BICS, while others are more exclusively school centered.

A look at an elementary classroom shows the integrated work that takes place across these CALP areas.

> Mrs. Gómez found in her second-grade transitional bilingual class that, although the students were fairly fluent English conversationalists, they were performing poorly in academic tasks. Students seemed to understand English when pictures and other visual clues were present. However, when she gave instructions or briefly reviewed concepts, the students appeared lost. She became aware that students needed to be provided with lessons that eased them along the continuum from their interpersonal language usage to the more abstract academic requirements. She noticed that Linda and several of her classmates enjoyed jumping rope during recess. Mrs. Gómez wrote down many of the patterned chants the girls were reciting. She transferred these to wall charts and read and recited them with the children. Next she introduced poems with more extensive vocabulary on wall charts, supplementing the charts with tapes that children could listen to in learning centers. At the same time, the class was studying the ocean. Mrs. Gómez set up other learning centers with shells, dried seaweed, fish fossils, and other ocean objects. The instructions for these centers featured patterned language similar to that already encountered in the rhymes and poems. Gradually Mrs. Gómez was able to record more complex and abstract instructions in the learning centers. This progression and integration of activities helped the children to move along the continuum from BICS to CALP.

The difficulty that English learners have in acquiring CALP reinforces the need for maintenance bilingual programs in which students do not transition into English abruptly. Although critics of bilingual education have charged that educating children in the primary language reduces their opportunity to acquire English, this argument assumes that proficiency in English is separate from proficiency in a primary language. The assumption is that content and skills learned through the primary language do not transfer to English. This notion of "no interrelationship between languages" (Cummins, 1981b) has been termed *separate underlying proficiency (SUP)*. The contrasting notion, "significant interrelationship between languages," asserts that cognition and language fundamentals, once learned in the primary language, form a basis for subsequent learning in any language. This position assumes a *common underlying proficiency (CUP)* and is characterized by the belief that a second language and the primary language have a shared foundation. For example, children learning to read and write in Korean develop concepts about print and the role of literacy that make learning to read and think in English easier, despite the fact that these languages do not share a similar writing system. The surface differences in the languages are less important than the deeper understandings about the function of reading and its relationship to thought and learning. Cummins (1981b) cites much evidence to support the idea of a common underlying proficiency. Once a student has a strong foundation in the native language, learning a second language—and learning in general—readily builds upon this foundation. Students do not have to relearn in a second language the essentials of schooling: how to communicate, how to think critically, and how to read and write (Association for Supervision and Curriculum Development, 1987).

Age. The age of the learner is an important factor to be considered in the discussion of language. Second language acquisition is a complex process that occurs over a long period of time, and the optimum age for its inception has been widely debated. Although many people believe that children acquire a second language more rapidly than adults, recent research counters this notion. It is true that natural exposure to second languages during childhood can lead to higher second language proficiency than exposure that begins in the adult years, but this generally pertains only to pronunciation (see Point/Counterpoint on page 35). Contrary to popular belief, adults proceed through early stages of syntactic and morphological development faster than children do; older children acquire a second language faster than younger children (Collier, 1987; Krashen et al., 1979). Cummins (1980) suggests that older learners acquire cognitive/academic proficiency more rapidly than younger learners because the CALP in their first language (L1) is better developed.

Language Acquisition Processes.   These processes involve mental activities that people employ to be able to communicate ideas. Two of these processes are directly related to the general cognitive mechanism that individuals use in any type of learning: *transfer* and *generalization*. Transfer is applying old learning to new situations, and generalization involves inferring or drawing conclusions in order to make a response to a situation.

In language learning, transfer is most noticeable when learners use rules from their first language that are not applicable to the second. This has been called *negative transfer.* After working with second language learners, most teachers have numerous examples, often humorous, of sentences, phrases, or words students have transferred from their first language that have no direct equivalence in their second. One of the authors (Weed), for example, once mistakenly referred to a coconut as *coco-noix* instead of *noix de coco.* She was using English word order (adjective + noun) instead of the French pattern (noun + attribute). Meaning, however, was not lost. Weed's French friends knew exactly what she was talking about; she had the correct concept and had used it in the correct situation. The "negative" element was merely the surface representation. Unfortunately, the emphasis on negative transfer of surface grammatical or pronunciation errors can hide the more powerful *positive transfer* that occurs and allows people to respond appropriately and meaningfully in new language situations.

Point/Counterpoint

What is the best age for second language acquisition?
Those of us who, as adults, have tried to learn a second language have found it a some-times frustrating and difficult experience. We look to children, who seem to smoothly roll impossible sounds off their tongues and to interact fluently with their neighbors, and wonder why we no longer have these seemingly facile abilities. Is there a best age for learning a second language?

Point: **Children learn second languages easily.**
Those who argue that a child can learn a second language more rapidly than an adult gen-erally ascribe to the *critical period* hypothesis postulated by Lenneberg (1967). He asserted that the brain has a language acquisition processor that functions best before puberty. Despite the fact that the critical period hypothesis has not been proved, people continue to use Lenneburg's work to assert that the child's brain is better able to learn language rapidly.

Evidence from child second language studies indicates that the language children speak is relatively simple compared to that of adults—it has shorter constructions with fewer vocabulary words. This is one reason for its more fluent appearance. People also believe that children are less inhibited than adults when speaking a second language, but this is not so. Children are just as likely to be embarrassed around their peers as are adults, and are more likely to be shy when speaking before adults (McLaughlin, 1992).

One area in which prepubescent youth may have an advantage is in the acquisition of native-speaker–like pronunciation skills. Research (Oyama, 1976) has found that the earlier a person begins to learn a second language, the closer the accent will become to that of a native speaker. Older learners may not have an advantage in the areas of oral fluency and accent.

Counterpoint: **Adults learn languages more skillfully than children.**
Research comparing adults to children has consistently demonstrated that adolescents and adults outperform children in controlled language learning studies (e.g., Snow & Hoefnagel-Hoehle, 1978). Adults have access to more memory strategies; are, as a rule, more socially comfortable; and have greater experience with language in general. The self-discipline, strategy use, prior knowledge, and metalinguistic ability of the older learner create a distinct advantage for the adult over the child in language acquisition.

A recent article (Marinova-Todd, Marshall, & Snow, 2000) analyzed misconceptions about age and second language learning and reached the following conclusions: "Older learners have the potential to learn second languages to a very high level and introducing foreign languages to very young learners cannot be justified on grounds of biological readiness to learn languages" (p. 10). "Age does influence language learning, but prima-rily because it is associated with social, psychological, educational, and other factors that can affect L2 proficiency, not because of any critical period that limits the possibility of language learning by adults" (p. 28).

Much research has been carried out and numerous studies have been made comparing various features (phonological, syntactic, and semantic) of languages. Contrastive analysis, a tool for analyzing and learning that emphasizes comparisons between the first and second language, rests heavily on behaviorist and structuralist tenets. Classroom materials based on this approach encourage comparisons of those structural elements deemed by the materials developer to be the most troublesome. Contemporary theory recognizes the importance of the first language in a global sense and does not encourage learners to compare minute surface forms of the first and second languages as they learn.

The second general cognitive strategy used by all learners is generalization—the act of drawing a conclusion or making an inference. In first language acquisition, this process is seen when young children begin to acquire concepts and put labels to them. "Dada," a child may say to any male, or "ball" about any round object. The child has understood an aspect of the concepts *father* and *ball* and generalized the terms to all objects representative of the understood aspect. In second language acquisition, the term *overgeneralization* is more frequently used and refers to situations in which the learner incorrectly generalizes a rule to cases where it does not apply. English learners may say, for example, "I don't can do that." In this case, the student has overgeneralized the rule "insert *do* in negative clauses." In another example, the student may say, "He asked me that should he go." Here, the student has overgeneralized the question–word-order rule.

As parallels between first and second language acquisition have become more evident, a shift has occurred in understanding second language acquisition processes. Learners are no longer seen as second language bumblers whose every mistake needs "fixing." Instead, they are recognized as intelligent, hypothesis-forming individuals who use the knowledge of their first language and a growing awareness of the second to progress toward native-like second language fluency. The precise way in which knowledge of the first language affects second language acquisition is not certain (see Point/Counterpoint on page 37).

The language produced by second language learners is an intermediate language, a form that features some combination of constructs carried over from the first language with elements of the second. Selinker (1972) calls this an "interlanguage." Corder (1978) calls this "language-learner language" and characterizes it as a different language from that of the native speaker but very similar to that of other language learners. Instead of criticizing language-learner language as error-ridden and deficient, full of overgeneralizations and negatively transferred elements, a teacher can recognize it as a dynamic system that is in constant progression toward increased proficiency. Interlanguage is a continuum stretching from the mother language to the target language. Teachers knowledgeable about this interlanguage help students progress along this continuum, correctly assessing the strengths of the learner and providing additional mediation of elements still unmastered.

Stages of Development.   Second language learners are individuals who vary greatly in their acquisition of a second language. However, there appear to be some generally accepted stages of development through which learners progress. These

Point/Counterpoint

How does a person's first language affect learning a second language?
Individuals who have learned more than one foreign language sometimes find that a first foreign language interferes with a second: In trying to say the pronoun *il* ("he") in French, for example, one could mistakenly use the word *el* (Spanish). More difficult to sort out is the influence of the first language on the second. Much was made of error analysis in the 1960s, as teachers sought to document a predictability in the errors made by native Japanese speakers, for example, when learning English. What is the effect of the first language on learning a second language?

Point: **Skill in a first language helps second language learning.**
Current research has shown that learning the first language and learning a foreign language resemble each other to some extent. The "mistakes" that both children and adults make in the second language are similar to the errors that children make in learning their native language. In many ways, learning the first language accomplishes a rich foundation for learning another tongue. Learning that things have names, that language classifies reality, and that language is a means for sharing experience with others—none of these insights need to be discovered anew in the second language. A learner can immediately begin to transfer concepts from the first language to the second. Knowledge of the world, as well as knowledge of language (metalinguistic awareness), enables a learner to streamline language learning the second time around.

Cummins (1981b) emphasizes that students who have the opportunity to develop cognitive and academic skills in their first language before being asked to develop these skills in the second language are more successful in school. Moreover, students who receive a high level of academic support from parents in the home are more likely to develop academic language skills in the second language. When children and parents share a common language, such support is more likely.

Counterpoint: **The first language interferes with second language learning.**
The idea that early learning, such as learning a native language, interferes with later learning (such as a second language) is called *proactive interference.* Such interference has been explained by Schunk (1991) as confusion resulting from the same or similar schema or script being used on different occasions. Many terms in a second language cannot be translated directly into the first language, and attempts to form cognates interfere with understanding rather than facilitate comprehension. For example, who can fully translate the Russian word for *comrade,* with its associated connotations in the world-experience of an ex-Soviet?

According to Skutnabb-Kangas (1981), many bilinguals feel that their second language is somehow impoverished, that it is poorer in emotion and feels colder, more alien, more superficial, and less rich in words than the first language. In some sense, the first language has interfered with learning the second; the native language has taken up the role most central to the heart, leaving little emotional space for the second. No matter how rich the experience of learning the second language, the first dominates the personality. For others, however, the second language represents new learning opportunities and experiences not available in the first language. For these learners, the second language augments, rather than interferes with, the first language.

stages include *preproduction, early production, speech emergence,* and *intermediate fluency.* In preproduction—also called the silent period—the learner is absorbing the sounds and rhythms of the new language, becoming attuned to the flow of the speech stream and beginning to isolate specific words. For the most part, learners in the silent period feel anxious when expected to produce speech. Once a learner feels more confident, words and phrases are attempted—the early production stage. Responses can consist of single words ("yes," "no," "O.K.," "you," "come") and two- or three-word combinations ("where book," "no go," "don't go," "teacher help"). Students can sometimes recite simple poems and sing songs at this point. In the third stage, speech emergence, learners respond more freely. Utterances become longer and more complex, but as utterances begin to resemble sentences, syntax errors are more noticeable than in the earlier stage ("Where you going?" "The boy running"). Once in intermediate fluency, students begin to initiate and sustain conversations and are often able to recognize and correct their own errors.

Specific guidelines for language behaviors of students at various levels of proficiency can be found in Richard-Amato's (1996, pp. 99–100) *Making It Happen.* These include specific suggestions for classroom activities that match the language acquisition level. Using the designations *beginning, intermediate,* and *advanced,* Richard-Amato divides each level into low, mid, and high. Regardless of the scale, it is now recognized that, in natural situations, learners progress through stages in their acquisition of a second language. These stages are predictable, and learners advance through them at their own pace. Undue pressure to move through the stages rapidly only serves to frustrate and retard language learning.

Learning Styles.   Many researchers have documented differences in the manner in which learners approach the learning task. "Learning styles are the preferences students have for thinking, relating to others, and for particular types of classroom environments and experiences" (Grasha, 1990, p. 23). These preferences serve as models for instructors in their efforts to anticipate the differing needs and perspectives of students. Once learning styles have been identified, instructors can use the information to plan and to modify certain aspects of courses and assignments. Hruska-Riechmann and Grasha (1982) offer six learning styles: competitive versus cooperative, dependent versus independent, and participant versus avoidant. For Sonbuchner (1991), learning styles refer to information-processing styles (preferences for reading, writing, listening, speaking, visualizing, or manipulating) and work environment preferences (differences in motivation, concentration, length of study sessions, involvement with others, level of organization, prime times for study, amount of noise, amount of light, amount of heat, and need for food/drink). Table 2.2 lists learning style variables that have been divided into four different categories—cognitive, affective, incentive, and physiological—according to Keefe (1987).

Although in the typical classroom it is not possible to tailor instruction precisely to meet individuals' needs, some modification may be made that takes learning styles into account. If students score high on dependency and competitiveness, for example, assignments that enhance other characteristics (such as collaborative

TABLE 2.2   **Learning Style Variables**

Cognitive	Affective	Incentive	Physiological
■ Field independent/ Field dependent ■ Scanning (broad attention) vs. focusing (narrow) ■ Conceptual/analytical vs. perceptual/concrete ■ Task constricted (easily distracted) vs. task flexible (capable of controlled concentration) ■ Reflective vs. impulsive ■ Leveling (tendency to lump new experiences with previous ones) vs. sharpening (ability to distinguish small differences) ■ High cognitive complexity (multidimensional discrimination, accepting of diversity and conflict) vs. low cognitive complexity (tendency to reduce conflicting information to a minimum)	■ Need for structure ■ Curiosity ■ Persistence ■ Level of anxiety ■ Frustration tolerance	■ Locus of control (internal—seeing oneself as responsible for own behavior, or external—attributing circumstances to luck, chance, or other people) ■ Tendency to imitate others ■ Risk taking vs. caution ■ Competition vs. cooperation ■ Level of achievement motivation ■ Reaction to rewards and punishment ■ Social motivation arising from family, school, and ethnic background ■ Personal interests	■ Gender-related differences (typically, males are more visual-spatial and aggressive, females are more verbal and tuned to fine-motor control) ■ Personal nutrition ■ Health ■ Time-of-day preferences ■ Sleeping and waking habits ■ Need for mobility ■ Needs for and response to varying levels of light, sound, and temperature

Source: Based on Keefe (1987).

and independent learning) might be developed. Teachers who are aware of the dimensions of difference in how learning takes place can use a variety of learning activities to accommodate distinct learning styles.

Learner Strategies.   Aside from general language acquisition processes that all learners use, there are individual strategies that learners adopt to help them in the acquisition process. Second language acquisition research divides individual learner strategies into two types: communication and learning. *Communication strategies* are employed for transmitting an idea when the learner cannot produce precise linguistic forms, whereas *learning strategies* relate to the individual's processing, storage, and retrieval of language concepts (Brown, 2000). This distinction between *output* and *input* helps distinguish these two types of strategies since research in this area of second language acquisition is still ongoing and sometimes confuses the two terms.

The work by Chesterfield and Chesterfield (1985) that was summarized in Chapter 1 provides a list of communication strategies that Mexican American children used to learn English. (Chesterfield and Chesterfield call them learning strategies.) These verbal strategies relate to the actual utterances children were heard to make. Brown (2000) examines five broad categories of communication strategies based on Tarone's work (1981). These strategies make conscious use of both verbal and nonverbal devices.

- *Avoidance:* Evading the use of sounds, structures, or topics that are beyond current proficiency. For example, a student may avoid sharing plans because of an inability to use the future tense.
- *Prefabricated patterns:* Memorizing stock phrases to rely on when all else fails.
- *Cognitive and personality styles:* Employing one's personality to compensate for unknown language structures. An example of this is the compliant, quiet student who does not volunteer yet who is not called on because she or he does not present a control problem for the teacher.
- *Appeals for help:* Asking a native speaker for help or pausing to consult a dictionary.
- *Language switch:* Falling back on the primary language for help in communication.

This last strategy, often called *code switching,* has been studied extensively because it permeates a learner's progression in a second language. Code switching—the alternating use of two languages on the word, phrase, clause, or sentence level (Valdés-Fallis, 1978)—now has been found to be used for a variety of purposes, not just as a strategy to help when expressions in the second language are lacking. Baker (1993) lists 10 purposes for code switches: (1) to emphasize a point, (2) because a word is unknown in one of the languages, (3) for ease and efficiency of expression, (4) as a repetition to clarify, (5) to express group identity and status and/or to be accepted by a group, (6) to quote someone, (7) to interject in a conversation; (8) to exclude someone, (9) to cross social or ethnic boundaries, and (10) to ease tension in a conversation. Code switching thus serves a variety of intentions beyond the mere linguistic. It has important power and social ramifications.

A recent Spanish-speaking immigrant to the United States might acquire whole phrases or words in English from a fellow student and then intersperse these when speaking Spanish to gain access to his peer group. Children speaking English on the playground have been heard to repeat in Spanish something just said in English, perhaps to clarify what was said or to identify with two groups. The use of target language vocabulary is particularly noticeable in bilingual classrooms in which children are learning concepts in two languages and pick the term in one language as a preferred usage. The content of the course, the interpersonal link between speakers, and the speech community's values are factors in language choice. Very often, one language may be associated with certain activities, situations, or social practices of the speakers. Words or phrases from this language are used when discussing such activities in a second language (Peñalosa, 1980). In many models of bilingual schooling, students are encouraged to use only English or only the primary language in certain contexts. Language purists look down on language mixing. A more fruitful approach might be to let children learn in whatever manner they feel most comfortable, so that anxiety about language will not interfere with concept acquisition.

The second category of individual learner strategies is learning strategies. These include the techniques a person uses to think and to act in order to complete a task. Extensive work in identifying learning strategies has been done by O'Malley and Chamot (O'Malley, Chamot, Stewner-Manzanares, Kupper, & Russo, 1985a, 1985b), who have incorporated specific instruction in learning strategies in their Cognitive Academic Language Learning Approach (CALLA). They have organized learning strategies into three major types: metacognitive, cognitive, and social-affective (Chamot & O'Malley, 1987). These will be discussed in Chapter 4.

Cognitive Style. This is the last intrapersonal factor to be discussed that bears relevance to one's acquisition of a second language. A cognitive style refers to "consistent and rather enduring tendencies or preferences *within* an individual" (Brown, 1987, p. 79). Long lists of cognitive styles—including such constructs as sensory modality strengths, types of information processing, motivation, attributes, and value judgments—have been assembled by educators and psychologists. For the teacher of English learners, however, elements that have shown cultural differences are the ones to note. Tharp (1989b) suggests two cognitive styles that have relevance for classrooms: visual/verbal and holistic/analytic. On a continuum from visual to verbal and from holistic to analytic, it is the latter element in these two styles that schools expect and reward. For students who have a more visual orientation, and whose previous learning consisted of observing and learning by doing rather than through verbal instructions, schools may be mystifying until they catch on to a different cognitive style. Similarly, students with more holistic thought processes understand pieces of a process through knowledge of the pattern as a whole. "Wholistic comprehension proceeds by incorporating phenomena into ever-expanding circles of context, rather than by reducing phenomena to their disassembled parts" (Tharp, 1989b, p. 353). Many aspects of cognitive style have been demonstrated to show cultural differences (see Cohen, 1969), although other researchers have considered the connection between cognitive styles and cultural styles to be overrated (O'Neil, 1990).

Types of Bilingualism and Related Cognitive Effects. Early studies on bilingualism have reported both positive and negative cognitive and academic effects. To account for this inconsistency, Cummins (1979b) analyzed the language characteristics of the children studied and suggested that the level of bilingualism attained is an important factor in educational development. *Limited bilingualism,* or subtractive bilingualism, can occur when children's first language is gradually replaced by a more dominant and prestigious language. This has also been called semilingualism (Díaz, 1983). In this case, children may develop relatively low levels of academic proficiency in both languages. *Partial bilingualism,* in which students have achieved a native-like level in one of their languages, has neither positive nor negative cognitive effects. The most positive cognitive effects are experienced in *proficient bilingualism,* when students attain high levels of proficiency in both languages. This is also called *additive bilingualism.*

Whether or not bilingualism presents a cognitive advantage has been actively researched (see Point/Counterpoint below). Cummins (1976) posits a *threshold hypothesis*: Children must attain a critical level, or threshold, of linguistic proficiency in order to avoid cognitive deficit and allow their bilingualism to benefit their cognitive growth. There are actually two thresholds. Attaining the first generally ensures that negative cognitive effects will not occur, and attainment of the second may lead to accelerated cognitive growth. A variety of researchers have found that proficient bilinguals who have high levels of primary and second language outperform monolinguals on a variety of cognitive tasks (Duncan & DeAvila, 1979; Kessler & Quinn, 1980). This research indicates that a strong bilingual program provides an important prerequisite to subsequent academic success. Chapter 6 discusses bilingualism and bilingual education in greater detail.

Point/Counterpoint

How does being bilingual affect learning?
The Bilingual Education Act of 1968 authorized funds for the education of students who were "educationally disadvantaged because of their inability to speak English." This law was explicitly compensatory in nature; it attempted to remediate the "handicap" of being bilingual. Does being bilingual cause learning problems, or does it involve associated cognitive strengths?

Point: **Bilingual children are hampered in school because of cognitive interference.**
Early research on bilingualism concluded that speaking two languages was so taxing on the mental development of the child that cognitive abilities suffered. Díaz (1983) summarized research performed prior to 1962, which built a case for a "language handicap" in bilingual children. Researchers found evidence that bilingual children had "poorer vocabulary," "deficient articulation," "lower standards in written composition," and "more grammatical errors" that nonbilinguals. One interpretation was that bilingualism caused "linguistic confusion" that deeply affected children's intellectual ability and academic performance.

Counterpoint: **Being bilingual may have cognitive advantages.**
Cummins (1976) found early studies that claimed a "language handicap" were often flawed by the failure to separate the economic status of children from the measure of their academic ability. Moreover, Díaz (1983) found that these studies systematically failed to define *bilingual* in a satisfactory manner, often confusing such factors as parents' birthplaces and family name with bilingual proficiency.

A number of studies have shown that bilingual children perform better than monolinguals on tests that measure various aspects of cognitive and linguistic development. In a study involving 10-year-old French-Canadian children, Peal and Lambert (1962) showed a positive correlation between bilingualism and general intelligence. In this research, however, the students chosen as subjects had equally developed French and English skills; critics have charged that these students were likely to have been gifted and therefore naturally scored highly on a test of general intelligence.

Subsequent research has shown that higher degrees of bilingualism are correlated with increased cognitive abilities in such areas as concept formation, creativity, knowledge of the workings of language, and cognitive flexibility (Díaz, 1983; Galambos & Goldin-Meadow, 1990). Skutnabb-Kangas (1981) has summed up other research that shows a positive effect of bilingualism on general intellectual development, including the mixed results of research on bilingualism and divergent thinking.

Sociocultural Factors

Language learning and language teaching occur within social and cultural contexts. As one masters a language, one is also becoming a member of the community that uses this language to interact, learn, conduct business, love and hate, and participate in a myriad of other social activities. A part of the sense of mastery and enjoyment in a language is acting appropriately and understanding cultural norms. Learners adapt patterns of behavior in a new language and culture based on experiences from their own culture. They carry from their home culture certain patterns of behavior that are used automatically as they learn a new language. These patterns of behavior can be both helpful and limiting in learning the second language community's patterns of interaction.

Culture includes the ideas, customs, skills, arts, and tools that characterize a given group of people in a given period of time (Brown, 2000). One's own culture forms the template of reality; it operates as a lens that allows some information to make sense and other information to remain unperceived. When two cultures come into contact, misunderstandings can be created because members of these cultures have differing perceptions, behaviors, customs, and ideas. Thus, sociocultural factors—how people interact with each other and how they carry out their daily business—play a large role in second language acquisition.

If, as many believe, prolonged exposure to English is sufficient for mastery, then why do so many students fail to achieve the proficiency in English necessary for academic success? Some clues to this perplexity can be found beyond the language itself, in the sociocultural context. Do the students feel that their language and culture are accepted and validated by the school? Does the structure of the school mirror the students' mode of cognition? A well-meaning teacher, with the most up-to-date pedagogy, may still fail to foster achievement if students are socially and culturally uncomfortable with, resistant to, or alienated from schooling.

As students learn a second language, their success is dependent on such extralinguistic factors as the pattern of acculturation for their community; the status of their primary language in relation to English; their own speech community's view of the English language and the English-speaking community; the dialect of English they are hearing and learning and its relationship to standard English; the patterns of social and cultural language usage in the community (see Labov, 1972); and the compatibility between the home culture and the cultural patterns and organization of schools. These issues are explored here with a view toward helping teachers facilitate student learning by bridging the culture and language gap.

Acculturation Variables

Acculturation is the process of adapting to a new culture. English learners in the United States, by the mere fact of living in this country and participating in schools, learn a second culture as well as a second language. How the acculturation proceeds depends on factors beyond language itself and beyond the individual learner's motivation, capabilities, and style. Moreover, acculturation may not be a desirable goal for all groups.

In studying students' differential school performance, Ogbu (1978) draws a distinction between various types of immigrant groups. *Caste-like minorities* are those minority groups that were originally incorporated into society against their will and have been systematically exploited and deprecated over generations through slavery or colonization. Caste-like minorities traditionally work at the lowest paying and most undesirable jobs, and they suffer from a job ceiling that they cannot rise above regardless of talent, motivation, or achievement. Thus, academic success is not always seen as helpful or even desirable for members of these groups. *Immigrant minorities* who are relatively free of a history of deprecation, on the other hand—such as immigrants to the United States from El Salvador, Guatemala, and Nicaragua—believe that the United States is a land of opportunity. These immigrants do not view education as irrelevant or exploitative but, rather, as an important investment.

Schumann (1978a) has developed the acculturation model that asserts that "the degree to which a learner acculturates to the target language group will control the degree to which he acquires the second language" (p. 34). He lists the following social variables that he concludes are important factors in acculturation:

- The primary language and the English language groups view each other as socially equal, of equal status.
- The primary language and the English language groups both desire that the L1 group assimilate.
- The primary language and the English language groups expect the primary language group to share social facilities with the English language group.
- The primary language group is small and not very cohesive.
- The primary language group's culture is congruent with that of the English language group.
- Both groups have positive attitudes toward each other.
- The primary language group expects to stay in the area for an extended period.

The positive attitudes between groups of speakers (primary language and English-speaking groups), as well as the small numbers of primary language individuals, help these students acquire English; if these factors are not present, primary language students can be hindered. Therefore, if a classroom has large groups of primary language speakers whose language is not valued by English speakers, then English language acquisition is not promoted despite the teacher's best intentions.

Differential Status of Languages

In the previous section, reference was made to status and how a group's status may affect members' school performance. A related issue is that of the status of a group's language. In modern U.S. culture, the social value and prestige of speaking a second language varies with socioeconomic position; it also varies as to the second language that is spoken. Many middle-class parents believe that learning a second language benefits their children personally and socially and will later benefit them professionally. In fact, it is characteristic of the elite group in the United States who are involved in scholarly work, diplomacy, foreign trade, or travel to desire to be fully competent in two languages (Porter, 1990). However, the languages that parents wish their children to study are often not those spoken by recently arrived immigrants (Dicker, 1992). This suggests that a certain bias exists in being bilingual—that being competent in a "foreign language" is valuable, whereas knowing an immigrant language is a burden to be overcome.

In the following informal sociolinguistic ranking task, rank from 1 to 4 the following language situations according to the probable socioeconomic status of an individual in that situation (1= highest socioeconomic status):

_____ A child in a Miami neighborhood speaks Haitian French.
_____ A child in a Washington, D.C., suburban preschool learns French.
_____ A student in an El Paso middle school is placed in a Spanish-for-native-speakers class.
_____ A student in a Minneapolis high school studies Spanish as a second language.

Did you rank the preschool child as representing the highest socioeconomic class? In the United States, members of the upper middle class in the diplomatic communities in New York and Washington place great value on the acquisition of French, to the extent of enrolling young children in preschools that feature French instruction. In contrast, a native speaker of French from Haiti receives very little social status from the knowledge of French because it is not acquired in the context of possible use in the upper classes. In fact, the Haitian immigrant may represent one of the lowest economic classes in the United States (rank = 4 on this 1–4 scale). Middle-class students in U.S. high schools routinely enroll in French, German, or Spanish classes to meet college entrance requirements. Therefore, this middle-class language acquisition probably represents a ranking of 2 on the exercise. Spanish-speaking students in the Southwest do not need Spanish taught as a foreign language, but their social status as Spanish speakers is paradoxically lower than that of mainstream U.S. students who acquire Spanish as a foreign language. This task illustrates the differential social status of second languages in the United States.

Not only are second languages differentially valued, so too are various aspects of languages. Judgments are made about regional and social varieties of languages, "good" and "bad" language, and such seemingly minor elements as voice level and speech patterns. Native Americans may value soft-spoken individuals and interpret European Americans' loud voice tone as angry. The standard middle-class speech patterns of female teachers may be considered effeminate by lower-class adolescent boys and thus rejected (Saville-Troike, 1976). The video "American Tongues" (information available at http://www.cnam.com/more_info/ameri3 .html) provides an informative overview of various American dialects and their impact on others. It has been a useful teaching tool for helping students and workers hear examples of regional speech and attitudes and relate them to their own lives.

There are many ways in which a second-class status is communicated to speakers of other languages, and, since language attitudes usually operate at an inconspicuous level, school personnel and teachers are not always aware of the attitudes they hold. It is not possible to inventory completely those factors that influence language attitudes and the practices perpetuated because of those attitudes. The sensitive teacher can, however, learn areas where there may be differences in language use and where those differences might create friction because the minority groups use may be deemed "inferior" by the majority. Furthermore, teachers can be honest with themselves about their own biases, recognizing that they communicate these biases whether or not they are aware of them. Everyone has biases, so being aware of them and being candid about changing injurious biases can go far in affecting the climate of the school and the perception of students regarding their own value. Generally, attitudes toward second languages need to be broadened. If Americans, consciously or unconsciously, are going to maintain certain "foreign" languages as the prestige languages in this new century, they are cutting themselves off from the social and economic advantages available to those who value a wide range of languages and cultures.

Value Systems

As student populations in U.S. schools become increasingly diversified both linguistically and culturally, teachers and students have come to recognize the important role that attitudes and values play in school success. Values, like attitudes, operate at an intuitive level and unknowingly permeate all interactions.

> Amol is a third-grade student whose parents were born in India. As the only son in a male-dominant culture, he has internalized a strong sense of commitment toward becoming a heart surgeon. His approach to classwork is painstaking. His writing is particularly labored. Although English is the dominant language in the home, Amol's writing in English is slow and careful. Often, he is the last one to be finished with an assignment during class. His teacher places great emphasis on speed

in learning and considers time a critical factor in the display of capability. The teacher's main frustration with Amol is that he cannot quickly complete his work. (Do we want the future heart surgeon to be quick?)

In this example, the teacher epitomizes a mainstream U.S. value: speed and efficiency in learning. This value is exemplified in the use of timed standardized testing in the United States. Teachers often describe students of other cultures as being lackadaisical and uncaring about learning, when in fact they may be operating within a different time frame and value system.

Other values held by teachers and embodied in classroom procedures have to do with task orientation. The typical U.S. classroom is a place of work in which students are expected to conform to a schedule, keep busy, maintain order, avoid wasting time, conform to authority, and achieve academically in order to attain personal worth (LeCompte, 1981). Working alone is also valued in school, and children spend a great deal of time in activities that do not allow them to interact verbally with other people or to move physically around the room.

Children need to find within the structure and content of their schooling those behaviors and perspectives that permit them to switch between home and school cultural behaviors and values without inner conflict or crises of identity (Pérez & Torres-Guzmán, 1992). Teachers need to feel comfortable in the values and behaviors of their students' cultures in order to develop a flexible cultural repertoire within the context of teaching. In order to begin to understand the values placed on various aspects of interaction, teachers can examine the importance of the following dichotomies in their classrooms—cooperation versus competition, aggression versus compliance, anonymity versus self-assertion, sharing time versus wasting time, and disorder versus order (Saville-Troike, 1976)—and examine their feelings about them in order to understand their personal value system.

The danger of excluding the students' culture(s) from the classroom is that cultural identity, if not included, may become oppositional. Ogbu and Matute-Bianchi (1986) describe how oppositional identity in a distinctly Mexican American frame of reference influences the performance of Mexican American children. They attribute achievement difficulties on the part of some Mexican American children to a distrust of academic effort. When schools were segregated and offered inferior education to this community, a general mistrust of schools caused a difficulty in accepting, internalizing, and following school rules of behavior for achievement. Parents in this community, who may have experienced rejection themselves and who do not view schooling as a source of success, may unknowingly and subtly communicate ambivalence and disillusionment about the value of academic effort to their children. Deviant behavior, in Ogbu and Matute-Bianchi's perspective, is a reflection of the destructive patterns of subordination and social and economic deprivation of the minority group. Doing well in school, for some students, is not a part of the code of conduct that wins them affirmation among their peers in the community. This element of resistance or opposition is not always overt but often takes the form of mental withdrawal, high absenteeism, or reluctance to do classwork.

Schools with high concentrations of English learners often deprive children of using their cultural knowledge and experience, even when staff are well meaning. It is easy to give lip service to the validation of the students' cultures and values. However, if teachers consistently use examples drawn from one culture and not another, use literature that displays pictures and photographs of one culture only, and set up classroom procedures that allow some students to feel less comfortable than others, these students will be forced to accept alienation from home, family, and culture. This is unfair and damaging. The concept of a rich and flexible cultural repertoire is the theme that can allow cultures to mix constructively and promote achievement.

Dialects and Standard Languages

All speakers have three or more levels in their language usage—levels of which they may or may not be aware. There is an intimate speech used in the home; an informal but slightly restrained speech used in semipublic situations; and the carefully prepared, deliberate, formal speech of public addresses. Some of this speech may belong to the standard dialect, some to other regional or social dialects. The terms *standard* and *dialect* indicate that certain forms are more acceptable than others. It is not the case, however, that certain forms are inadequate for the task demanded of them. All languages and dialects are adequate. It is only that people believe certain forms are "better." "The community's choice of what shall count as the norm and what shall be rated as 'bad' . . . is an arbitrary choice, so that usage is never good or bad but thinking makes it so" (Joos, 1967, p. 14). What, then, is the standard dialect and what characterizes other dialects? And where does the interlanguage used by students as they learn English fit into the standard/dialect mix?

Standard English operates on both a formal and an informal level. The formal standard follows a prescribed code, is relatively homogeneous, and is largely confined to the style used when writing, giving public speeches, or talking on television. It is the form taught in schools for expository or argumentative writing and is characterized by a restrained vocabulary; strict adherence to grammatical elements such as subject-verb agreement, pronoun-antecedent relationships, and tense sequences; and use of complex sentence structures. The informal standard is more subjective and flexible and is sensitive to the context in which it is used. The language used in a store when asking for assistance, the talk at the office water cooler, and the conversation at parties and receptions are examples of informal standard. It has a written form—personal correspondence and business and social notes (Pooley, 1977).

A dialect is a variety of a language, usually regional or social, that is distinguishable from other varieties by differences in pronunciation, vocabulary, and grammar. Everyone speaks a dialect, and, as stated previously, no dialect is good or bad in itself. The difference in the prestige of certain dialects comes from the prestige of the speakers of that dialect.

Teachers in general often feel that their role is to enforce the phonology, semantics, and syntax of standard English in the classroom (Roberts, 1985) and not to accept or validate other dialects. Teachers may take one of three philosophical positions on the teaching of Standard English:

- *Replacive or eradicationism:* Standard English supplants the dialect of vernacular-speaking students. Following this philosophy, teachers see their role as correcting students' "errors."
- *Additive or bidialectialism:* Maintains both the standard and vernacular variety for use in different social situations. Following this philosophy, teachers may encourage students to use colloquialisms to lend flavor to creative writing or dialog, while reserving Standard English for formal classroom contexts.
- *Dialect rights:* Rejects the necessity to learn and practice standard spoken English. Following this philosophy, teachers do not teach Standard English. (Wolfram, 1991)

Regardless of teachers' attitudes toward nonstandard dialects, the language spoken by a child—whether standard or nonstandard—is the best means of direct communication between teacher and child. An understanding of the child's language is a necessary first step toward understanding a student (Labov, 1969).

In 1974, the National Council of Teachers of English (NCTE) took a strong position on students' language rights:

> We affirm the students' right to their own patterns and varieties of the language—the dialects of their nurture or whatever dialects in which they find their own identity and style. Language scholars long ago denied that the myth of a standard American dialect has any validity. The claim that any one dialect is unacceptable amounts to an attempt of one social group to exert its dominance over another. Such a claim leads to false advice for speakers and writers, and immoral advice for humans. A nation proud of its diverse heritage and its cultural and racial variety will preserve its heritage of dialects. We affirm strongly that teachers must have the experiences and training that will enable them to respect diversity and uphold the right of the students to their own language. (College Composition and Communication, 1974, pp. 2–3)

One issue raised concerning dialects has been their effect on basic educational skills such as reading and writing. An important question for educators has been: Does language variation contribute to educational failure or problems in a significant way? The answer is probably no. Attitudes appear to play a larger role in student success and failure than do dialectal differences. If teachers use dialect to evaluate students' potential or use proficiency in Standard English to predict school achievement, then it is possible that the teachers' own attitudes toward the students' dialects—either positive or negative—have more to do with students' cognitive and academic achievement than does the dialect. Speaking a dialect other than Standard English may cause miscommunication between the student and teacher. For example, a student may say "wif" and not "with" or read "She didn't pay no attention" when the text has "She didn't pay attention." If the teacher makes a correction, the student may not hear it or even understand why the teacher has interrupted. All the child will remember is that the teacher interrupted. A continuing pattern of such interruptions can serve to silence the child. Transformations such as those cited have not been found to interfere with comprehension. Ultimately, a greater block to comprehension may be a lack of prior knowledge about a topic, a factor that may be attributed to the sociolinguistic aspect of the dialect: Certain speech communities have access to prior knowledge that others do not (Wolfram, 1991).

The interlanguage of English language development students may be considered a dialect of English. If teachers devalue the accent students use as they learn English, English language learners receive the message that their dialect is not accepted. Using the philosophy underlying the Natural Approach (Krashen & Terrell, 1983), an English teacher can model correct usage without overt correction, and the student, in time, will self-correct—*if* the student chooses Standard English as the appropriate sociolinguistic choice for that context.

Cultural Patterns and Organization of Schools

Often, minorities in U.S. society experience school failure. Several conflicting hypotheses try to explain this. One is that students of these groups are unmotivated—the students and/or their parents are uninterested in education and unwilling to comply with teacher-assigned tasks. A second hypothesis is that students who grow up as native speakers of another language are handicapped in learning because they have not acquired sufficient English. A third hypothesis is that there are cultural differences, a cultural mismatch, between the ways children learn at home or among their peers and the ways they are expected to learn at school. A fourth hypothesis is that teachers have lower expectations for their non-European American students and thus provide them with a less rigorous instructional program. A fifth hypothesis is that schools operate in ways that advantage certain children and disadvantage others, and that these distinct outcomes align with social and political forces in the larger cultural context. In this section, organization and patterns within the school are examined to explore the fifth hypothesis and extend the understanding of sociocultural factors that influence schooling for English learners.

Some social theorists see the culture of the school as maintaining the poor in a permanent underclass and as legitimizing inequality (Giroux, 1983). In other words, schooling is used to reaffirm class boundaries. McDermott and Gospodinoff (1981) postulate that students who come to school without an orientation toward literacy present organizational and behavior problems to teachers who are pressured to produce readers. Both teachers and students use systematic miscommunication to achieve a compromise around this difficulty. This compromise creates an educational class system in which minority students—or any students who are not successful in the classroom—emerge from their schooling to occupy the same social status as their parents.

An incident that demonstrates the way schools use language to perpetuate social class inequality was recorded by Erickson (1977).

> The fourth-grade class was electing student council representatives. Mrs. Lark called for nominations. Mary, a monolingual English-speaking European American student, nominated herself without bothering

to follow the class rules of raising her hand and waiting to be called on. Mrs. Lark accepted Mary's self-nomination and wrote her name on the board. Rogelio, a Spanish-speaking Mexican American child with limited English proficiency, nominated Pedro. Mrs. Lark reminded the class that the representative must be "outspoken." Rogelio again said, "Pedro." Mrs. Lark announced to the class again that the representative must be "a good outspoken citizen." Pedro turned red and stared at the floor. Mrs. Lark embarrassed Rogelio into withdrawing the nomination. No other Mexican American child was nominated, and Mary won the election. Pedro and Rogelio were unusually quiet for the rest of the school day and avoided making eye contact with the teacher.

Incidents like this one are generally unintentional on the teacher's part. Teachers have specific ideas and guidelines about appropriate conduct, deportment, and language abilities. If students are not aware of the teacher's values and intention, miscommunication can occur. A beginning step in helping all students be an integral part of the class and the learning environment is for teachers to become sensitive to their own cultural and linguistic predispositions.

Nieto (2000) identifies numerous structures within schools that affect student learning: tracking, testing, the curriculum, pedagogy, the school's physical structure and disciplinary policies, the limited roles of both students and teachers, and limited parent and community involvement.

■ *Tracking* (placement of students in groups of matched abilities), despite its superficial advantages, in reality often labels and groups students for years and allows them little or no opportunity to change groups. Unfortunately, these placements can be based on tenuous, ad hoc judgments. A study of inner-city primary students showed how teachers classified, segregated, and taught students differently beginning from their first weeks in school (Rist, 1970). Secondary school personnel who place ESL students in low tracks and/or in nonacademic ESL classes preclude those students from any opportunity for higher-track, precollege work. Furthermore, tracking systems serve to divide a campus and can increase prejudicial and racist feelings. Gibson (1987) found that non-English-speaking Punjabi students in the ESL track were treated with hostility by the majority students, who believed that ethnic relations would improve if the Punjabis would give up their values and conform to European American norms. Faculty and staff at the high school gradually became aware that the majority students needed crosscultural understanding in order to help the immigrants adjust to their new environment.

■ *Testing* impedes equity in schools by affecting the way teachers present curriculum to various groups. Students who respond poorly on standardized tests are often given "basic skills" in a remedial curriculum that is basically the same as the one in which they were not experiencing success.

■ *Curriculum* design is often at odds with the needs of learners. Only a small fraction of knowledge is codified into textbooks and teachers' guides, and this is rarely the knowledge that English learners bring from their communities. In addition, the curriculum is systematically watered down for the "benefit" of children in language minority communities through the mistaken idea that such students cannot absorb the core curriculum. As a result, students' own experiences are excluded from the classroom, and little of the dominant culture curriculum is provided in any depth.

■ *Pedagogy* is often tedious and uninteresting, particularly for students who have been given a basic skills curriculum in a lower-track classroom. The pressure to "cover" a curriculum excludes learning in depth and also frustrates teachers of lower-track classes.

■ The *physical structure* of the school also determines the educational environment. Many inner-city schools are built like fortresses to forestall vandalism and theft. Rich suburban school districts, by contrast, may provide more space, more supplies, and campus-like schools for their educationally advantaged students.

■ *Disciplinary policies* often discriminate against certain students, particularly those who wear high-profile clothing, have high physical activity levels, or tend to hold an attitude of resistance toward schooling. Williams (1981) observed that students in urban African American ghetto schools may skillfully manipulate the behavioral exchanges between peers to test, tease, and sometimes intimidate teachers. By interpreting this as delinquency, teachers leave these interpersonal skills undeveloped, and students may become more disruptive or rebellious. Rather than defining students' predilections as deviant or disruptive, teachers can channel these interactions into cooperative groups that allow children to express themselves and learn at the same time.

■ The *limited role of students* excludes them from taking an active part in their own schooling, and alienation and passive frustration may result. In classrooms on the Warm Springs (Oregon) Reservation, teacher-controlled activity dominated. All the social and spatial arrangements were created by the teacher: where and when movement took place; where desks were placed and even what furniture was present in the room; and who talked, when, and with whom. For the Warm Springs students, this socialization was difficult. They preferred to wander to various parts of the room, away from the lesson; to talk to other students while the teacher was talking; and to "bid" for each other's attention rather than that of the teacher (Philips, 1972).

A time-honored activity in mainstream classrooms is the small reading group, where participation is usually mandatory, individual, and oral. For Native American children, this structure was particularly ill fitting. They frequently refused to read aloud, did not utter a word when called on, or spoke too softly to be audible. On the other hand, when students controlled and directed interaction in small group projects, they were much more fully involved. They concentrated completely on their work until it was completed and talked a great deal to one another in the group. Very little time was spent disagreeing or arguing about how to go about a task. There was, however, explicit competition with other groups. A look at the daily life of the Warm Springs children revealed several factors that would account for their willingness to work together and their resistance to teacher-directed activity. First, they spend much time in the company of peers with little disciplinary control from older relatives. They also spend time in silence, observing their elders and listening without verbal participation. Speech seems to be an optional response rather than a typical or mandatory feature of interaction. One last characteristic of community life is the accessibility and openness of communitywide celebrations. No single individual directs and controls all activity, and there is no sharp distinction between audience and performer. Individuals are permitted to choose for themselves the degree of participation in an activity (Philips, 1972). Schooling became more successful for these students when they were able to take a more active part.

■ The *limited role of teachers* excludes them from decision making just as students are disenfranchised. This may lead teachers to have negative feelings toward their students.

■ *Limited parent and community involvement* may characterize inner-city schools with large populations of English learners. Parents may find it difficult to attend meetings, may be only symbolically involved in the governance of the school, or may feel a sense of mismatch with the culture of the school just as their children do. In circumstances like these, it is simplistic to characterize parents as being unconcerned about their children's education. School personnel, in consultation with community and parent representatives, can begin to ameliorate such perceptions by talking to each other and developing means of communication and interaction appropriate for both the parent and school communities.

Teaching and learning in mainstream classrooms is often organized with social structures that deny the ways in which students are most likely to learn. Tharp (1989b) describes the typical North American classroom. Students are seated in ranks and files, and a teacher-leader instructs the whole group. Individual practice and teacher-organized individual assessment are parts of this practice. Many students are not productive and on task in this environment. Instead, they may pay little attention to teachers and classwork and seek attention from peers. Cultures that feature collaboration, cooperation, and assisted performance may find the traditional U.S. classroom a detriment to learning. Other cultures may find the grouping of boys with girls to be contrary to cultural values. In the case of the Punjabis, for example, teenage boys and girls avoid conversation in mixed company and girls do not speak up in the presence of males. Coeducational physical education classes were particularly torturous for the girls, who have been taught to avoid physical activity and to keep their legs fully covered (Gibson, 1987).

Cooperative learning has positive results in the education of minority students (Kagan, 1986). Positive race relations among students and socialization toward prosocial values and behaviors are potential outcomes of a cooperative learning environment. Classroom structures that emphasize individual performance, the teacher as controlling authority, and little or no student control of participation may be "culturally incongruent" with the background of many groups (Cazden, 1988; Erickson & Mohatt, 1982; Heath, 1983b; Philips, 1972). Cooperative learning may restore a sense of comfort in the school setting to children of a variety of cultures. Students may gain psychological support from each other as they acquire English, and this support can help the students work as a group with the teacher to achieve a workable sociocultural compromise between the home culture and the culture of the school.

CHAPTER

3 Language Structure and Use

The first time that I saw you.
I was paralized [sic] with emotion
that everything I didn't expected [sic].
I was in love with you
and because of anything
My eyes were telling you beautiful things.
Everything started from the first time
I saw you.
I felt as if I had found
What I was looking for.
I never before had so much happiness in
my life.
I have found in you many reasons to live
maybe because with you I have learn [sic]
what's love.
You have showed me new happiness
having you, I can't ask for more
    for all of this.
    I love you!

—ESL high school student

Language—what it can do for us! It allows us to express deep feelings, as this student has done in her love poem. It takes us beyond the here and now, allowing us to recall past events and to anticipate the future. It is a means of connection between one individual and another. It communicates the heights of joy and the depths of despair. Language belongs to everyone, from the preschooler to the professor. There is almost no aspect of a person's life that is not touched by language: Everyone speaks and everyone listens. People argue about language, sometimes quite passionately and eloquently. Language is universal, and yet each language has evolved to meet the experiences, needs, and desires of that language's community.

It is important for teachers to understand language structure in order to help their students to learn (see Figure I.1). All languages share certain features—such as the ability to label objects and to describe actions and events—and certain functions—such as the facility to obtain favors, to make demands, to express imagination, and to make apologies. This chapter explores the subsystems that make up languages in general, paying attention to those elements particular to the English language, and the use to which languages are put. Components of nonverbal communication are also discussed in order to highlight the power of the nonverbal system.

Language Universals

According to Woodbury (1997), there are roughly 5,000 to 6,000 languages spoken in today's world. Although not all of these have been intensely studied, enough investigations have been carried out by linguists over the centuries to posit the following list of some universal facts about language:

- Wherever humans exist, language exists.
- There are no "primitive" languages. All languages are equally complex, capable of expressing any idea, and expandable to include new words for new concepts.
- All languages change through time.
- The relationships between the sounds and meanings of spoken languages or between gestures and meanings of sign languages are, for the most part, arbitrary.
- All human languages use a finite set of sounds or gestures that are combined to form meaningful elements or words that then combine to form an infinite set of possible sentences.
- Every spoken language uses discrete sound segments and has vowels and consonants.
- Speakers of any language are capable of producing and comprehending an infinite set of sentences.
- All grammars contain rules for the formation of words and sentences.
- Similar grammatical categories are found in all languages.
- Every language has a way of referring to past time; the ability to negate; the ability to form questions, issue commands, and so on.
- Semantic universals, such as "male" or "female," are found in every language in the world.
- Every normal child, born anywhere in the world, of any racial, geographical, social, or economic heritage, is capable of learning any language to which he or she is exposed. (Fromkin & Rodman, 1993, pp. 25-26)

The Structure of Language

Language has been divided into various subsystems that allow one to study distinct components. These include *phonology,* the study of the sound system of a language; *morphology,* the study of how words are built; *syntax,* the study of the structure of sentences; *semantics,* the study of the meanings of a language; and *pragmatics,* the use of language in social contexts. One of the fascinating facts about language is that speakers learn all these subsystems of their first language without realizing it. Thus, native speakers can converse fluently, but cannot explain a sound pattern or a grammatical point. To them, that is "just the way it is." For English language development (ELD) teachers, however, a basic knowledge of these various subsystems will help in understanding the various components of a language in order to pinpoint student needs and to provide appropriate instruction. Such knowledge also helps teachers recognize the richness and variety of students' emerging language.

Phonology: The Sound Patterns of Language

The phonology of a language is the way in which speech sounds form patterns. Speakers' phonological knowledge enables them to form meaningful utterances and to recognize what is or what is not a sound in their own language. In the following list of nonsense words, native English speakers can immediately pick out which three "words" *do not* conform to English sound patterns and thus could never become English words, and which three "words" *do* conform to English sound patterns and thus could become English words: ldang, bluck, stuoin, trawr, gobsmacked, fulf.

Phonemes. Phonemes are the sounds that make up a language. These are distinctive units that "make a difference" when sounds form words. For example, in English, the initial consonant sounds /t/ and /d/[1] are the only difference between the words *tip* and *dip* and are thus phonemes. The number of phonemes in a language ranges between 20 and 50; Hawaiian is a language with one of the fewest (18), whereas English has a high average count (from 34 to 45, depending on the dialect).

Each language has permissible ways in which phonemes can be combined. These are called *phonemic sequences.* In English, /spr/ as in *spring,* /nd/ as in *handle,* and /kt/ as in *talked* are phonemic sequences. Languages also have permissible places for these sequences. They may occur initially (at the beginning of a word), medially (between initial and final position), finally (at the end of a word), or in a combination of these positions. Spanish, for example, uses the sequence /sp/ medi-

---

1. A convention of linguistic notation is to use a phonetic alphabet to represent sounds and to place the phonetic symbols between slashes. This avoids confusion between spelling conventions and phonemic representation. This convention is used in this text.

ally—*español*—but never initially. This would explain why, in speaking English, native Spanish speakers may say *"espeak."* English speakers have a similar problem when confronted with African words beginning with sequences such as /ts/ or /ng/. These sequences occur in final position in English—*cats, purring*—but never in an initial position. On the other hand, in English, the sequence /st/ occurs initially and finally—*stop, forest*. Not all of the permissible sequences are used in every pattern. For example, English has *cr* and *br* as initial consonant clusters. *Craft* is a word but at present *braft* is not, although it would be phonologically permissible. *Nraft*, on the other hand, is not permissible because *nr* is not an initial cluster in English.

Phonemes occur in predictable groups called *natural classes*. Speech sounds can be described in terms of their characteristic point of articulation (tip, front, or back of the tongue), whether the vocal cords vibrate or not (voiced and voiceless sounds), and the manner of articulation (the way the airstream is obstructed). Table 3.1 shows the English stops (sounds that are produced by completely blocking the breath stream and then releasing it abruptly). The point placements given in the chart relate to the positions in the mouth from which the sound is produced. Other languages—for example, Spanish—have different qualities to the stop sounds. Not all languages distinguish between voiced and voiceless sounds, which are distinctive to native English speakers. Arabic speakers may say *barking lot* instead of *parking lot* because, to them, *p* and *b* are not distinguishable.

Pitch. Besides the actual formation of sounds, other sound qualities are important in speech. Speakers of all languages vary the pitch of their voices when they talk. In English, pitch is important in distinguishing meaning within a sentence: "Eva is going," as a statement, is said with a falling pitch, but when it is used as a question, the pitch rises at the end. This use of pitch to modify the sentence meaning is called *intonation*. Languages that use the pitch of individual syllables to contrast meanings are called *tone languages*. Most of the languages of the world are tone languages: There are more than 1,000 tone languages in Africa alone. Chinese, Thai, and Burmese are tone languages, as are many American Indian languages (Fromkin & Rodman, 1993). Pitch, whether at the word or at the sentence level, is one of the phonological components of a language that plays an important role in determining meaning.

TABLE 3.1   Point of Articulation for Voiced and Voiceless English Stops

		Labial		Dental			
Point		*Bilabial*	*Labiodental*	*Interdental*	*Alveolar*	*Palatal*	*Velar*
Manner	*Voicing*						
Stop	voiceless	*p*			*t*		*k*
	voiced	*b*			*d*		*g*

Stress.   Stress, another phonological component of languages, can also occur at the word or the sentence level. Within words, specific syllables can be stressed. In the following examples, the stressed syllable is indicated by the accent mark ´ :

> *pérfect*   adjective, as in "She handed in a perfect paper."
> *perféct*   verb, as in "It takes so long to perfect a native-like accent."
> *rébel*   noun, as in "James Dean played the role of a rebel."
> *rebél*   verb, as in "Adolescents often rebel against restrictions."

Like pitch, stress modifies the meaning of words. Stress can further be used at the sentence level to vary emphasis. For example, the following sentences all carry different emphases:

> Shé did that.
> She díd that.
> She did thát.

When words are combined into phrases and sentences, one of the syllables receives greater stress than the others. Students who learn a second language sometimes find difficulty in altering the sound of a word in the context of whole sentences. Current language pedagogy, along with the whole language philosophy, discourages the teaching of words isolated from the context of sentences and paragraphs. Not only is the meaning of the word difficult to learn in isolation from context but also the sound of a word can differ when it is pronounced in normal conversation than when it occurs in a vocabulary list. For example, in a vocabulary list, *west* is pronounced /wɛst/ whereas in the phrase "she's flying to the West Coast on Monday," it is pronounced /wɛs/. The final /t/ is deleted.

Native speakers are seldom, if ever, taught explicitly the phonological rules of their language, yet they know them. Phonological knowledge is acquired as a learner listens to and begins to produce speech. The same is true in a second language.

Morphology: The Words of Language

Morphology is the study of the meaning units in a language. Many people believe that individual words constitute these basic meaning units. However, many words can be broken down into smaller segments that still retain meaning.

Morphemes.   Morphemes, small, indivisible units, are the basic building blocks of meaning. *Terrorizers* is an English word composed of four morphemes: *terror + ize + er + s* (root + verb-forming suffix + noun-forming suffix + plural marker). Morphemes can be represented by a single sound, such as *a*, meaning *without*, in *amoral* or *asexual;* a syllable, such as the noun-forming morpheme *-ment* in *amendment;* or two or more syllables, such as *tiger* or *artichoke.* Two different morphemes may have the same sound, such as the *-er* as in *dancer* ("one who dances") and the *-er* in *fanci<u>er</u>* (comparative form of *fancy*). A morpheme may also have alternate phonetic forms: The regular plural *-s* can be pronounced either /z/ (*bags*), /s/ (*cats*), or /iz/ (*bushes*).

Morphemes are of different types and serve different purposes. *Free morphemes* can stand alone (*envelop, the, through*), whereas *bound morphemes* occur only in conjunction with others (*-ing, dis-, -ceive*). Most bound morphemes occur as *affixes.* (The others are bound roots.) Affixes at the beginning of words are *prefixes* (*un-* in the word *unafraid*); those added at the end are *suffixes* (*-able* in the word *believable*); and *infixes* are morphemes that are inserted into other morphemes (*-zu-* in the German word *anzufangen,* "to begin"). Bound morphemes are of two types: derivational and inflectional. *Derivational morphemes* can change the meaning of a word. For example, adding *ex-* to the noun *champion* means "former champion." Derivational morphemes can also change a word's part of speech. By adding *-ance* to the adjective *clear,* the noun *clearance* is formed. *Inflectional morphemes* (of which English has only eight), on the other hand, only qualify the word in some manner. An *-s* is added to a verb to indicate third-person singular or an *-ed* to indicate past action; an *-s* is added to a noun to indicate more than one or an *-'s* to indicate possession; *-er* and *-est* are added to adjectives to indicate comparison or superlative.

Students who learn English as a second language may profit from learning sets of words at one time that share a similar root morpheme or *root word.* Learning the verb *authorize* can lead to the use of the root *author-* to generate the related words *authority, authorization, authoritarian, author, authoritative, unauthorized,* and *authoritatively.* This is a way for students learning English to expand their vocabulary quickly. Compounds can be learned in a similar manner, although in English many compounds no longer connote the original roots—for example, *household, cupboard,* and *breakfast.*

English has historically been a language that has welcomed new words— either borrowing them from other languages or coining new ones from existing words. A useful exercise for teachers as well as students is to make charts of English words that EL students use in their first language and words English has borrowed from the students' native languages. This activity increases everyone's vocabulary and often generates interesting discussions about food, clothing, cultural artifacts, as well as the ever-expanding world of technology. Students may also become motivated to use bound or free morphemes creatively: Those who play computer video games or read comic books may enjoy making up names for new characters, which are often formed from English morphemes combined with standard suffixes, such as Phoenixmon or Machinemon.

Helping students understand other processes for word coinage also heightens interest in vocabulary building. Understanding *clipping,* a process of shortening words, such as *prof* for *professor* or the slangy *teach* for *teacher,* gives students a sense that they are learning two words for one as well as both colloquial and academic speech. *Product names* often include a word evoking an important feature of the product, such as Brillo, *brilliant;* Jello, *gel;* and Kleenex, *clean. Acronyms* are plentiful in English and many are already familiar to students—UN, CIA, and NASA, for example. A growing list of acronyms helps students increase their vocabulary of both the words forming the acronyms and the acronyms themselves. Introducing students to *blends,* words formed from parts of two words—for example, *smog* from smoke + fog and *brunch* from breakfast + lunch—can turn students into word detectives and they often discover new ones through shopping (Wal-Mart?) or advertisements.

Syntax: The Sentence Patterns of Language

Syntax refers to the structure of sentences and the rules that govern the correctnessof a sentence. Sentences are composed of words that follow accepted patterns, but sentence meaning is more than the sum of the meaning of the words. Sentence A, "The teacher asked the students to sit down" has the same words as sentence B, "The students asked the teacher to sit down" but not the same meaning. Not every sequence of words is a sentence—for example, sentence C, "*asked the the teacher to down students sit"[2] has no syntactic rules and thus has no meaning.

All native speakers of a language can distinguish syntactically correct from incorrect combinations of words. Even very young English-speaking children know that "the paper is on the desk" is meaningful, but sentence C (above) is not. This syntactic knowledge in the native language is not taught in school but is constructed as native speakers acquire their language as children. This internal knowledge allows speakers to recognize the sentence "'Twas brillig and the slithy toves did gyre and gimble in the wabes" in Lewis Carroll's "Jabberwocky" as syntactically correct English, even though the words are nonsense. Fortunately, speakers of a language with this knowledge of correct and incorrect sentences can, in fact, understand sentences that are not perfectly formed. Sentences that contain minor syntactic errors, such as the high school student's poem cited at the beginning of this chapter, are still comprehensible.

Besides grammaticality and word order, syntactic knowledge accounts for double meaning, or *ambiguity,* as in the sentence "She is a Chinese art expert," for recognizing when sentences of different structures mean the same thing ("She is easy to please"; "Pleasing her is easy"; "It is easy to please her") and for permitting speakers to understand and produce novel utterances, the *creative* aspect of language.

Whereas syntax refers to the internally constructed rules that make sentences, *grammar* looks at whether a sentence conforms to a standard. An important distinction for ELD teachers to keep in mind is the one between standard and colloquial usage. Many colloquial usages are acceptable sentence patterns in English, even though their usage is not standard—for example "I ain't got no pencil" is acceptable English syntax. It is not, however, standard usage. Through example and in lessons, teachers are promoting the standard dialect, but need to be aware that students' developing competence will not always conform to that standard, and that students will also learn colloquial expressions that they will not always use in the

---

2. In linguistic notation, an asterisk (*) is used before a word or string of items to indicate it is not a possible combination in the language cited.

appropriate context (see Appropriateness in this chapter). Learning the syntax of a language is a dynamic process in which progress is made toward grammatical accuracy. The learner acquires syntactic knowledge, semantic meanings, and phonological accuracy simultaneously, and good teaching supports this acquisition.

Semantics: The Meanings of Language

Semantics is the study of meanings of individual words and of larger units such as phrases and sentences. Speakers of a language have learned the "agreed-upon" meanings of words and phrases in their language and are not free to change meanings of words at will—which would result in no communication at all (Fromkin & Rodman, 1993).

Some words carry a high degree of stability and conformity in the ways they are used (*kick* as a verb, for example, must involve the foot—"he kicked me with his hand" is not semantically correct). Other words carry multiple meanings, ambiguous meanings, or debatable meanings (*marriage,* for example, for many people can refer only to heterosexual alliances and to use it for nonheterosexual contexts is not only unacceptable but inflammatory). For second language acquisition, the process of translating already recognized meaning from one language to the next is only part of the challenge. New semantic meanings must be continually acquired if the mind is to develop while second language learning takes place.

Recognizing the meaning of words involves various kinds of knowledge about words. Table 3.2 illustrates the kind of judgments that a language user can make.

TABLE 3.2   Semantic Properties of Words

Property	Meaning	Example
ambiguity	having more than one sense	She cannot bear children.
anomaly	incongruous in context	They remodeled the dog.
contradiction	opposite in nature	odorless pine scent
redundancy	using surplus words	return back
related meaning	sharing one or more elements	dazzle, shimmer, sparkle, gleam, shine
specificity	narrowing the meaning	fall—tumble; furniture—chair
entailment	logically related to previous meanings	She is his mother → He is her son
connotation	implying suggested meanings	pig → sloppy, dirty, messy
association	frequently connected meanings	The wealthy are privileged.

Part of the difficulty in learning English as a second language is that the English language is extraordinarily rich in synonyms. The *Oxford English Dictionary* lists about 500,000 words; a further half million technical and scientific terms are not included in this tally (compared with French, with fewer than 100,000 words) (McCrum, Cran, & MacNeil, 1986). The challenge when learning this vast vocabulary is to distinguish denotations, connotations, and other shades of meaning.

In addition, speakers of a language must make semantic shifts when writing. It may be understandable when a speaker uses the colloquial "And then she goes..." to mean "she says," but in written English, one must make a semantic shift toward formality, using synonyms such as "she declared," "she remarked," and "she admitted." A teacher who encourages this type of semantic expansion helps students acquire semantic flexibility. Bolinger and Sears (1981) give the example of a series of terms (*coax, persuade, convince*) that are synonymous but that have varying implications. "I was convincing him to go" could be used only if the result was successful. "Persuade," however, puts the result in doubt: "I was persuading him to go" also tells nothing about the result, but emphasizes his reluctance. To go further, "twisting his arm" would imply a more extreme reluctance as well as more extreme persuasion.

Part of the semantic knowledge people receive in a conversation is carried by the intonation used by the speaker: Contrast "*You* went?" with "You *went?*" The meaning of words, therefore, comes partially from the stored meaning and partially from the meaning derived from context. The *lexicon* is the sum total of the meanings stored, the association of these meanings with the correct context, the ability to pronounce the word correctly, the knowledge of how to use the word grammatically in a sentence, and the knowledge of which morphemes are appropriately connected with the word. This knowledge is acquired as the brain absorbs and interacts with the meaning in context.

Pragmatics: The Influence of Context

The general study of how context affects the user's interpretation of language is called *pragmatics*. Pinker (1994) defines pragmatics as "how language is used in a social context, including how sentences are made to fit in with the flow of a conversation, how unspoken premises are inferred, and how degrees of formality and politeness are signaled" (p. 480). If language were only a matter of sounds, words, and grammar, then the following exchange would not seem to make sense.

A: The door!
B: I'm on the phone.
A: OK. I'll get it.

However, through knowledge of the context of this exchange, one might deduce that it occurred in a building, that someone has just knocked on the door, and that A, by announcing this with the short phrase "the door," expects a response from B regarding opening the door. B's response never mentions the door, but instead, incongruously from a cohesion point of view, tells A what B is doing. This information signals to A that B is occupied and is in no position to answer the door. This prompts the final statement that A will answer.

For ELD purposes, an important part of pragmatic knowledge is the way in which patterns of interaction vary depending on culture. Two areas of pragmatics discussed here are *scripts* and *cultural context.*

Scripts.   Every situation carries with it the expectations of the speakers involved and a script that carries out those expectations. In a restaurant, for example, the customers pause at the front counter to see if someone will escort them to their seat. They anticipate being asked, "How many [people in the party]?" To continue the script, when they are seated, they expect to be approached by a waitress or waiter, given a menu, and asked if they would like a drink before ordering. This interchange follows a predictable sequence, and pragmatic knowledge is needed to carry out the parts of the dialogue. Obviously, a fast-food restaurant has a very different script.

Classroom procedures also have scripts, and one of the important tasks of kindergarten and first-grade teachers is to teach children how to initiate and respond appropriately in the school setting. Confusion and possibly a sense of alienation can arise for English learners who are used to the school scripts in their own countries and find a different one in U.S. schools. A knowledgeable teacher recognizes that these students are acting from the school scripts with which they are familiar. It may take time—and explicit coaching—for students to learn the set of behaviors appropriate for a U.S. school context.

Cultural Context.   Pragmatics implies a cultural context in which the language is embedded. Introductions in Japanese contain a mandatory bowing behavior that varies in depth in relation to the status of the participants. The process of making introductions in Japan, therefore, pragmatically differs from that in the United States. The speech acts performed during introductions are conjoined with the many social conventions controlling what participants expect from one another. To illustrate the pragmatics of a classroom situation, consider the following: A teacher calls out to a child who is sitting at her seat, "Are you finished with your work?" In some cultures, the child might expect praise for having completed the work but in most classrooms in the United States, this question implies that the student should find something else to do and not "waste time." The pragmatic context of the situation implies that the child should display the cultural values of industriousness and self-direction. Many times, teachers make judgments about students' academic potential on the basis of their ability to respond to pragmatic features of classroom discourse. If this is the case, explicit attention paid to these features will benefit students' classroom success ("When I say, 'It's time for lunch,' I mean, put your books away and take out your lunch money"). This will help students gain an awareness of how to respond appropriately in given contexts—pragmatic features of language.

Discourse: Oral Interaction

Maintaining a conversation in a second language requires the ability to take turns; to initiate relevant topics and to understand and respond appropriately to a topic that has been introduced; to repair misunderstanding; and to tailor the interaction suitably to the gender, status, age, and cultural background of the conversational participants. These aspects of language acquisition are often overlooked, but are obviously necessary elements for smooth interaction.

Taking Turns. Speakers of a language have implicitly internalized the rules of when to speak, when to remain silent, how long to speak, how long to remain silent, how to give up the floor, how to enter into a conversation, and so on. Linguistic devices such as intonation, pausing, and phrasing are used to signal an exchange of turns. Some groups of people wait for a clear pause before beginning their turn to speak, whereas others start while the speaker is "winding down" (Tannen, 1997). It is often this difference in when to "take the floor" that causes feelings of unease and sometimes hostility. A speaker may constantly feel that he is being interrupted or pushed in a conversation or, conversely, that he has to keep talking because his partner does not join in when appropriate. By becoming more aware of turn-taking behavior, the ELD teacher can help students make significant gains in their interactional comfort level.

Topic Focus and Relevance. These elements involve the ability of conversationalists to explore and maintain each other's interest in topics that are introduced, the context of the conversation, the genre of the interchange (story telling, excuse making), and the relationship between the speakers.

Conversational Repair. This involves techniques for clearing up misunderstanding and maintaining the conversation. For example, a listener confused by the speaker's use of the pronoun *she* might ask, "Do you mean Sally's aunt or her cousin?" With English learners, the alert teacher will notice quizzical looks rather than specific conversational interaction that signal lack of understanding.

Appropriateness. In general, this may cover all other aspects of conversational discourse, including gender, status, age, and cultural background of the speakers. The term *speech register* is often used to denote the varieties of language that take these factors into consideration. For example, in the classroom in which the teacher's assistant is an older woman who shares the language and culture of their children, students may converse with her in a manner similar to the interactions with their own mothers, whereas their discourse with the teacher could reflect usage reserved for more formal situations. A reverse of these registers would be inappropriate.

Discourse: The Written Genre

Some of the same principles that apply to oral discourse can be seen in written text. In some ways, creating a coherent paragraph or essay is similar to having a conversation with the reader. Some shared knowledge can be assumed, but writing has to be more explicit because there is no pragmatic feedback from the reader, such as scratching the head, wrinkling the nose, or giving a blank look. As in oral discourse, register and cohesion are important elements. The register of a written text must be appropriate for the audience, for the context, and for its function. Cohesion involves five areas: reference, substitution, ellipsis, conjunction, and lexical cohesion (Halliday & Hasan, 1976).

Reference.   Reference involves devices in the text that signal the need to retrieve information elsewhere (outside the text, preceding or following text). For example, a student writing a brief summary of a guest speaker's presentation might begin, "She showed us pictures of dolphins." A teacher's reaction might be, "Who showed us? Begin with Mrs. Quiles's name." The student's writing indicated she expected the reader to know who "she" was. The teacher's reaction was an attempt to have the student learn to write for an audience beyond those present for the speaker or, more specifically, to learn that a pronoun must refer to a preceding noun.

Substitution.   Substitution allows the writer to avoid repeating elements in a text. For example, one child wrote: "Henry got video games for Christmas. I did too." By using the cohesive device substitution, the child was able to avoid repeating "got video games for Christmas."

Ellipsis.   Ellipsis allows the writer to assume certain information without making it explicit. The student writes, "For the Homecoming dance, I was on the decorating committee and Julio was on refreshments." The word *committee* is understood after *refreshments* and does not need to be repeated.

Conjunction. Conjunction includes devices that are additive (*and, besides, furthermore*); expository (*that is, in other words*); comparison (*similarly, as . . . as*); contrastive (*however, on the other hand*); causal (*so, therefore*); temporal (*next, after that*); and many others.

Lexical Cohesion. Lexical cohesion involves such areas as vocabulary use and incorporating synonyms when repeating the same term would be stylistically boring (*sundown* for *sunset*).

   For Internet users interested in further general information about linguistics, the ERIC Digest *What Is Linguistics?* (http://www.cal.org/ericcll/digest/cal00001.html) gives a clear overview. The Linguistic Society of America provides *Fields of Linguistics* (http://www.lsadc.org/web2/fldfr.htm), which contains 22 short articles explaining the discipline of linguistics to the general public.

Language Functions

Since Halliday's (1978) seminal work in observing his young son and distinguishing seven different functions for language (*instrumental, regulatory, representational, interactional, personal, heuristic,* and *imaginative*), other researchers (Shafer, Staab, & Smith, 1983; Tough, 1977) have observed children's language use and posited categories of functions. Christie, Enz, and Vukelich (1997) have studied and compared these investigations and propose three broad domains of language use, each including specific functions.

- Reveal or assert needs/wants; satisfy personal needs; accomplish goals; direct self/others; control self/others
- Connect with self and others; share information about self/others; interact with others; direct self/others; express feelings
- Create, comprehend, and expand knowledge; learn—find out information; communicate information to self/others; pretend and fantasize (p. 23)

The ELD teacher who is aware of this wide range of functions provides multiple opportunities for English learners to express themselves. Too often the traditional classroom limits student interaction to providing short answers to teacher-initiated questions. Although this latter is an important facet of schooling, it is not sufficient to provide English learners with a broad range of language experiences. For a list of instructional strategies that promote language functions, see Pinnell's (1985) article, "Ways to Look at the Functions of Children's Language."

Language Change

One last, sometimes ignored, universal language principle is that of language change. The English language, which in its current form is about 500 years old, has changed considerably even from Middle English to Modern English. Words for common tools have come and gone. Who knows today what an *adz* is, or a *tang* or the *heft* of a knife? The grandparents of the current teachers in the schools may have never dreamed that a *chip* would be a minuscule bit of computer architecture. These lexical changes are immediately noticeable, but languages change in every system—phonology, morphology, syntax, semantics, and pragmatics.

As English evolved from its roots in the Germanic branch of the Indo-European family of languages, certain sound shifts took place such as the gradual loss of the guttural *ch*. Thus, the Germanic *ich* became the English *I*. Similarly, as English absorbed the French influence after the Norman invasion, many words beginning with *p* became *f*: French *poisson* became English *fish*. Morphological change occurred with the gradual elimination of declension endings in English nouns and verbs. Only the change in form of the third person *he goes* remains in the declension of present-tense verbs, and the plural shift remains in the inflection of nouns. Syntactically, as the inflections dropped off nouns, word order became fixed. Pragmatically, the fusing of the English second person into the single form *you* avoided many of the status distinctions still preserved in European languages. This may have accompanied the loss of other deferential behaviors (bowing, removal of the hat) that occurred with the rise of mercantilism and the decline of feudalism.

For a very readable article on language change directed toward teachers, see Gadda's chapter "Language Change in the History of English: Implications for Teachers" in Durkin (1995). He makes the point that teachers need to understand language change to counteract the "unfortunate popular attitude that sees all change in language as decay" (p. 263).

Nonverbal Communication

A discussion of language would not be complete without mention of the vast nonverbal system that accompanies, complements, or takes the place of the verbal. "An elaborate and secret code that is written nowhere, known by none, and understood by all," is Edward Sapir's definition of nonverbal behavior (quoted in Miller, 1985). This nonverbal system, estimated to account for up to 93 percent of communication (Mehrabian, 1969), involves sending and receiving messages through gestures, facial expressions, eye contact, postures, and tone of voice. Everyone is adept at sending and receiving these nonverbal messages, but, again—like oral language— the meaning people get from them is unconsciously learned. Because this nonverbal system accounts for a large part of the emotional message given and received, ELD teachers find it helpful to learn about various aspects of nonverbal communication and to begin to recognize when students' nonverbal messages may or may not fit in with expected school norms.

Body Language

The *American Heritage Dictionary* (1992) defines *body language* as "the bodily gestures, postures, and facial expressions by which a person communicates non-verbally" (p. 211). Body language is one way in which teachers communicate their authority in the classroom. Standing in front of the room, they become the focus of attention; standing arms akimbo communicates impatience with students' disorder; passing from desk to desk as students are working communicates individual attention to students' needs. In turn, students' body language communicates that they are paying attention ("eyes up front, hands folded" is the standard way teachers expect attentive students to act). Students who look industrious are often seen as more effective academically, and a student who approaches obsequiously to ask permission to leave the classroom will often receive the permission that was denied a more abrasive interrupter. In a parent conference, cultural differences in body language may impede communication. For example, parents may need to be formally ushered into the classroom and not merely waved in with a flick of the hand. Parents from a culture that offers elaborate respect for the teacher may become uncomfortable if the teacher slouches, moves her chair too intimately toward the parent, or otherwise compromises the formal nature of the interchange.

Gestures. Gestures—expressive motions or actions made with hands, arms, head, or even the whole body—are culturally based signs that are often misunderstood. They may or may not occur in conjunction with speech, but they always carry meaning. Gestures are commonly used to convey "come here," "good-bye," "yes," "no," and "I don't know." In European American culture, for example, "come here" is signaled by holding the hand vertically, palm facing the body, and moving the index finger rapidly back and forth. In other cultures, it is signaled by holding the hand in a more horizontal position, palm facing down, and moving the fingers rapidly back and forth. "Yes" is generally signaled by a nod of the head, but in some places a shake of the head means "yes." This can be particularly unnerving for teachers if they constantly interpret the students' head shakes as rejection rather than affirmation. Teachers may want to examine gestures they frequently use or expect in their classroom, and then discuss with their students what gestures they use and what the teacher's gestures mean to them.

Facial Expressions. Through the use of eyebrows, eyes, cheeks, noses, lips, tongues, and chins, people nonverbally signal any number of emotions, opinions, and moods. Although some facial expressions of happiness, sadness, anger, fear, surprise, disgust, and interest appear to be universal across cultures (Ekman & Friesen, 1971), other expressions are learned. Smiles and winks, tongue thrusts, and chin-jutting can have different meanings depending on the context within a culture as well as across cultures. Americans, for example, are often perceived by others as being superficial because of the amount of smiling they do, even to strangers. In some cultures, smiles are reserved for close friends and family.

Eye Contact. Eye contact is another communication device that is highly misunderstood. Both insufficient and excessive eye contact create feelings of unease, yet it is so subject to individual variation that there are no hard and fast rules to describe it. Generally, children in European American culture are taught not to stare but are expected to look people in the eye when addressing them. Teachers expect a child who is paying attention to have the eyes "up front." In some cultures, however, children learn that the correct way to listen is to avoid direct eye contact with the speaker. In the following dialogue, the teacher incorrectly interprets Sylvia's downcast eyes as an admission of guilt because, in the teacher's culture, eye avoidance signals culpability.

> TEACHER: Sylvia and Amanda, I want to hear what happened on the playground.
>
> AMANDA: (looks at teacher) Sylvia hit me with the jump rope.
>
> TEACHER: (turning to Sylvia) Sylvia, did you hit her?
>
> SYLVIA: (looking at her feet) No.

TEACHER: Look at me, Sylvia. Am I going to have to take the jump rope away?

SYLVIA: (continuing to look down) No.

By being aware that eye contact norms vary, teachers can begin to move beyond feelings of mistrust and can open lines of communication. For informative and sometimes humorous information about nonverbal communication, see Givens (2000).

Communicative Distance

People maintain distance between themselves and others—an invisible wall or "bubble" that defines a person's personal space. This distance varies according to relationships. Generally, people stand closest to relatives, close to friends, and farther from strangers. This distinction is commonly found across cultures, although differences occur in the size of the bubble. South Americans stand closer to each other than do North Americans, who in turn stand closer than do Scandinavians. Violating a person's space norm can be interpreted as aggressive behavior. In the United States, an accidental bumping of another person requires an "excuse me" or "pardon me." In Arab countries, such inadvertent contact does not violate the individual's space and requires no verbal apology. In classrooms, which are already crowded places, teachers can learn about students' distance requirements by organizing activities that move students ever closer to each other and asking them to signal when they are at comfortable speaking distances.

Arias's (1996) article entitled "Proxemics in the ESL Classroom" discusses perception and use of space and provides activities teachers can use to help themselves and their students learn about their "cultural bubbles" (available online at http://exchanges.state.gov/forum/vols/vol34/no1/p32.htm).

Conceptions of Time

In the mainstream culture of the United States, individuals' understanding of time may be at odds with that of students of other cultures. Hall (1959) points out that, for speakers of English, time is an object rather than an objective experience. Time is handled as if it were a material. English expressions include "saving time," "spending time," and "wasting time." Not only is time a commodity, but those who misuse this commodity earn disapproval. Teachers reprove students for idling and admonish students to "get busy." Standardized tests record higher scores for students who work quickly. In fact, teachers correlate rapid learning with intelligence. Teachers allocate time differently to students in classroom recitation, giving more time for answers to students from whom they expect more.

With an awareness of mainstream U.S. conceptions of time, teachers become more understanding of students and their families whose time values differ from their own, and are willing to make allowances for such differences. In oral discourse, some students may need more time to express themselves, not because of language shortcomings per se, but because the timing of oral discourse is slower in their culture. Parents who were raised in cultures with radically different concepts of time may not, for example, be punctual to the minute for parent conferences. One group of teachers allowed for this by not scheduling specific individual conference times. Instead, they designated blocks of three hours when they would be available for conferences, and parents arrived when they could.

The many varieties in language, both verbal and nonverbal, and the phenomenon of language change allow for rich and dynamic expression. The classroom is a home for the language of students, and the teacher is a liberal and stimulating language host. In a classroom that promotes English language development, the primary language is welcome as an alternative vehicle for self-expression, yet an overarching theme is the encouragement of English as the common idiom. English, the language of one small island in Europe, is now the international lingua franca, a language that appears on most of the world's T-shirts and caps, the language used by air traffic controllers, the language of science, the official language in 63 countries (and the unofficial second language in many of the rest), and the language of Shakespeare as well as of Elvis. English—with its vast store of technical terminology, its idiosyncratic spelling system, its penchant for accepting and using words from a multiplicity of cultures, and its many international dialects, including computer languages such as Java and Visual Basic—is the passport to a world beyond the borders of the classroom. The sensitive teacher advances the students' language skills by accepting and promoting the students' voice. Students writing journals, publishing newspapers and books, giving speeches, acting in dramas, singing songs, working within the community, debating timely issues, discussing world events—these literacy and language development events give students a voice to the world.

CHAPTER

4 English Language Development

> . . . the learner needs
>   expectation of success,
>   the confidence to take risks and make mistakes,
>   a willingness to share and engage,
>   the confidence to ask for help,
>   an acceptance of the need to readjust,
> and the teacher needs
>   respect for and interest in the learner's language, culture, thought and
>   intentions,
>   the ability to recognize growth points, strengths and potential,
>   the appreciation that mistakes are necessary to learning,
>   the confidence to maintain breadth, richness and variety, and to match these
>   to the learner's interests and direction (i.e., to stimulate and challenge),
>   a sensitive awareness of when to intervene and when to leave alone.
>
> —*English for Ages 5–11* in Dwyer, 1991

Language that is understandable and relevant to the learner fosters language acquisition and learning. In classroom situations, the teacher plays a central and crucial role in providing a learning environment in which language can be understood. This environment is rich with activities and materials that allow for language to be used and learned within a meaningful context. But the meaning that a teacher provides and the meaning that a student interprets are seldom identical. The teacher and the student must negotiate a compromise. The teacher not only provides information but also acts as a coach and facilitates the student's efforts toward meaning. The student receives information and actively constructs a personal knowledge framework. As the student learns a second language, the meaning that is constructed becomes a personal compromise between the native speaker's fluency and accuracy and the learner's attempts at comprehension and production. Using the most current English language development (ELD) methodologies, teachers acknowledge and build on the student's meaningful efforts, while at the same time maintaining a challenging pace of exposure to English.

With the increase of second language learners into the nation's K–12 system, more attention is now being paid to instruction for these students. Standards documents are being written to help schools address the needs of English learners. Teachers have a wide repertoire of methods that provide meaningful lessons for their students. They are knowledgeable about how their own speech patterns (delivery) can be modified to facilitate student understanding. Because of the labor-intensive nature of beginning language instruction, they often have others who assist in instruction. Orchestrating teaching assistants and parent and community aides is an important part of organizing and managing an ELD classroom. This chapter addresses these aspects of the changing nature of ELD methodology.

English Language Development Standards

The impetus to develop standards in various disciplines came from the 1989 Education Summit in Charlottesville, VA, in which President Bush and the nation's governors proposed a long-term national education strategy (often referred to as *Goals 2000*). Standards documents were subsequently written to define what students should know and be able to do in various disciplines in each grade. Unfortunately, these documents did not provide educators with directions and strategies to assist English learners. As a consequence, the international professional organization TESOL, Inc. (Teachers of English to Speakers of Other Languages, Inc.) developed an ESL standards document (TESOL, 1997) to draw attention to English learners' needs. The document serves as a complement to other standards documents and specifies those language competencies English-learning (EL) students need in order to become fully fluent in English. The standards are organized around three goals, each subdivided into three standards (see Figure 4.1). The goals and standards, divided into grade-level clusters (pre-K–3, 4–8, and 9–12) are explained through descriptors, sample progress indicators, and classroom vignettes. An important component is the provision made for students who enter schools at later grades with little formal schooling.

Numerous states have also produced documents to assist teachers working with English learners. California, for example, has prepared *English Language Development Standards* (1999a) to ensure that English learners develop proficiency in both the English language and the concepts and skills contained in the English-Language Arts (ELA) Content Standards. Although this document is more limited in scope than the TESOL standards (which consider all disciplines), it provides teachers with guidelines to move students toward fluency within the language arts curriculum.

The importance of these standards documents is that teachers now have specific behaviors and goals to help them work with English learners. They can work with students through a developmental framework, recognizing that students cannot be forced to produce beyond their proficiency level, but knowing that students are expected to attain certain levels of competency commensurate with their proficiency.

FIGURE 4.1   **ESL Goals and Standards**

Goal 1:   To use English to communicate in social settings
- Use English to participate in social interaction
- Interact in, through, and with spoken and written English for personal expression and enjoyment
- Use learning strategies to extend . . . communicative competence

Goal 2:   To use English to achieve academically in all content areas
- Use English to interact in the classroom
- Use English to obtain, process, construct, and provide subject matter information in spoken and written form
- Use appropriate learning strategies to construct and apply academic knowledge

Goal 3:   To use English in socially and culturally appropriate ways
- Use the appropriate language variety, register, and genre according to audience, purpose, and setting
- Use nonverbal communication appropriate to audience, purpose, and setting
- Use appropriate learning strategies to extend . . . sociolinguistic and sociocultural competence

Source: Copyright © by TESOL (1997).

Methods for English Language Development

Instructing students in a second language has a long and distinguished history. Scholars in the universities and preparatory schools of medieval and Renaissance Europe routinely learned Greek and Latin; in seventeenth- and eighteenth-century Europe, use of the vernacular became more acceptable as a medium of instruction, yet French was widely taught because it was the language of Western intellectual exchange. A well-educated person was expected to have mastered several languages; Elizabeth I of England, for example, spoke Latin, French, Spanish, Italian, and Flemish.

As scientific knowledge about the human body, mind, and language developed and changed, language teaching methodology mirrored the current thinking. When the mind was viewed as a muscle, exercise in the form of grammar drills and translations dominated language teaching. When the mind was viewed as an "empty slate," the teacher's job was to pour information into students in the form of drill and practice, particularly emphasizing oral repetition. Contemporary views of the mind hold that it has a meaning-making, pattern-seeking function. Teaching that follows this view supplies rich linguistic input in a meaningful context and encourages students to communicate ideas. Many of the techniques of past eras survive in some form in modern second language instruction—grammar-translation, audiolingual, and direct methods all use classic techniques, sometimes with a modern twist. Communicative methods include the Natural Approach and Total Physical Response, as well as some lesser-known techniques. Current approaches include content-based ESL, language and literacy, the Cognitive Academic Language Learning Approach, and computer-assisted language learning. An overview of ELD methods is given in the next section, including specific strategies and classroom examples.

Historical Methods of ELD Instruction

Languages have been taught for thousands of years. In the Western world, because Greek and Latin were essential for the educated man, an analysis of their grammatical elements undergirded methods for instruction. In the mid-twentieth century, Skinnerian behaviorism influenced language teaching and learning: If language could be learned as a process of habit formation, the appropriate response could be conditioned and available when needed. These are but two of the prevailing influences in language instruction that spawned language teaching methodologies. Historical methods of language instruction share the following commonalities: (1) teacher centered and teacher controlled; (2) carefully structured; (3) sequenced according to grammatical structures; (4) discrete language units taught separately (part to whole); (5) focus on correct form; (6) learner considered a passive recipient of knowledge; (7) little focus on language for communicative purposes; and (8) language taught as a subject by itself (Ovando & Collier, 1998). Three methods are considered here: *grammar translation, audiolingual,* and *direct.*

Grammar-Translation Method. The earliest pedagogy for second language instruction depended largely on students' laborious translation of classical texts. The prevailing medieval European philosophy of instruction was derived from the belief that man was a sinful creature; young scholars had to be severely disciplined if they were to be saved from ignorance. Long hours bent over manuscripts completing word-by-word translations of Latin or Greek texts were considered an appropriate training that strengthened the will. An emphasis on teaching grammar accompanied translation, because both Greek and Latin were languages in which declensional word endings were necessary to establish meaning.

This instructional method was the most popular foreign language instruction in the Western world until the mid-twentieth century (Richard-Amato, 1996). Teachers used the students' native language to explain grammar, define vocabulary, and translate passages. Students were expected to learn long lists of vocabulary words, memorize noun declensions and verb conjugations, and translate texts. The emphasis on rules of grammar and perfect translation left little room to develop speaking proficiency. The major remaining vestige of this pedagogical legacy is the tendency for second language instructors to cling to grammatical structure as the hallmark of successful second language learning. This method is often used in classrooms in which the teacher is not a native English speaker and does not feel comfortable speaking the language.

The Audiolingual Method. As a reaction to the grammar-translation method, which focused on reading and writing ability in a second language, audiolingual instruction was designed to create facile speakers in a second language. This method used carefully ordered structures in the target language, which were incorporated into dialogues and pattern drills, in an attempt to develop correct language habits by repetitious training. The role of the teacher was to direct and control students' behavior, provide a model, and reinforce correct responses (Doggett, 1986). Students parroted the teacher, repeating sentences and making teacher-indicated grammatical transformations with little or no consideration of meaning. Errors were corrected immediately to discourage "bad" habit formation. Reading and writing were often delayed until the student had an adequate oral base. A language lab was used so students could mimic sounds, phrases, and drills heard on audiotapes. The audiolingual method can still be incorporated into the instruction of idioms and formulaic greetings and exchanges ("Hi! How are you?" "I'm fine. And you?") because these exchanges are often predictable and patterned. The weakest feature of audiolingual instruction is the lack of creative communication when patterned drills are used. The strength of the method is probably its focus on correct pronunciation.

The Direct Method.   In the direct method, students are immersed in the target language through listening to discourse and responding to questions. Using short sentences, they eventually build up long sentence strings. This methodology, begun in the mid-nineteenth century, was based on the way children were perceived to learn their native language—through the direct association of words and phrases with words and actions (Omaggio, 1986). No translation is allowed in this method. Students are expected to understand meaning directly from the target language without using the native language. Grammar is taught inductively as students experience a variety of sentence forms. Teachers pantomime and use visual aids to convey vocabulary, and students use only the target language to convey comprehension. The culture associated with the target language is also taught inductively (Doggett, 1986). The best known user of this method is the Berlitz language program.

Communicative Approaches

Based on research in first and second language acquisition, approaches developed during the 1960s, 1970s, and 1980s emphasized language as communication. These approaches contributed to important changes in the nature of second language teaching: (1) a reduced emphasis on teaching grammatical structures, (2) a reconception of the teacher/student relationship, (3) a recognition of the range of language functions, and (4) an appreciation of language as embedded in social contexts. In communicative approaches, teacher and students work collaboratively. The teacher guides the students, organizes resources, and sets up procedures and activities so that a communicative process among all participants in a classroom furthers learning. The students, in turn, take responsibility for their own learning and share that responsibility with other students and the teacher. However, these approaches do not necessarily preclude formal practice (see the Point/

Counterpoint below) and vary among themselves in the degree to which they ascribe to such principles. This section discusses *the Natural Approach, Total Physical Response, Suggestopedia,* and *the Silent Way.*

The Natural Approach.   The Natural Approach (Krashen & Terrell, 1983) uses as its underlying theory Krashen's Monitor Model (see Chapter 1). This method, which closely resembles the way a child acquires a first language, is based on four principles: (1) comprehension precedes production, (2) production emerges in stages, (3) activities are central, and (4) the affective filter is low. The key element is for the teacher to provide comprehensible input and to be alert to patterns and behaviors that indicate that students are listening and comprehending. Speech is of secondary importance in the early stages, and when it does emerge, errors are not corrected.

Point/Counterpoint

Is repetitious practice the best way to learn language?
Many of the activities that take place in English-as-a-second language classes allow students to engage in practicing new features of the language (vocabulary, grammatical forms, interactions, etc.) in order to develop confidence and ease in English. The role of formal practice activities has changed as language teaching methodologies have been updated. What is the best kind of practice to gain specific skills in the second language?

Point: **Language skills become automatic through repeated drill and practice.**
In the behaviorist teaching methodology popular in the 1960s, "structured drills" were designed to enable students to form new language habits. These drills revolved around morphological or syntactic features. For example, pattern drills guided students through a series of verb forms in highly structured ways. A typical drill might work on the present tense: "He *plays* soccer. (We) We *play* soccer. (I) I *play* soccer." It was thought that by using extensive drill, language use would become automatic and students would be able to access the forms acquired through drill practice to use in everyday interaction and academic work. These formal drill activities were considered most suitable for students at the beginning of second language acquisition.

Counterpoint: **Language is learned more readily through communication.**
When cognitive theory became popular in the 1970s, pattern drills were replaced with structured but meaningful practice activities in order for students to integrate language subskills into their internal representation. Rather than learning subskills based on forms and structures, learners were instead encouraged to acquire language strategies. These strategies included facility in communicating. Learning to carry on conversations, modifying language to fit various contexts, and choosing the best style of speech for each interaction are examples of the strategies needed for effective communication. One might think of this type of practice as "creative automatization" (Gatbonton & Segalowitz, 1988). Formal practice activities are still suitable in order to develop accurate usage; this type of practice is incorporated into activities that encourage communicative competence.

Terrell (1981) describes three techniques that help with listening comprehension skills: (1) Total Physical Response (TPR) (discussed next); (2) use of people and objects in the immediate environment; and (3) use of pictures rather than actual objects. The essential elements in these techniques are the *context* (everything talked about can be seen), the *intent* (students know the subject and the teacher's expectations of them prior to the lesson), and the *key vocabulary* (emphasized through intonation, pauses, and repetition). Initially, it is expected that students will understand the *ideas* (70 percent according to Terrell), but not necessarily the *specifics* of the language. What they are learning is the important developmental step of "partial comprehension"—listening for general meaning. Figure 4.2 provides examples of Natural Approach activities for three stages of language development: preproduction, early production, and speech emergence.

FIGURE 4.2   Activities for the Natural Approach

Preproduction Stage

Materials: 3–5 pictures

1. Introduce the pictures to the entire class one at a time. Focus on one aspect of each picture. Introduce one to five new words while describing the picture.
2. Pass the picture to a student in the class.
3. Ask questions such as: "Who has the picture of the boy in red?" "Who has the picture of the wave?" The students only have to reply with the appropriate classmate's name.

Early Production Stage

Materials: pictures

The following is an example of *teacher-talk* based on pictures. The words in parentheses are expected student responses.

"Is there a woman in this picture?" (yes). "Is there a man in the picture?" (no). "Is the woman old or young?" (young). "Yes, she's young, but very ugly." (no, pretty). "That's right, she's not ugly, she's pretty. What is she rocking?" (baby). "Yes, she's rocking her baby. Is the baby sitting or standing?" (standing). "Yes, the baby is standing. What is the baby holding?" (mother's hands). "Yes, she's holding her mother's hands. She is standing on her mother's knees, holding her hands, and rocking."

Speech Emergence Stage

Use either/or questions ("Is that a map or a globe on the wall?"), identification statements ("On the wall, there is a _____."), and pattern frames ("Diana likes to _____. Timoteo likes to _____. Daniel and Voltario like to _____.") Use charts and advertisements to supplement pictures and objects.

Total Physical Response (TPR). Total Physical Response is based on the association between language and body movement and can be an engaging, lively addition to classroom techniques. In studying children learning their first language, Asher (1982) noted three elements that he made the basis for his approach:

1. Listening, and hence understanding, precedes speaking.
2. Understanding is developed through moving the body.
3. Speaking is never forced.

In TPR, students respond to an oral command that has simultaneously been modeled. For example, the teacher says "Stand" while standing up and "Sit" while sitting down, and the students follow along. The instructor repeats the commands followed by the appropriate action until students perform without hesitation. The instructor then begins to delay his or her own action to allow students the opportunity to respond and thus demonstrate understanding. Eventually, students, first as a whole group and then as individuals, act on the instructor's voice command alone. The number of commands is gradually increased (Asher recommends three as an optimal number of new commands). Novel commands are given that combine previously learned commands in a new way. For example, if the students were familiar with "Run" and "Walk to the chair," they might be given "Run to the chair." Students continue to respond in a nonverbal manner until they feel comfortable issuing their own commands.

Reading and writing are also introduced through commands. The instructor may write on the board "Stand" and gesture to the students to perform the action. After practice with the written form in class, students can be given lists of familiar commands that they can then manipulate in their own fashion. The concrete, hands-on methodology recommended by Asher is associated with early stages of second language learning and is recommended by Krashen and Terrell (1983) for promoting comprehension in a low-anxiety environment. TPR techniques have been successfully incorporated into content lessons. The art lesson in Figure 4.3 demonstrates how this can be done.

Suggestopedia. Georgi Lozanov, a Bulgarian psychotherapist and physician, introduced Suggestopedia as a method that would fully utilize the capabilities of the human brain. Lozanov (1982) believed several tenets of ordinary education were contrary or inconsistent with the physiological and psychological functions of the personality: emphasis on the intellect at the expense of the emotional and motivational aspects of the personality; either studying parts with no consideration of the whole or studying the whole without paying attention to the parts; and learning directed only to the conscious level, ignoring that which can be learned spontaneously and intuitively. By contrast, Suggestopedia incorporates three psychophysiological aspects: the global participation of the brain, the simultaneous processes of analysis and synthesis, and the simultaneous and indivisible participation of the conscious and paraconscious processes.

FIGURE 4.3   TPR-Based Art Lesson

*Introductory Lesson on **Line**, One of the Design Elements in Art*

Level: Beginning-intermediate level students

Responding Physically as Kinds of Line

1. Depending on the age and willingness of the students, have students stand at their desks or remain seated. (Those standing will use their whole body to become a line. Those seated can use their arms.)
2. While giving verbal instructions, model, then draw a type of line and write the word on the board or on butcher paper.

Verbal Instructions	*Physical movements*
Pretend your body (arm) is a line.	Model, draw, write "line"
Be (Make) a vertical line.	Model, draw, write "vertical"
Be (Make) a horizontal line.	Model, draw, write "horizontal"
Be (Make) a diagonal line.	Model, draw, write "diagonal"
Be (Make) a curved line.	Model, draw, write "curved"
Be (Make) a zigzag line.	Model, draw, write "zigzag"

3. Randomly repeat instructions. Gradually delete modeling and point to the graphic and word. Encourage students to observe others as necessary.

Identifying the Elements of Line

4. Display art reproductions or slides. Depending on students' proficiency, either point to a line and ask students to identify or ask them to find one and describe it so others will identify it.
5. If using art reproductions, provide one to groups of 3–4 students. Ask groups to identify the types of line. (Circulate. For more advanced students, suggest adding characteristics such as long, short; wide, thin; rough, smooth; direction line is moving; degree of curve—gradual, wavy, spiral.)

Producing Own Lines and Works of Art

6. Collect reproductions and distribute one blank paper per student.
7. Ask students to fold paper in sixths. Model folding.
8. On overhead or on board, draw each type of line while saying, "These are vertical lines. I am drawing vertical lines. Draw vertical lines in the first section of your paper." Do not label at this point. After all five types have been drawn, point to each and ask students to name the type of line. Add the words as students say them and direct them to write them on their paper.
9. Distribute the second blank paper and ask students to create their own drawing using the types of line learned.

Describing Their Creations

10. When finished, ask small groups or pairs to share their drawings, describing the lines they used. Circulate and make suggestions for additional descriptors as necessary.
11. Ask if anyone would like to share with the whole group.
12. For homework, ask students to observe their environment and report on the types of lines they find and where they find them.

Source: K. Weed, "The Language of Art, the Art of Language" in D. Brinton & P. Master (Eds.), *New Ways in Content-Based Instruction* (Alexandria, VA: Teachers of English to Speakers of Other Languages [TESOL], 1997). Reprinted by permission.

Key conditions of any Suggestopedic language program are the absence of tension and the inclusion of relaxation elements. Such conditions allow students "undisturbed intellectual and creative activity" (p. 155), tapping into those mental reserves untapped in other learning environments. Concentration is directed to the whole of the teacher's message, to its communicative aspect. Pronunciation, vocabulary, and grammar remain on what Lazanov characterizes as the "second" plane. They are assimilated and learned along with the whole structure. Music is a vital element in the lesson—classical and early Romantic music of an emotional nature; preclassical of a more philosophic nature. Once material is introduced in a relaxed, supportive atmosphere, students engage in "elaborations"—reading dialogue, songs, games, and conversations. Role playing is another important aspect of the program. Students can take on new identities when they wish but are never forced to perform. There is no obligatory homework, and the textbook contains "a light-hearted story with a pleasant, emotional plot" (p. 158).

The Gregorio Esparza Accelerated Elementary School in San Antonio, Texas, bases its curriculum on Lozanov's principles. For information about Accelerated Teaching and Learning and the program at the school, see http://www.northside. isd.tenet.edu/esparww/s-accel1.htm. Current language instruction may benefit from Suggestopedic techniques, such as the relaxation methods, the vocabulary presentation, and the use of creative skits and the involvement of students' personalities.

The Silent Way.   In this method, no first language is used. Simple linguistic situations allow learners to observe and then describe the actions performed. The teacher concentrates on the students' pronunciation and word flow and encourages personal production of the language. Students use their own judgment to listen, voice, and correct their own language. According to Gattegno, the developer of the method, the teacher provides little vocabulary, yet the students are able to produce much language. Gattegno (1982) describes a typical lesson:

> The box of colored rods that the teacher places on his desk is all he carries. He opens it and draws out of it one rod and shows it to the class while saying in the foreign language the word for rod. . . . He puts it down in silence and picks up another of a different color and says the same (one or two) words again, and so on, going through seven or eight rods and never asking for anything. The intrigued students have attentively noted the events and heard some noises which to them will seem the same while their eyes see only different objects and a repetition of the same action. Without any fuss the teacher then lifts a rod and asks in mime for the sounds he uttered. Bewildered, the class would not respond, in general, but the teacher says "a rod" and asks again in mime for another effort from the class. Invariably someone guesses . . . that the teacher wants back what he gave. When in his own way the pupil says something approximating what the teacher said, the teacher may smile or nod, showing how content he is at being understood. At the next trial almost the whole class repeats the sounds for a rod. . . . The teacher does not inquire whether some students are thinking of a piece of wood, others of lifting something, or something different. (p. 197)

In this method, students must develop their own criteria for correctness. Errors are expected as a normal part of learning. Through teacher silence, students are encouraged to take the initiative and be self-reliant, and to do most of the talking and interacting (Doggett, 1986).

Current ELD Approaches

Although the contributions of the communicative approaches changed the focus to learner-centered, meaningful, interactive educational practices, the contributions of the current approaches move language education into the content realm. No longer is the sole function of the language class to teach language. With the increase of English learners in K–12 schools, school personnel recognized that EL students needed to keep up academically with their native English-speaking peers while in the process of learning English. Current approaches vary in emphasis, but all support the following principles: (1) integration of language and content teaching, (2) use of authentic language and materials, (3) recognition of student diversity and learning styles, (4) development of cognitive strategies, (5) use and support of students' first languages and cultures, (6) importance of interaction and collaborative learning; and (7) student engagement in purposeful learning tasks. The following approaches are discussed in this section: *content-based ESL, literacy instruction for English learners, the Cognitive Academic Language Learning Approach,* and *computer-assisted language learning.*

Content-Based ESL.   In content-based ESL classrooms, ESL teachers, often in collaboration with content teachers, organize learning objectives around academic subjects drawn from grade-level curricula. They use instructional materials, learning tasks, and classroom techniques that not only develop language proficiency but also content knowledge. In addition, teachers help students with cognitive strategies and study skills. In content-based ESL classrooms, students participate in activities and on material that they often deem more relevant and meaningful to their academic progress. Content-based ESL classes are taught by ESL teachers who often make up part of a core team. Thus, for example, ESL, English, social studies, and math teachers may work together to integrate their curricula and provide continuity for students as they move between the classes.

Although the students in content-based ESL classrooms are all English learners and are therefore not competing directly in the class with native English-speaking peers, the range of ability within any one class can still be enormous. The challenge to help all students with English and grade-level expectations is overwhelming. One teacher successfully accepted and met this challenge in her fifth/sixth-grade class of 26 children (Igoa, 1995). She describes her program as follows:

> I put all State Framework curriculum on hold until the children had advanced in language arts first—reading, writing, spelling—and numeracy. I took all the skills a child would normally learn in first grade and made sure the children mastered them alone or in study groups. I gradually moved them up the grades; it took approximately two months for each grade level.... All the children went through this pro-

cess of learning all the skills from ground up—first grade onward. . . . In the afternoon, I alternated between science, history, and finishing up the morning's work. . . .

By the end of January, almost all the children were reading at third grade level comfortably, quickly, and without hesitation. . . . I brought in American history books written at the third grade level. Slowly the transfer of skills from reading literature to reading history began to take place. We discussed how to look at history with a critical mind and to see it as an extension of storytelling. . . . As they became comfortable with reading history and as the study groups became well established, I periodically brought in science books they could read and showed them how to transfer reading skills to science reading. . . . By March and April, the children were developing fourth grade skills. By May they were beginning to do some fifth grade work. (pp. 165–166)

Content-based ESL is currently one of the methods that helps students learn English and the subject matter required for school. It is also one of the methods for English learners that helps them achieve some of the national standards. In the Standards document developed by TESOL (1997) mentioned earlier, three standards relate to EL students being able to use English to achieve academically in all content areas. These include being able to (1) use English to interact in the classroom; (2) use English to obtain, process, construct, and provide subject matter information in spoken and written form; and (3) use appropriate learning strategies to construct and apply academic knowledge.

Burkart and Sheppard (2001) have developed a training packet for content-based ESL (http://www.ncbe.gwu.edu/miscpubs/cal/contentesl/) that includes, along with model programs and lesson plans, guidelines for every aspect involved in developing content-based ESL classrooms. TESOL has also published a four-volume series *Integrating the ESL Standards into Classroom Practice* (information available online at http://www.tesol.org/assoc/k12standards/index.html), which show through teacher-designed and implemented units how to incorporate the standards into classroom practice.

Literacy Instruction for English Learners. Literacy instruction is a crucial aspect of K–12 schooling in the United States. How to help children learn to read and read to learn has been hotly debated for decades. The topic of English learners and how best to instruct them has not been immune to the loud and sometimes nasty debates. However, a complicating factor that is sometimes not considered by monolingual reading researchers is the varying background experiences that English learners bring to the reading task. California TESOL (CATESOL, 1998) provides the following five classifications for English learners that help put this background into perspective:

- Young learners [K–3] whose beginning literacy instruction is in their primary language
- Young learners [K–3] acquiring initial literacy in English because they do not have access to primary language reading instruction

- Older learners with grade-level primary-language literacy, who are beginning to develop literacy in English
- Older learners with limited formal schooling in their home country
- Older learners with inconsistent school history, with limited development of either the primary language or English (p. 1)

Even when these variables are recognized, standards documents, such as the one for California (California Department of Education, 1999a), expect teachers to "catch English learners up" to monolingual English speakers. The document specifically states that the ELD standards "are designed to move all students, regardless of their instructional program, into the mainstream English-language arts curriculum" (p. 2). Beginning teachers are now being tested on their knowledge of reading instruction prior to receiving certification. Content specifications for the California Reading Instruction Competence Assessment (RICA) include statements relating to English learners. "The beginning teacher understands that the goal of reading instruction is to develop reading competence in all students, including English language learners" (2.2) and

> The beginning teacher is able to interrelate the elements of language arts instruction to support the reading development of English language learners (e.g., using preview-review, visual aids, charts, real objects, word organizers, graphic organizers, and outlining). The teacher knows general ways in which the writing systems of other languages may differ from English (e.g., that not all writing systems are alphabetic, that English is less regular phonetically than some other alphabetic languages). The teacher understands factors and processes involved in transferring literacy competencies from one language to another (e.g., positive and negative transfer) and uses knowledge of language similarities and differences to promote transfer of language skills (e.g., through scaffolding strategies, modeling, and explicit instruction) (11.4). (California Department of Education, 1998a)

What, then, characterizes literacy instruction for English learners? Evidence from research in second language acquisition indicates that the natural developmental processes that children undergo in learning their first language (oral and written) also occur in second language acquisition (oral and written). For reading, these processes include using knowledge of sound/symbol relationships (graphophonics), word order and grammar (syntax), and meaning (semantics) to predict and confirm meaning, and using background knowledge about the text's topic and structure along with linguistic knowledge and reading strategies to make an interpretation (Peregoy & Boyle, 2001).

Classrooms that support the literacy learning of English learners share the following general practices: Students are engaged in activities that are meaningful to them, and they often jointly negotiate with the teacher. Instruction is cognitively demanding, yet is "scaffolded" to ensure student success. A scaffold is temporary support, provided by a more capable person, for new concepts and skills that students are not able to perform unassisted. As students become more proficient, the scaffold is gradually removed (Chamot & O'Malley, 1994; Peregoy & Boyle, 2001). Learning is organized into topics and themes so that students can build on previous learning of vocabulary and grammatical structures as well as academic concepts and skills. Students work collaboratively and grouping is flexible. Students participate in different kinds of groups throughout their day, which affords them the opportunity to see other learners' styles of problem solving. Students are further immersed in a print-rich environment so that they have constant opportunities to interact with the written word. Specific strategies for EL students' literacy instruction, techniques for students without literacy in first or second languages, and transferring literacy from first to second languages are explained in Strategic Teaching: Reading and Writing later in this chapter.

Cognitive Academic Language Learning Approach (CALLA).   This approach, designed for EL students at the advanced beginning and intermediate levels of English language proficiency, incorporates explicit teaching of learning strategies within academic subject areas. Its purpose is to enrich the language that students may use for academic communication while furthering their ability to comprehend the language and discourse of different subject areas. The CALLA model includes three components: topics from the major content subjects, the development of academic language skills, and explicit instruction in learning strategies for both content and language acquisition (Chamot & O'Malley, 1994). The content topics, aligned with the all-English curriculum, are introduced gradually, emphasizing those which have extensive contextual supports or reduced language demands. Chamot and O'Malley suggest science instruction that uses a discovery and hands-on approach first, because students are often intrinsically interested in science. The second component, academic language skills, includes all four language modes in daily content lessons. Students learn not just vocabulary and grammar, but also important concepts and skills using academic language. In addition, they learn language functions important for the specific curricular areas, such as analyzing, evaluating, justifying, and persuading.

The third—and central—component is instruction in learning strategies. These strategies are divided into three major categories: *metacognitive, cognitive,* and *social-affective.* The metacognitive strategies help students to plan, monitor, and evaluate their learning processes. Teachers help students learn to preview the main concepts in material to be learned, plan the key ideas that must be expressed orally or in writing, decide in advance what specific information must be attended to, check comprehension during listening or reading, and judge how well learning has been accomplished when completed.

Cognitive strategies include using reference materials resourcefully; taking effective notes; summarizing material adequately; applying rules of induction or inference; remembering information using visual images, auditory representation, or elaboration of associations to new knowledge; transferring prior skills to assist comprehension; and grouping new concepts, words, or terms understandably. Social-affective strategies teach how to elicit needed clarification, how to work cooperatively with peers in problem solving, and how to use mental techniques or self-talk to reduce anxiety and increase a sense of personal competency.

An indispensable resource for teachers interested in using CALLA is *The CALLA Handbook: Implementing the Cognitive Academic Language Learning Approach* (Chamot & O'Malley, 1994). This book introduces the approach, provides guidelines for establishing a CALLA program, and explains procedures for implementing CALLA in the classroom, as well as model units in science, mathematics, social studies, and literature and composition. In addition, the article "Learning Strategy Instruction in the Bilingual/ESL Classroom" (Stergis & Perrin, 1997) provides a sample of activities and effective strategies used with Haitian and Vietnamese middle and high school students.

Computer-Assisted Language Learning (CALL). The Digital Revolution is changing the way people spend their free time—playing video and computer games, chatting on the Internet, conducting business transactions, and much more. The social changes of the Digital Revolution, many cultural observers believe, will be as vast and far-reaching as those generated by the Gutenberg Revolution with the advent of the printing press (Hanson-Smith, 1997). Language classrooms can be similarly transformed with the capabilities now available through multimedia computing, the Internet, and the World Wide Web. Computer-assisted language learning has the potential for extending learning beyond the four walls of the classroom to include the whole world.

Probably the word that comes to mind most quickly when considering the capabilities of the computer is *vast*. The range, variety, and potential are almost unfathomable. However, language teachers have effectively used and benefited from this resource with a little guidance and direction.

Computer-assisted language learning supports the trends in language teaching mentioned at the beginning of this section. For example, word processing supports the writing process by allowing students to organize, draft, revise, edit, and even publish their work without going through the painstaking tasks of manually writing and rewriting. Students can work collaboratively, using presentation or authoring software to create a professional-looking presentation. They can email or chat with keypals in different areas of the world.

Classrooms involved in CALL use both software programs and online resources to help students achieve their language learning goals. Software programs include the following: traditional drill-and-practice programs that focus on vocabulary or discrete grammar points; tutorials; games; simulations that present students with real-life situations in the language and culture they are learning; productivity tools, such as word processing, databases, spreadsheets, graphics, and desktop publishing (DTP); and presentation or authoring programs. Material from encyclopedias and even the *National Geographic* is available on CD-ROMs (Compact Disk-Read Only Memory).

Instant communication afforded through the Internet connects students with other parts of the world, with speakers of English, and with information. Through email, chat groups, and list serves (electronic discussion groups on specific topics and/or resources), students can connect with their classmates, schoolmates, or students in other parts of the globe. A useful link to access various list serves is http://alabanza.com/kabacoff/Inter-Links/listserv.html. The World Wide Web delivers authentic materials, including texts, images, sound recording, video clips, virtual reality worlds, and dynamic, interactive presentations. Streaming audio and video connects students with native speakers and authentic audiovisual materials by virtually transporting the target language environment to the second language classroom. Students can listen to live radio stations from around the world or hear prerecorded broadcasts of music, news, sports, and weather (see Media Info at http://emedia1.mediainfo.com/emedia/ and Leloup & Ponterio [2000]). Search engines (e.g., Yahoo, Altavista, Excite), described by Leloup and Ponterio as "online private eyes," help the student find authentic materials on classroom, group, or individual research topics.

The computer is not to be viewed as something students use without benefit of teacher guidance. Instead, it is a powerful learning tool that requires the teacher to organize, plan, teach, and monitor. Hanson-Smith (1997) finds that computer technology can provide students with the means to control their own learning, to construct meaning, and to evaluate and monitor their own performance. She describes three levels of CALL implementation in the classroom, noting the teacher's role in each. At a modest level, language learning software can provide a passive listening experience accompanied by a search apparatus so that students may click on a word or sentence to hear it repeatedly, look up a meaning, analyze grammar, see a related picture or video clip, and/or read a related text. The teacher monitors students' progress, encouraging, instructing, and modeling as appropriate. At a somewhat higher level, students may listen to a sentence, compare their voices to a computer model of the correct response or have the computer judge the accuracy of their responses. This type of software needs teacher intervention to guide students through the material and to suggest strategies for using supplemental references. Students benefit from reporting weekly progress to the teacher or aide and discussing computer scores in order to guide their continuing learning. At a still higher level, students may research current events, historical and cultural topics, business matters, art or literature, weather or geography—any topic of interest to them and to the learning goals of the class. They may talk to native speakers through email and Telnet sites and collaborate with learning teams, both native and nonnative English speakers.

Computer-assisted language learning teachers caution that they must help students carefully plan and organize learning experiences, rehearse useful language, and understand not only some of the physical operation of the Internet and Web but also the conventions and codes that have become "netiquette" for such communications. For a well-organized, highly readable guide for using the computer in the language classroom, see *Internet for English Teaching* (Warschauer, Shetzer, & Meloni, 2000).

Integrating the Language Skills: A Classroom Example

The various principles, standards, and strategies presented in this chapter come together in the following case study (adapted with permission from Weed & Ford, 1999). The teacher explains practices used during an immigration unit in her multigrade (2, 3, 4), multilingual (Spanish, English, Samoan, Tongan, Armenian, Indonesian) classroom.

Within the context of the social studies curriculum, reading, listening, speaking, and writing are integrated as students first explore and develop their ideas and later shape these ideas into formal presentations. They listen for a purpose, exchange ideas in large- and small-group settings, write based on their growing understanding, and read each other's work. The teacher facilitates the process and, importantly, also provides specific lessons on skills the students need. The teacher describes the lessons as follows:

> As part of our immigration unit, the children and I read *How Many Days to America?* (Bunting, 1988). Because so many of the children had immigrated to our southern California community, they had a lot to share about their own experiences. Prior to reading our next book, *If You Sailed on the Mayflower in 1620* (McGovern, 1969), we looked at a detailed poster of a drawing of the *Mayflower.* This familiarized the children with the different parts of the ship and the story we would be drawing, talking, writing, and reading about.
>
> I then started the story. After reading a segment, I stopped and asked the children to draw what they thought was most important about what they had heard. They quickly sketched their main ideas, knowing they could go back later to add details (similar to writing a rough draft). We continued for several days until we finished the book.
>
> At the end of each daily reading and sketching session, the children got together in groups and shared a drawing that the group discussed. If a child did not fully understand a concept, the group discussed it, offering a context for all group members of clarify their understanding. During this small-group time, I rotated among the different groups and prompted where necessary, "What more can you tell me about your picture?" "Why did you decide to include this detail?" "Why do you think your friend had that interpretation of your drawing?" and, in situations where one group member had given an original interpretation, often quite different from that of the other students, "What could you do differently to make your ideas clearer?"
>
> Although the text and my questions were in English, the students' discussion ranged across languages. Often, a long exchange occurred in Indonesian or Spanish or Tongan as the students sorted

out ideas, clarified their interpretations, and then drafted their written work. I was not concerned about these primary language explorations; I knew from my experience that the students were gaining rich conceptual knowledge through their talk. Notions understood through the English medium were being massaged and expanded in the primary language.

After their discussions, the artists wrote a sentence or two about the drawing, pulling from their own and their group members' ideas. By the end of the week, the children had a series of drawings in a folder. They reviewed their drawings and took out those that included their writing. They got into groups again and collectively sequenced their pictures. They were creating their own book based on the story of the *Mayflower*.

More discussion went on during this group work. Although the published work would be in English, pairs and trios of students continued to discuss in their primary languages, and the braver, sometimes the more proficient, would present ideas in English to the whole small group. I often saw three- and four-way conversations—discussion in first language, tentative idea presenting in English, some exploring among members in English, with questions and discussion going back and forth in various respective primary languages. From their initial "story map," students elaborated on their writing, adding details and clarifying thoughts. The editing evolved as a part of group discussion as students prepared their story for publication. They also refined their artwork, adding details, checking the poster, and going back to the book for ideas.

Throughout this sequence of activities, the children generated ideas through different systems. Writing would prompt new ideas for pictures, and pictures generated new ideas for writing. Discussion clarified, suggested, and supported. Sometimes students would even completely change a picture or their writing based on a new understanding. I noticed that often a student who was reticent in speaking was nonetheless an important idea-generator for a group.

During the editing sessions, I introduced small strategy lessons depending on the group's needs. These lessons focused on issues, questions, and dilemmas that had come up in the natural course of discussion and writing. In this manner, specific skills were able to be addressed in the context of the students' writing.

When the final products were ready, a representative from each group read the group's book aloud and showed the illustrations. These students were not always the most proficient in English, but rather those whom the group decided would best represent it. The books were then placed in the classroom library for all to read. These student-produced books were so popular that they often wore out.

Strategic Teaching

Developing proficiency in English is a multifaceted task. Not only must students *read* and *write* at a level that supports advanced academic success but they must also use their skills of *listening* and *speaking* to gain information and demonstrate their knowledge. A fifth necessary skill is the ability to *think* critically and creatively. The teacher's role is to integrate these separate, but interrelated, skills in a unified curriculum that moves students from beginning to advanced proficiency in classroom English.

Both communicative and current approaches to language teaching emphasize the integration of all four language modes. There are times, however, when the teacher finds that students need work in a particular area. This section addresses the four language modes and provides specific strategies for each.

Listening

Part of the knowledge needed to comprehend oral discourse is the ability to separate meaningful units from the stream of speech. Although listening has been classified along with reading as a "receptive" skill, it is by no means a passive act. The cognitive approach to learning promotes listening as an act of constructing meaning. Listeners draw on their store of background knowledge and their expectation of the message to be conveyed as they actively work at understanding conversational elements. The role of the teacher is to set up situations in which students feel a sense of purpose and can engage in real communication. In this way, students can develop a personal agenda—their own purposes and goals—for listening, and the English that they acquire is most useful in their daily lives. Although the current emphasis is on communicating for authentic purposes, a number of guided listening techniques that come from more traditional language teaching methodologies may be helpful for teachers. Activities will be discussed under the categories of listening to repeat, listening to understand, and listening for communication.

Listening to Repeat: The Audiolingual Legacy. A common audiolingual strategy is *minimal pair* pattern practice, in which students are asked to listen to and repeat simple phrases that differ by only one phoneme—for example: "It is a ship"/ "It is a sheep." "He is barking"/"He is parking." Another typical listen/repeat format is *backward buildup*: Students are given the end of a sentence or phrase to repeat; when they are successful, earlier parts of the sentence are added until the complete phrase is mastered ("store/the store/to the store/walked to the store/ Peter walked to the store"). Both these procedures require that the student hear the word and/or sentence elements and be able to accurately reproduce them. Backward buildup provides additional practice in sentence intonation. Little attention, however, is paid to meaning.

Current methods encourage students to listen to minimal pairs within meaningful contexts. Teachers can use poems, nursery rhymes, and songs to introduce "rhyming words," which differ by only one phoneme. Students can be asked to fill in the blanks at the end of lines, demonstrating their knowledge of the sound and the word within the context. In addition, teachers can read aloud wordplay books, alliterative books, and books with tongue twisters, and encourage students to talk about how the author manipulated words. Such activities not only help students hear the language but the work with sounds also provides opportunities for preliterate students to develop phonemic awareness, "the insight that every spoken word is made up of a sequence of phonemes" (California Department of Education, 1999b, p. 278) and considered by many to be a prerequisite for learning to read (Tunmer & Nesdale, 1985; Yopp, 1985).

To provide students with sentence intonation patterns in a meaningful context, jazz chants provide rhythmic presentations of natural language. "The rhythm, stress, and intonation pattern of the chant should be an *exact* replica of what the student would hear from a native speaker in natural conversation" (Graham, 1992, p. 3).

Listening to Understand: The Task Approach.   Gradually, listening to repeat is replaced with other uses for listening as the audiolingual tradition fades. Instead, students are asked to perform tasks such as writing the correct response or selecting the correct answer to demonstrate comprehension (Morley, 1991a). To be successful, they must listen carefully. Typical classroom tasks are listening to an audiotape and completing true/false exercises based on the content, listening to a prerecorded speech and circling vocabulary items on a list as they appear in the text, and listening to a lecture and completing an outline of the notes.

For a more interactive adaptation of these listening procedures, the teacher and students can discuss the topic of an upcoming talk by a guest speaker and brainstorm questions and comments the students might like to make. During the talk, students listen for answers to their questions. The talk is also tape-recorded and the tape subsequently put into a listening center. Students can then re-listen, making note of ideas they want to share in the class follow-up activities. The tape also serves as a mediator when students have varying recollections of a particular point. The students can listen carefully to the tape in order to reconcile their points of view.

Listening for Communication: The Comprehension Approach. Now that language teaching methods emphasize the interactional aspects of language and recognize the importance of the listener's construction of meaning, the first stage to language acquisition is now seen as listening rather than repeating. During the initial "silent period," learners actively listen, segmenting the sound stream, absorbing intonation patterns, and becoming comfortable in the second language environment. Students are no longer expected to mimic previously prepared speech or to respond to comprehension checks. They demonstrate comprehension through nonverbal means. With this methodology, academic subjects can be included, even in the early stages of language acquisition (see TPR and Natural Approach discussed earlier in this chapter).

Once beyond the initial stage, interviews are often used to augment listening skills in the communicative approach. *The Complete ESL/EFL Cooperative and Communicative Activity Book* (Sloan, 1991) offers various interview formats and subjects that can be used cooperatively among students. Listening can also be used in problem-solving situations. Teachers can give students riddles, logic puzzles, and brain teasers as well as more traditional mathematical problems to listen to and solve (Morley, 1991a). Listening, far from a mere receptive skill, can be successfully combined with other language modes as part of an integrated approach to English acquisition.

Table 4.1 provides listening comprehension activities within each of the three categories discussed.

Speaking

Speaking involves a number of complex skills and strategies, but, because spoken language leaves no visible trace, its complexity and organizational features had previously never been realized. With the invention of the tape recorder, however, a means became available to study and analyze spoken language. Spoken discourse involves not only the stringing together of words in proper grammatical sequence but also the organizing of those strings into coherent wholes. This produces an oral text, one which has an inherent form, meaning, and a set of characteristics that determine its purpose and function. Spoken discourse can be informal, such as conversations between friends, or formal, such as lectures or presentations. Informal conversations are interactive; speaker and listener share common knowledge and support one another with nonverbal cues. On the other hand, in a formal presenta-

TABLE 4.1   Activities for Listening Comprehension

Repetition	Understanding	Communication

To hear sound patterns:
 Rhyming poems
 Songs
 Couplets
 Tongue twisters
 Jingles
 Alliterative poems
     and books
 	
 To listen to sentences:
 Jazz chants
 Dialogues
 Skits
	Listening to answer factual
	 questions orally or in writing:
	     Dialogues
	     Talks
	     Lectures
	     Arguments
	
	 Listening to make notes:
	     Support an argument
	     Persuade
		Playing games:
		     Twenty Questions
		     Pictionary
		     Password
		     Simon Says
		     Mother May I?
		
		 Open-ended sentences
		
		 Conversation starters
		
		 Cooperative problem-
		     solving activities:
		     Riddles
		     Logic puzzles
		     Brainteasers

tion, the speaker assumes the listener can supply a complex background or context. In a formal context, the listener is less able to interact with the speaker to negotiate meaning.

Part of the role of the teacher is to help students assimilate and produce discourse not only for the purpose of basic interpersonal communication (informal) but also for the comprehension and production of cognitive/academic language (formal). In addition, the teacher provides opportunities for students to express themselves in the wide range of language functions (see Chapter 3).

Situations for Spoken Discourse.   Students need opportunities to talk in natural interactional contexts and for a variety of purposes: to establish and maintain social relationships; to express reactions; to give and seek information; to solve problems, discuss ideas, or teach and learn a skill; to entertain or play with language; or to display achievement (Rivers & Temperley, 1978). In addition, students learn needed discourse skills by interacting with different conversational partners: other students, the teacher, other adults at school, cross-age peers, guests, and so on.

In order for students to have the opportunity to practice and develop discourse proficiency, teachers create environments that challenge students to use language to meet the social, emotional, and cognitive demands of their lives in and out of school. The following three principles (Dudley-Marling & Searle, 1991) help teachers set up such environments:

1. *Consider the emotional setting.* Speaking is risky and some students who are developing fluency in English can fear ridicule from their colleagues as well as corrections from the teachers. Teachers set up a climate of trust and respect by encouraging students to respect the language of their peers, by listening respectfully when students speak, and by working with students to establish classroom rules of respect and support.
2. *Create a physical setting for talk.* Classrooms need to be arranged so that students have flexibility in working and interacting. Some desks can be replaced with round or rectangular tables; other desks can be arranged in clusters; rows may be maintained in part of the classroom with work stations and centers in other parts. In addition, classrooms contain things to talk about. A science class has fish tanks and nature displays; a social studies class has flags, maps, and artifacts from the unit under study; all classrooms have a variety of print material.
3. *Group students for instruction.* Students need frequent opportunities to talk. Flexible grouping allows students to work with a variety of classmates; cross-age tutors provide one-on-one time with an older student; and aides, parent volunteers, and volunteer "grandparents" can lead small group discussions.

Resources for Spoken Discourse.   Teachers can provide opportunities for oral discourse, ranging from those that are carefully constructed to those that are completely student generated. Several texts are available to help teachers include speaking activities in their daily lessons.

Cooperative Learning (Kagan, 1989), a classic in the field, provides numerous activities that help students learn important conversational and group skills such as taking turns, interrupting, asking for clarification, looking interested, and changing the topic of conversation.

"Oral Communication in TESOL: Integrating Speaking, Listening, and Pronunciation" (Murphy, 1991) provides a wide range of activities for actively teaching oral communication. These include problem solving in small groups, enacting sociograms, and practicing persuasive or entertaining speeches.

Jazz Chants (Graham, 1978a) and subsequent jazz chant books by Carol Graham (1978b, 1986, 1988, 1992) offer entertaining verbal interchanges set to catchy rhythms. Students soon request their favorite segments, such as the toe-tapping singalong, "I'll have a chicken salad sandwich on toast" or the woeful, "I'm sorry, I'm so sorry, I'm really sorry, I'm terribly sorry." Graham (1988) has also put fairy tales into jazz chant form so that younger and less proficient students have the opportunity to work with longer texts.

Conversation Inspirations: Over 2000 Conversation Topics (Zelman, 1996) is an invaluable source of conversation topics arranged into six types of activities: role plays, interviews, chain stories, talks, problems, and discussions.

Discussion Starters (Folse, 1996) offers speaking activities that build oral fluency using exercises specifically designed for group participation. The discussion prompts are based on role play, "finish-the-story" situations, problems that can be solved only if members of a group work together, and real court cases for groups to play "You Be the Judge."

Talk It Up! (Koryrev, 1998) and *Talk It Through!* (Koryrev & Baker, 2000) focus on developing students' ability to communicate fluently and accurately by integrating listening, speaking, and pronunciation practice. Topics such as Privacy and Weird Science present skills in anticipating questions, understanding suggestions, and note taking.

So to Speak 1 & 2 (Webster & DeFilippo, 1999) include crosscultural and communicative pair and group exercises based on daily conversational situations that motivate students to integrate listening, speaking, and pronunciation practice. The lessons can be easily adapted for elementary-age students.

Can't Stop Talking (Rooks, 1990) presents serious and challenging dilemmas for students to solve. Students take on the roles of those involved in solving such problems. Examples include "Making the Punishment Fit the Crime!" and "Let's Put Some Pizzazz in the TV Schedule!"

Table 4.2 has organized representative oral activities into the three categories suggested by Allen and Vallette (1977). These categories range from tightly structured on the left to freely constructed on the right.

Improving Oral Proficiency. English learners must have a comprehensible control of the English sound system. Pronunciation involves the correct *articulation* of the individual sounds of English as well as the proper *stress* and *pitch* within syllables, words, and phrases. Longer stretches of speech require correct *intonation* patterns (Pennington & Richards, 1986). However, the goal of teaching English

TABLE 4.2 Formats for Oral Practice in the ELD Classroom

Guided Practice	Communicative Practice	Free Conversations
Formulaic exchanges	Simulations	Discussion groups
Greetings	Guessing games	Debates
Congratulations	Group puzzles	Panel discussions
Apologies	Rank-order problems	Group picture stories
Leave-taking	Values continuum	Socializing
Dialogues	Categories of preference:	Story telling/retelling
Mini-conversations	Opinion polls	Discussions of:
Role plays	Survey taking	Films
Skits	Interviews	Shared experiences
Oral descriptions	Brainstorming	Literature
Strip stories	News reports	
Oral games	Research reports	
	Story telling	

pronunciation is not necessarily to make second language speakers sound like native speakers of English (Celce-Murcia & Goodwin, 1991). In fact, the goal of the learners themselves often has more to do with their eventual approximation of native speaker pronunciation than do special teacher-directed exercises. Some English learners do not wish to have a native-like pronunciation but prefer instead to retain an accent that indicates their first language roots and allows them to be identified with their ethnic community (Morley, 1991b). Still others may wish to integrate actively into the mainstream culture and thus are motivated to try to attain a native accent in English. Teachers need to recognize these individual goals and enable learners to achieve a quality of pronunciation that does not detract significantly from their ability to communicate.

Over a period of many months, teachers may find that students' attempts to reproduce correct word stress, sentence rhythm, and intonation may improve by exposure to native speaker models. Particularly with younger students, teachers may not explicitly teach such discourse patterns but instead may allow for interactive contact with native English speakers to provide appropriate patterns. The teacher's role, in this case, is to create a nonthreatening environment that stimulates and interests students enough that they participate actively in producing speech. In other cases, however, teachers may want to intervene actively. Clarification checks may be interjected politely when communication is impaired. Correction or completion by the teacher may be given after the teacher has allowed ample "wait time." Older students may be given the task of comparing speech sounds in their native language with a sound in English in order to better understand a contrastive difference. Students' attempts to produce English may be enhanced if they are encouraged to produce alternative vocabulary, simplified sentence structures, and approximate sounds to English.

Reading and Writing

Many teachers consider reading to be the intellectual foundation of academic work. As such, it involves much more than merely decoding text; it is a construction of meaning. Meaning does not exist on the page, independent of the reader. The construction of meaning is an interaction between the text and the reader's experience. This constructive process requires that readers be able to draw on short- and long-term memory to match the meaning of the text to their prior knowledge, linguistic ability, and experience (Barnitz, 1985; Rumelhart, 1977, 1980). They must also be familiar with the discourse community from which the text is drawn. Thus, through acquiring and practicing literacy, readers are dealing with more than the mechanics of reading and comprehension. They are going beyond the narrow act of "reading" itself. They are acquiring knowledge. This process can be accomplished more effectively through reading in a larger context, in which students engage in group activities, work collaboratively, and read and write texts for communicative purposes.

Writing is more than an exercise for the teacher to assign and critique. It is an opportunity for students to link with the social and cultural heritage of English and to begin communicating effectively across cultures. At the heart of the classroom writing task is its relation to the real world. Through writing, students perform a purposeful social action, an action that takes them beyond a mere school assignment. Communicating with one another—with others outside the classroom, with home and family, with presidents and corporate officers, with city officials and nursing home residents—establishes real discourse and helps students to convey information that is real and necessary. This is the essence of writing as a communicative task.

Strategies for English Learners' Literacy Instruction.   An explanation of all the strategies appropriate for EL students is beyond the scope of this book. However, certain strategies that encompass the main principles for suitable instruction with English learners are explained here. These include prereading activities that help build students' background knowledge prior to working with text; Language Experience Approach (LEA), a strategy particularly helpful for nonliterate students; directed reading-thinking activity (DR-TA), a strategy that develops students' abilities to predict text; literature response group, a postreading strategy that invites active student participation; and the writing process, which engages students in developing their own texts. The interested reader will find an excellent compilation of literacy procedures for English learners in Peregoy and Boyle's third edition (2001) *Reading, Writing, and Learning in ESL.*

Prereading activities provide a means of connecting the learner with the cultural context of a book or passage and give learners the background information they need to be able to interact effectively with the text. These prereading activities may include group brainstorming; use of pictures, charts, and realia; field trips, nature walks, guest speakers, and other types of community contacts; and/or recall of previous readings on related topics. Such experiences help students to build their knowledge of the topic and to anticipate the content of the text. They further allow students to understand vocabulary and concepts within a rich linguistic environment so that the whole of the text is comprehensible, not merely individual vocabulary items.

The *Language Experience Approach (LEA)* encourages students to respond to events in their own words, which the teacher writes down and reads back so that students can eventually read the text for themselves. Because the students are providing their own phrases and sentences, they find the text relevant and interesting, and generally have little trouble reading it. The importance of LEA in developing the language of English learners cannot be overemphasized. It connects students to their own experiences and activities by having them express themselves orally; it reinforces the notion that sounds can be transcribed into specific symbols and that those symbols can then be used to recreate the ideas expressed; and it provides texts for specific lessons on vocabulary, grammar, writing conventions, structure, and more. The following is one teacher's account of a LEA lesson the class engaged in after having studied the Qin dynasty.

> After finishing the lesson on the Qin dynasty, I had my sixth-grade class brainstorm key ideas. I wrote their points on the board and then asked them to tell a story about a fictional family of three living during that era. The only restrictions I put on was that they had to keep in mind the key points. Their story follows:
>
>> Chang, Li, and their son, Wei, lived during the Qin dynasty. Li was excited because Chang was able to *buy* the family some *land*. A few days later, Chang was taken by the emperor to go *build* the *Great Wall*. Li and Wei were sad. They did not like the emperor, because he had strict *laws* and *punishments*. Li wrote Chang a letter telling him how the emperor tried to bring the people in China together by *standardizing writing, money,* and *measurement*. Chang never received the letter because he died on the long walk to the Great Wall. Li and Wei grew crops so they could survive. They hoped a new and better emperor would come and *overthrow* the mean one.
>
> After the class decided they were finished with their story, they read it out loud many times. They then chose the 12 key words (emphasized above) they wanted to focus on. I erased the key words from the story, leaving blanks where they were supposed to go. The class read the story again. The next day, I had individual copies for the students. We worked with the story again by reading, matching key words to the appropriate blanks, and so on. (Bowen, personal communication, May 11, 1999)

Directed Reading-Thinking Activity (DR-TA) is an activity that helps students understand that proficient readers actively work with text by making predictions as they read. DR-TA is a teacher-guided activity that leads students through the prediction process until they are able to do it on their own. The teacher asks students to make predictions and then read to confirm their ideas. Although initially students believe there are absolute "right" and "wrong" predictions, through teacher guidance, they begin to see how the text helps them predict and understand that general ideas serve equally as well as specific details. The following is an example of a DR-TA activity using Viorst's poem "Talking" (1981):

> I use the overhead projector and a piece of paper to slowly uncover the parts of the poem after students have made their predictions. In order to help me, I have made a green dot at the end of each line where I want to stop. I reveal the title "Talking" and ask students, "What is this poem about?" The wise-guys always say "talking," but other students give some specific examples. I move the paper down to reveal the first line of the poem and ask, "What will happen in this poem?" Responses range from what "they" do to curtail the author's talking to students' experiences with their own too-much talk. Next I show three lines and ask, "What might the author say next?" I listen to students' responses, noting that I will go back when we're done to point out the colon at the end of the last line and how that might be a clue to what will be coming—not the specifics necessarily, but certainly the idea of a list. After revealing the next four lines, I stop and ask, "Based on what you've read so far, who is the author?" I hope students will recognize some issues from childhood and predict that this is written from the point of view of a child. If not, here's another teaching point. The next section I show ends with "And ten things that I love the most." My simple question is, "What's next?" Generally, all students are able to say at this point that there will be a list of 10 things. I reveal 9 of them and my second to the last question is, "And what will the last thing be?" Frequently, there is a chorus of the answer, "Talking!" but if not, I have another teaching point. My last question is always, "Was there anything you didn't understand?" For this poem, the questions generally focus on vocabulary ("scabby," "erg") but, with other texts, students may often ask about whole phrases or sentences or even concepts. We then go back and note words, phrases, and sentences in the text that lead to predictions. When a student's response is completely plausible from the context but not what the author has written, I always point out that the author has *chosen* to write what he or she did, but could have written what the student suggested. This reinforces the thinking and creative aspect of both the writing and the reading processes. (Kathryn Weed)

The key to DR-TA lessons is to accept all student responses. The teacher's goal is to help students see that correctness is not as important as plausibility, and that they need to check the text continually as new information is revealed.

Literature response groups can develop a community of readers and help students understand the richness of the literacy experience. After having read a piece of literature (depending on the proficiency level of the student, different strategies are used to help the student read the text—teacher, other adult, or cross-age tutor reads; buddies read together; student reads individually), the teacher and a small group meet to discuss the piece. Each student is given an opportunity to express ideas about the story before a general discussion begins. The teacher listens and, after each student has had a turn, opens the discussion with a thought-provoking question. As points are made, the teacher guides the students to deeper understandings by, for example, asking them to support their point with words from the text and asking what words or devices the author used to invoke a mood, establish a setting, describe a character, move the plot along, and so on. In the following excerpt, the teacher talks about her first experience with this type of discussion. The students had read *Now One Foot, Now the Other* by dePaola (1981).

> In planning this lesson, I was a bit apprehensive about the students' overall reaction to this type of discussion. However, I found that they enjoyed discussing the story in a more intimate setting as opposed to a whole class discussion. The use of higher-order thinking skills was encouraged and I found that these second-graders were indeed up to the challenge. In my mind, I had already anticipated some very sad and tearful remarks, but, to my surprise, these students were capable of handling the sad emotions that were evoked. I also had to refrain from trying to clarify what I thought a student was trying to state. This was very hard for me. I had to remember that one of my objectives was for the students to verbalize their thoughts and convey meaning. They need practice in doing so.
>
> Two of the students were not sad. They felt very proud to be the "teacher" in this reverse situation. The ability to be the leader and show their leadership skills made them feel like grown-ups. This opened up more discussion on how they have been helpful at home.... They could tell me about helping with the wash or cooking. Sometimes they have to be responsible in cleaning up so they can all live together. This, indeed, allowed for a diverse discussion. This provided an excellent avenue for my verbal communicators and opened up a safe environment for those students who do not like to respond verbally. They seemed less intimidated in the small group. I found that my students had definite ideas about major issues—illness, hospitals, family members, working, being responsible, and being good friends. I found out that their concerns were very important in their lives and that this piece of literature and forum for discussion provided an opportunity for them to talk. I have found another avenue of teaching! (Dotts, personal communication, November 18, 1998)

The writing process has become increasingly accepted as an alternative to the "product" view of writing. The shift from a focus on product to a focus on process is "the most significant single transformation in the teaching of composition" (Kroll, 1991, p. 247). It changes the way students compose, provides situations where language can be used in a meaningful way, and emphasizes the act of writing rather than the result. The process approach is particularly important for English learners who are developing their oral language skills at the same time as their written skills, because it involves more interaction, planning, and reworking. Students are not moving from topic to topic quickly, but have an opportunity to work with a topic (and therefore vocabulary and structures) over a period of time. The three general stages—the planning or *prewriting, writing,* and *editing*—allow students to organize, develop, and refine concepts and ideas in ways that the product approach to writing does not. For example, during prewriting, students are involved in oral language experiences that develop their need and desire to write. These activities may include talking and listening about shared experiences, reading literature, brainstorming, or creating role plays or other fantasy activities (Enright & McCloskey, 1988).

During the writing stage, students write quickly to capture ideas, doing the best they can in spelling, vocabulary, and syntax without a concern for accuracy. They then rewrite and redraft as necessary, again working with other students and/or the teacher to share, discuss, expand, and clarify their ideas. In the last stage, editing, students are helped to fix up their mechanics of usage and spelling, particularly when their writing is going to be shared in a formal way. If a perfected or final version is not necessary, students may file their rough drafts in a portfolio. The process has generated writing that is satisfying in its ability to capture and share ideas—the essence of writing for the purpose of communication. If, however, the writing is published or publicly shared, students also achieve the pride of authorship. Ways of publishing may vary: a play performed, a story bound into a book for circulation in the class library, a poem read aloud, an essay posted on a bulletin board, a video made of a student reading aloud, a class newspaper circulated to the community, and so on (Enright & McCloskey, 1988).

Techniques for Students without Literacy in First or Second Languages. Preschoolers without a knowledge of print, older students without previous schooling, and the partially literate who may have acquired some decoding skills in their primary language but whose overall level of literacy does not provide them useful access to print—these groups need special treatment. Research continues to indicate that literacy in the primary language is an important precursor to school success. "Children who are dominant in a language other than English acquire academic language and literacy skills rapidly and better in both the native language and English when they attain literacy proficiency in the first language" (Flood, Lapp, Tinajero, & Hurley, 1997). However, it is not always possible to provide primary language literacy instruction. For this situation, Hamayan (1994) outlines seven instructional procedures that lead students to literacy in their second language. (Although these strategies are especially important for preliterate second language learners, they are also helpful for English learners in general—even those who are literate in their first language.)

First, the classroom is saturated with meaningful environmental print. Students see labels, announcements, names, and signs with as many contextual clues as possible. Such labels are often written by the students themselves, giving them pride of ownership and purposeful writing opportunities. Labels can be bilingual or trilingual, thus incorporating students' native languages into their beginning literacy experiences. Second, literacy activities move from the "known" to the "unknown." They revolve around content of interest to the learners. One way of starting with the "known" is to base literacy activities on the children's oral language (see earlier discussion on LEA). Third, literacy is allowed to emerge naturally. Students go through a silent period in reading—often mouthing words while the teacher reads aloud. Similarly, in writing, they start in a rudimentary fashion without always writing well-formed letters and perfectly spelled words. Dialogue journals are a means to allow language to emerge in a natural developmental way. Fourth, effective literacy environments are free of anxiety. Children's attempts at reading and writing are greeted with enthusiasm. When they see their efforts are rewarded, students feel encouraged to continue. Fifth, activities are motivating. Children sense the intrinsic worth of reading when it leads to a dramatic presentation or sharing with a buddy. They enjoy writing when they know they will have a comment, not a correction, from the teacher. Sixth, students' attention is focused on specific structures and forms of written language within the context of meaningful activities. Their own oral language stories, dialogue journals, and so on provide the basis for specific instruction. Seventh, content area instruction is integrated with literacy. Vocabulary, grammatical structures, and language functions needed in academic areas are incorporated into literacy activities. Table 4.3 provides examples of materials, reading, and writing activities that have been found to support English learners.

Phonics in Literacy Instruction for English Learners. A discussion of literacy would not be complete without mention of the role of phonics, "a system of teaching reading and spelling that stresses basic symbol-sound relationships and their application in decoding words" (California Department of Education, 1999b, p. 278). Phonics is again being touted as an important means to help children learn to read. For example, the California Reading Task Force included the following as the second of the four components of a balanced, comprehensive approach to reading: "an organized, explicit skills program that includes phonemic awareness (sounds in words), phonics, and decoding skills" (California Department of Education, 1999b, p. 11). The first component, it should be noted, was "a strong literature, language, and comprehension program that includes a balance of oral

TABLE 4.3 Materials and Activities to Support EL Students' Literacy Development

Materials	Activities with a Reading Focus	Activities with a Writing Focus
Literature, literature, and more literature	Read-aloud	Dialogue journals
Big books	Readers' Theater	Writing workshop
Pattern books	Story telling	Response groups
Wordless picture books	Sharing	Peer editing groups
Ads, posters, pamphlets, brochures	Oral reading activities:	Author's chair
Utility bills	Choral reading	Classroom/school newspaper
Song books	Buddy reading	Literature response journals
Poetry	Repeated reading	Content area journals
Rhymes, riddles, tongue-twisters, jokes	Independent reading	Developing scripts for Readers' Theater
Jump-rope rhymes, finger-play	Directed reading-thinking activity (DR-TA)	Language Experience Approach (LEA)
Journals, diaries	Language Experience Approach (LEA)	
Magazines		
Comic books		
How-to books		
Dictionaries, encyclopedias		

and written language" (p. 11). Phonemic awareness (discussed earlier in Listening to Repeat: The Audiolingual Legacy) is found to be an important precursor to native English speakers' success in learning to read, and once children grasp the principles that words are made of phonemes and that letters represent these phonemes, they can benefit from phonics instruction (Grossen, 1997). Importantly, this research is with native English speakers. For English learners, instruction in phonics is not so clear-cut and lists of practices appropriate for them do not include phonics work (Flood et al., 1997; Hudelson, 1994). Hamayan (1994) cites four reasons why structural approaches (phonics based and grammar based) fail to meet the needs of preliterate EL students: (1) they do not meet the learner's need to acquire an understanding of the functional aspects of literacy, (2) literacy is forced to emerge in an unnatural way and in an artificial form, (3) a focus on form and language structures without a functional context makes learning abstract and thus meaningless and difficult, and (4) literacy becomes a boring chore.

However, it cannot be denied that written English is based on the alphabetic principle and that children do need to understand that sounds and letters correspond. Teachers of English learners are encouraged to provide students with rich language experiences, including wordplay, which lead them to understandings of sound/symbol correspondences. During and after read-alouds, for example, teachers point out specific sound and letter patterns that occurred in the texts. According to Peregoy and Boyle (2001), specific instruction in sound/symbol correspondence emerges best through students' own writing. Their invented or temporary spelling represents "an important step on the way to conventional spelling while providing individualized phonics practice that will assist both reading and writing development" (p. 153).

In the following excerpt, an elementary teacher reacts to what he perceives as the problems of a phonics-based program: Success for All^tm (SFA). This program for teaching elementary students reading and writing emphasizes prevention and intervention to ensure achievement for every child. (For information about the program, see http://www. successforall.net/curriculum/index.htm.)

> While the adoption of SFA was well-intended, my observations as an educator, as an ESL professional, and as a graduate student of language education is that SFA is a uniquely inefficient means of literacy instruction. As part of the philosophy behind SFA, its founder, John [sic] Slavin, separates the act of reading from the act of comprehension. But language has evolved specifically for the purpose of human communication. It is a basic premise of language education that successful communication only occurs as the result of comprehensible input. Although it can be argued than phonics based instruction has its value, SFA uses phonics as the sole medium for reading instruction. The identification of certain sounds and sound blends takes precedence over coherent, logical reading material. In the short illustrated stories written for SFA, words containing a specific story's target sound or sound blend are preferred to commonly occurring English words and natural language use. As a result, the stories written for SFA frequently make little or no narrative sense.
>
> For ESL students in SFA, this use of awkward syntax provides only unnatural input, which either serves to contradict their growing knowledge of the spoken lan-

guage (as it does with their native English-speaking peers) and/or reinforces the use of problematic language. I frequently experience students substituting a more commonly heard word or phrase for the awkward one SFA employs for the sake of phonic continuity when reading the SFA stories aloud. As a language professional, I recognize such utterances to be signs of genuine language acquisition and development despite the conflict with SFA. In such instances, the students' utterances are technically incorrect according to the SFA rubric. By attributing greater importance to students' knowledge of English phonics than to a more naturalized acquisition of language, SFA hinders students' ability to develop their literacy as an extension of their spoken language. I believe that its [SFA's] phonics, rather than comprehension, based approach is both alienating and inappropriate for ESL and native English-speaking students. (Lee, 2000, reprinted with permission)

Transferring Literacy from First to Second Languages. During the era in which the audiolingual method of second language instruction was in vogue, it was customary to anticipate that certain learners would experience predictable kinds of difficulties in learning English, depending on their first language. For example, it is difficult for native speakers of Japanese to distinguish the phonemes /r/ and /l/, because Japanese does not feature such a distinction. Likewise, native speakers of Mandarin or Cantonese forms of Chinese might have difficulty mastering the definite and indefinite article in English because Chinese employs a very different way of marking nouns. This reasoning about predictable difficulties, called *contrastive analysis,* is no longer a primary strategy in second language acquisition theory. Contemporary views deemphasize L1–L2 transfer or interference and instead emphasize meaningful communication in the second language.

The idea of contrasting the native language with English in order to predict possible interference or transfer has been carried into the domain of writing instruction. *Contrastive rhetoric* is a term used to denote the process of understanding ELD students' writing by comparing typical texts in the native language with that of English (see Grabe & Kaplan, 1990). Kaplan (1967) indicates that a language such as Arabic may show a text structure that depends on elaborate parallel structures and embedded references to moral teaching to create points of rhetoric. Arabic students learning English tend to use very little subordinating structures and instead rely on parallelism and metaphor. Other writing instructors have commented that Chinese students tend to use circular rhetoric structures when writing in English, and use relatively few linear or "logical" beginning-to-end arguments that are common in English texts. Teachers of writing may find their students' thought structures more understandable by noting what typical rhetoric structure in the primary language contributes to thought.

Teacher Delivery

In a language classroom, the focus of teacher and students is on language development. In a content classroom, teacher and students are concerned with the subject being studied. In ELD classrooms, teachers and students focus on both language and content. Through modifications in their own talk, conscious attention to clarification, appropriate questioning strategies, and an understanding of when and where to deal with grammar and treat errors, teachers can provide a rich learning environment that promotes both language and content knowledge.

Comprehensible Input

One of the primary tasks of any teacher is to ensure that students understand. In working with students who learn English at home, the teacher's task is to help them understand new concepts. English acts as an invisible medium used to accomplish this task. For students whose first language is not English, teachers are confronted with developing content knowledge through a foreign medium—English. The amount of English that is learned depends somewhat indirectly on the amount of time spent in English language development classes (see Point/Counterpoint on page 105). It becomes the responsibility of the teacher to supply understandable language. This is Krashen's "comprehensible input" (see input hypothesis, discussed in Chapter 1). In order to provide comprehensible input just above students' current abilities, teachers can consider four means: (1) embedding language within a meaningful context, (2) modifying the language presented to the student, (3) judiciously using paraphrase and repetition, and (4) involving the students in multimodal learning activities.

Krashen's notion of comprehensible input has been an important contribution to understanding language acquisition and to developing ways for teachers to provide such input. More recent research (Gass, 2000) also points to the role of the learner in negotiating, managing, even manipulating conversations to receive more comprehensible input. Thus, negotiation between the conversational partners leads to understanding and acquisition. Comprehensible input to the student stimulates the student's language output. By means of this output, students actively solicit more input. The knowledgeable teacher tries to "stretch" the student's proficiency by staying just slightly ahead of the language the student produces. Thus, the classroom learning becomes a two-way exchange that builds English proficiency.

To illustrate this collaboration and negotiation of meaning between student and teacher, witness the following one-to-one exchange:

STUDENT: I put it here. (points to microscope slide on mounting platform)

TEACHER: You mounted the slide.

STUDENT: Yes, it has it—it has plant.

TEACHER: You mounted a leaf on the slide?

STUDENT: No, not leaf. The plant, um, ground (gestures to indicate under the ground).

TEACHER: Oh. You mounted a plant *root* on the slide.

STUDENT: Yes. Root.

Point/Counterpoint

Does immersion in a second language promote acquisition?

Several methods of ESL teaching work on the immersion principle, in which only the target language is used in language instruction. If students hear, speak, read, and write directly in the target language, learning supposedly is quicker. But is this the case?

Point: **The more time spent in a second language context, the more language is learned.** The time-on-task research performed by educators in the late 1970s and early 1980s promoted the idea that the more academic time was devoted to a subject, the more of that subject was mastered (Doyle, 1983). This theme has been evoked by English-only advocates, who promote English-only immersion education with the argument, "the more time spent in English, the more English is learned."

In some ways this argument is reminiscent of the mind-as-a-muscle metaphor that was common in medieval language teaching. Latin was taught as a way of disciplining the mind, on the grounds that repeated practice was the key to language learning or mental strength. Chomsky's argument (1959) against B. F. Skinner's reinforcement theory was that grammar was learned not through repeated exposure to language, drill, or practice, but through the ability of the mind to extract meaningful rules from disparate stimuli and to make sense of language. Repeated exposure to language is useful only if the exposure makes sense.

Counterpoint: **Comprehensible language is more important than time.** The principle that the more academic time was devoted to a subject, the more of that subject was mastered does not necessarily hold true for language learning. Research indicates that increased exposure to English does not necessarily speed the acquisition of English. Children who are educated in their primary language to the point where they are able to function at a high cognitive level, make sense out of academic tasks, and apply prior knowledge to learning new knowledge are able to learn a second language more rapidly.

Krashen's input hypothesis (1981) emphasizes that classroom language that is understandable to a student will promote more rapid language acquisition than language that is incomprehensible. The more usable context the student can be provided, the more language will be learned. This means that classroom language must match the learner's level of understanding, combined with ways to make the learning familiar. The exposure to a second language must be the kind that is conducive to learning.

TEACHER: Can you draw what you see? (she makes drawing movements on an imaginary paper) . . . Make a drawing.

STUDENT: Make a drawing for the root.

Language Contextualization.   The foregoing conversation demonstrates the basic principles of language contextualization and modification. The conversation is focused on the immediate task, using vocabulary about that task. Both the teacher and the student are negotiating meaning: The teacher, in this case, tries to understand what the student has done and then guide her to the next step; the student attempts to explain what she has already done. In the process, the teacher uses sentence structures that expand the student's output by supplying needed phrases and vocabulary. The teacher uses gestures to convey instructions. The teacher does not correct the student's speech but concentrates on understanding and communicating with the student about the task. Thus, English is being acquired through the natural process of communication. Of course, the subtle meanings that are conveyed through language structure require many such conversations before the student shows mastery. What is most important in this dialogue is that the student has used language to accomplish a task and has increased language proficiency as a by-product of this interaction.

The teacher ensures that the English provided to the student is embedded within an understandable context by focusing on the task rather than the language. This context can be a learning activity (experimenting, drawing, map making); it can be a cooperative project (a play, a game, a group report); and it can involve other contexts and persons (field trips or guest speakers who demonstrate specific skills and talents).

Language Modification.   Language modification is an important means of creating comprehensible input in second language classes. Numerous studies have examined how teachers adapt their speech. Such adaptation has been found to exist at all linguistic levels—phonological (using precise pronunciation); syntactic (less subordination; shorter sentences that follow subject-verb-object format); semantic (more concrete, basic vocabulary); pragmatic (more frequent and longer pauses; exaggerated stress and intonation); and discourse (self-repetition; slower rate). Although these elements are widely used and have value, they have not been conclusively proved to aid comprehension. Elaboration, in which the teacher supplies redundant information through repetition, paraphrase, and rhetorical markers, may prove more effective than simplifying grammar and vocabulary (Nunan, 1991).

Repetition and Paraphrase.   An important part of providing a comprehensible learning environment for students is the teacher's use of repetition and paraphrase. Repetition involves not merely verbal repetition, but organizational repetition as well. Verbal repetition does not mean that the teacher repeats the same directions five or six times consecutively but that he or she uses the same type of direction throughout various lessons. For example, an elementary teacher may say, "Today we are going to continue our work on. . . . Who can show me their work from yesterday?" These sentences can be repeated throughout the day to introduce lessons.

Organizational repetition involves the structure of the day and the format of lessons. Lessons that occur at specific times and places help orient students to procedures. Lessons that have clearly marked boundaries—nonverbal, such as a location change or materials gathering, as well as verbal ("Now it's time to. . .")—also provide a basis for understanding. Students know what to expect and how to proceed. They are then able to turn their attention to content and language instruction (Wong-Fillmore, 1985).

Paraphrases of simple instructions can give students yet another opportunity to process spoken input. Repeating important words and phrases need not be dull. Wong-Fillmore (1990) gives an example of an important point that was communicated to students using simple, repetitious phrases.

TEACHER: Who remembers the person who came to speak to us yesterday?

CLASS: The mayor [Diane Feinstein, mayor of San Francisco].

TEACHER: Good. And what was special about the mayor?

CLASS: She is a woman.

TEACHER: Yes! The mayor is a woman. A woman can be a mayor. What else can a woman be?

CLASS: President.

TEACHER: O.K., a woman can be president. What else can a woman be?

CLASS: Governor.

TEACHER: Yes, a woman can be governor. Very good.

Use of Media, Realia, Manipulatives, and Other Modalities. Not all students are principally verbal learners. Most students can benefit from the use of media, realia, manipulatives, and other modalities—visual and hands-on activities that make language more comprehensible. For example, diagrams in science books represent structures and functions in a graphic way. Models that construct the human alimentary system make concrete the abstract process of digestion. With the availability of computers, software programs and the Internet offer sights, sounds, and experiences that provide excellent language (and content) learning opportunities. Table 4.4 provides a list of both object and human resources for the classroom.

Clarification Checks

Clarification checks at intervals give the teacher a sense of the students' ability to understand. A teacher might pause during instruction to ask, "Do you understand?" or "Is this clear?" Students can raise their hands if they are following. Similarly, the teacher might pause to ask a question requiring a simple response, such as, "Show me how you are going to begin your work." For a more complex instruction, the teacher might ask an individual student to restate the instruction using his or her own words. These clarification checks are an important means of maintaining a two-way process of instruction. Those students who seem to lack comprehension may be paired with a "buddy" who can supplement the teacher's instructions.

The teacher may also find it necessary to teach students how to verbalize their understanding. Students need to know not only what to say to signal understanding but also how and when to send these messages. Teachers may need to find ways

TABLE 4.4   Classroom Elements That Foster Language Learning

Object Resources	Human Resources
Picture files	Cooperative groups
Maps and globes	Pairs
Charts and posters	Cross-age tutors
Printed material:	Heterogeneous groups
Illustrated books	Community resource people
Pamphlets	School resource people
News articles	Parents
Catalogs	Pen pals (adult and child)
Magazines	Keypals
Puzzles	
Science equipment	
Manipulatives:	
M & Ms	
Buttons	
Cuisenaire rods	
Tongue depressors	
Gummy bears	
Costumes	
Computer software	
Internet	

in which English learners can voice their need for clarification, such as accepting questions that are written on index cards or allowing students to speak for others (Díaz-Rico, 1991). The ability to ask for help when needed involves cultural norms and discourse competence. Just as kindergarten and first-grade teachers recognize that part of their task is to socialize students to school procedures, so too must ELD teachers, at all levels, recognize that their students need to be taught the appropriate context and procedures for speaking.

Appropriate Questioning Strategies

Questions are a staple in U.S. classrooms, and it is generally through skilled questioning that teachers lead discussions and ascertain students' understanding. However, standard questioning strategies can be fraught with peril in working with English learners. Two general areas are considered here. The first concerns the way questions are framed relative to students' proficiency levels; the second has to do with sociocultural aspects of displaying knowledge.

Generally, a teacher can consider a linguistic hierarchy of question types. For students in the "silent period," a question requiring a nonverbal response—a head movement, pointing, manipulating materials—will elicit an appropriate and satisfactory answer. Once students are beginning to speak, either/or questions provide the necessary terms, and the student needs merely to choose the correct word or phrase to demonstrate understanding: "Is the water evaporating or condensing?" "Did explorers come to the Americas from Europe or Asia?" Once students are more comfortable in producing language, *wh-* questions are appropriate: "What is happening to the water?" "Which countries sent explorers to the Americas?" "What was the purpose of their exploration?"

The common practice in teacher-directed classrooms is for students to bid to answer a teacher's question or for the teacher to call on a specific individual. Both procedures can be problematic for English learners, who may be reluctant to bring attention to themselves, either because they see such an action as incompatible with group cohesiveness and cultural norms, or because they may be reluctant to display knowledge in front of others.

The following story written by a student from Vietnam portrays differences in teaching styles between his country and the United States:

> Call me Henry. I grew up in Vietnam, where we usually don't ask questions or have much contact with the teacher. Rarely will a student raise his hand. From the day I entered kindergarten and all the way through high school, I just listened and took notes in class. Each evening it was my responsibility to memorize the materials that were presented in class that day. There were no discussions, debates, or challenges to the teacher's point of view. The teacher was always right because he was the teacher. He knew the stuff better than me.
>
> When I came to the United States the school system surprised me. My classes were hardly ever quiet. One day we had a discussion on the topic of gun control. Everyone participated in it. The class atmosphere was exciting and fun. The arguing went on until the end of the class, and everyone seemed to enjoy it. To my surprise the teacher encouraged the discussion and listened to what the students had to say. This felt very different to me. The teacher was treating the students like friends, not like in Vietnam where teachers kept their distance from the students. (Dresser, 1993)

Teachers who are sensitive to varying cultural styles organize other means for students to demonstrate language and content knowledge, and act as observers and guides rather than directors or controllers of student activity.

Treatment of Errors

In any endeavor, errors are inevitable, and language learning is certainly no exception. Often, people accept errors (or do not even notice them) when children are learning their first language, but teachers expend much energy noting, correcting, and designing lessons to address errors when students are learning a second language. Often, no allowance is made for the learners' age, level of fluency, educational background, or risk-taking behavior. These, however, are relevant factors in determining how a teacher should deal with language errors.

In the early stages of language learning, fluency is more important than accuracy. A teacher who is uncomfortable with less than perfect speech only adds unnecessary anxiety to the developing proficiency of the ELD student. Thus, the teacher, instead of monitoring and correcting, should converse and model appropriate language. When a student says "My pencil broken," the teacher's response is, "Go ahead and sharpen it." In this interchange, language has furthered meaning despite the imperfection of syntax. Error correction is not necessary. The teacher focuses on the student's message and provides correction only when the meaning is not clear. Younger children, particularly, appear to learn more when teachers focus on meaning rather than form. Older students, who are more aware of school procedures and who are able to apply learned rules, may profit from specific lessons or feedback on recurring errors (Yorio, 1980).

Apart from the personal factors just mentioned, teachers need to be aware of the types of errors their students are making (Walz, 1982). According to Yorio (1980), errors can occur in two general categories: systematic (appearing with regularity) or random (caused by memory lapse, inattention, or inadequate rule acquisition). The teacher can observe systematic errors in the class and discuss them with the class, with small groups who display the same error, or with individuals. By observing systematic errors, the teacher will recognize that random errors do not need to be corrected.

Error correction strategies should serve to enhance the student's self-correction abilities. As mentioned before, probably the best overall strategy is for the teacher to focus on meaning and provide communicative contexts in which students can hear, produce, and learn.

Treatment of Grammar

Historically, grammar has been seen as the organizational framework for language and, as such, has been used as the organizational framework for language teaching. In many classrooms, second language instruction has been based on learning the correct use of such items as the verb *to be*, the present tense, definite articles, possessive adjectives and pronouns, subject-verb agreement, and so forth (see Allen & Vallette, 1977). Ellis (1988) calls this the "structure of the day" approach (p. 136). Linguists dispute the value of such a structured approach for the attainment of grammatical competence, and some research (Dulay, Burt, & Krashen, 1982) indicates that teaching may have a very limited effect on the order of development of at least some grammatical structures. The effectiveness of formal instruction may depend on the nature of the grammatical rule that is being taught (Ellis, 1988). Students, who have acquired the first language through communicative interaction, often miss the intent of the teacher's corrective comment because they are searching for meaning, not correction. In addition, the teacher's effort to describe correct syntax may prescribe a narrow view of correctness, a view that may not be universally agreed on. This may inadvertently communicate to students that their usage is substandard.

The effective language teacher, therefore, organizes instruction around meaningful concepts—themes, topics, areas of student interest—and deals with grammar as the need arises. This is done on an individual basis or, when the teacher notices a systematic problem among several students, direct instruction. Practice on the grammar point may be directed to a small group or, when necessary, the class as a whole.

Working with Paraprofessionals

Paraprofessional educators may be instructional aides, volunteers from the parent community, tutors from other grades, or senior citizens and other community volunteers. Students from high school service organizations or university students may work in classrooms as part of community outreach programs. Language teaching is a labor-intensive enterprise, and having a variety of assistants means that more can be accomplished during school time. Involving paraprofessionals requires careful organization to recruit skillful helpers and to utilize them effectively. Prudent planning is needed to maintain high-quality instruction and to ensure that assistants in the classroom feel valued.

Organizing for Assistance

A paraprofessional works alongside the teacher to assist in preparing materials, doing clerical work, monitoring small groups of students, giving tutorial help, or providing basic instruction under teacher supervision. Many bilingual education programs rely on teacher aides to deliver primary language instruction; or, in a classroom in which the teacher delivers the primary language instruction, the aide may be involved with pull-out ELD tutoring for those students most in need of English instruction. The quasi-instructional duties, such as tutoring and assisting small groups of students, provide an extension of teacher expertise. It is the teacher's responsibility to see that instructional quality is maintained, that the aide is effective in promoting student achievement, and that students receive as rich instruction from the aide as they might from the teacher.

Although aides who are hired and placed by the school district or principal are often assigned to classrooms without prior input from the teacher, at other times the teacher can choose who will be helping. The strongest criteria are that an aide be reliable, helpful, and sincerely desire to work with students (Charles, 1983). Beyond these personal characteristics, paraprofessionals in bilingual and ELD classrooms should possess good English language skills, a working knowledge of classroom management, and "cultural savvy"—an understanding of both the host culture and the students' (Law & Eckes, 2000). Volunteers who speak the students' native language(s) can be selected to serve as role models, giving a greater sense of worth to English learners. Although it is certainly desirable for the volunteer to have good English language skills, those who do not speak English well can read to and with children in the primary language or can preteach necessary subject matter vocabulary and concepts that will subsequently be taught by the teacher in English.

To locate classroom volunteers other than district-provided personnel, teachers may approach other colleagues to request that older students be assigned as cross-age tutors. Helpful peers with good English abilities can be used as "buddies." Parents may be recruited through invitations sent home with students or through personal contacts at open house activities, student conferences, or home visits. The local high school and university can be contacted for a list of outreach organizations and names of contact people. Also, many communities have a city worker to coordinate senior citizen activities. This person can be contacted to suggest volunteers.

Classroom professionals have responsibility for all instruction and classroom behavior. By right of their position, they have authority in these areas. Disciplining students in groups supervised by the aide is certainly the responsibility of the aide; the teacher must support such discipline while ensuring that students are treated with courtesy. Instruction provided by the aide likewise is valid and important and should be considered as such by the students. However, smooth management and major teaching in the classroom ultimately rests on the teacher's shoulders.

Often, teacher assistants who are brought into the classroom to offer primary language instruction may share the students' cultural background. These individuals can provide valuable linguistic and emotional support for students as they learn English. On the other hand, such aides may subtly modify the teacher's educational intentions (Williams & Snipper, 1990). For example, Mr. Burns, a fifth-grade teacher in a bilingual classroom, had a Laotian aide who was the mother of four students in the school. While working in cooperative groups, the students were expected to exchange ideas and information as well as compose and deliver group reports. Mr. Burns began to notice that the Laotian students did not speak voluntarily but waited to be called on. In observing the aide work with these students, he found that she discouraged students from speaking unless they received permission to do so. In a conference with the aide, Mr. Burns discovered, to his chagrin, that she believed that speaking out undermined the teacher's authority. The aide and the teacher came from different cultural backgrounds, with different views of what constitutes respectful behavior. A compromise had to be negotiated that would encourage students to develop speaking proficiency.

Planning Assisted Lessons

All individuals working with the teacher provide a challenge in planning activities and monitoring student achievement. Teachers who value the help provided by assistants must be willing to invest time in both planning and supervising in order for such individuals to be employed effectively.

The tasks carried out by the aide should be planned by the teacher. A paraprofessional should not be expected to plan and prepare materials without teacher supervision. Moreover, student achievement should not be evaluated solely by the paraprofessional; this is a responsibility of the classroom teacher.

All paraprofessionals should have a classroom space provided for their tutoring or group work. Often, aides are given a table or desk where the teacher places materials for the paraprofessional's use. The teacher should arrange work that allows classroom aides to make the greatest contribution during the hours they work (Williams & Snipper, 1990). The number of students for which an aide is responsible may vary during this period, from one-to-one tutoring to supervising the entire class while the teacher is involved in conferences or individual student contact. Should the aide be unavailable, the teacher must have backup plans so that the day's activities can be modified.

It is not easy to be a classroom assistant and to work under someone else's supervision. Feeling accepted and valued is an important component of the sense of belonging that makes the role rewarding. Making the aide feel part of the instructional team is an important aspect of morale. To do this, aides need to be engaged in meaningful work from which they can derive a sense of accomplishment. Their duties should not be relegated to tedious and menial tasks. They need to be given clear directions and understand not only what is expected of them but also what is expected of the students. It is important that they participate in instructional planning and can be involved in seeing certain activities through to closure. They are also a source of valuable feedback to the teacher on students' needs and accomplishments. For their efforts, paraprofessionals deserve appreciation, whether it is a spoken "thank you" and a pat on the back or an occasional gift or token of esteem (Charles, 1983). The box below provides guidelines for teachers who are working with a paraprofessional.

Guidelines when Working with and Supervising a Paraprofessional Teaching Assistant

- Develop a daily schedule of activities.
- Inform your paraprofessional about your expectations of him or her.
- Demonstrate and verbally explain specific teaching tactics to be used for particular lessons and students.
- Be sure that the paraprofessional is fully informed about every aspect of classroom activity. Maintain full communication.
- Be open to suggestions from your paraprofessional.
- Take time to observe the aide's performance.
- Provide praise or corrective feedback for specific actions.
- Determine who evaluates the paraprofessional's performance and try to do so in writing on a regular basis (at least monthly). Make sure someone reviews the evaluation with him or her.
- Provide remedial attention for any documented weak areas and keep a record of effort spent working on these areas.
- Do not criticize the paraprofessional, especially in front of the students. When criticism is necessary, make it constructive and private.
- Deal immediately with any problems that may arise.

Source. Adapted from Westling and Koorland (1988).

The ELD classroom is a complex environment. The classroom teacher orchestrates a wide variety of language acquisition activities, involving students whose English language abilities vary greatly. Within a single class period, a teacher may employ many differing methods depending on the communicative goals desired. Teaching assistants can help teachers meet the needs of particular groups of students. The joy of working in classrooms with English learners lies in the progress that students make daily.

CHAPTER

5

Content Area Instruction

School started the day after Labor Day. Our enrollment suddenly included 150 Hmong who had recently immigrated to our school district. We had neither classrooms nor teachers to accommodate such a large influx, and no one was qualified to deliver instruction in Hmong. By October, it was obvious that our policy of placing these students in regular content classes was not working. The students were frustrated by their inability to communicate and keep up with class work and teachers felt overwhelmed and inadequate to meet the needs of students who were barely literate and did not know English. A typical student was Khim, who, though better off than most Hmong because she could communicate her basic needs in English, could not cope with the reading and writing demands of eleventh-grade history, math, and science. She did not have the background knowledge or the study skills required for these classes and thus could not meet graduation requirements. On October 15, the faculty meeting was abuzz with discontent and resolve: We needed a new approach to delivering classes for the language minority students who were our new challenge.

—High school teacher journal entry

This vignette illustrates the situation facing many schools and teachers today—how to help the growing number of second language students flooding the nation's schools. Fortunately, programs that include sheltered instruction—said to be the most influential instructional innovation since the 1970s, particularly because it addresses the needs of secondary students (Faltis, 1993)—address this specific need. *Sheltered instruction* is an approach used in multilinguistic content classrooms to provide additional language support to students while they are learning academic subjects, rather than expecting them to "sink or swim" in a content class designed for native English speakers. Sheltered instruction may take place in mainstream classes made up of native and nonnative speakers of intermediate proficiency, or in classes consisting solely of nonnative speakers who operate at similar English proficiency levels (Echevarria, Vogt, & Short, 2000). Sheltered instruction is, ideally, one component in a program for English learners that includes ELD classes for beginning students, primary language instruction in content areas so students continue at grade level as they learn English, and content-based ESL classes.

Sheltered English, or Specially Designed Academic Instruction in English (SDAIE), combines second language acquisition principles with those elements of quality teaching that make a lesson understandable to students (Sobul, 1994). Such instruction enables them to improve listening, speaking, reading, and writing through the study of an academic subject. SDAIE is the preferred method used by both intermediate and high schools when native language instruction is not available or is offered only in one primary language (Minicucci & Olsen, 1992). A SDAIE classroom has subject content and objectives identical to those of a mainstream classroom in the same subject, but, in addition, includes language objectives and sociocultural awareness. Instruction is modified for greater comprehensibility. The distinction between SDAIE and content-based English instruction is that SDAIE features content instruction taught by content area teachers with English language support. Content-based ESL, taught by ELD teachers, features the use of content area materials as texts for ESL lessons. The difference between SDAIE and mainstream content instruction is the subject of this chapter.

Principles of Specially Designed Academic Instruction in English (SDAIE)

English learners can succeed in content area classes. They do not need to learn English by studying it formally as an isolated activity. If they can follow and understand a lesson, they can learn content matter, and the content area instruction—if modified to include English language development—becomes the means for acquiring English. Basically, SDAIE addresses the following needs of English learners: (1) to learn grade-appropriate content; (2) to master English vocabulary and grammar; (3) to learn "academic" English (i.e., the semantic and syntactic ways that English is used in content subjects); and (4) to understand and use appropriate classroom behavior, such as turn taking, participation rules, and established routines (Echevarria, Vogt, & Short, 2000).

In order to accomplish these goals, SDAIE teachers provide a context for instruction that is rich in opportunities for hands-on learning and student interaction. Teachers devote particular attention to communication strategies. Variety in instructional techniques helps students to master demanding content areas. By altering the means of presenting material to make it more accessible and understandable, the teacher maintains a challenging academic program without watering down or overly simplifying the curriculum. In general, sheltered instruction incorporates fundamental principles of good teaching—the ability to communicate, to organize instruction effectively, and to modify complex information to make it understandable to students. Often, experienced teachers remark that SDAIE is "just good teaching"; however, it is more than just good teaching. SDAIE teachers have knowledge of second language acquisition and instructional techniques for second language learners that teachers working with native speakers do not possess. In mainstream elementary and content classrooms, English is an invisible medium. In SDAIE classrooms, English is very much present and accounted for. SDAIE teachers extend practices of good teaching to incorporate techniques that teach language as well as content.

It is sometimes helpful to understand a concept by defining what it is *not*. In the case of SDAIE, which often was implemented as the need arose and suffered from the lack of knowledgeable and adequately prepared teachers and program administrators, this is particularly true. The following statements put SDAIE into perspective by stating what it is *not:*

- SDAIE is *not* submersion into English-medium classrooms; that is, placing students in mainstream classes in which the teacher makes *no* modifications to accommodate the students' nonnative background.
- SDAIE is *not* a substitute for primary language instruction. Even in a sheltered classroom, students still are entitled to, and need support in, their primary language for both content and literacy development.
- SDAIE is *not* a watered-down curriculum. The classroom teacher continues to have the responsibility to provide all students with appropriate grade-level content learning objectives.

Additionally, SDAIE may not be the most appropriate program option for all English learners.

A SDAIE Model

The following model for SDAIE provides a frame for discussing appropriate instruction in sheltered classes (see Figure 5.1). This model originally used the four critical components of the Los Angeles Unified School District (1993) SDAIE model—content, connections, comprehensibility, and interaction—as a guiding framework. However, after working with teachers and teacher candidates, it became obvious that something was missing. It was found that a person could be technically proficient in many of the SDAIE elements, yet not be successful with the students. Discussion and observation revealed that the teacher's attitude played such a critical part in the success of the class that it needed to be explicitly incorporated into the model. Thus, teacher attitude was added as an overarching component.

In addition to the model, an observation form (Figure 5.2) was developed that provides more explicit elements and strategies within each component and that allows teachers to focus on, observe, and incorporate SDAIE elements into their lessons. Many teachers have also used the form as a checklist for lesson planning. They recognized they did not and could not use every aspect in every lesson, but by working within the overall frame they were more assured of providing appropriate learning opportunities for their English learners.

FIGURE 5.1   A Model of the Components of Successful SDAIE Instruction

Teacher Attitude	
The teacher is open and willing to learn from students.	
Content Lessons include both subject and language objectives. Material is selected, adapted, and organized with language in mind.	**Connections** Curriculum is connected to students' background and experiences. Learning strategies are deliberately taught and used.
Comprehensibility Lessons include explicit strategies that aid understanding: Contextualization Modeling Teacher speech adjustment Frequent comprehension checks	**Interaction** Students have frequent opportunities to: Talk about lesson content Clarify concepts in their home language Re-present learning through a variety of ways

Source: Adapted from Los Angeles Unified School District (1993).

FIGURE 5.2   Specially Designed Academic Instruction in English Observation Form

Date: _____   Subject: _____

Duration of observation: _____   Number of students: _____

SDAIE Component	✓	Evidence (describe with specific evidence the components observed)

CONTENT
Content objective
Language objective
Materials and text
  Clear and meaningful
  Support both objectives		

CONNECTIONS
Bridging1
  Concepts/skills linked to student experiences
Bridging2
  Examples used/elicited from students' lives		

FIGURE 5.2 Continued

SDAIE Component	✓	Evidence (describe with specific evidence the components observed)

Schema building
   New learning linked to old through
      scaffolding strategies (webs,
      semantic maps, visual organizers)
Metacognitive development
   Learning strategies deliberately
      taught and practiced
   Opportunities for students to use
      processing skills		

COMPREHENSIBILITY
Contextualization
   Use of pictures, maps, graphs, charts,
      models, diagrams, gestures, labels,
      dramatizations to illustrate con-
      cept clearly
   Appeal to variety of learning styles
Modeling
   Demonstration of skill or concept to
      be learned
Speech adjustment
   Slower rate
   Clear enunciation
   Controlled use of idioms
   Repetition of key words and phrases
Comprehension checks
   Variety of methods used		

INTERACTION
Opportunities for students to talk about
lesson content
   Teacher to student
   Student to teacher
   Student to student
   Student to content
   Student to self
Clarification of concepts in L1
   Primary language material
   Student interaction
Re-presentation of understanding
   Students transform knowledge
      through illustration, dramatiza-
      tion, song creation, dance, story
      rewriting, critical thinking		

The scope of this book does not permit an exhaustive discussion of SDAIE. For an excellent, in-depth treatment, refer to *Making Content Comprehensible for English Language Learners: The SIOP Model* (Echevarria, Vogt, & Short, 2000).

Teacher Attitude

Previous chapters have mentioned affective aspects of learning and classroom environments that foster meaningful language acquisition, but have not specifically addressed the role of the teacher's attitude. Teachers are no different from the rest of the population when faced with something new or different. Many recoil—dig in their heels—refuse to change. But teachers have also chosen to work with people, and they frequently find delight and satisfaction with their students' work, behavior, and learning. It is this sense of delight that is important to capture in working with all learners, particularly English learners.

What aspects characterize a successful attitude in working with second language learners? First, teachers believe that all children can learn. They do not assume that, because a child does not speak English, he or she is incapable of learning. Second, they recognize that all children have language. Children have successfully learned their home language and have understandings and skills that transfer to their second language. Teachers demonstrate the same attitudes that parents have about their children's initial language learning—the conviction that they *will* learn. These teachers *nurture* development rather than teach it. Third, teachers recognize that a person's self-concept is involved in his or her own language and at times students need to use that language. Teachers are not afraid of this happening in their classrooms (Weed & Sommer, 1990). In SDAIE classrooms, it is not only the students who are learning. Successful teachers themselves are open and not only are they *willing* to learn but they also *expect* to learn.

Content

Content involves the careful planning of both content and language objectives and the selecting, modifying, and organizing of materials and text that support those objectives. Objectives are necessary to guide teaching. A lesson with a clear objective focuses the instruction by concentrating on a particular goal and guides the teacher to select those learning activities that accomplish the goal. If the teacher is not clear on the objectives of a lesson, then it is difficult to assess student learning. Once objectives are clearly stated, then the teacher selects material that will help students achieve those objectives.

Content Objectives.   Planning begins by the teacher first specifying learning goals and identifying competencies students must develop. Standards documents that spell out what students should know and be able to do are available to provide an overview of the goals. State agencies, district planners, and school officials have developed curricular programs that follow the goals put forth in the documents.

The teacher divides these overall goals for the year into units. These units are further divided into specific lessons. Each lesson contains the essential content area objectives.

Objectives may include more than one content area. For example, students placed in a high school biology class may be helped to learn content by the use of art. High school math that incorporates abstract designs is another use of art to teach content. Music can also be analyzed as a math activity, thereby enriching one content area with another. A recent approach to middle school instruction encourages teachers to plan thematic units that integrate basic skills and content areas (Short, 1991). Elementary teaching is particularly enriched by and lends itself to cross-subject thematic units.

In developing their sequence of content objectives, teachers want to keep two important questions in mind: (1) Have I reviewed the objectives for the year and organized them for thematic flow? and (2) Have I considered the sequence of objectives and rearranged them, if necessary, putting more concrete concepts before more abstract ones (i.e., those that can be taught with hands-on materials, visuals, and demonstrations before those that are difficult to demonstrate or that require more oral and/or written skills)?

Language Objectives. In addition to considering content area goals, a SDAIE course also includes language acquisition objectives and takes into account the particular language demands of the content area. Again, teachers can refer to the standards document developed by TESOL (1997) as a guide to help them with these goals. The teacher considers the various tasks that language users must be able to perform in the different content areas (e.g., describing in a literature lesson, classifying in a science lesson, justifying in a mathematics lesson, etc.). Importantly, a language objective takes into account not only vocabulary but also the language functions and discourse of the discipline.

In working with teachers, Short and Echevarria (1999) note that incorporating language objectives has been problematic for both content teachers who tend to see language as vocabulary development and for ELD-trained teachers who concentrate so much on the content objectives that they lose track of the language ones. For many content teachers, language is still an invisible medium. *The CALLA Handbook* (Chamot & O'Malley, 1994) is a valuable resource for helping teachers understand the language demands of various disciplines. Each of the subjects—science, mathematics, social studies, and literature and composition—has a chapter in which the authors specifically address the language demands.

In reviewing their language objectives, teachers can keep the following questions in mind: (1) What is the concept load of the unit and what are the key concepts to demonstrate and illustrate? (2) What are the structures and discourse of the discipline and are these included in the language objectives? and (3) Are all four language modes included in the planning (listening, speaking, reading, writing)?

An example of appropriate content and the language objectives for an elementary life cycles unit is provided in Figure 5.3.

FIGURE 5.3   **Life Cycles Unit: Content and Language Objectives**

Science
To study the life cycles of various animals
To compare life cycles for similarities and differences
To study the effect of the surrounding environment on an animal's life cycle
To study the ways in which humans have influenced the life cycles of various animals

Language
To use strategies for reading nonfiction text
To understand the purpose and use of an index
To learn note-taking skills
To compare the report genre with the informational narrative genre
To construct in a small group an informational narrative about the life cycle of butter-
flies
To write individually an informational narrative or a report about the life cycle of a
chosen animal
To read and interpret diagrams to assist in the comprehension of factual text
To study the ways in which authors and publishers use graphics and layout features
in factual text

Source: Adapted from Hornsby (1991).

Materials and Texts.   A critical aspect of any lesson is the proper selection and use of materials. Textbooks have become a central tool in many classrooms, but they often need to be supplemented by other materials. The SDAIE teacher must select, modify, and organize text material to best accommodate the needs of English learners.

Selecting materials involves an initial choice of whether the teacher wishes to have one primary content source or a package of content-related materials (chapters from various texts, video- and audiotapes, magazine and newspaper articles, encyclopedia entries, literary selections, Internet sources, software programs, etc.). Regardless of what is chosen, however, the teacher must consider two main criteria: Are the content objectives for the lesson adequately presented by the material? Is the material comprehensible to English learners?

To present the content sufficiently, the text must be up to date and thorough in its treatment of the desired material. The tasks required of students should be appropriate to the discipline and should promote critical thinking. The style of the text should be clearly organized, with attractive print and layout features that assist students' comprehension. Study questions and other guides should be included, along with a teacher's guide and/or answer key. The text should appeal to a variety of learning styles. Sources represented in the text should include various literary genres (e.g., narrative, descriptive, and analytic).

To make the text comprehensible, the language should be straightforward, without complex syntactic patterns, idioms, or excessive jargon. New content vocabulary should be clearly defined within the text or in a glossary. Diagrams should show vocabulary pictorially. Graphs and charts need to be clearly labeled. Overall, the text should engage the student. For further guidelines on selecting texts for content-based courses, Brinton, Snow, and Wesche (1989) provide a checklist. Chapter VII of the *Foreign Language Framework* (California State Department of Education, 2000) lists criteria for evaluating instructional materials in ESL.

Content area teachers must also consider the use of primary language resources such as dictionaries, books, software programs, and Internet sites, as well as people resources such as cross-age tutors, parents, and community volunteers in helping students to understand concepts. English learners in the content class are continually exposed to new content material and often find a native language dictionary helpful. Students may bring two dictionaries to class: a bilingual dictionary and a dictionary in their native language with definitions. For an elementary student, picture dictionaries such as Amery and Milá's *The First Thousand Words in Spanish* (1979) and Amery's *The First Thousand Words: A Picture Word Book* (1979) have been found to be very useful. Other primary language resources such as encyclopedias, textbooks, and illustrated charts can supply support for teaching content area concepts.

Modifying materials may be necessary to assist English learners in comprehending connected discourse. Some learners may need special textual material, such as excerpts taken from textbooks or chapters from the readings that have been modified. In modifying text, the goal is to improve comprehensibility without watering down the curriculum. Through the use of simplifications, expansions, direct definitions, and comparisons, elements that aid in comprehension can be built into a text. The following examples, from Richard-Amato and Snow (1992), come from a history lesson:

> *Simplification:* "The government's funds were depleted. It was almost out of money."
>
> *Expansion of ideas:* "The government's funds were depleted. It had spent a lot of money on many things: guns, equipment, help for the poor. It did not have any more money to spend on anything else."
>
> *Direct definition:* "The government's funds were depleted. This means that the government spent all of its money." (p. 151)

For beginning English learners, present, simple past, and simple future verb tenses as well as commands can be used to eliminate complexity. The word order in sentences should rely on the common subject-verb-object format, with few subordinating clauses. The <u>verb + not</u> structure is more easily understood than other negations such as *hardly, no longer,* and *no more.* Paragraphs should be carefully structured so that the main idea is easily recognized and supporting information follows immediately. Markers for logic structure should be simple: Terms such as *first, next,* and *then* indicate sequence; *but* indicates contrast; *because* indicates cause and effect. These adaptations increase readability. As students' language proficiency increases, so should the complexity of their reading material. The goal is to move students toward the ability to work with unmodified texts.

Rewriting text selections to increase readability for English learners requires a sizable time investment. An alternative approach is to supply an advance organizer for the text that brings out the key topics and concepts, either in outline form, as focus questions, or in the form of concept maps. Changing the modality from written to oral is another possible modification. By reading aloud, the teacher models the process of posing questions while reading to show prediction strategies used when working with text (see Directed Reading-Thinking Activity in Chapter 4). Selected passages can be tape-recorded for students to listen to as they read along in the text. If modified text is necessary, some of the native English-speaking students can be assigned the task of simplifying the textbook by rewriting portions. This serves as a review for the students who do the rewriting. They can also be asked to duplicate their class notes for the benefit of the English learners (Richard-Amato & Snow, 1992).

Organizing materials increases clarity. When a variety of materials is used rather than one main text, the materials should be grouped by concept to demonstrate similarity and contrast in points of view, genre, or presentation, for example. Materials for the social studies theme "acculturation" can include primary documents, personal histories, and literature. Students who research specific concepts related to acculturation—such as immigration assimilation, culture shock, job opportunities, or naturalization—may find that each document features a unique voice. A government document presents a formal, official point of view, whereas a personal or family story conveys the subject from a different perspective. In addition, numerous pieces of literature such as Bunting's (1988) *How Many Days to America?* or Yep's (1975) *Dragonwings* offer yet other points of view. The teacher's role is to help students recognize the similarities of concept in the various genres.

Connections

Students engage in learning when they recognize a connection between what they know and the learning experience. Thus, a critical element of the SDAIE lesson is the deliberate plan on the teacher's part to elicit information from and help make connections for the students. This can be accomplished in several ways: *bridging*—linking concepts and skills to student experiences (bridging1) or eliciting/using examples from students' lives (bridging2); *schema building*—using scaffolding strategies to link new learning to old; and *metacognitive development*—using strategies that help students think of the steps involved in a learning task.

Bridging: Developing Experiences.   Teachers provide new experiences that arouse interest and attention to a topic. These may include field trips, guest speakers, films and movies, experiments, classroom discovery centers, music and songs, poetry and other literature, computer simulations, and so on. By engaging in experiences with their classmates, students can focus on the topic and begin to associate what they already know with these new experiences. In order to deepen these experiences, the teacher can guide the students to talk and write about them.

This prewriting can be shared with others for comment, elaboration, and extension of ideas.

Bridging: Linking from Students' Lives. Prior knowledge of a topic may be tapped to determine the extent of students' existing concepts and understandings. Many students may have experiences to share that are relevant. This allows them to place new knowledge in the context of their own episodic memories rather than storing new information solely as unrelated concepts. Some prior knowledge may include misconceptions; there may be some "unlearning" that has to take place. Also, some prior knowledge may be based on experiences and conceptualizations of the students' home cultures that are beyond the teacher's experience. Background knowledge may be activated or developed through classroom activities that include all of the language processes. Brainstorming and KWL (What do I *k*now? What do I *w*ant to learn? What have I *l*earned?) procedures are two such activities.

Brainstorming helps to determine how much students know about the topic. The procedure can be done either as a whole class activity or within student groups. The essential element in any brainstorming session is that all ideas be accepted. This is especially true for English learners. A comment made by a student may be highly relevant within that student's experience or cultural background, but may appear inappropriate to the teacher. The teacher needs to accept the comment and then, in the follow-up to brainstorming, ask the student to give more detail about the comment. "Can you tell me more about what you said here?" allows the student to explain without feeling there was something amiss with the comment. Once ideas are exhausted, the students and teacher together can organize the list, grouping and selecting appropriate category labels. The class and teacher then have a beginning model from which they can work and learn.

KWL not only taps into what students already know but also ascertains what they would like to learn. The students list everything they know about a topic. They then tell the teacher what they would like to learn. When the unit is completed, they return to the chart and talk about what they have learned. The chart is kept up throughout the duration of the unit and students refer to it from time to time. They have the opportunity to make additions and changes. In the initial "this-is-what-we-know," it is important for the teacher to write what the students say, even if the information is incorrect. Such information will be corrected in a natural way during the unit, allowing students to see that ideas and facts need to be investigated and substantiated.

Schema Building. If there is little prior knowledge about the topic at hand, students will need more instructional support. By using scaffolding techniques, teachers can help students build schema—that is, construct a framework of concepts that show the relationships of old and new learning and how they are connected.

Graphic organizers help students order their thoughts by presenting ideas visually. Semantic mapping and webs are ways of presenting concepts to show their relationships. After a brainstorming session, the teacher and students could organize their ideas into a semantic map, with the main idea in the center of the chalkboard and associated or connected ideas as branches from the main idea. The teacher and students collaborate to put together supporting ideas using brainstormed words to capture details. Alternatively, a teacher could be more directive in creating a map by writing the central topic and branching out from it with several major subtopics. Students could provide information that the teacher then writes into the appropriate category. Figure 5.4 shows the results of a brainstorming session after second-grade students had heard *Cloudy with a Chance of Meatballs* (Barrett, 1978). They brainstormed on the questions "What junk food can you think of?" and "What is in junk food that our bodies don't need?"

Metacognitive Development. Metacognitive development involves direct teaching of strategies that help students think of the steps involved in the learning task. It involves thinking about how one learns. Chamot and O'Malley (1994) divide metacognitive strategies into three areas: planning, monitoring, and evaluating. Planning strategies help students learn how to organize themselves for a learning task. For example, by teaching students to skim through a text before they read it, they can get the main ideas; by teaching students to scan for specific information, they learn that they do not have to read laboriously through pages of text to find a specific piece of information. Monitoring strategies help students to think while listening, speaking, reading, and writing. They learn to check their comprehension in listening and reading and their production while speaking and writing. Evaluating strategies teach students how to assess their own performance on a task. They can use learning logs or reflections to keep track of their progress.

Because working with text can be problematic for English learners, this is an area in which students can benefit from help with metacognitive strategies. Students need to understand the structure of a text as well as the actual content. Teach-

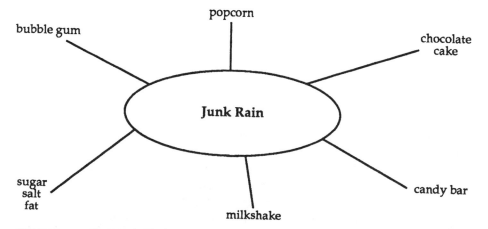

FIGURE 5.4   Semantic Web Created While Brainstorming "Junk Food" after Reading *Cloudy with a Chance of Meatballs*

ers teach students how to preview or "walk through" a text by noting the structure of the assigned chapter(s), including the main headings, subheading, maps, graphs, and pictures that are included to assist comprehension (Law & Eckes, 2000).

Teachers should also familiarize students with the difference in the style and structure of texts depending on the particular discipline. Stories have a rhetorical style based on characterization, plot, and setting; in contrast, expository writing uses such devices as cause and effect, comparison and contrast, and main ideas with additive details. Content texts are more information-packed than stories; have specialized organizing principles that may be discipline specific; and use abstract, specialized, and difficult vocabulary. The language may feature complex sentence structures, and reference may be made to background knowledge that is restricted to that discipline (Addison, 1988; Gunderson, 1991). Visual aids (graphs, maps, charts) may be unique to each discipline, and, although certainly valuable for English learners, these items can cause interpretation difficulties if not specifically addressed.

English learners benefit from a systematic approach to studying instructional texts, such as Thomas and Robinson's (1972) SQ4R, an acronym for *survey, question, read, reflect, recite,* and *review.* Such a system uses a range of metacognitive strategies. Students first scan a text, paying attention to headings and subheadings to look for major topics. Headings are used to invent questions using the *wh-* words: *who, what, why, where, when.* Then students read the material. They reflect on what has been read, trying to relate the material to information already known. Asking and answering questions (recite) puts the major ideas into focus. Finally, an active review necessitates re-reading only material that has not yet been learned.

Comprehensibility

A key factor in learning is being able to understand. Throughout all phases of a lesson, the teacher ensures that students have plenty of clues to understanding. This is one of the aspects of SDAIE that makes it different from that of the mainstream. Teachers are aware that they need to present concepts in a variety of ways. They choose key ideas and plan for depth rather than breadth. They increase the comprehensibility of lessons in four ways: *contextualization* (strategies that create a parallel to speech and/or text through pictures, realia, dramatizations, etc.); *modeling* (demonstration of the skill or concept to be learned); *speech adjustment* (strategies to adjust speech from the customary native speech patterns); and *comprehension checks* (strategies to monitor listening and reading comprehension).

Contextualization. The verbal presentation of a lesson is supplemented by the use of manipulatives and visual backup as teachers write key words and concepts on the chalkboard or butcher paper; use graphs, pictures, maps, and other physical props to communicate; or imaginatively use the overhead projector or a computer hooked to a television monitor. Lectures need to be well organized and succinct, supplying only the knowledge that students need in order to extend or modify their previous knowledge or clarify misunderstandings. There is a one-to-one correspondence between the concept and the clue to minimize student misunderstandings.

Concepts should be presented numerous times through various means and in a rich visual and/or kinesthetic (e.g., through drama and skits) environment.

In a biology class, for example, when teaching about flowers, a teacher may refer students to the explanation in the text (paragraph form), a diagram of a flower in the text (graphic form), a wall chart with a different flower (pictorial form), a text glossary entry (dictionary form), and actual flowers that students can examine. Through these numerous media, the concepts *petal, stamen, pistil,* and *sepal* are understood and provide a basis for future study about life forms. The teacher's task here is to ensure that these multiple sources are organized to communicate clearly each concept.

In addition to contextualizing the content of a lesson, teachers of English learners must also make accessible the organization and management procedures in the classroom. During the lesson, verbal markers provide structure so students can understand what is expected of them. Markers for key points, such as *now, note this, for instance,* and *in conclusion,* cue students to material that is especially important. Terms such as *first, second,* and *last* clearly mark the steps of a sequence. To help students with these verbal markers, teachers can provide them with a list and ask them to listen for them during a lesson. In groups, students can later discuss when, how often, in what context they found them and what they mean. To help with directions, teachers can determine the 10 most frequently used verbal markers and provide mini-TPR-type lessons to help students learn them. The teacher might also learn how to say all or some of these 10 simple directions in the students' language(s). This helps students overcome the anxiety of not understanding a teacher's directions and provides a bond between teacher and students as the students recognize and appreciate the teacher's attempts to include them and know something about their language.

Besides these key words and phrases heard in lesson presentations, there are also *key direction words* (Kinsella, 1992) that students need to know—for example, *analyze, compare, contrast, define, describe, discuss, explain, evaluate, illustrate, justify, state,* and *summarize.* By initially working together to complete short tasks that incorporate these different words, students can become familiar with these terms. Teachers can then use the overhead projector to share work samples generated from the tasks and the class as a whole can pinpoint specific examples of these direction words within their appropriate contexts and in conjunction with content material.

Modeling. Demonstrating new concepts can involve hands-on, show-and-tell explanations in which students follow a careful sequence of steps to understand a process. This can include having students work with materials at their seats in order to accompany the demonstration. The teacher ensures that the demonstration illustrates the concept clearly and that there is a one-to-one correspondence between the teacher's words and the demonstration. The teacher is prepared to redemonstrate as needed. In addition, the teacher continues to use the chalkboard, overhead, butcher paper, or computer to write key terms, concepts, and/or sequential elements.

Speech Adjustment. Teachers in SDAIE classrooms modify their speech to accommodate the various proficiency levels of their students. One way they do this is by monitoring their own language usage and reducing the amount of their talking in the classroom. Reduction of teacher talk provides more opportunities for students to talk both with the teacher and among themselves and for them to affect the type of input they receive (see Comprehensible Input in Chapter 4). Teachers also modify their language by slowing their delivery, which, when combined with clearer articulation, allows English learners greater opportunity to separate words and process the language. Krashen (1980) compares this to other kinds of language simplification, such as caretaker speech and foreigner talk (a term coined by Ferguson, 1975). Many native speakers unconsciously alter and simplify speech addressed to a nonnative speaker by slowing their speech, and teachers can do this consciously.

Another means of modifying input is by exaggerating intonation and placing more stress on important new concepts. Again, this is similar to caretaker speech, in which nouns and verbs in a sentence are emphasized more than the smaller function words (*the, a, in, on*). The use of exaggerated stress and intonation allows the teacher and student to share a focus on the topic at hand and to continue or extend an instructional conversation for as long as needed (Richards, 1978). Teachers also monitor their vocabulary usage and sentence structure. They control their use of idioms and/or teach idiomatic expressions. They simplify their syntax, often keeping to a subject-verb-object structure with little or no embedded clauses.

As students become more proficient in English, teachers again adjust their speech, this time increasing speed and complexity. Ultimately, English learners will need to function in an all-English-medium classroom; therefore, over time, SDAIE teachers need to lessen the speech modification scaffolds they use to accommodate their students' evolving proficiency.

Comprehension Checks. Teachers use strategies to continuously monitor students' listening and reading comprehension. During formal presentations, they use devices such as asking students to put their thumbs up or down, to paraphrase to another student, or to dramatize, write, or graph their understanding. Occasionally asking students to "vote" on their understanding of what has been said by a show of hands helps to maintain interest and check for understanding. Depending on student response, teachers may need to rephrase questions and information if the students do not initially understand. Clarification checks are also discussed in Chapter 4.

Interaction

The organization of discourse is important for language acquisition in content classes. "Teacher-fronted" classrooms (Harel, 1992) are dominated by teacher talk. The teacher takes the central role in controlling the flow of information, and students compete for the teacher's attention and for permission to speak. In these classrooms, English learners are dependent on their ability to understand the teacher's explanations and directions. Classrooms that feature flexible grouping patterns, by contrast, permit students greater flexibilty in the flow of information. Students have an easier communication task when they talk and listen to their peers. In such classrooms, the style of teacher talk often changes: Teachers assist students with the learning task (emphasizing content) rather than providing error correction; moreover, teachers give fewer commands and impose less disciplinary control (Harel, 1992).

The teacher orchestrates tasks so that students use language in academic ways. Students are placed in different groups for different activities. For example, when learning new and difficult concepts, English learners who speak the same language are placed together so they can use their native language, whereas students of varying language backgrounds and abilities are grouped for tasks that require application of key concepts and skills. Teachers themselves work with small groups to achieve specific instructional objectives (e.g., in literature response groups, as discussed in Chapter 4, or in instructional conversations, discussed next).

In planning for interaction in the SDAIE lesson, the teacher considers opportunities for students to talk about key concepts, expects that students may clarify the concepts in their primary language, and allows a variety of means through which students can demonstrate their understanding.

Student Opportunities to Talk. Classrooms in which teachers use SDAIE are noisy places as students engage in a variety of opportunities to explore, express, debate, chat, and laugh. Teachers ensure that students have numerous conversational partners and opportunities to interact with the content of lessons. Interaction patterns include teacher to student, student to teacher, student to student, student to content, and student to self.

Cooperative learning activities, both formally and informally structured, allow English learners to work with each other in a noncompetitive, equal opportunity environment (Holt, Chips, & Wallace, 1992). In the Complex Instruction model (Cohen, Lotan, & Catanzarite, 1990), students are assigned well-defined roles that rotate among all members. Equal opportunity at all roles eliminates notions of high and low status within the group. Students further practice cooperative rules while working with content materials.

Individual work expands the students' abilities to follow through on their specific areas of interest. Once areas of inquiry have been determined through pre-teaching activities, students can choose specific topics that they want to pursue. The teacher's role is to facilitate their access to resources and their ability to direct their focus.

Probably one of the most powerful strategies teachers can use to ensure both content and language development in an interactional setting is the instructional conversation (IC). The lessons in this discussion-based strategy focus on an idea or concept that has educational value as well as meaning and relevance for students. The teacher encourages expression of students' own ideas, builds on students' experiences and ideas, and guides them to increasingly sophisticated levels of understanding (Goldenberg, 1991). Based on extensive analysis of the research and literature in education and diversity, the Center for Research on Education, Diversity, and Excellence (CREDE) has developed five standards for effective pedagogy and learning. One of them is "teaching through conversation"—engaging students through dialogue, especially the instructional conversation (CREDE, 1999).

Creating a Community of Scholarship with Instructional Conversations in a Transitional Bilingual Classroom (Patthey-Chavez, Clark, & Gallimore, 1995) and *Enacting Instructional Conversation with Spanish-Speaking Students in Middle School Mathematics* (Dalton & Sison, 1995) are two articles about IC's, both available on the Internet, that provide both information about implementing instructional conversations and actual classroom transcripts. The box below summarizes use of the IC in the classroom.

Clarification of Concepts in the Primary Language. In SDAIE classrooms, students are afforded opportunities to learn and clarify concepts in their own language. Where possible, the teacher provides primary language resources (print, electronic, personnel) that can help students with key concepts. While SDAIE teaching involves presenting subject matter in English, teachers continue to provide opportunities throughout the lesson for students to clarify their understanding using their primary language.

Use of the primary language is still a controversial issue and many teachers shy away from it on the mistaken belief (perpetuated by decades of language teach-

Instructional Conversation

Teachers using instructional conversations make the following instructional modifications:

1. Arrange the classroom to accommodate conversation between the teacher and a small group of students on a regular and frequent schedule.
2. Have a clear academic goal that guides conversation with students.
3. Ensure that student talk occurs at higher rates than teacher talk.
4. Guide conversation to include students' views, judgments, and rationales, using text evidence and other substantive support.
5. Ensure that all students are included in the conversation according to their preferences.
6. Listen carefully to assess levels of students' understanding.
7. Assist students' learning throughout the conversation by questioning, restating, praising, encouraging, and so forth.
8. Guide the students to prepare a product that indicates that the goal of the instructional conversation was achieved.

Source: CREDE (1999).

ing methodology that actively discouraged it) that if students use their primary language, it detracts from developing English proficiency. However, research continues to show that when students are able to use their first language, they make more academic gains in both content and language than if they are prohibited from using it (Collier, 1995). As Saville-Troike (1984) states regarding the children in her study, "Most of the children who achieved best in content areas, as measured by tests in English, were those who had the opportunity to discuss the concepts they were learning in their native language with other children and adults" (p. 216).

Re-Presentation of Understanding.   After students have had the opportunity to learn new material in a meaningful way, they can transform that knowledge through other means, such as making illustrations, doing dramatizations, creating songs, dancing, and rewriting stories. By re-presenting information in another form, students must review what they know, and think about how to organize and explain their knowledge in the new format. By sharing their discoveries in a variety of manners—in learning centers; through dramatic, visual, or oral presentations; by staging a Reader's Theater; by developing slide, video, or computer-based audiovisual shows; through maps and graphs—they also use their developing language skills in a more formal occasion.

Re-presentation of knowledge is also an important means for teachers to assess student learning and to pinpoint areas for reteaching, expansion, and/or modification. In this manner, assessment becomes a part of the learning cycle instead of something divorced from classroom practices.

SDIAE offers English learners an important intermediate step between content instruction in the primary language, an environment in which they may not advance in English skills, and a "sink-or-swim" immersion, in which they may not learn key content-related concepts. Although standards-based instruction emphasizes the acquisition of content, SDAIE requires additional lesson objectives that foster English language acquisition. This supplementary focus on language development is the key that unlocks the core curriculum for English learners.

Content Area Application

Each content area has a specialized knowledge base, vocabulary (consider, for example, the different meanings for *foot* in mathematics, biology, geography, furniture construction, poetry, theater), and particular graphic and verbal means for organizing information. Each content area has standards that guide curriculum development. However, only the English language arts standards document attempts to address the needs of English learners. Applying the standards for English learners has been a thorny issue. Are they expected to achieve the same standards as their native English-speaking peers? Should they have different standards? How do they have access to the same challenging content as their peers? How do they meet the standards? While native English-speaking students are learning content, English learners have the dual task of learning content *and* language, sometimes in sheltered classes, but more frequently in mainstream ones (McKeon, 1994).

The following case study (Giacchino-Baker, 1992), drawn from the domain of social studies, is presented here to illustrate some of the "dos and don'ts" of effective content instruction for English learners. Following the case study, individual content areas are discussed. In each, reference is made to the respective content standards and then strategies organized around the model discussed in the first part of this chapter are presented as specific means to help teachers provide challenging and accessible content to their English learners.

> Gabriela, who finished high school (*la preparatoria*) in Mexico, had arrived in California only six weeks previously. She struggled to make sense of classroom activities in U.S. History, one of the "sheltered" classes she was taking at Capital High. Gabriela's ESL 1 teacher identified her as being at the early production stage of language proficiency, yet she was being asked to function in a "mainstream" history class, where all presentations, readings, and written assignments were done in English. The bilingual history teacher, Mr. Ortega, sometimes accepted students' questions and/or responses in Spanish. However, three out of the thirty-one students in the class were not Spanish speakers.
>
> Mr. Ortega asked Gabriela to retake a test when she received an "A." His suspicion of cheating was unfounded, however, because she was able to explain orally all of the test items in Spanish. Gabriela was happy to explain her note-taking and test-taking strategies to her teacher. She said that she copied every word that the teacher wrote on the blackboard, even though she understood very few of them. When she got home, she asked her U.S. cousins to translate the words into Spanish so she could study them and then memorize the English words. Gabriela explained that she could rarely follow oral activities in class because she was too busy taking notes, and the teacher spoke too quickly. She depended almost entirely on the text and translated class notes for information. Because students were not allowed to take the class set of books home, Gabriela spent most of her time studying her notes. High school in Mexico had been even more demanding, so this chore did not seem onerous.
>
> Mr. Ortega encouraged Gabriela to see him after class whenever she had questions about class activities. At that time, he explained difficult concepts in Spanish whenever necessary. He also encouraged her to try to listen to his explanations rather than read or write as he spoke in class. He told her that he underlined key items on the board as he spoke, and he always explained test formats and content.
>
> Gabriela was highly motivated and well educated. Her prior knowledge enabled her to make comparisons between the U.S. and Mexican systems of government and to make connections between the

histories of the adjoining countries. This "sheltered" class, however, did not provide enough linguistic support for her needs, despite occasional tutoring by her teacher. Gabriela would have benefited from the use of more audiovisual support and vocabulary and concept development strategies in Mr. Ortega's presentations. Because this class contained students with a wide range of English language proficiencies, she would have learned more English through formal and informal collaborative activities with her fellow students—activities that focused on historical issues and students' experiences.

Social Studies

According to the social studies standards document *Expectations for Excellence,* the primary purpose of social studies is to help young people develop the ability to make informed and reasoned decisions for the public good as citizens of a culturally diverse, democratic society in an interdependent world (National Council for the Social Studies, 1994).

This purpose represents a tall order for teachers working with English learners who may have limited background with the social studies program in U.S. schools. However, by implementing certain strategies on a regular basis, teachers have found that their English learners are able to achieve the goals outlined in the social studies standards documents.

Content: Flexible, Thematic Curriculum. A recent trend in many public schools has been to recognize the wholeness of knowledge and to organize instruction around broad themes. Based on students' interests and questions, these themes engage students in meaningful activities that focus on the area of inquiry rather than a specific skill. Students learn social studies by researching, reading, and experimenting to answer real-world questions that they have posed themselves. This view is student centered rather than teacher centered, and involves as much student-student interaction as teacher-student interaction. The "question-driven" or problem-posing format forces a reconceptualization of the curriculum away from a narrow focus on subject areas to broader concepts that connect to significant ideas and issues (Freeman & Freeman, 1998). For English learners, this reconceptualization is felicitous, as it allows for more interactive engagement with a number of other speakers, for continuous concept development, and for an expanding base of vocabulary and language structures that can be used in a variety of contexts.

This move to a thematic approach to instruction, however, has taken place primarily at the elementary level, although middle schools have also been reorganizing so that content teachers can collaborate on instruction and can work together with the same groups of students. For examples of thematic integration at middle school, see Berman, Minicucci, McLaughlin, Nelson, and Woodworth (1995) online at http://www.ncbe.gwu.edu/miscpubs/schoolreform/index.htm. High schools, however, have tended to retain classes organized around subject areas. Academic work at the secondary level is particularly challenging for students whose native language is not English. Modifying instruction for these students at the high school level is imperative in order for these students to have access to the core curriculum and to be able to graduate with the same depth of knowledge as their native English-speaking peers.

Thematic units provide a natural environment for the practice of language skills as students learn concepts in the social studies curriculum. For example, students studying a fifth-grade unit on "Settlement of the West" can examine the legal issues involved in the Treaty of Guadalupe-Hidalgo, compare the various cultures that came into contact in the Southwest, delve into the history of land grant titles, and pursue many more issues of interest. Through means such as filmstrips, films, videos, computer simulations, literature, nonfiction texts, and oral discussions, students are able to develop conceptual knowledge. Such a unit incorporates history, geography, sociology, economics, values, information-seeking skills, group participation, and perhaps dramatic skills as students act out the signing of treaties and other cultural events.

Connections: Linking to Prior Knowledge.   As mentioned and discussed in the model for SDAIE instruction (Bridging: Linking from Students' Lives), students learn more rapidly and with greater understanding when new concepts are related to what they already know. By starting each class with an activity that actively engages students in reviewing their own experiences relevant to the topic, the teacher not only gains valuable insights that can help in teaching but he or she also gives students an opportunity to see how their experiences fit into the realm of social studies. In the classroom example presented in Chapter 4, the teacher presented the immigration unit by first having the children talk about their own experiences in immigration, including what type of transportation they used and how long the journey took (Weed & Ford, 1999). This introduction provided a focus for the students, introduced vocabulary and concepts, and actively prepared them to relate their experiences to those of the Pilgrims.

Using an oral history approach actively involves students in gathering information from their families and communities. Furthermore, not only do students learn that history is composed of their own and their family's stories but also, by delving into their own background, they may learn about complex issues, such as religious persecution, tyranny of autocratic rulers, and the rights and responsibilities of self-governance. Through such oral history projects, students are engaging in many of the historical thinking skills outlined in the U.S. history standards (e.g., chronological thinking, reading historical narratives, describing the past through the perspectives of those who were there, and preparing an historical analysis and interpretation) (Anstrom, 1999a). For more information about oral history projects, read "Junior Historians: Doing Oral History with ESL and Bilingual Students" (Olmedo, 1993).

Comprehensibility: Contextualizing Instruction. Specific strategies can increase the ability of English learners to understand content and to experience history "come alive." Graphic organizers provide students with visual means to represent their content knowledge. A time line can be used to place important events in chronological sequence. A population graph can show the effect of events on people, and maps can place significant events in their geographical locale. Pictures from a variety of sources can bring past events to life. Skills in working with text—such as previewing a social studies chapter by following the visual material (pictures, charts, diagrams) or scanning for specific information—help students identify main concepts. Classmates can help each other evaluate the information they read in order to write group reports. Johnston and Johnston's *Content Points* (1990) offers a variety of specific strategies for social studies content units that are based on Chamot and O'Malley's CALLA strategies.

Interaction: Cooperative Learning.   Social studies topics in particular have been difficult for English learners because the topics are generally abstract, cognitively complex, and highly language dependent. Therefore, the use of visuals, hands-on props and manipulatives, and other projects to supplement the lesson content is a necessity. However, the teacher must be aware that the use of such materials may inadvertently be misused to water down content, a practice that decreases the information available to students rather than increases the students' ability to comprehend a complex content. To avoid such a situation, cooperative learning can be used to structure the classroom so that English learners have increased opportunities to verify their comprehension by receiving explanations from their peers and sharing prior knowledge. Encouraging students to exchange information helps them to clarify and familiarize themselves with the lesson content. In this way, students are involved in their own learning and teachers can rely less on lectures and worksheets. In "Cooperative Learning and Social Studies," Olsen (1992) discusses five cooperative structures that engage students actively in content and language learning: three-step interview, roundtable, think-pair-share, solve-pair-share, and numbered heads.

Re-Presenting Knowledge: Linking Instruction to Assessment.   Many of the tasks, projects, and role plays that students are engaged in to learn the content can be further used in assessment. Such authentic tasks provide a richer means of assessing students who are still struggling with the language than the traditional paper-and-pencil tests. In one fifth-grade class, the students produced a news program with a U.S. Civil War setting. The program included the show's anchors; reporters in the field interviewing generals, soldiers, and citizens; a weather report; and reports on sports, economics, and political conditions. There were even commercial breaks. The students engaged in much research in order to be historically accurate, but enthusiasm was high, as they shared their knowledge in a format they knew and understood. In addition, students were able to work in the area of their particular interest.

A useful resource for teachers who wish to ensure that their social studies program meets the needs of English learners is Anstrom's (1999a) "Preparing Secondary Education Teachers to Work with English Language Learners: Social Studies" available online at http://www.ncbe.gwu.edu/ncbepubs/resource/ells/social. htm.

Literature

Of the 12 standards in the *Standards for the English Language Arts* (International Reading Association & National Council of Teachers of English, 1996), 2 provide support for English learners: Standard 9, "Students develop an understanding of and respect for diversity in language use, patterns, and dialects across cultures, ethnic groups, geographic regions, and social roles"; and Standard 10, "Students whose first language is not English make use of their first language to develop competency in the English language arts and to develop understanding of content across the curriculum." In addition, Standard 1 calls for wide reading, including texts about the cultures of the United States and the world. In her *Call to Join the Literacy Compact,* NCTE president Beverly Chin (1996) reiterated the central goals of the standards document: that students experience writing to real readers for real purposes, that they read often from a broad range of literature, and that students who speak more than one language use their literacy in their first language to build literacy in English, while continuing to develop expertise in their first language.

Teachers using literature in their classrooms or those whose main focus is to teach literature may find that English-language literature does not elicit the same responses from English learners as from native English speakers. By selecting materials judiciously, slowing the pace slightly, portioning work into manageable chunks, and increasing the depth of each lesson, the teacher can ensure that English learners have a fulfilling experience with literature.

Content: Material Selection.   An appropriate selection of genre may be one way to help English learners develop their conceptual and linguistic schemata. The literature curriculum can be a planned sequence that begins with familiar structures of folktales and myths and uses these as a bridge to more complex works of literature. Myths and folktales from many cultures are now commonly available in high-quality editions with vibrant illustrations. These tales often evoke a familiar response from students despite their various nationalities. Students can move from these folktales and myths to selected short stories by authors of many cultural backgrounds, then to portions of a longer work, and then to entire works (Sasser, 1992).

Connections and Comprehensibility: Into, Through, and Beyond.   A common framework now used in working with literature is *into, through,* and *beyond.* Activities prior to reading prepare students to get "into" the literature. Teachers provide students with specific strategies to help them read "through" the material, and, finally, follow-up activities help students organize and retain their understanding "beyond" the act of reading.

"Into" activities activate students' prior knowledge by drawing from their past experiences or develop background knowledge through new experiences. Films, texts, field trips, visual aids, and graphic organizers can be interwoven to clarify and enhance meaning and help students appreciate the work. Once students are ready for the text, they can make predictions about the story. Some teachers put these predictions into "time capsules" that can be opened and analyzed once the text has been read. Students can discuss what happened later in the book to confirm or disprove their original predictions.

"Through" activities help students as they work with the text. Teachers find reading aloud a useful strategy that gives the students an opportunity to hear a proficient reader, to get a sense of the format and story line, and to listen to the teacher "think aloud" about the reading. In the "think aloud," teachers can model how they monitor a sequence of events, identify foreshadowing and flashback, visualize a setting, analyze character and motive, comprehend mood and theme, and recognize irony and symbols (Anstrom, 1998a). To help students develop a sense of inflection, pronunciation, rhythm, and stress, a commercial tape recording of a work of literature can be obtained for listening and review or native English-speaking students or adult volunteers may be willing to make a recording.

To sustain students' interests in a longer work of literature, class time may be used to recapture the narrative to date and compare students' understanding of the assigned reading. Students find it eye-opening to hear others' differing interpretations of the same text and fruitful discussions often arise. A preview of the next reading can feature interesting aspects of the new passage. In *Literature in the Language Classroom,* Collie and Slater (1987) suggest several ways in which a teacher can structure literature homework. One suggestion is the "gap summary," a technique in which the teacher provides an almost-complete and simply phrased description of the main points of the section assigned for home reading. Gaps are usually key words or expressions that only a reading of the passage can reveal. This gives students a focus for their reading assignment.

Many kinds of graphic organizers can also be used to help students focus their thoughts and reactions to a literature piece. Semantic webs, T-graphs (which cite selected passages and ask for students' reactions), and Venn diagrams allow students to organize their understandings of the text. To tie together students' appreciation of the longer text, an ongoing diary of what each character is feeling helps students step within the character. Students can also be encouraged to make inferences about missing aspects of the story: What were the characters like at school? What were their favorite subjects? Did they have friends? Were they close to their parents?

"Beyond" activities are designed to extend the students' appreciation of literature. Authentic written responses encourage students to reflect on the piece of literature and to express their interpretations to an audience beyond the classroom. Poems can be written and shared with other classes or parents at a "Poetry Night." Reviews of literature works can be written for the school or classroom newspaper. Letters can be written to authors expressing students' reactions to the story or to pen pals recommending certain pieces of literature. Students can pretend to be movie critics and view the film representation of a text studied in class. They can then compare the differences and draw conclusions about the pros and cons of the different media. Favorite parts of selections can be rewritten as a play and enacted for other classes as a way to encourage other students to read that piece of literature.

Students can plan a mock television show and devise various formats that include ideas from the literature studied. For example, a weather announcer can talk about the weather and climate, a newscaster can give the lastest update on the characters, and a game show host can ask contestants to answer questions or to act as characters or objects in the story.

Interaction: Varying Groups. Teachers working in mixed-ability classrooms can plan group activities that help students in different ways. Students can work in homogeneous groups when the goal of the activity is accuracy and in heterogeneous groups when the goal is fluency (Peck, 1992). For example, to develop accuracy, first-grade students can listen to a reading of the story "The Three Little Pigs." A group of beginning students can retell the story using pictures and then talk about the pictures. Intermediate students can retell the story to the teacher or a cross-age tutor. The teacher writes their story for them, and then students can reread, illustrate, and rearrange the story from sentence strips. A group of more proficient students can create a new group story.

Heterogeneous groups encourage language development when fluency is a goal. Mixed groups of children can experience activities in learning centers and talk about the experience with one another. In the book *Literature and Cooperative Learning,* Whisler and Williams (1990) detail a variety of cooperative learning activities that have been adapted for the literature classroom.

Interaction: Maintaining the First Language. As the standards document makes clear, students are encouraged to use and develop their native language. This seems difficult and frequently uncomfortable for teachers who do not share the same language(s) as their students. However, there are several strategies teachers can use that support students' first language within the context of the classroom program. Aides and tutors can assist in explaining difficult passages and helping students summarize their understanding. Native language books, magazines, films, and other materials relating to the topic or theme of the lesson can support and even augment students' learning (Tikunoff, Ward, Romero, Lucas, Katz, Van Broekhuisen, & Castaneda, 1991). Students can also keep reading logs or journals in their native language.

In "Multicultural Children's Literature: Canon of the Future," Monroe (1999) offers four approaches that give voice and a sense of accomplishment to her students. The approaches include genre approach, author-illustrator studies, theme approach, and issues approach.

Mathematics

In 2000, the National Council of Teachers of Mathematics (NCTM) updated their standards document originally published in 1989. The new document, *Principles and Standards for School Mathematics* (NCTM, 2000), reflects what has been learned since the first document was released, and strengthens and furthers the messages of the original document (without replacing them). Of its six principles (equity, curriculum, teaching, learning, assessment, and technology), those specifically relevant for English learners (although they are never specifically addressed) include equity (high expectations and strong support for all students); teaching (challenging and supporting students to learn mathematics well); and learning (actively building new knowledge from experience and prior knowledge to learn mathematics with understanding). Two suggestions from the document support what is known about teaching English learners. The first suggests depth over breadth: "Curricula can be offered so that students can explore mathematics more deeply rather than more rapidly. This model allows them to develop deep insights into important concepts that prepare them well for later experiences instead of experiencing a more cursory treatment of a broader range of topics" (p. 368). The second relates to grouping: "Students can effectively learn mathematics in heterogeneous groups if structures are developed to provide appropriate, differentiated support for a range of students. Structures that exclude certain groups of students from a challenging, comprehensive mathematics program should be dismantled" (p. 368).

For nonnative speakers of English, specially designed activities and teaching strategies must be incorporated into the mathematics program in order for them to have the opportunity to develop their mathematics potential. Additionally, although common wisdom holds that mathematics is a language in itself and can be learned by those who do not speak the language of instruction, in fact the language of mathematics contains numerous difficulties for English learners. The next section discusses these difficulties, followed by sections suggesting specific teaching strategies to help English learners in their mathematics learning.

The Language of Mathematics.   Instead of being "language neutral," mathematic vocabulary poses numerous problems for English learners. These difficulties lie in four major areas: vocabulary skills, syntax, semantics, and discourse features.

Vocabulary in mathematics includes words of a technical nature such as *denominator, quotient,* and *coefficient,* and words such as *rational, column,* and *table* have a meaning different from everyday usage. Often, two or more mathematical concepts combine to form a different concept: *least common multiple* and *negative exponent.* The same mathematical operation can be signaled with a variety of mathematics terms: *add, and, plus, sum, combine,* and *increased by* all represent addition. Moreover, special symbols are used for vocabulary terms (Dale & Cuevas, 1992).

Syntax problems occur when students try to translate directly from English word order to the corresponding mathematical expression (Dale & Cuevas, 1992). For example, the expression "8 divided by 2" might be translated as $8\overline{)2}$; however, the correct expression is $2\overline{)8}$. This may pose difficulty for students who tend to write mathematical sentences in the same manner in which they read and write English. A further difficulty is the complex sentence structures often used in mathematical problems to signal logical connectors and other propositions. For example, "if...then" and "either...or" statements must be translated into logical symbols before problems can be completed, posing additional linguistic difficulty for English learners.

Semantic problems occur when students are required to make inference from natural language to the language of mathematics. Students need to be able to identify key words and determine how other words are linked to the key words. For example, in the problem "Five times a number is two more than ten times the number," students must recognize that "a number" and "the number" refer to the same quantity. However, in the problem "The sum of two numbers is 77. If the first number is ten times the other, find the number," students need to know they are dealing with two numbers (Dale & Cuevas, 1987).

Discourse features that are unlike natural language characterize the texts used in mathematics. The tendency to interrupt for the inclusion of formulae is confusing and perhaps frightening to the reader of mathematics textbooks. Such texts require a reading rate adjustment because they must be read more slowly and require multiple readings. Charts and graphs are an integral part of the text, not a supplement, and technical language has precise, codified meaning. Reading such text may require up-and-down as well as left-to-right eye movements. Unfortunately, most students receive very little explicit instruction in mathematics text processing (Bye, 1975).

In "A Naturalistic Look at Language Factors in Mathematics Teaching in Bilingual Classrooms," Khisty (1993), found online at http://www.ncbe. gwu.edu/ncbepubs/symposia/third/khisty.htm, provides further information and classroom examples of the language of mathematics and its impact on students.

Content: Clustering Objectives.   Many English learners enter U.S. schools after third grade. These students are expected to "catch up" in order to be on a par with their classmates. One way of helping them to do this is to cluster objectives. Similar learning objectives can be clustered across grade-level boundaries. Such clusters make the most efficient use of students' time and recognize that, often, older students do not require as much time to master objectives taught in lower grades. Such clustering can also reduce the artificiality of structuring lessons where, for example, students solve only problems that involve numbers less than 100 and do not require regrouping (Buchanan & Helman, 1997).

Connections: Using Students' Experiences.   Teachers can find out from their students what activities they engage in after school and then capitalize on those for mathematics instruction. For example, those students who participate in sports can learn to calculate their batting average, points per game, race times, average speed, and so on. At home, students can keep charts of expenditures for utilities, payments, and so forth over a period of time, comparing present usage with past, calculating savings in interest if payments are made early. Older students with after-school jobs can use their pay stubs to figure the percentages of their various withholding categories (Anstrom, 1999b). Younger students may be able to assist their parents with shopping by helping to keep purchases within the budget and/ or determine the best priced item. They can also help calculate the tax that will be added to the total.

Comprehensibility: Modeling Technology and Other Tools.   Many English learners are unfamiliar with the basic tools associated with mathematics (rulers, protractors, calculators, computers, etc.) (Buchanan & Helman, 1997). After demonstrating each, teachers can provide students with real-life opportunities to use them. For example, students are told that the classroom needs to be recarpeted. They first have to estimate the area, then check their estimates with the actual tools (using both standard and metric measuring instruments as they will not know which system the carpet company uses), and then use calculators to find the percentage of error in their estimates. Computer programs may also be used to provide estimates and calculations.

Comprehensibility: Checking for Comprehension.   A teacher whose classroom contains students in various stages of language acquisition can modify comprehension questions and tailor these questions to elicit different responses. For example, when showing students a box holding four red cubes and three blue ones, the teacher may ask a preproduction student a question such as, "Are there more red or blue cubes?" (The answer can be expressed by holding up a red or blue card.) To students in the stage of speech emergence, the question can elicit the response "blue" or "red." For those students in intermediate stages of fluency, a harder question might be: "Do you think that more than half the cubes are blue? More than 50 percent?"

Interaction: Working in Groups.   Strategies for reading math texts and for supplementing students' math with language instruction involve more student interaction and small group work. Students need to be encouraged to think aloud about mathematics and talk with one another about the processes involved. In this way, they use language as a tool for tackling mathematics concepts (Crandall, Dale, Rhodes, & Spanos, 1987). Working in groups, students can discuss with one another the activities in which they engage at math centers or stations in various parts of the classroom. This gives them an opportunity to try out ideas and learn various mathematical strategies from their peers.

Re-Presenting Knowledge: Alternative Assessment.   Alternative assessment requires students to perform tasks similar to those used to teach and learn the material. In mathematics, tasks such as asking students to develop a series of graphs based on student characteristics, to run a school store, or to pretend playing the stock market (Anstrom, 1999b) keep students actively engaged in mathematics while allowing the teacher to assess their understanding.

In their article "Reforming Mathematics Instruction for ESL Literacy Students," Buchanan and Helman (1997; online at http://www.cal.org/ericcll/digest/buchan01.html) offer specific guidelines with examples for teaching mathematics to English learners. "A Mathematical Problem: How Do We Teach Mathematics to LEP Elementary Students?" by Mather and Chiodo (1994; online at http://www.ncbe.gwu.edu/miscpubs/jeilms/vol13/math13.htm) provides a list of mathematical terms in English and Spanish, suggestions for appropriate instruction, and recommended teacher resources.

Science

The National Science Education Standards (National Research Council, 1996) emphasizes inquiry as the means for students to become scientifically literate. Inquiry is described as

> a multifaceted activity that involves making observations; posing questions; examining books and other sources of information to see what is already known; planning investigations; reviewing what is already known in light of experimental evidence; using tools to gather, analyze, and interpret data; proposing answers, explanations, and predictions; and communicating the results. Inquiry requires identification of assumptions, use of critical and logical thinking, and consideration of alternative explanations. (p. 23)

Working in inquiry classrooms with EL students can be challenging but extremely rewarding for teachers who recognize the connections between inquiry and SDAIE and who organize learning activities to maximize their students' experiences. English learners bring multiple views of the world to a learning setting. Their prior experiences, personal and cultural, offer insights into the domain of science inquiry. Teachers need to recognize that as English learners construct science knowledge, they have linguistic and cultural demands placed on them over and above those placed on native English-speaking students (Kessler & Quinn, 1987; Kessler, Quinn, & Fathman, 1992).

In a paragraph about instruction for EL students, the addendum to the standards document, *Inquiry and the National Science Education Standards* (Olson & Loucks-Horsley, 2000), notes that "learner-centered environments in which teachers build new learning on the knowledge, skills, attitudes, and beliefs that students bring to the classroom, are critical to science learning of English language learners" (p. 122).

In the following sections, the language of science and the problems it can pose for students are presented. Specific strategies that need to be incorporated to facilitate the EL students' science learning are then provided.

The Language of Science.   The four major language areas (vocabulary, syntax, semantics, discourse features) detailed in the section on mathematics are also relevant for science. Students not only have to learn scientific definitions of some common words they may already know (*energy, sense, work,* etc.) but they must also learn complex syntactic structures, which include passive voice, multiple embeddings, and long noun phrases (Chamot & O'Malley, 1994). Furthermore, EL students need to understand the structure of scientific writing. Generally, science articles describe a process; a hypothesis is made, data are gathered, ideas are confirmed, and conclusions are reached. A number of types of text structures are common in science content materials. The *cause-effect structure* links reasons with results or actions with their consequences. The *compare-contrast structure* examines the similarities and differences between concepts. The *time order structure* shows a sequential relationship over the passage of time (Pérez & Torres-Guzmán, 1992). To assist in their comprehension, students can receive special training in following written instructions for procedures or experiments and can be shown ways to organize their recognition of science vocabulary.

Content: Common Themes.   Organizing instruction around broad themes—such as the nature of matter, or pollution and purification of water, or the impact of drugs on the physiology and behavior of living organisms—puts science in a comprehensible context that can have relevance to students' lives. Such contextualizing increases the probability that students will continue to want to learn science on their own; extends the time a single topic is studied, thus allowing more time for understanding and reflection as well as repetition of key English words and phrases; and reduces the tendency of superficial treatment of subjects (Sutman, Guzmán, & Schwartz, 1993).

In planning around themes, teachers often prepare a choice of projects for students to complete to strengthen their comprehension of difficult science material. Caution needs to be made in developing the list of projects, however. Each project needs to be tied to a central objective. For example, if students are to understand the basic properties of a cell, the list of projects might include drawing and labeling a cell diagram, preparing an oral report on the structure and function of a cell, or summarizing the current research on cloning (Lynch in Anstrom, 1998b). Sometimes, lists are made of fun activities that do not provide equal access to the central objectives and concepts. Teachers need to review project lists and be clear on the objectives.

Connections: Using Everyday Examples.   One way to make science relevant to students is to point out its role in their everyday lives—for example, how water gets into their faucets or how heat gets into their radiators. Explaining the food chain through students' own diets and referring to agricultural practices in their native countries also links science to students' experiences (Sutman, Guzmán, & Schwartz, 1993). Using information from students and then organizing it into diagrams and charts can explain classification and scientific processes and helps students begin to see scientific inquiry in their own lives.

Students may come to science class with naïve theories of heat, energy, and other concepts that are either inconsistent or incompatible with current scientific knowledge (Chamot & O'Malley, 1994). Thus, teachers need to elicit knowledge from students to elucidate their misperceptions. The KWL strategy is particularly applicable in these situations. In a nonthreatening way, teachers can find out and note what students know about a topic (being sure to list all their ideas exactly). By analyzing their misconceptions, the teacher can then provide materials, experiences, and projects that will help the students, on their own, reorganize their erroneous thinking and change it.

Connections: Metacognitive Development.   Developing learning strategies is extremely important in scientific inquiry. As noted earlier, inquiry involves posing questions; examining sources of information; planning investigations; gathering, analyzing, and interpreting data; explaining and predicting; and communicating results. In *The CALLA Handbook,* Chamot and O'Malley (1994) outline and explain 12 strategies for the steps in the scientific method that address the above concepts. These include such strategies as questioning for clarification, making a logical inference based on prior knowledge and research, grouping and classifying data according to features or attributes, and self-evaluation (comparing the answer derived through observation and experimentation with the original hypothesis and reporting on changes in understanding).

Comprehensibility: Modeling. If the teacher feels the need to lecture, a helpful strategy for English learners is to videotape the lesson. Students should be encouraged to listen to the lecture, concentrating on understanding and writing down only questions or parts of the lecture they do not understand. Later, the videotape is played and the teacher and several students take notes on the board. The teacher can model the type of outline that emphasizes the main ideas and clearly indicates supporting details. The students use whatever strategies are comfortable for them, including use of their native language. After a few minutes, the videotape is stopped and the notes compared. The discussion then highlights various note-taking strategies and provides new strategies for everyone involved. This activity can be used on a periodic basis to determine students' ability in comprehending lectures and taking effective notes (Adamson, 1993).

Interaction: Group Participation. Teachers of EL students frequently worry that their students do not contribute enough to group discussions. Native English-speaking students may dominate a learning group by outtalking other students. Kagan (1989) describes a strategy that can equalize the conversation in a cooperative learning group. Each person uses his or her pen or pencil as a designated marker that serves as a pass to speak. The student wishing to speak puts the pen in the middle of the group table. The next person who wishes to talk then puts down a pen. This technique gives each group member an equal opportunity to be heard. When everyone has taken a turn, the pens are picked up and another round of speaking begins.

The Visual and Performing Arts

The California *Challenge Standards for Student Success, Visual and Performing Arts* (California State Department of Education, 1998c) contains five standards: (1) Artistic Perception, (2) Creative Expression, (3) Historical and Cultural Context, (4) Aesthetic Valuing, and (5) Connections, Relations, Applications (p. x).

The visual and performing arts are often used as a medium for EL students to illustrate their understandings of concepts. Ideas that were originally presented in linguistic form can be translated into the artistic medium so that students can demonstrate their comprehension. However, arts lessons in themselves help students develop language skills. The *Challenge Standards* provide specific objectives and sample tasks for each of the standards. Teachers knowledgeable about SDAIE techniques can organize instruction so that it meets the content objective while addressing the needs of English learners. For example, English learners in any of the primary grades would be able to participate in the following, learning not only artistic principles but also vocabulary. For the theater objective "Replicate the sound and movement of objects, animals, and people," the following is a sample task: "After a walk around the school during which students have observed the movement of natural objects, they pantomime the actions of such objects as leaves, branches, clouds, and the animals they saw" (p. 81). For Creative Expression (Music), third-graders need to "sing or play, with increasing accuracy, a varied repertoire of music, alone and with others" (p. 58). Obviously, songs from their own cultures can be included in this repertoire. English learners can find their culture valued as well by the objective in Historical and Cultural Context (Dance): "Learn and perform dances from their own and other cultures" (p. 11). Teachers can browse through the *Challenge Standards* (available online at http://www. cde.ca.gov/challenge/vpa.html) to organize their arts curriculum around the five standards and to provide their English learners with the challenging but rewarding knowledge that goes with artistic knowledge. In addition, SUAVE (Socios Unidos para Artes Via Educación [United Community for Arts in Education]), a cultural partnership program for teachers, is an arts-integrated program in multicultural and multilingual settings. This program, which uses the arts as a medium for instruction, offers students a forum for translating ideas and creating representations and metaphors (Goldenberg, 1999)—exactly the kind of instruction that engages English learners. Information about the program can be found at http:// www.csusm.edu/SUAVE/index.htm.

Physical Education

The *Challenge Standards for Student Success, Physical Education* (California State Department of Education, 1998b, p.vi) divides its seven standards into three areas: movement skills and movement knowledge, self-image and personal development, and social development. Students who participate in a high-quality physical education program can expect the following: to develop various motor skills and abilities related to lifetime leisure skills; to value the importance of maintaining a healthy lifestyle; to improve their understanding of movement and the human body; to know the rules and strategies of particular games and sports; and to gain self-confidence and a sense of self-worth in relation to physical education and recreation programs.

Standard 7 pertains to the interrelationship between history and culture and games, sports, play, and dance. Teachers can elicit from students what they know about their own culture's games, sports, and so on, invite guest speakers to demonstrate various activities, and build their curriculum from their students' own knowledge base.

Additionally, physical education activities can be carefully structured to motivate students' cooperation and sense of group cohesiveness. This is particularly important in a class in which English learners of various cultures are together.

Torbert and Schneider (1992) call these activities *Positive and Effective Multicultural Interaction (PEMI).* Bonding among students occurs over time using games that encourage collaboration, group identification, equalization of opportunity rather than elimination, a focus on participation rather than winning, and inclusion of players at various ability levels. An example of such an activity is "Chaotic Team Juggle," in which students toss 8 to 15 soft "trash" balls (made of loosely packed paper held together with a rubberband or two). The only rule in tossing is that the passer must make eye contact with the receiver before throwing. There are so many balls (about one for every three students) that students are constantly involved and the eye contact "seems to support a subtle bonding effect between players" (p. 359).

A caution for teachers working with children from different cultures: Sometimes physical education can put an unexpected burden on students. For example, as mentioned in Chapter 2, coeducational activities were stressful for Punjabi girls who were expected not to engage in physical activity and not to show their legs (Gibson, 1987). Chapter 10 provides guidelines to help teachers learn about their students' customs.

Instructional Needs Beyond the Classroom

To be successful in their academic courses, EL students often need assistance from organizations and volunteers outside of the classroom. This assistance can come from academic summer programs, additional instructional services such as after-school programs and peer tutoring, and Dial-a-Teacher for homework help in English and in the primary language. Support in the affective domain may include special home visits by released time teachers, counselors, or outreach workers and informal counseling by teachers. Monitoring of academic progress by counselors helps to encourage students with language needs (Romero, 1991).

Escalante and Dirmann (1990) explicated the main components of the Garfield High School Advanced Placement Calculus course in which Escalante achieved outstanding success in preparing Hispanic students to pass the AP Calculus examination. Importantly, Escalante's success was not solely due to outstanding classroom teaching; he was the organizer of a broad effort to promote student success. In his classroom, he set the parameters: He made achievement a game for the students, the "opponent" being the Educational Testing Service's examination; he coached students to hold up under the pressure of the contest and work hard to win; and he held students accountable for attendance and productivity. But beyond this work in the classroom was the needed community support. Community individuals and organizations donated copiers, computers, transportation, and souvenirs, such as special caps and team jackets. Parents became involved in a campaign against drug use. This helped Escalante emphasize proper conduct, respect, and value for education. Past graduates served as models of achievement. They gave pep talks to students and acted as hosts in visits to high-tech labs. The support from these other individuals combined to give students more help and encouragement than could be provided by the classroom teacher alone. Students saw concentrated, caring, motivated effort directed toward them—something they had rarely before experienced. The results were dramatized in the unforgettable feature film *Stand and Deliver*.

Escalante's successful mathematics program at Garfield High School involved much more than excellent classroom instruction. It is not surprising that the five key features of SDAIE were incorporated in his teaching: *content* and language teaching, the latter through extensive attention to specific mathematics vocabulary; *connections* between the math curriculum and the students' lives and development of appropriate schema when background was lacking; *comprehensibility* through use of realia and visual support for instruction and modification of teacher talk; *interaction* with each other through cooperative learning; and *teacher attitude,* a positive coaching approach that conveyed high expectations. This is the instructional enhancement that opens the door to success for English learners.

6 Theories and Methods of Bilingual Education

When we hear the child speak, we see only what is above the surface of the water, the water lily itself. But the roots of the mother tongue lie deep beneath the surface, in the more or less unconsciously acquired connotative and nonverbal meanings. When the child learns a foreign language, that language easily becomes . . . a splendid water lily on the surface which superficially may look just as beautiful as the water lily of the mother tongue. . . . But it is often the case that for a very long time the second language is a water lily more or less floating on the surface without roots.

    If at this stage we allow ourselves to be deceived by the beautiful water lily of the foreign language into thinking that the child knows this language . . . well enough to be able to be educated through it . . . the development of the flower of the mother tongue may easily be interrupted. If education in a foreign language poses a threat to the development of the mother tongue, or leads to its neglect, then the roots of the mother tongue will not be sufficiently nourished or they may gradually be cut off altogether. . . . [A] situation may gradually develop in which the child will only have two surface flowers, two languages, neither of which she commands in the way a monolingual would command her mother tongue. . . . And if the roots have been cut off, nothing permanent can grow any more.

            —Skutnabb-Kangas, 1981, pp. 52–53

Bilingual education has existed in the United States since the colonial period, but over the more than two centuries of U.S. history it has been alternately embraced and rejected. The immigrant languages and cultures in North America have enriched the lives of the people in American communities, yet periodic waves of xenophobia and language restrictionism have virtually eradicated the capacity of most U.S. citizens to speak a foreign or second language. For English learners, English-only schooling has often brought difficulties, cultural suppression, and discrimination even as English has been touted as the key to patriotism and success. Only as recently as 1968 did Congress signal its first commitment to bilingual education by enacting the Bilingual Education Act as a means of addressing the needs of students whose first language was not English. Beginning in 1970, landmark court cases mandated special language instruction for children with a limited command of English. However, although federal legislation, through continuing reauthorization of the 1968 Bilingual Education Act, has supported the right of English learners to learn in their native language, individual states have sometimes moved to restrict bilingual education (e.g., California's 1998 Proposition 227 and Arizona's 2000 Proposition 203).

Despite the argument—and the evidence—that bilingual education helps students whose home language is not English to succeed in school, bilingual education continues to be an area of contention. Knowledge of a foreign language is not the accepted norm for much of U.S. society, and those individuals who speak languages associated with immigrant status are looked on with disfavor. Many people feel that any tolerance of linguistic diversity undermines national unity. However, others hold the view of the United States as a "salad bowl," featuring a mixture of distinct textures and tastes, instead of a "melting pot," in which all cultural and linguistic diversity is melted into one collective culture and language. Bilingual education in the 1990s became bilingual/bicultural education, and is rapidly becoming multilingual/multicultural.

The classrooms of the United States are increasingly diverse, with students coming from many countries of the world to be educated as Americans. The challenge to any English language development program is to cherish and preserve the rich cultural and linguistic heritage of the students as they acquire English. One means of preserving and supplementing the home languages of our nation's children is through bilingual education. Bilingual education has been considered by many to be a teaching method but it can also be considered a policy—a way in which instruction is organized and managed (see Figure I.1).

Foundations of Bilingual Education

The progress of bilingual education in the United States has advanced on three fronts: cultural, legislative, and judicial. Culturally, the people of the United States have seemed to accept bilingualism when it has been economically useful and to reject it when immigrants were seen as a threat. Legislative and judicial mandates have reflected this ambivalence. In periods when the economic fortunes of the United States were booming, European immigrants were welcome and their languages were not forbidden (immigrants of color, however, faced linguistic and cultural barriers as they strove for assimilation). In times of recession, war, or national threat, immigrants, cultures, and languages were restricted and/or forbidden. Periodically throughout history, English has been proposed as the national language (e.g., the bill entitled "Declaration of Official Language Act of 1999" [H. R. 50]), yet this has never been enacted into law. Although the United States has no official language, 23 states have passed laws proclaiming English as official (English First, 1999).

Because the states reserve the right to dictate educational policy, bilingual education has depended on the vagaries of state law. When the U.S. Congress enacted legislation to begin Title VII of the Elementary and Secondary Education Act, federal funding became available for bilingual education programs. Almost simultaneously, the courts began to rule that students deprived of bilingual education must receive compensatory services. Together, the historical precedents, federal legislative initiatives, and judicial fiats combined to establish bilingual education in the United States. However, it has been left to the individual states to implement such programs and this has at times caused conflict.

Historical Development of Bilingual Education

Early Bilingualism.   In 1664, at least 18 colonial languages were spoken on Manhattan Island. German, Dutch, Swedish, and Polish could be heard in the armies of the American Revolution, and Spanish was dominant in the Spanish lands of the New World. Bilingualism was common both among the working and educated classes, and schools were established to preserve the linguistic heritage of new arrivals. The Continental Congress published many official documents in German and French. German schools were operating as early as 1694 in Philadelphia, and by 1900, over 4 percent of the United States elementary school population was receiving instruction either partially or exclusively in German. In 1847, Louisiana authorized instruction in French, English, or both, upon the request of parents. The Territory of New Mexico authorized Spanish-English bilingual education in 1850 (Crawford, 1999).

Language Restrictionism.   Although there were several such pockets of acceptance for bilingual education, other areas of the country effectively restricted or even attempted to eradicate immigrant and minority languages. Under an 1828 treaty, the U.S. government recognized the language rights of the Cherokee tribe. Eventually, the Cherokees established a 21-school educational system that used the Cherokee syllabary to achieve a 90 percent literacy rate in the native language. In 1879, however, the federal government forced the Native American children to attend off-reservation, English-only schools where they were punished for using their native language. In the East, as large numbers of Jews, Italians, and Slavs immigrated, descendants of the English settlers began to harbor resentment against these newcomers. New waves of Mexican and Asian immigration in the West brought renewed fear of non-English influences. Public and private schools in the new U.S. territories of the Philippines and Puerto Rico were forced to use English as the language of instruction (Crawford, 1999).

World War I brought anti-German hysteria, and various states began to criminalize the use of German in all areas of public life (Cartagena, 1991). As World War I ended, Ohio passed legislation to remove all uses of German from the state's elementary schools, and mobs raided schools and burned German textbooks. Subsequently, 15 states legislated English as the basic language of instruction. This repressive policy continued in World War II when Japanese-language schools were closed. Until the late 1960s, "Spanish detention"—being kept after school for using Spanish—remained a formal punishment in the Rio Grande Valley of Texas, where using a language other than English as a medium of public instruction was a crime (Crawford, 1999).

Assimilationism.   Although the U.S. Supreme Court, in the *Meyer* v. *Nebraska* case (1923), extended the protection of the Constitution to everyday speech and prohibited coercive language restriction on the part of the states, the "frenzy of Americanization" (Crawford, 1999) had fundamentally changed public attitudes toward learning in other languages. European immigrant groups felt strong pressures to assimilate and bilingual instruction by the late 1930s was virtually eradicated throughout the United States. This assimilationist mentality worked best with northern European immigrants. For other language minorities, especially those with dark complexions, English-only schooling brought difficulties. Discrimination and cultural repression became associated with linguistic repression.

After World War II, writers began to speak of language minority children as being "culturally deprived" and "linguistically disabled." The "cultural deprivation" theory rejected genetic explanations for low school achievement for English learners and pointed to such environmental factors as inadequate English language skills, lower class values, and parental failure to stress educational attainment. On the basis of their performance on IQ tests administered in English, a disproportionate number of English learners ended up in special classes for the educationally handicapped.

Rebirth of Bilingual Education.   Bilingual education was reborn in the early 1960s in Dade County, Florida, as Cuban immigrants, fleeing the 1959 revolution, requested bilingual schooling for their children. The first program at the Coral Way Elementary School was open to both English and Spanish speakers. The objective was fluency and literacy in both languages. Subsequent evaluations of this bilingual program showed success both for English-speaking students in English and Spanish-speaking students in Spanish and English. Hakuta (1986) reported that by 1974, there were 3,683 students in bilingual programs in the elementary schools and approximately 2,000 in the secondary schools.

The focus of bilingual education on dual-language immersion and developmental bilingualism that had been featured in the Dade County bilingual programs was altered when the federal government passed the Bilingual Education Act of 1968 (Title VII, an amendment to the 1965 Elementary and Secondary Education Act). This act was explicitly compensatory. Children who were unable to speak English were considered to be educationally disadvantaged, and bilingual education was to provide the resources to compensate for the "handicap" of not speaking English. From its outset, federal aid to bilingual education was seen as a "remedial" program rather than an innovative approach to language instruction (Wiese & García, 1998). The focus shifted again in 1989, when developmental bilingual programs were expanded. Maintaining and developing the native language of students became an important goal for bilingual education.

The English-as-Official-Language Movement. This movement supplied the chief opposition to bilingual education in the late twentieth century. The goals of the English-only movement are the adoption of a Constitutional amendment to make English the official language of the United States, repeal of laws mandating multilingual ballots and voting materials, restriction of bilingual funding to short-term transition programs, and universal enforcement of the English language and civics requirement for naturalization (Cartagena, 1991). One English-only organization, U.S. English, Inc., believes that "the passage of English as the official language will help to expand opportunities for immigrants to learn and speak English, the single greatest empowering tool that immigrants must have to succeed" (U.S. English, 2000). To achieve this goal, U.S. English has financed the drive at the state level to have English as the official language of each state. For example, the organization spent more than $700,000 on California's 1986 Proposition 63, which instructed public officials "to ensure that the role of English as the common language in the State of California is preserved and enhanced." Critics of this initiative charged that the climate created by this measure was responsible for California's failure to reauthorize a bill mandating bilingual education in the state.

The closest to success the English-only groups have reached at the federal level was when the House passed the "Bill Emerson English Language Empowerment Act of 1996" (H.R. 123), which declared English the official language, required U.S. government officials to conduct official business in English, repealed bilingual voting rights, and required all naturalization ceremonies to be performed entirely in English.

However, at the state level, these groups have met with more success. English First, a national, nonprofit lobbying organization whose goals are consistent with those of U.S. English, lists the 23 states that have enacted English-only laws. Of these, however, two laws are being challenged in the courts (Alabama and Alaska) and one has been overturned (Arizona). Five other states are not considered in these statistics, as they have enacted an "English Plus" stance (Hawaii, New Mexico, Oregon, Rhode Island, and Washington) (English First, 1999).

Emergence of a New Nativism. Many U.S. communities are feeling the pressure not only of increased immigration but also of immigration from underdeveloped nations. In 1998, for example, over 660,000 legal immigrants were admitted to the country. Of these, over one-third were from North America, which includes the Caribbean, Central America, and Mexico (38.3 percent), one-third from Asia (33.3 percent), and only 13.7 percent from Europe (United States Immigration and Naturalization Service, 1999). Since the mid-1980s, language loyalties have become a subtle means of reframing racial politics, and bilingual education has become an integral part of the issue. The English-only lobby has labeled "un-American" the effort to provide language support to other language speakers. The English-only movement also plays on the fears of monolingual English teachers, raising the specter that the effort to recruit qualified teachers, redesign curricula, and reorganize class schedules to provide a bilingual program will lead to reassignment and loss of status for nonbilingual staff. Bilingual education is a subject that is bound up with individual and group identity, status, intellect, culture, and nationalism. As a people, Americans have limited experience with bilingualism, and some find it hard to justify or support spending resources on dual language instruction.

Bilingualism in the Modern World. Many countries in today's world are officially bilingual, including Canada, Belgium, Finland, Cameroon, Peru, Singapore, and South Africa. Official bilingualism, however, does not imply that all inhabitants of a country are bilingual; it simply means that more than one language may be used in government or education. However, as the world becomes progressively smaller and more and more regions interact in economic, political, and cultural exchanges, bilingualism, and even multilingualism, has become a fact of daily life. In the global society, proficiency in more than one language is a highly desirable trait (Glick, 1988).

Legal Evolution

The use of English and other languages in public life, particularly language use in the schools, has been affected by "cycles of liberalism and intolerance" (Trueba, 1989) in which conflicting beliefs and policies about language have influenced legislation and judicial actions.

Federal Law and Judicial Decisions. Given the tensions already mentioned between those who are concerned that language diversity leads to disunity and thwarts efforts at social assimilation, and those who consider bi- and multilingualism to be an important asset of the nation, it is not surprising that legislative and judicial decisions vary between the two extremes. According to Wiese and García (1998), "The most salient feature of the polemic between assimilation and multiculturalism has been language, particularly the role of native language instruction" (p. 2). These opposing viewpoints are evident in the 35 years represented by legislation directed toward English learners and how best to help them achieve the American dream. Since the initial legislation in 1968, there have been five reauthorizations of the Bilingual Education Act, and numerous court cases upholding or clarifying the rights of language learners.

The Civil Rights Act: Title VI (1964) set a minimum standard for the education of any student by prohibiting discrimination on the basis of race, color, or national origin in the operation of a federally assisted program (NCBE, 1995). The Title VI regulatory requirements have been interpreted to prohibit denial of equal access to education because of an English learner's limited proficiency in English (United States Office for Civil Rights, 1999).

The Bilingual Education Act: Title VII of the Elementary and Secondary Education Act (1968) was the first federal law relating to bilingual education that recognized the unique educational disadvantages faced by non-English-speaking students. It authorized $7.5 million to finance 76 projects serving 27,000 children. The goal of these funds was to support education programs, train teachers and aides, develop and disseminate instructional materials, and encourage parental involvement. This legislation, which built on the 1964 Civil Rights Act, was compensatory in nature. English learners were perceived as "culturally deprived" and in need of remediation.

The May 25 memorandum from the United States Department of Health, Education, and Welfare (1970) informed school districts with more than 5 percent national-origin minority children that the district must offer some kind of special language instruction for students with a limited command of English; prohibited the assignment of students to classes for the handicapped on the basis of their English language skills; prohibited placing such students in vocational tracks instead of teaching them English; and mandated that administrators communicate with parents in a language they can understand.

Serna v. *Portales Municipal Schools* (1972) was the first case in which the federal courts began to enforce Title VI of the Civil Rights Act. A federal judge ordered instruction in native language and culture as part of a desegregation plan.

Lau v. *Nichols* (1974) was a landmark case in which the U.S. Supreme Court ruled:

> There is no equality of treatment merely by providing students with the same facilities, textbooks, teachers and curriculum, for students who do not understand English are effectively foreclosed from any meaningful education.

Although this case established the right of students to differential treatment based on their language minority status, it did not require a particular instructional approach.

The Equal Education Opportunities Act (EEOA) of 1974 was a civil rights statute passed by the U.S. Congress to define what constitutes a denial of constitutionally guaranteed equal educational opportunity (Wiese & García, 1998):

> No individual can be denied equal educational opportunity on account of race, color, sex, or national origin by ... (f) the failure of an educational agency to take appropriate action to overcome language barriers that impede equal participation by its students in its instructional program. (EEOA, 1974)

Title VII Reauthorization (1974) specifically linked equal educational opportunity to bilingual education. "The Congress declares it the policy of the United States to establish equal educational opportunity for all children (a) to encourage the establishment and operation ... of education programs using bilingual education practices techniques, and methods" (Bilingual Education Act, 1974). Bilingual education was defined as "instruction given in, and study of, English, and, to the extent necessary to allow a child to progress effectively through the educational system, the native language" (Sec. 703[a] [4] [A] [i]).

Lau Remedies (1975) were guidelines from the U.S. Commissioner of Education that told districts how to identify and evaluate children with limited English skills, what instructional treatments to use, when to transfer children to all-English classrooms, and what professional standards teachers need to meet (United States Office for Civil Rights, 1976).

Ríos v. *Read* (1977) was a federal court decision that a New York school district had violated the rights of English learners by providing a bilingual program that was based mainly on ESL and that included no cultural component (Crawford, 1999). Although no specific remedy was mandated, the U.S. Office for Civil Rights began to visit school districts with large numbers of English learners to ensure that districts met their responsibilities.

Between the time of the reauthorization in 1974 and the subsequent ones, public opinion moved toward the assimilationist position that public funds should be used for English language acquisition and assimilation toward the mainstream (Crawford, 1999). Title VII 1978 Reauthorization added to the definition of bilingual education: Instruction in English should "allow a child to achieve competence in the English language," and English-speaking students in bilingual programs were to "assist children of limited English proficiency to improve their English language skills." Additionally, parents were included in program planning, and personnel in bilingual programs were to be proficient in the language of instruction and English (Wiese & García, 1998).

Castañeda v. *Pickard* (1981) tested the EEOA statute. The Fifth Circuit Court outlined three criteria for programs serving EL students. District programs must be (1) based on "sound educational theory," (2) "implemented effectively" through adequately trained personnel and sufficient resources, and (3) evaluated as effective in overcoming language barriers. Qualified bilingual teachers must be employed, and children are not to be placed on the basis of English language achievement tests. The outcome of the *Idaho Migrant Council* v. *Board of Education* (1981) case was a mandate that state agencies are empowered to supervise the implementation of federal EEOA requirements at the local level.

Plyler v. *Doe* (1982) was a Supreme Court decision that a state's statute that denies school enrollment to children of illegal immigrants "violates the Equal Protection Clause of the Fourteenth Amendment" (NCBE, 2000).

Keyes v. *School District #1* (1983) established due process for remedies of EEOA matters.

Title VII Reauthorization (1984) provided for two types of bilingual programming: transitional and developmental. *Transitional programs* were defined as providing "structured English-language instruction, and, to the extent necessary to allow a child to achieve competence in the English language, instruction in the child's native language." *Developmental programs* provided "structured English-language instruction and instruction in a second language. Such programs shall be designed to help children achieve competence in English and a second language, while mastering subject matter skills." Thus, for the first time, the goal of bilingual education was competence in two languages; however, no funding was provided for these programs (NCBE, 1995).

Gómez v. *Illinois State Board of Education* (1987) was a court decision that gave state school boards the power to enforce state and federal compliance with EEOA regulations. Children must not sit in classrooms where they cannot understand instruction, and districts must properly serve students who are limited in English. In none of the rulings did the courts mandate a specific program format, but in all they clearly upheld the notion that children must have equal access to the curriculum.

Title VII Reauthorization (1988) increased funding to state education agencies, placed a three-year limit on participation in transitional bilingual programs, and created fellowship programs for professional training (NCBE, 1995).

Improving America's Schools Act (IASA) (1994) amended and reauthorized the Elementary and Secondary Education Act of 1965 within the framework of the Goals 2000: Educate America Act (1994), whose purpose was to "improve learning and teaching by providing a national framework for education reform." The comprehensive educational reforms called for in Goals 2000 entailed reconfiguration of Title VII programs, with new provisions for reinforcing professional development programs, increasing attention to language maintenance and foreign language instruction, improving research and evaluation at state and local level, supplying additional funds for immigrant education, and allowing participation of some private school students. IASA also modified eligibility requirements for services under Title I so that English learners became eligible for services under that program on the same basis as other students (NCBE, 1995; United States Office for Civil Rights, 1999).

The Proposed Title VII Reauthorization (2000) will continue to help English learners to meet challenging state content and performance standards by providing increased funding to develop, implement, expand, or enhance comprehensive preschool, elementary, or secondary education programs serving limited English proficient students (United States Senate Committee on Health, Education, Labor, and Pensions, 2000).

"Federal Policy, Legislation, and Education Reform: The Promise and the Challenge for Language Minority Students" (Anstrom, 1996, online at http://www.ncbe.gwu.edu/ncbepubs/resource/fedpol.htm) provides a clear discussion of educational reform and the Goals 2000 legislation as it relates to English learners.

State Law.   Although federal protections of the rights of English learners are still in effect, many states have weakened or eliminated their requirements regarding bilingual education. According to a 1999 survey of state education agencies, 43 states[1] and the District of Columbia have legislative provisions for limited English proficient student instructional programs (NCBE, 1999). These provisions, however, do not necessarily include bilingual programs, but may instead specify ESL instructional programs, bilingual/dual language instructional programs, or both.

---

1. The seven states that have no provisions for programs for English learners include Alabama, Hawaii, Louisiana, Michigan, New Mexico, Tennessee, and West Virginia.

In 1998, California, with a school enrollment of approximately 1.4 million limited English proficient children, passed Proposition 227, a measure rejecting bilingual education. The Proposition stipulates that

> all children in California public schools shall be taught English by being taught in English. In particular, this shall require that all children be placed in English language classrooms. Children who are English learners shall be educated through sheltered English immersion during a temporary transition period not normally intended to exceed one year.... Once English learners have acquired a good working knowledge of English, they shall be transferred to English language mainstream classrooms. (California State Code of Regulations, 1998 Article 2, 305)

Provision 310 provided parents with waiver possibilities if their children met criteria spelled out in the law: "Under such parental waiver conditions, children may be transferred to classes where they are taught English and other subjects through bilingual education techniques or other generally recognized educational methodologies permitted by law."

Unfortunately, laws such as this one often result in a lack of support for the education of English learners. Dismantling bilingual education and expecting children to learn English (along with academic subjects) in one year flies in the face of contemporary research on language acquisition (see, in particular, Collier, 1995). After 35 years of legislation supporting the rights of English learners, it can only be assumed that such laws will be found to infringe on students' rights.

Educational Issues

What obligation does a community have toward newcomers—in particular, non-native, non-English-speaking children? When education is the only means of achieving social mobility for the children of immigrants, these young people must be given the tools necessary to participate in the community at large. When school dropout rates exceed 50 percent among minority populations, it seems evident that the schools are not providing an adequate avenue of advancement. Clearly, some English learners do succeed: Asian American students are overwhelmingly represented in college attendance, whereas Hispanic Americans are underrepresented (Suarez-Orozco, 1987). Individual states are addressing the obligation to educate all students by adhering to content standards documents, written by mandate of the Goals 2000 legislation. These documents specify that which *all* students are expected to know and be able to do. Nevertheless, children continue to receive differential treatment in the public schools. The structure of schooling creates equity problems, all the way from the tracking procedures that segregate students of "lower" ability from those of "higher" ability to the day-to-day operation of classrooms, in which some students' voices are heard while others are silenced. These structural components of schools must be addressed lest the belief continue that achievement problems reside solely within students.

The success and/or failure of ethnic minority students has caused concern and has prompted various explanations for students' mixed performances. A genetic inferiority argument assumes that certain populations do not possess the appropriate genes for high intellectual performance. The cultural deficit explanation attributes lower academic achievement to deficiencies in the minority culture. The cultural mismatch perspective maintains that cultures vary and that some of the skills learned in one culture may transfer to a second but that other skills will be of little value or, worse, will interfere with assimilation to the new culture. The contextual interaction explanation posits that achievement is a function of the interaction between two cultures—that the values of each are not static, but adapt to each other when contact occurs.

In schools, three phenomena occur in which minority students are disproportionately represented: underachievement, dropping out, and overachievement. These phenomena may be occurring because of the ways schools and classrooms promote unequal classroom experiences for students. In response to the perception that some students "underachieve" or "overachieve" or "drop out" or are "pushed out," schools have designed various mechanisms to help students to succeed. Some of these have been successful, others problematic.

Underachievement.   Several measures of achievement reveal discrepancies in the achievement of Whites in comparison with ethnic minorities. On the National Scholastic Assessment Test in 1998, the average scores for Whites on the verbal subtest was 526, whereas those of all ethnic minority groups (Hispanics, Blacks, Asian and Pacific Islanders, and Native Americans) were between 28 and 92 points lower. With the exception of Asian Americans (average score 562), all ethnic groups were lower than Whites on the mean score of the mathematics subtest (College Entrance Examination Board, 1999).

Ethnic minority groups, except for Asian Americans, attain lower levels of education. Hispanic Americans, for example, are particularly hard hit by the phenomenon of educational underachievement. In 1998, for example, of the 65 percent of high school graduates who attended college, 53 percent were White and only 5 percent were of Hispanic origin (United States Department of Labor, 1999). Of college students in 1996, Hispanic Americans represented 11.7 percent of community college students and only 5.7 percent in four-year institutions. In addition, Hispanic Americans represent only a small number of faculty members and administrators in higher education; they hold 2.5 percent of such positions (United States Department of Education, 1998). Low educational levels have resulted in poor subsequent incomes and a lower likelihood of high-prestige occupations. A survey by the Hispanic Association on Corporate Responsibility found that Latinos hold only 81 of 11,881 executive positions in the top 500 industrial corporations in America (Fortune 500) (Ross, 1993).

A study by the United States Commission on Civil Rights (1978) found that Asian Americans were frequently "overqualified" for their jobs and that Whites with lesser qualifications held the same jobs as Asian Americans. Thus, it is unclear that underachievement is the real problem. Even ethnic minorities who achieve in school may not be able to attain positions of responsibility in society. Exploitation and discrimination in society are linked with underachievement in schools.

Dropouts.   There is a disparity in graduation and dropout rates among various ethnic groups in the United States. Table 6.1 shows the graduation rate for the year 1996–1997 and the high school dropouts among persons 16 to 24 years old in October 1998. An important marketplace repercussion from graduation and dropout statistics is the differential rate of employment of these two groups: 61 percent of high school dropouts are in the labor force versus 80 percent of graduates who were not in college (United States Department of Commerce, 1999).

Noting the alarmingly high percentage of Hispanic dropouts, U.S. Secretary of Education Richard W. Riley, in 1995, initiated a special project to study issues related to the problem. In its final report, *No More Excuses* (Hispanic Dropout Project, 1998), the Hispanic Dropout Project explicated the continuing stereotypes, myths, and excuses that surround Hispanic American youth and their families:

> What we saw and what people told us confirmed what well-established research has also found: Popular stereotypes—which would place the blame for school dropout on Hispanic students, their families, and language background, and that would allow people to shrug their shoulders as if to say that that was an enormous, insoluble problem or one that would go away by itself—are just plain wrong. (p. 3)

The report contains findings and recommendations at local, state, and national levels, and is addressed to school personnel, families, community, business, and other stakeholder groups. Teachers, the Hispanic Dropout Project found, make one of two poor choices: either they blame the students and their families for school failure or they excuse the students' poor performance, citing factors such as low socioeconomic status or lack of English proficiency. This latter attitude, although well-meaning, is particularly harmful, as it does not allow students access to cognitively demanding instruction (Lockwood, 2000). The three recommendations for teachers are consistent with the principles, concepts, and strategies of this present text: (1) provide high-quality curriculum and instruction, as explained in Part Two of this book; (2) become knowledgeable about students and their families,

TABLE 6.1   Percent of Graduation in 1996–1997 and of High School Dropouts among Persons 16 to 24 Years Old, October 1998

	White	Hispanic	Black	Asian/Pacific Islander	Native American
Graduation	72%	10%	13%	4%	Less than 1%
Dropouts	7.7%	29.5%	13.8%	Not available	Not available

Sources: United States Department of Commerce (1999) and United States Department of Education (2000).

as discussed in Part Three of this book; and (3) receive high-quality professional development—an ongoing task in which this entire text can be an impetus and a base. *Transforming Education for Hispanic Youth: Exemplary Practices, Programs, and Schools* (Lockwood & Secada, 1999; online at http://www.ncbe.gwu.edu/) provides more in-depth information about, and examples of, exemplary schools for Hispanic American youth.

Overachievement.   The Hispanic Dropout Project speaks of the damage to students' education attainment by the "excuse" mentality. An equally pernicious view is that which ascribes exceptional achievement to a specific group, such as is the case for Asian Americans. The term *model minority* has been evoked for Asian Americans, connoting a "super group" whose members have succeeded in U.S. society despite a long history of racial oppression. Asian American students are seen as academic superstars who win academic distinction and are overrepresented in elite institutions of higher education (Suzuki, 1989). This stereotype plays out in at least two ways with equally damaging results. First, ascribing a "whiz kid" image to students can mask their individual needs and problems and lead the teacher to assume a student needs little or no help. This may ultimately lead to neglect, isolation, delinquency, and/or inadequate preparation for the labor market among these students (Feng, 1994). Second, by lumping all Asian Americans together into this stereotype, it ignores the differential cultural, language, economic, and immigration status of the various groups and severely limits those most in need of help. Among the Southeast Asian students, the Khmer and the Lao have a grade point average (GPA) below that of White majority students, whereas Vietnamese, Chinese-Vietnamese and Hmong students are well above this GPA. Japanese, Korean, and Chinese students are also well above White students in terms of GPA (Trueba, Cheng, & Ima, 1993).

Two general factors may contribute to academic success for certain minority groups: the groups' views about the place of education for the group, and the school's bias toward viewing the group as academically successful. In the first instance, the success of the Punjabi (Sikhs from rural northwest India who settled in northern California), for example, may be due to the groups' resistance to assimilation into mainstream society and to the strong family support for students who are harassed or who experience other cultural conflicts in the schools (Gibson, 1987).

In the second case, school personnel may act toward Asian Americans in ways that support the model minority attribution. Wong-Fillmore (1980) documents the behavior of Chinese American students as being more in accord with teachers' expectations than, for example, that of Hispanic American students. Asian American children may comply with authority, but this compliance may afford them less opportunity to acquire the networking and social skills needed to advance in the workplace.

Teachers can actively move away from the model minority myth in their practices and interactions through a number of specific actions. They can treat students as individuals and not ascribe high or low expectations to them as members of groups based on national origin or ethnicity. By recognizing that Asian/Pacific American students speak different languages and come from different cultural areas, teachers can avoid lumping them together as one homogeneous group. Instead, teachers who take time to learn about the languages and cultures of these students will appreciate their differences (Nash, 1991). "Asian-American Children: What Teachers Should Know" (Feng, 1994; online at http://ericps.ed.uiuc.edu/eece) provides general information about Asian American children and a list of practices to help teachers become more knowledgeable about Asian cultures. Equally helpful is O'Connor's (1999; online at http://faculty.ncwc.edu/toconnor) "Understanding Discrimination against Asian Americans."

Placement.   Educators have responded to these educational issues by developing special programs and procedures and/or by placing students in special classes. *Special education* referrals and placements for culturally and linguistically different students have been disproportionate (Cummins, 1984; Rodriguez, Prieto & Rueda, 1984). Explanations for this overreferral include the following: low level of acculturation, inadequate assessment, language problems, poor school progress, academic/cognitive difficulties, and special learning problems (Malavé, 1991). Biased assessment has resulted in negative evaluation of English learners, largely because intelligence testing has been derived from models of genetic deficiency, cultural deprivation, and other deficit models (Payan, 1984; Rueda, 1987).

In situations where students are legitimately placed in special education classes, Bransford and Baca (1984) recommend alternative bilingual special education model programs that build on students' language and cultural strengths. Successful instructional programs for culturally and linguistically diverse special education students focus on building higher-order thinking skills; encouraging creative tasks that allow the expression of ideas through the native culture and language; providing student-to-student interaction and meaningful social contact; using comprehensible input in the second language; and allowing enhanced social contact with native speakers and mainstream students (Malavé, 1991). Chapter 12 of this text provides a more in-depth discussion of the issues and challenges facing special education for EL students and their teachers.

Retention/promotion policies are not carried out with equity. Unfortunately, some students begin falling behind their expected grade levels almost immediately upon entering school. In 1995, of the 13.7 percent of children who spoke a language other than English in the home, 10 percent were retained at least one grade. (The same percentage was also true for children who speak English at home.) However, retention rates for English learners differed according to language: Spanish, 10.4 percent; other European, 4.3 percent; Asian, 2.4 percent; and other, 6.6 percent (United States Department of Commerce, 1997). And, as the Department of Commerce warns, students who repeat at least one grade are more likely to drop out of school.

On the other side of the coin, students are also differentially distributed in advanced placement courses, a type of "in-house" promotion. Table 6.2 illustrates this distribution.

TABLE 6.2   **Percentage of High School Graduates Taking Advanced Placement Courses in High School, by Race/Ethnicity, 1998**

	White	Black	Hispanic	Asian/Pacific Islander	Native American
AP calculus	7.5	3.4	3.7	13.4	0.6
AP/honors biology	16.7	15.4	12.6	22.2	6.0
AP/honors chemistry	4.8	3.5	4.0	10.9	0.9
AP/honors physics	3.0	2.1	2.1	7.6	0.9

Source: United States Department of Education (2000).

Tracking offers very different types of instruction depending on students' placement in academic or "general" education courses. To justify this, educators have argued that tracking is a realistic, efficient response to an increasingly diverse student population. However, tracking often creates class and race-linked differences in access to learning and has been found to be a major contributor to the continuing gaps in achievement between minorities and Whites (Oakes, 1985, 1992).

Segregation in schools has been steadily increasing, with particularly disastrous effects on minority students. Although during the 1970s and 1980s, districts were working at desegregating their schools, the 1990s witnessed an increasing number of court cases that released districts from these efforts (Weiler, 1998). Inequity follows segregation. Although students in only 5 percent of segregated White schools face conditions of poverty, students do so in more than 80 percent of segregated African American and Latino schools (Orfield, Bachmeier, James, & Eitle, 1997). In addition, segregation makes it difficult for English learners to be grouped with native speakers of English during the school day.

Compensatory education was the impetus behind the success of the Bilingual Education Act; bilingual education was presented as a compensatory program, one that would help students whose English was limited. A compensatory view of bilingual education assumes that students whose native language is not English are deprived and in need of special programs. However, compensatory programs are often reduced in scope, content, and pace, and students are not challenged enough, nor given enough of the curriculum to be able to move to mainstream classes (Mehan, Hubbard, Lintz, & Villanueva, 1994).

At the federal level, another major compensatory program is Title I of the Elementary and Secondary Education Act (ESEA), which provides funding for low-income students. Until the 1994 reauthorization of the ESEA, EL students had been largely excluded from access to Title I programs because of the designation of language deficiency. However, in line with the reform efforts, the 1994 reauthorization did away with this exclusion in order to help districts coordinate their efforts for all students and develop inclusionary programs.

ESL as compensatory education is all too common. Because of the emphasis on a rapid transition to English, bilingual education has traditionally been confined to grades K–3. In recent years, however, with the influx of primary language students of high school age, bilingual education has become necessary for older students as well. As a part of these programs, a portion of the instructional day has been reserved for ESL instruction. Unfortunately, ESL has been identified with remediation of linguistic deficiencies.

Submersion in English is too often an alternative to bilingual education: English learners are placed with native speakers in classrooms where teachers have no training in language teaching pedagogy or sheltered content practices (McKeon, 1994). Research has shown that parents of students in submersion programs have been less involved in helping their children with homework than parents of students in bilingual programs (Ramírez, 1992). Thus, viewing ESL as remedial education or expecting children to acquire English without help has long-term adverse consequences for school achievement.

Inclusion of English learners in mainstream classrooms is now the trend. Although many of the previously mentioned placement procedures for EL students have negatively impacted their educational achievement, inclusionary procedures have integrated them into challenging educational programs. In a study of "good educational practice for LEP students," researchers found numerous schools that have successfully been educating EL students to high standards (McLeod, 1996). In these schools, programs for EL students were an integral part of the whole school program, neither conceptually nor physically separate from the rest of the school.

> The exemplary schools have devised creative ways to both include LEP students centrally in the educational program and meet their needs for language instruction and modified curriculum. Programs for LEP students are so carefully crafted and intertwined with the school's other offerings that it is impossible in many cases to point to "the LEP program" and describe it apart from the general program. (p. 4)

Several reform efforts have attempted to dismantle some of the compensatory education and tracking programs previously practiced in schools. These have included accelerated schools, cooperative learning, restructured schools, and detracking. A particularly noteworthy high school program is Advancement Via Individual Determination (AVID). This "untracking" program places low-achieving students (who are primarily from low-income and ethnic or language minority backgrounds) in the same college-preparatory academic program as high-achieving students (who are primarily from middle- or upper-middle-income and "Anglo" backgrounds) (Mehan et al., 1994).

Teacher Expectations and Student Achievement.   Jussim (1986) offers a general framework for the relationship between teacher expectations and student achievement. Teachers develop initial expectations based on a student's reputation, on previous classroom performance, or on stereotypes about racial, cultural, and linguistic groups. These expectations, which often resist change despite evidence to the contrary, form the basis for differential treatment of students and for the rationalization for such treatment. Students, in turn, react to this differential treatment in ways that confirm the teacher's expectations. Thus, teachers have a high degree of effect on student achievement: Student effort and persistence are shaped, in part, by students' perception of the teacher's expectation.

Teachers' expectations for student performance are culturally based, as are their criteria for evaluation. Pedagogical training may enable teachers to organize instruction that more accurately allows diverse students access to the curriculum.

> As an Anglo teacher in a reservation school, Patricia Osborn was acutely aware that her Native American students disliked writing in English. She often noted that these pupils had difficulty developing ideas when writing essays, and seemed to lack organization. As she sat down with David Littlebear, principal at the school, she reviewed her critique of the students' writing. "They don't develop a topic from beginning to end," Patricia complained. "There is little sequence, whether time-order, cause and effect, problem-solution, or comparison and contrast. I have difficulty getting them to summarize the main points at the end of the writing."
>
> David Littlebear replied, "In tribal speaking, our elders seldom address a topic directly. Suggestions are made indirectly and the listener must make the connection. The speaker does not presume to point out the relevance of the example to the topic. The presentation is more of a collage of related ideas with the inclusion of references to stories and narratives that members of the culture share. Before you conclude that the students cannot write, try to develop a kind of writing that incorporates the speaking style of our people. Perhaps then the students will measure up to your expectations." (Scafe & Kontas, 1982)

In this case study, the Native American students were modeling writing based on experience with public speaking that is not linear in progression. Because of their stature, tribal elders may not be required to verify their sources explicitly. Credence is not determined by citing written proof, because for generations, transmission of the culture was maintained through the spoken word (Scafe & Kontas, 1982). Teachers from the dominant White culture prescribe behaviors for success with which minority students may have little experience or practice; in some cases, this behavior may be directly contrary to accepted behaviors in other cultures.

Access for English Learners. School programs that recognize the rights and abilities of minority students and strive to reverse the discriminatory patterns of the society at large have proved more successful in helping these students through the schooling process (Cummins, 1984, 1989). With the implementation of the Goals 2000 and IASA legislation in 1994, school districts are being encouraged to create comprehensive school reform plans. Programs for English learners can be integrated within the core program. *School Reform and Student Diversity: Exemplary Schooling for Language Minority Students* (McLeod, 1996) details features of exemplary schools, goals for ensuring access to high-quality teaching, ways to improve teaching and learning for EL students, and an appendix of the featured schools.

Parent and Community Participation

"Strong parent involvement is one factor that research has shown time and time again to have positive effects on academic achievement and school attitudes" (Ovando & Collier, 1998). Yet, for various reasons, on the part of both schools and communities, this has sometimes been an elusive goal. The growing number of EL students in the school system, however, clearly requires that efforts continue to establish communication, develop partnerships, and involve parents, families, and communities. Fortunately, over the past decade, successful programs have developed and various guidelines are available to help school personnel, parents, and communities work together to ensure parental rights, parental involvement, successful programs, and school/community partnerships that benefit students.

Recognizing Parental Rights. Parents have numerous rights that educators must respect and honor in spite of the challenges they may present to the school. These include (1) the right of their children to a free, appropriate public education; (2) the right to receive information concerning education decisions and actions in the language parents comprehend; (3) the right to make informed decisions and to authorize consent before changes in educational placement occur; (4) the right to be included in discussions and plans concerning disciplinary action toward their children; (5) the right to appeal actions when they do not agree; and (6) the right to participate in meetings organized for public and parent information (Young & Helvie, 1996).

Issues in Parental Involvement. Schools attempting to increase parental involvement have encountered issues in five areas of concern: language, survival and family structure, educational background and values, knowledge about education and beliefs about learning, and power and status. Ovando and Collier (1998) offer questions within each area that can provide a valuable guide as school personnel begin to address and overcome misconceptions regarding parents and that will open dialogue for fruitful collaborations and programs (see Table 6.3).

Programs in Action. As schools and parents have looked for ways in which they can partner in order to help children achieve success in school, several have developed family literacy projects. One of the first was the Párajo Valley Family Literacy project in Watsonville, California. Project founder and author Dr. Alma Flor Ada designed a parental involvement program that would help parents recover a lost sense of dignity and identity. She began with a "meet the author" program by telling her own stories and explaining her feelings about writing in Spanish. Each subsequent session included reading and discussing children's books and sharing experiences. Videotapes showing parents discussing and enjoying the books were circulated in the community. Parents eventually replaced teachers as facilitators in the discussions and parents were encouraged to write their own stories. As a result, those parents increased in self-confidence and self-expression. They gave presentations at regional migrant education conferences and

TABLE 6.3   Questions Regarding Parental/School Relationships

Area of Concern	Questions
Language	How does educators' language (jargon?) affect home/school communication?
	Do community members support the use of the home language in school?
Family structure	How do the struggles of day-to-day survival affect the home/school partnership?
	How will differences in family structure affect the relationship?
Educational background, attitudes toward schooling	Do school expectations match the parents' educational backgrounds?
	What do educators assume about the attitudes of parents
Knowledge and beliefs about education	How do parents learn about school culture, their role in U.S. schools, and the specific methods being used in their child's classroom? Would they be comfortable reinforcing these methods at home?
	How do parents and teachers differ in the perception of the home/school relationship?
Power and status	How does the inherent inequality of the educator/layperson relationship affect the partnership?
	Do programs for parents convey a message of cultural deficiency?
	To what degree are language minority community members a part of the school in instructional and administrative positions?

Source: Adapted from Ovando and Collier (1998, pp. 301–309).

circulated lists of books to buy in Spanish. The major components of this project were the collaboration of the school and parents in a shared enterprise and the reciprocal interaction between parents and children that encourages both to enjoy literature (Ada, 1989).

A second such project is the Hmong Literacy Project, initiated by Hmong parents in Fresno, California. As their children became more assimilated in the United States and less appreciative of their cultural roots, the parents felt the need to preserve their oral history and maintain their culture through written records. Thus, they asked for literacy lessons in Hmong (a language that has been written for about only 30 years) and in English. Throughout the program, they developed not only the asked-for literacy skills but also skills in math and computers that allowed them to help their children academically. Through the Hmong Parents Newsletter, communication was increased between the school and the community, leading to greater parent participation in school activities (Kang, Kuehn, & Herrell, 1996).

A different type of program is the Parent Resource Center in Texas. It provides a system of social and educational support for language minority parents. Based on a needs assessment, the parent community identified four priorities: (1) ESL instruction, (2) strategies to help their children at home, (3) understanding the school system, and (4) understanding their rights and responsibilities (Bermúdez & Márquez, 1996). The words of one of the program participants serves to illustrate the value of such a program not only in helping immigrant parents but also in dispelling negative stereotypes regarding parents.

> Learning English helps us overcome the obstacles we encounter in this country. It gives us the opportunity to go to a doctor without having to find an interpreter.... Look, my children are growing, I need to learn to help my children with their school work. Although I only completed nine years of school in my country [Guatemala], one day I want to go back to school so I can obtain a job. This is my dream. We are very appreciative of all that the program has done for us. We are in this country and we need to communicate with others in their language. (Bermúdez & Márquez, p. 4)

School/Community Partnerships.   In addition to developing partnerships with parents, schools are also reaching toward communities to help them in educating all children. Community-based organizations (CBOs)—groups committed to helping people obtain health, education, and other basic human services—are assisting students in ways that go beyond traditional schooling (Dryfoos, 1998). Adger (2000) found that school/CBO partnerships supported students' academic achievement by working with parents and families, tutoring students in their first language, developing students' leadership skills and higher education goals, and providing information and support on issues such as health care, pregnancy, gang involvement, and so on.

Communities can foster a climate of support for EL students by featuring articles in local newspapers and newsletters about their achievements in the schools and prizes they have won, by sponsoring literature and art exhibitions that feature students and by publishing their stories written in both languages. Students can be invited to the local library to offer their stories, books, and poetry to other students, again in both English and the primary language. In this way, support for bilingualism and bilingual education programs is orchestrated in the community at large.

Organizational Models: What Works for Whom?

Bilingual education is an umbrella term used to refer to various types of programs and models. It is a term used in two ways: first, for education that promotes academic and linguistic development in two languages; and second, to denote programs that include students who speak languages other than English. In the first instance, bilingualism is being fostered; in the second, English learners are present but bilingualism is not a goal of the curriculum (Baker, 1993). Obviously, the school experience for English learners varies depending on the aim of the program in which students participate. The program can support and extend the home language and culture, or it can consider the students' language and culture irrelevant to schooling.

The various program models (discussed next) vary in degree of support for the home language. The least supportive is submersion, in which there is no support for the home language and culture. The most supportive is dual language instruction, which actively promotes bilingualism, biliteracy, and biculturalism. The models reflect different goals—for example remediation or enrichment—as well as the influence of federal, state, and local policies.

Submersion

The default mode for educating English learners in U.S. classrooms is submersion. These are mainstream classrooms in which no provisions are made for the language and academic needs of EL students. Students in such a program receive instruction in English, with English monolingualism as the goal. The associated social difficulties experienced by minority students in an ELD classroom are not addressed. As a result, the strongest of these language minority students may survive or even succeed academically (they "swim"), but the majority do not have the cognitive and academic foundation in the primary language at the time of education in English and thus do not attain the level of success educators might wish (they "sink"). In addition to being academically disabling, submersion denies students their rights under law:

> Submersion is not a legal option for schools with non-native English speakers; however, oversight and enforcement are lax, and many smaller schools with low populations of NNS [non-native-speaking] students are simply unaware that they are required to provide some sort of services to these students. Parents of these children, for cultural and other reasons, tend not to demand the services their children are entitled to; thus it is not uncommon to find submersion in U.S. public schools. (Roberts, 1995, pp. 80–81)

English as a Second Language

All bilingual models have an English-as-a-second-language component. However, if that is the only component, then the program is not a bilingual program. ESL instruction is delivered in a variety of ways and studies have shown varying degree of student success depending on the program model (Thomas & Collier, 1997).

Pull-Out ESL.   Associated with the submersion model is the separation of English learners for remedial instruction in English. This often takes the form of separate half-hour per day classes in which students leave their home classroom and receive instruction in vocabulary, grammar, oral language, and/or spelling. Such instruction rarely is integrated with the regular classroom program; and, when they return to the home classroom, children usually are not instructed on curriculum they missed while they were gone. This lack only exacerbates an already difficult learning situation. Of the various program models, ESL pull-out is the most expensive to operate because it requires hiring an extra resource teacher (Chambers & Parrish, 1992; Crawford, 1997). It has, however, been the most implemented and the least effective model (Thomas & Collier, 1997).

ESL Class Period.   Although pull-out ESL is normally found at the elementary level, students in the secondary school often have separate ESL classes that help them with their English skills. Unfortunately, these classes may focus entirely on the English language and do not help students with their academic subjects. The effect of such segregation is that students can be maintained in an "ESL ghetto" and never have the possibility of receiving rich academic instruction.

Content-Based ESL.   Although these classes are still separate and contain only EL students, students learn English through academic content in a curriculum organized around grade-level academic objectives (see Chapter 4). The most effective of these models is when the ESL teacher collaborates with content area teachers and some team teaching occurs (Ovando & Collier, 1998).

Sheltered Instruction or SDAIE.   As discussed in Chapter 5, sheltered instruction is provided by teachers who have both content background and knowledge of second language acquisition. Lessons have both content and language objectives. EL students and native English speakers are often together in sheltered classrooms, lessening the stigma of EL students being in a separate, remedial course.

    In none of the ESL models is the primary language of the students explicitly acknowledged or used. Individual teachers may have second language competencies with which to support students on an individual basis, but this is not part of the program design.

Transitional or Early-Exit Bilingual Education

The overriding goal of transitional bilingual education (TBE) programs is to mainstream students into English-only classrooms. In these programs, students receive initial instruction in most, if not all, content areas in their home language while they are being taught English. Most of these programs last only two to three years, long enough for students to achieve Basic Interpersonal Communication Skills (BICS) but not long enough for children to build Cognitive Academic Language Proficiency (CALP) either in their native tongue or in English. As a consequence, they may not be able to carry out cognitively demanding tasks in English, and may be considered to be "subtractively bilingual."

There are numerous problems with a TBE program. It may be perceived as a remedial program and/or another form of segregated, compensatory education. Teachers may "water down" the curriculum in order to be able to cover both the content and the English language objectives. It rests on the common misconception that two or three years is sufficient time to learn a second language for schooling purposes (Ovando & Collier, 1998).

Maintenance or Developmental Bilingual Education

A bilingual program that supports education and communication in the students' primary language as well as students' heritage and culture is a maintenance bilingual education (MBE) design, also known as developmental bilingual education. The major assumption in such a program is that bilingualism is a valuable asset, not only for the individuals who are bilingual but also for society as a whole. Students in an MBE design are not quickly transitioned but are encouraged to be proficient in both English and their native tongue. Literacy in two languages is often an important goal (Roberts, 1995). These goals enhance self-concept and pride in the cultural background. Developmental programs have mainly been implemented at the elementary level with programs in K–5 or K–6 depending on the configuration of the district. They are rarely continued into the intermediate grades. Programs that offer continuing support for students' academic learning in their first language have also been called *late-exit* to distinguish them from the transitional *early-exit* programs (Ramírez, 1992).

A particularly compelling use of maintenance bilingual programs is in the education of Native Americans. There are 74 schools operated by Native American organizations under grants or contracts with the Bureau for Indian Affairs that place a high priority on cultural and linguistic preservation (Reyhner, 1992). The attempt to increase the number of speakers of Native American languages is sometimes called "restorative" bilingual education. Primary language maintenance is carried out in school systems in the U.S. possessions of Guam and the Marshall Islands, as well as in the state of Hawaii.

Immersion

Immersion education provides academic and language instruction in two languages ideally from grades K–12. The goal of immersion programs is for students to be proficient in both languages—to achieve additive bilingualism. The term has come from program models in Canada, where middle-class, English-speaking children are instructed in French. In the United States, English-only submersion programs for English learners are sometimes mischaracterized as immersion. This misconception has led to confusion. Canadian immersion is not and never has been a monolingual program, because English is incorporated into the programs both as a subject and as a medium of instruction (Lambert, 1984). In addition, the social context of French immersion is the upper middle class in Quebec Province, where both English and French have a high language status for instructional purposes. In contrast, when EL students are submerged in mainstream English classes, instruction is not given in their home language, and they do not become biliterate and academically bilingual.

Enrichment Immersion.   In the United States, a comparable social context to Canadian-style immersion is found in the exclusive private schools of the upper class, in which foreign languages are highly supported, even to the extent of instruction being delivered directly in a foreign language. This program model can be labeled *enrichment immersion.*

Dual or Two-Way Immersion.   The enrichment immersion model is inadequate for EL students in the United States because the low status of the students' primary language puts it at risk for suppression (Hernández-Chávez, 1984). A two-way immersion model enhances the status of the students' primary language by providing instruction in that language to native English speakers. This allows EL students to be in a position to help their English-speaking peers (see Point/Counterpoint on page 173).

In the two-way immersion design, a high level of academic competence is achieved in two languages by both EL students and native English speakers. Both groups of students participate in content area instruction in the minority language as well as in English, although the two languages are not mixed. Both groups receive language instruction in both their native and the second language. An example of a highly successful dual-language program is that at the Valley Center-Pauma Joint Unified School District in California. Information about this program is available at http://www.cal.org/db/2way/. In addition, the National Clearinghouse for Bilingual Education (NCBE) has a wealth of information about two-way programs at http://www.ncbe.gwu.edu/library/twoway.htm.

Newcomer Centers

Newcomer programs offer recent immigrants an emotionally safe educational atmosphere that fosters rapid language learning, acculturation, and enhancement of self-esteem (Friedlander, 1991; Olsen & Dowell, 1989). Common goals for various newcomer program models include helping students acquire enough English to move into the regular language support program, developing students' academic skills, and helping them gain an understanding of U.S. schools and educational expectations. Additional goals may include developing students' primary language and introducing students to their new communities. Programs may be organized as a school-within-a-school, as a separate program in its own location,

Point/Counterpoint

Does dual immersion enhance English learning?

Dual immersion programs are designed to provide an enriched program of academic and language study in which students and teachers use both languages as the medium of communication for specific areas of the curriculum. This encourages EL students to develop their primary language and native English-speaking students (for example, Spanish language learners [SSLs]) to attain advanced levels of functional proficiency in the second language by performing academic tasks in that language. But do immersion programs help English learners to develop English skills?

Point: Dual immersion promotes English learning.

Research has shown that students who enter school in the United States with limited or no proficiency in English make more progress in acquiring English and in developing academically if they receive schooling in their primary language as they are introduced to English as a second language (Cummins, 1981b; Ramirez, 1992; Thomas & Collier, 1997). Strong literacy skills in the primary language can be applied to the acquisition of English literacy. Dual language immersion schools help EL students develop their primary language fully while adding proficiency in English through enriched, challenging curriculum. Students who act as language hosts—for example, Spanish-speaking children who serve as language models for native English-speaking students in a dual immersion program—gain self-esteem and increased cultural pride (Lindholm, 1992), leading to increased motivation to learn. Careful attention to a high-quality bilingual program in the context of primary language maintenance is key (Veeder & Tramutt, 2000).

Counterpoint: Dual immersion delays English learning.

Although dual immersion programs do not segregate primary-language students, as do traditional bilingual programs, critics charge that these programs fail to teach English to English learners. Because programs teach content in the primary language, they do not emphasize communication in English, as do transition bilingual programs. Amselle (1999) argues that "dual immersion programs are really nothing more than Spanish immersion, with Hispanic children used as teaching tools for English-speaking children." Experts concede that the greatest challenge in two-way bilingual programs is to "reduce the gap" between the language abilities of the two groups (EL students and SLLs). This gap appears as content classes in English are modified (slowed down) for English learners to "catch up," or as content delivery in the primary language is slowed for SSLs. As Molina (2000) advises, "Without a watchful approach to the quality of two-way programs, schools will find themselves tragically exploiting the English learners they had hoped to help for the benefit of the language majority students."

or in district intake centers (Genesee, 1999; Short, 1998). Programs vary in both length of day and length of time in program. Some are full day, in which students have various content courses along with ESL, whereas others are half-day or after school. The majority of newcomer programs operate for one year, although some may last four years, and others only one semester or one summer. Programs also distinguish themselves by whether they are primarily ESL or bilingual, and by the manner in which they exit students (Genesee, 1999; Short, 1998).

Research Studies on Program Effectiveness

Bilingual education continues to be controversial, entangled as it is with societal conceptions and misconceptions, issues of power and status, and climates of acceptance and fear. Thomas and Collier (1997) found three key predictors of academic success that appeared to prevail over other variables such as poverty, the school's location in an impoverished area, and the status (or lack thereof) of the language minority group. Those schools that incorporated all three predictors were "likely to graduate language minority students who are very successful academically in high school and higher education" (p. 15). The three predictors are as follows: (1) cognitively complex on-grade-level academic instruction through students' first language for as long as possible, combined with cognitively complex on-grade-level academic instruction through the second language (English) for part of the school day; (2) the use of current approaches to teaching the academic curriculum through two languages, including discovery learning, cooperative learning, thematic units, and activities that tap into the "multiple intelligences" (Gardner, 1983), and bridging techniques that draw on students' personal experiences; and (3) a transformed sociocultural context for EL students' schooling, with two-way bilingual classes frequently used to achieve this goal.

The task facing EL students is daunting. Consider that EL students need to acquire English and academic subjects while their native English-speaking (NES) peers are learning academic subjects. Each school year, the NES student sustains 10 months of academic growth. If the EL student initially scores low on tests in English (say two or three years below grade level), he or she has to outgain the NES student by making 15 months' progress (an academic year and a half) on the tests each year for five or six years in order to reach the average performance of a NES student. In studying the various program models for English learners, Thomas and Collier (1997) found that students who received on-grade-level academic work in their primary language were able to make these gains and, most importantly, sustain them.

For more information about successful schools and programs, interested readers can search NCBE's "Success Stories" link at http://www.ncbe.gwu. edu/ success/index.htm or read about outstanding programs in *Bilingual Education* (Christian & Genesee, 2001).

Instructional Strategies

Good classroom teaching must be a part of a bilingual classroom in the same way that good teaching is required in any classroom. When students are viewed as active participants in the learning process rather than empty receptacles to be filled with knowledge, then teachers organize classroom experiences for "reciprocal interaction" (Cummins, 1986). Teachers also recognize the importance of incorporating students' culture(s) into classroom tasks (see Chapter 10 for suggestions). In characterizing effective bilingual instruction, the following sections will focus on the use of two languages and exemplary means of classroom organization.

Language Management

If instruction is to be effective for children who potentially can function at a high level in two languages, the use of these languages must maximize cognitive and academic proficiency. Programs using two languages separate them by time, personnel, subject, and manner of delivery.

Time.   Bilingual programs may devote a specific time to each language. In an "alternate use" model, languages are used on alternating days: Monday, primary language; Tuesday, English; Wednesday, primary language; and so on. In a "divided day" model, the morning may be devoted to the primary language and the afternoon to English. In both these models, academic instruction is occurring in both languages.

Personnel.   Languages can be separated by teacher. In a team-teaching situation, one teacher may speak in English, the other in the primary language. When working with an aide, the teacher will use English and the aide the primary language. A caution in using this latter design is the association of the minority language with school personnel who do not have fully credentialed teaching status.

Subject.   Language may be organized by subject—primary language for mathematics, English for science, and so on. Again, for this model, school personnel need to be cognizant of which subjects are taught in which language. Models where the primary language is used only for language arts, music, and art, and English is used for science and mathematics, send a message about the status of the primary language.

Manner of Delivery.   The novice bilingual teacher may say everything twice, first in English and then in the primary language. This *concurrent translation* model has been found to be ineffective because students tune out when their subordinate language is spoken. Another approach is *preview/review,* in which the introduction and summary are given in one language and the presentation in the other. In situations where content area materials are not available in the minority language, preview/review has been found to be particularly useful (Lessow-Hurley, 1996).

Primary Language Use

In bilingual programs, the primary language can be used as the language of instruction in teaching students academic material, such as how English is used for native English-speaking students in mainstream programs, and it can be used to help students in their acquisition of English.

Academic Learning.   Primary language instruction is defined as "instruction focused on the development of the language itself (oral and literacy skills) through use of authentic written and oral literature and discourse as well as academic instruction through the primary language" (Sánchez, 1989, p.2). Instruction by means of the primary language allows students to capitalize on their life experiences and transfer their knowledge into an understanding of the purposes of reading and writing. Once they have a well-developed conceptual base in their primary language, they can translate into English concepts and ideas that are firmly established rather than facing the far more difficult task of learning fundamental concepts in an unfamiliar language (Lessow-Hurley, 1996). For example, hearing and reading familiar songs, poems, folktales, and stories in the native language exposes students to literary language and various genres. Once literacy is established in the native language, children can use these resources as they move into English, creating their own English texts, and reading English material written by others (Flores, García, González, Hidalgo, Kaczmarek, & Romero, 1985).

Language Acquisition.   There are several educationally sound as well as logical and psychological reasons for the judicious use of the primary language in learning English (and vice versa). Certainly in bilingual settings, in which two language groups are working and learning together, a disciplined approach to the use of L1 can enhance and facilitate language learning. The Point/Counterpoint on page 177 outlines the reasons for and against the use of L1 in learning L2.

Alternation of Languages

As students become more proficient in English, several factors help to determine which language they use. The primary factor is the students themselves. They are free to respond in whichever language is comfortable and appropriate to them. Teacher proficiency and material availability are other factors. In some cases, teachers may provide instruction in English while students, in their groups, talk and write in the home language. *Code switching*, the alternation between two languages, is accepted in this model, although students are expected to make final presentations, both oral and written, only in the language of instruction. Bilingual teachers and students may habitually alternate between the two languages that are used in

Point/Counterpoint

What Should Be the Role of L1 in Learning L2?

Many of the teaching techniques used for English language teaching in the twentieth century were developed for use in multilingual, often urban, classes where not a sole primary language was shared by the learners. In these classes the use of L1 was not feasible, or was strongly discouraged because of the belief that L1 would interfere with learning L2. However, in schools in the United States that feature a student population that shares an L1, this argument does not hold. Debate is now raging over the use of the learner's first language (L1) in the classroom: What should be the role of L1 in learning L2?

Point: **L1 is a useful tool in learning English.**

- Many words—especially concrete nouns—are learned fastest when translated. Teaching a simple word, such as *garlic,* involves a great deal of description or use of a picture. (Does every teacher have a picture of garlic?)
- L1 is useful to highlight false cognates (*embarazada* is not *embarrassed*).
- L1 can be used to discuss grammar differences between language (*English* does not use an article, as does *el ingles*) and abstract grammar ideas (how the rules of using the subjunctive differ in L1 and English).
- Use of L1 lowers stress in learning L2.
- Most learners naturally use L1; rather than creating a new language store, they mentally map the L2 directly on to the existing L1, drawing connections, contrasting ideas, and viewing the L2 through their L1.
- The L1 can be contrasted with L2; a knowledge of the L1 may give the teacher some advantage in predicting difficulties in learning the L2.
- If the teacher who does not speak L1 fluently tries to use L1—even poorly—it demonstrates to students that making mistakes is not a big deal.
- By trying to learn their L1, the teacher shows respect for the students' language and culture.
- Teachers who are not native speakers of English may nonetheless be valuable because they share the L2 learning experience with learners.

Counterpoint: **L1 is not useful in teaching L2.**

- Overuse on L1 can mean dependency.
- Learners may misunderstand an exact translation of a word's many meanings, especially because English has multiple synonyms for words.
- Use of L1 can also lead to a loss of useful language practice.
- Teachers who do not use English socially in class may communicate a low value for speaking and listening to English.
- Use of L1 may replace opportunities for listening and speaking practice in L2.
- Teachers who do not share the L1 with students may nevertheless receive preferential hiring because they are native speakers of English.

Source: Adapted from Buckmaster (2000).

their community (Valdés-Fallis, 1978). Code switching is regarded as a developmental aspect in acquiring a second language and/or a reflection of the community's language use. An excellent example of a fifth-grade bilingual class moving into English literacy while maintaining their first language is Hayes's (1998) *Literacy con Cariño: A Story of Migrant Children's Success.*

Classroom Organization

Recent studies on school reform and education for EL students all support the same findings: Students learn better when actively engaged in a nurturing environment that honors and respects their language and culture (McLeod, 1995; Nelson, 1996; Thomas & Collier, 1997). The active strategies and techniques outlined in Chapters 4 and 5 are equally valid for bilingual classrooms as for ELD and SDAIE classrooms, if not more so, as two groups of students are learning two different languages. Curriculum that is organized around themes, that strives for depth of a topic rather than breadth, that is cross-disciplinary, and that has meaning to students and is relevant to their lives provides students with the opportunity to achieve academic success. Every study makes mention of the importance of cooperative learning in helping students succeed.

Cooperative Groups. Cooperative grouping, in which EL students work cooperatively with native speakers of English, increases students' opportunities to hear and produce English and to negotiate meaning with others. Cohen's complex instruction (Cohen, Lotan, & Catanzarite, 1990) encourages equal access for all students in a cooperative group by assigning well-defined roles to each group member and ensuring that these roles rotate frequently. In addition to encouraging academic learning and language proficiency, cooperative learning also helps children learn classroom conventions and rituals and become an active part of the culture of the classroom. To be most effective, grouping needs to be flexible and heterogeneous in language, gender, ability, and interest.

Student-Centered Groups.   Certain formats of cooperative grouping encourage active student involvement and learning, whereas others continue to reinforce teacher-centered instruction. Cooperative Integrated Reading and Composition (CIRC) has been applied in a bilingual model (Calderón, Tinajero, & Hertz-Lazarowitz, 1990). The CIRC program consists of initial teacher-directed instruction in reading comprehension and then "Treasure Hunt" activities carried out by groups of students.

A contrasting program was implemented in a school in South Texas with a large number of migrant children (Hayes, 1998). During their fifth-grade year, students were empowered to teach themselves—they talked and wrote about their lives outside the classroom, about what they were learning and the effect this learning had on their lives. Students were given choices and opportunities to express themselves using daily journals and class-made books. Writing conferences helped them evaluate their own writing and that of their classmates. A rich supply of stories and nonfiction books encouraged them to read.

Collaborative Teaching. When teachers have the opportunity to collaborate, they can share interests and experiences and build on each other's strengths for the benefit of their students. An example of teachers working together is found in the Holistic English Literacy Program (HELP) at Elderberry Elementary School in Ontario, California. Three teachers—one in second grade, one in a bilingual third grade, and one in fourth/fifth grade—worked together to organize the school day to accommodate the needs of their English learners, to plan thematic units, and to support each other's areas of expertise (see Díaz-Rico & Weed [1995] for a more complete description).

Well-implemented bilingual education programs have been found successful in educating not only English learners but also native English-speaking students. In a world that is constantly getting smaller, in which the majority of people are bilingual, it is incumbent on the United States to utilize the linguistic facilities of its citizens and to develop these resources to their maximum potential. This argument speaks to the international arena. Equally important is the education of these citizens for the nation itself. As Thomas and Collier (1997) so eloquently express:

> By reforming current school practices, all students will enjoy a better educated, more productive future, for the benefit of all American citizens who will live in the world of the next 15–25 years. It is in the self-interest of all citizens that the next adult generations be educated to meet the enormously increased educational demands of the fast-emerging society of the near future. (p. 13)

7 Language and Content Area Assessment

A school is good when it moves away from factory-like processing procedures and toward more humanistic, individualized judgments.

The idea is to make evaluation a learning experience.

Testing should grow from what is taught, and what is taught should grow from who is taught.

—Postman & Weingartner, 1973

Reading tests do not test reading: They actually test similarity to the test writer.

—Edelsky, 1991

Assessment is a process for determining the current level of a learner's performance or knowledge. The results of the assessment are then used to modify or improve the learner's performance or knowledge. Ideally, a test informs educators about the strengths and needs of the language learner so that students are properly placed and appropriately instructed. Of course, assessment is also used for the purpose of informing school authorities, parents, or other concerned parties of the student's progress. Classroom instruction that is directly linked to placement tests for English learners permits teachers to use effective instructional practices as soon as students enter the classroom. Moreover, careful assessment ensures continuous progress toward mainstream instruction. In the current climate of standards-driven instruction, the results of assessment may also be used to assess the effectiveness of the teacher's instruction. In an English language development context, assessments can test language ability or content knowledge or both; in the process of testing these, one must take care that culture is not a hidden part of the test. In the model presented in Figure I.1, assessment has an impact on instruction, learning, and culture, and is itself affected by culture.

Various evaluation methods have been used with English learners. Some are required by government programs and legal mandates, and others, more informal, are devised by classroom teachers. Educators involved in assessment must be careful to ensure that tests are fair (free from cultural and linguistic bias) and valid (measuring what they purport to measure). Furthermore, tests must advance students' understanding and ability if they constitute a valid part of education. Tests should not be merely instruments of diagnosis for labeling and placing and designing remediation.

If testing is aligned with a curricular goal that emphasizes the production of well-formed English utterances over learner-centered communication, the learners may in fact relinquish control of the activity of learning English to the teacher and take no real responsibility for active intentional learning of the second language. Testing must therefore be an integral part of a learning environment that encourages students to seek meaning and use a second language to fulfill academic and personal goals.

Purposes of Assessment

Assessment instruments can be used for a number of purposes: *Proficiency tests* determine a student's level of performance; *diagnostic and placement tests* provide information to place students in the appropriate level of academic or linguistic courses; *achievement tests* assess the student's previous learning; and *competency tests* assess whether a student may be promoted or advanced. Teachers who use assessment skillfully can choose which methods of assessment are most useful for classroom decision making; develop effective grading procedures; communicate assessment results to students, parents, and other educators; and recognize unethical, illegal, and otherwise inappropriate assessment methods and uses of assessment information (Ward & Murray-Ward, 1999).

Proficiency Tests

Proficiency tests measure the test takers' overall ability in English, usually defined independently of any particular instructional program. These tests may help determine whether the test taker is ready for a job or ready to proceed to a higher level of education. Proficiency tests are sometimes divided into subskills or modes of language, including speaking, listening, writing, reading, vocabulary, and grammar. Within the last decade, experts in the field of second language acquisition have recommended that tests be a measure of communicative competence more than of grammar or vocabulary.

However, the proliferation of standardized tests has often resulted in an emphasis on the testing of decontextualized skills such as sentence-level punctuation, grammar, and spelling. Because the tests do not engage the learner's intrinsic interest by providing a story or feature article from which test items are drawn, the learner is required to focus on a series of individual sentences unrelated to one another. This undermines the mode in which cognition is most effective: the ability of the brain to seek out and assemble personal meaning. Therefore, a test that is not aligned with curriculum—that does not measure the extent to which a student has worked to acquire meaning—provides, at best, an uncertain measure of skill.

Proficiency tests are poor tests of achievement because, by design, their content has little or no relationship to the content of an instructional program. They may also poorly diagnose what specific knowledge a student has or is lacking. Educators should be cautious about using proficiency tests to predict academic or vocational success, because language is only one element among many that contribute to success (Alderson, Krahnke, & Stansfield, 1987).

Diagnosis and Placement Tests

Diagnosis and placement tests are administered to determine specific aspects of a student's proficiency in a second language. Most tests that purport to be diagnostic tests are in reality tests of relative proficiency in various skills (Alderson et al., 1987). Placement tests, which may be the same as proficiency tests, determine the academic level or the grade level into which students need to be placed. In addition to identifying students who are English learners and determining the level of proficiency, placement tests can be used to monitor progress of EL students in acquiring English and assist in redesignating EL students to mainstream classrooms (Slater, 2000).

Achievement Tests

An achievement test measures a student's success in learning specific instructional content whether language (knowledge about English) or another subject (mathematics, science). A curriculum-based achievement test is given after instruction has taken place and contains only material that was actually taught. The staff of the instructional program usually prepares such a test. The trend in achievement testing is away from testing samples of a student's storehouse of knowledge and toward testing a student's ability to think knowledgeably. For example, a beginning English learner may be given clues to a treasure hunt to practice the vocabulary associated with the schoolroom (eraser, chalk, globe), and a teacher may observe the student's ability to collect all the relevant items in an informal assessment. During the exercise, the student's English development is combined with critical and creative thinking.

However, the contemporary trend toward implementing national standards for achievement has caused a proliferation of achievement tests that are not aligned with specific curricular content. The pressure for students to perform well on these tests, which are often used by administrators as an index of academic success, may detract from time spent on language development activities. Educators have argued that these nationally normed tests penalize English learners, causing schools with large percentages of EL students to rank comparatively poorly on school achievement indices (Groves, 2000). Teachers who understand the needs of English learners can adjust their instruction to balance lesson planning with the need to prepare students to perform well on standardized achievement tests.

Competency Tests

Many states feature minimum competency testing programs that are used to identify students who may be promoted or graduate. In some states, such as Florida, English learners in certain grades who have been in an ESL program for two or fewer years may be exempt from the state minimum competency testing program. Other states offer modifications in the testing, such as extended time, a separate site, small group testing, or testing supervised by a familiar person (Evaluation Assistance Center—East, 1990). These provisions that modify or exempt testing for EL students may allow instructional progress until students are ready for standardized testing. Many school districts mandate remedial instruction between terms for students who fail to meet minimum competency standards. It is important that such supplementary instruction take into consideration the needs of English learners.

Methods of Assessment

One of the major activities in U.S. education is the comparison of children with one another to assess academic growth. Test scores, classroom grades, and teacher observation and evaluation are common bases for determining student progress. The judgments resulting from this testing may affect students' present adjustment to school and their future academic and social success. The social and economic pressures from testing often overshadow the curriculum and the affective goals of schooling. Performance-based testing is a growing alternative to standardized testing, although standardized testing will probably persist because of the economic and political investment in this type of assessment. For classroom purposes, teacher observation and evaluation—supplemented by other sources of data—remain potent allies for students' academic progress. Students can play a role in the assessment process by evaluating their own language development, content knowledge, and strategies for learning. This helps students become self-regulated learners who can plan their own learning activities and use of time and resources (O'Malley & Pierce, 1996).

The Role of Assessment in the Integrated Curriculum

The use of an integrated curriculum promotes language and academic development for EL students. Units of study in literature, math, science, and social studies may be combined into an interdisciplinary program in which students can use a variety of communication systems (language, art, music, drama) to pursue open-ended assignments. Students develop proficiency through activities such as silent reading, experiments, questioning, discussion, free writing, focused writing, and other integrated activities. Assessment is a natural part of this curriculum. Student outcomes are documented in a variety of ways—time capsules, surveys, creative works, posters, and so forth. Good records allow teachers to track individual progress and also reflect and store many observations about students' skills and interests. *Scenarios for ESL Standards-Based Assessment* (TESOL, 2001) uses actual classroom settings to illustrate how teachers integrate ongoing assessment with instructional activities.

Authentic Assessment

Assessments are considered "authentic" if they stem directly from classroom activities, allow students to share in the process of evaluating their progress, and are valid and reliable in that they truly assess a student's classroom performance in a stable manner. Such assessment is an ongoing process in which the student as well as the teacher make judgments about the student's progress in language using nonconventional strategies (Hancock, 1994). Although authentic or alternative assessments have been criticized as subjective and anecdotal, in fact through the involvement of the students in selecting and reflecting on their own learning, and through the use of multiple measures often stemming from nontraditional areas such as the arts, the teacher has a wider range of evidence on which to evaluate a student's competence. The advantage of authentic assessment is that it is directly related to classroom performance and permits teachers to design and offer the extra mediation that students may need as determined by the assessment.

Performance-Based Assessment

Performance-based testing is testing that corresponds directly to what is taught in the classroom. Most performance-based tests are production tasks, which require that students produce something. Performance-based testing procedures can easily be incorporated into classroom routines and learning activities. Methods for assessing performance can be divided into two main types: *standardized* (e.g., tests, checklists, observations, rating scales, questionnaires, structured interviews) and *less standardized* (e.g., student work samples, journals, games, debates, story retelling, anecdotal reports, and behavioral notes, in which the scoring is tailored to the product in a less standard fashion).

Students may be assessed through standardized means, such as teacher-designed examinations that are intended to be scored quickly. (These, of course, are not as elaborately "standardized" using national norms as are large-scale, commercially published tests.) Questionnaires and surveys can help teachers to learn about many students' skills and interests at once. An observation checklist allows teachers to circulate among students while they are working and to monitor specific skills, such as emergent literacy skills, word-identification skills, and oral reading (Miller, 1995). The advantage of standardized assessment is its speed of scoring, using predetermined questions and answer keys.

Less standardized, or open-ended, assessment, on the other hand, has been criticized for being time consuming, labor intensive, imprecise, and subjective even though much effort is put into developing acceptable concurrence among assessors

(Maeroff, 1991). Generally speaking, open-ended assessments may feature longer problem-solving exercises, assignments that involve reading and writing performances or exhibitions, and/or portfolios that contain student work gathered over a longer period of time, such as a semester. Despite the potential drawbacks of open-ended assessment, it can furnish valuable information about students' abilities. Not all open-ended assessments are difficult to grade; teacher-made *scoring rubrics* can be determined in advance of an assignment and assist both teacher and student by communicating in advance the basis for scoring (Jasmine, 1993). Using a combination of standardized and less standardized assessments provides a cross-check of student capabilities (Navarrete, Wilde, Nelson, Martínez, & Hargett, 1990). Navarrete and Gustke (1996; online at http://www.ncbe.gwu.edu/miscpubs/eacwest/performance/index.htm#contents) have written a practical guide to performance assessment that teachers will find useful in helping them develop sound performance assessment.

Classroom Tests. Classroom tests may reflect functional or communicative goals, whether they require a set of unrelated phrases or answers from students or solicit answers embedded in a naturalistic sequence of discourse. Tests may be highly convergent (one right answer required) or may be open ended, with many answers possible. By testing only outcomes of learning, these tests tend to divide knowledge into small pieces away from an applied context. On the other hand, more authentic tests of ability require students to have a repertoire of responses that call for judgment and skill in using language to meet challenges within the target culture.

Portfolio Assessment. Portfolio assessment is often used synonymously with the term *alternative assessment*. The purpose of portfolio assessment is to maintain a long-term record of students' progress, to provide a clear and understandable measure of student productivity instead of a single number, to offer opportunities for improved student self-image as a result of showing progress and accomplishment, to recognize different learning styles, and to provide an active role for students in self-assessment (Gottlieb, 1995). Portfolios may include writing samples (compositions, letters, reports, drawings, dictation); student self-assessments; audio recordings (retellings, oral think-alouds); photographs and video recordings; semantic webs and concept maps; and/or teacher notes about students (Glaser & Brown, 1993).

The Fairfax (VA) County public schools maintain portfolios in the ESL program to record students' progress in reading, oral language, and writing. The reading assessment component begins with an initial reading assessment. Group and individual checklists document reading-related behaviors, and reading samples are recorded for inclusion in the folder. The oral assessment includes opportunities for students to invent a story, to listen/retell, and to produce spontaneous speech. The oral language is scored in communicative stages. The writing assessment component includes rough drafts as well as final copies. The content is scored on a developmental scale with separate scoring rubrics for grades 2 through 6 and secondary school levels. Another comprehensive assessment for English learners is the District Writing Assessment developed by the Ontario-Montclair School District in Ontario, California, which uses holistic pre- and postassessment (administered in fall and spring of each academic year) to assess student proficiency in writing.

For further information about procedures to implement portfolios, see "A Portfolio Assessment Model for ESL" (Moya & O'Malley, 1994; online at http:// www.ncbe.gwu.edu/miscpubs/jeilms/vol13/portfo13.htm).

Standardized Tests

Standardized tests for second or foreign language teaching offer means for employing a common standard of proficiency or performance despite variations in local conditions or student abilities. For example, ESL curriculum in the United Kingdom uses a standard called the Graded Tests that advance students through various levels of ESL. These tests are produced by national examination boards and are used to determine ESL/EFL proficiency and readiness for entry into British universities. The Test of English as a Foreign Language (TOEFL), developed by the Educational Testing Service in Princeton, New Jersey, is a similar test used for nonnative speakers of English at eleventh grade or above. It is administered in more than 170 countries and areas for students wishing to study in universities and colleges in the United States. The benefits of standardized tests include speed in administration and convenience in scoring. They are also considered to be unbiased, although questions arise as to their impartiality.

Norm-Referenced Tests.   These tests compare student scores against a population of students with which the test has been standardized or "normed." Examples of norm-referenced tests are the Language Assessment Scales (LAS), a test designed to measure oral language skills in English and Spanish, and the Woodcock-Muñoz Language Assessment.

An example of a large, districtwide standardized content test is the Los Angeles Unified School District's (LAUSD) Comprehensive Assessment System, developed in conjunction with the National Center for Research on Evaluation, Standards, and Student Testing (CRESST). When completed, the LAUSD Comprehensive Assessment System will consist of norm-referenced content tests, as well as performance-based assessments in language arts, mathematics, history, and science at multiple grade levels. Results from the assessments will be used for multiple purposes, including school accountability and program improvement. It is unclear what provisions will be made for the equitable participation of EL students.

Criterion-Referenced Tests.   Criterion-referenced tests are used principally to find out how much of a clearly defined domain of language skills or materials students have learned. The focus is on how the students achieve in relation to the material, rather than to one another or to a national sample. Common examples of criterion-referenced tests are final examinations for a language course and tests included in teachers' editions of textbooks. On this type of test, all students may score 100 percent if they have learned the material well. In an ELD program with many levels, students may be required to pass criterion-referenced tests to progress from one level to the next.

Teacher Observation and Evaluation

Teachers are in the best position to observe and evaluate students on an ongoing basis. Moreover, teachers are responsible for communicating students' progress to administrators, parents, and students themselves. Documenting student progress and diagnosing student needs are two major purposes of teacher evaluation. Much of these data can be obtained as teachers design tests and observe students as they learn.

Observation-Based Assessment.   As students interact and communicate using language, an observant teacher can note individual differences. In addition to formal notes, teachers may record a cooperative or collaborative group working together; students telling a story, giving a report, or explaining information; or children using oral language in other ways. These observations of speaking and listening should extend across all areas of the curriculum and in all types of interactional situations. Observations may be formal (e.g., miscue analysis) or informal. They may be based on highly structured content or on divergent and creative activities. Multiple observations show student variety and progress (Crawford, 1993). One observational instrument that is used to assess students' oral proficiency is the Student Oral Language Observation Matrix (SOLOM). The teachers rate students' proficiency in comprehension, fluency, vocabulary, pronunciation, and grammar based on descriptors in a 1–5 scale.

Teacher-Made Tests.   Teacher-made tests are often the basis for classroom grading. Tests can assess skills in reading comprehension, oral fluency, grammatical accuracy, writing proficiency, and listening. Teacher-constructed tests may not be as reliable and valid as tests that have been standardized, but the ease of construction and administration and the relevance to classroom learning make them popular. Because of their own past testing experiences and the nature of tests connected with texts or text series, teachers may have a tendency to devise "discrete-point" tests—those that ask students for specific items of grammar or vocabulary. However, teachers can write for good communicative tests by using the following criteria:

- Use what is learned.
- The focus is on the message and function, not just on the form.
- Provide for group collaboration as well as individual work.
- Include authentic problems in language use, as opposed to contrived linguist problems.
- Ensure that testing looks like learning.

Grading.   A variety of approaches has been used to assign grades to English learners. Teachers sometimes experience frustration stemming from making these nontraditional students fit into a traditional evaluation system. Some schools in which all classes are taught in sheltered English assign a *traditional A–F grade scale* in accordance with grade-level expectations. Assignments are adjusted to meet the students' language levels. Students receive a separate grade in the subject areas of their ESL class and performance standards are not lowered in content classes. A *modified A–F grade scale* is used in schools where English learners are congregated in one ESL class regardless of grade level. During their time in this class, students' work is assessed with an A–F grade based on achievement, effort, and behavior with report card grades modified by a qualifier signifying work performed above, at, or below grade level. A third type of grade system is the *pass/fail grade scale* used by schools whose English learners are integrated into the regular classroom. This scale avoids comparing the English learner with English-proficient classmates ("From the Classroom," 1991).

Cautions about Testing

Tests are an influential part of the U.S. schooling system and are used in every classroom. When choosing standardized tests, teachers can consider the following guidelines (Worthen & Spandel, 1991) to help them determine the benefits and limitations of the test:

- Does the test correspond to the task that it measures?
- Does the score approximate the student's ability?
- How can the score be supplemented with other information?
- Does the test drive the curriculum?
- Is the test a fair sample of the students' skills and behaviors?
- Is the test being used unfairly to compare students and schools with one another?
- Are tests that involve minimum standards being used to make critical decisions regarding classification of students?

Identification, Assessment, and Placement of English Learners in the Schools

Twenty-nine states have specific laws and provide procedural guidelines regarding identification procedures for EL students. Many states also have procedures for redesignating students and for placing them in mainstream classes. Some states do not have state laws but do provide guidelines for the assessment of EL students. Generally speaking, students are first evaluated; then if identified as needing services, they are placed in suitable programs, if available. Ideally, the placement test results correspond directly to an instructional plan that can be implemented immediately by a classroom teacher. Once in a program, students are then periodically reevaluated for purposes of reclassification.

Identification Procedures for English Learners

A variety of methods are used to identify EL students needing services. The *home language survey*, a short form administered by school districts to determine the language spoken at home, is among the most frequently used methods to identify students whose primary language is not English. *Registration* and *enrollment* information collected from incoming students can be used to identify students with a home language other than English. Identification through *observation* is often done by a teacher or tutor who has informally observed a student using a language other than English. *Interviews* may provide opportunities to identify students, as may *referrals* made by teachers, counselors, parents, administrators, or community members (Cheung & Solomon, 1991). School districts are required by state and federal mandates to administer a placement test before assigning a new student to an instructional program if a home language survey indicates that the student's primary language is not English.

Assessment for Placement

Once students are identified, their level of English proficiency needs to be determined. Ideally, the assessment is done by staff with the language skills to communicate in the family's native language. Sometimes, however, assessment consists only of a conversational evaluation in English by an untrained person. Parents and students should be provided with orientation about the assessment and placement process and the expectation and services of the school system. Most important, the school staff needs to be trained, aware, and sensitive to the backgrounds and experiences of the student population.

Specific tests have been designed to help districts place EL students. For example, the Language Assessment Scales (LAS), a standardized test with mean scores and standard deviations based on various age groups, are designed to measure oral language skills in English and Spanish. Another frequently used proficiency test is the Bilingual Syntax Measure (BSM) I, which measures oral proficiency in English and/or Spanish grammatical structures and language dominance. The Basic Inventory of Natural Language (BINL) evaluates oral proficiency in English. Pictures are used to elicit natural speech, and spoken sentences are analyzed for fluency, average length of utterance, and level of syntactic complexity. The IDEA proficiency test also measures oral language proficiency in English. As students point to and name objects, complete sentences, and respond verbally, these responses are scored for accurate comprehension and production.

A more comprehensive instrument is the English Language Development Monitoring Tool, employed by Hacienda La Puente Unified School District in California. The tool has four components: listening, speaking, reading, and writing behaviors for each of the 6 levels of placement that correspond to the California English Language Development Standards. At each level, the placement chart indicates behaviors that show mastery; for example, at the Early Production level, "ability to understand basic survival sentences" is an indicator of performance. As a student demonstrates the corresponding behavior, the teacher attaches a sample of the student's work. The placement instrument travels with the student until the student is transitioned into the mainstream classroom, permitting a smooth transition from English Language Development services to mainstream instruction.

Additional sources of information about students' language abilities with which to make placement decisions are the following (Cheng, 1987):

- Observe students in multiple settings, such as classroom, home, and playground.
- With the help of a trained interpreter if necessary, obtain histories (medical, family, previous education, immigration experience, home languages).
- Interview current or previous classroom teachers for information about learning style and classroom behavior.
- Seek information from other school personnel (counselor, nurse), especially if they are capable of assessing the home language.
- Ask the student's parents to characterize a student's language and performance skills in the home and the community.

Educators who draw from a variety of information sources can see the students' needs in a broader context and thus design a language program to meet these needs. Although it is impossible for teachers to assemble detailed information on multiple criteria for each student, teacher-devised checklists and observational data gathered as students participate in integrated learning activities can be used to confirm or adjust student placement (Lucas & Wagner, 1999).

As a caution, teachers and school personnel need to be aware that even after administering these tests, appropriate academic placement may be difficult. First, placement tests only measure language proficiency. They say nothing about a student's academic background. Students may be highly prepared in certain subject areas and very weak in others. They may be very strong academically but have poor English skills, or, conversely, have excellent English skills and few academic skills. Placement by age can be a problem. Students may need much more time in the system to learn English, but placement in an earlier grade may lead to social adjustment problems.

Redesignation/Exit Procedures

School districts need to establish reclassification criteria to determine when EL students have attained the English language skills necessary to succeed in an English-only classroom. The reclassification process may utilize multiple criteria (Rico, 2000), including, but not limited to, all of the following:

- Be based on objective standards;
- Measure speaking, comprehension, reading, and writing;
- Ensure that all academic deficits are addressed; and
- Include district evidence that students can participate meaningfully in the general program.

Some districts organize bilingual education advisory committees to ensure ethnic parent representation and participation in implementing redesignation criteria that are reliable, valid, and useful. Norm-referenced tests using national norms or district, regional, or state nonminority norms can be employed for purposes of reclassification, as can standardized criterion-referenced tests. States set various cutoff scores on language and achievement tests that are used as criteria for proficiency in the process of redesignation.

Limitations of Assessment

Tests play a large role in placing and reclassifying EL students. Often, pressure is applied for programs to redesignate students as fluent English-speaking in a short period of time. Tests may be used to place EL students into mainstream programs before they are ready. Continuing support—such as tutoring, follow-up assessment, and primary language help—is often not available after reclassification.

Standardized tests, though designed to be fair, are not necessarily well-suited as measures of language ability or achievement for English learners. In fact, some have argued that the very use of tests is unfair because tests are used to deprive people of color of their place in society. As Sattler (1974) comments, "No test can be culture fair if the culture is not fair" (p. 34). The goal of tests notwithstanding, both the testing situation and the test content may be rife with difficulties and bias for EL students.

Difficulties in the Testing Situation

The context in which a test is administered needs to be examined to understand how students may be affected. Factors within the context of testing such as anxiety, lack of experience with testing materials, time limitations, and rapport with the test administrator may cause difficulties for culturally and linguistically diverse students.

Anxiety. All students experience test anxiety, but this anxiety can be compounded if the test is alien to the students' cultural background and experiences. Certain test formats such as multiple-choice tests, cloze procedures, and think-aloud tasks may provoke higher levels of anxiety because students may fear these assessments inaccurately reflect their true proficiency in English (Oh, 1992; Scarcella, 1990). Allowing students to take practice exams may familiarize them with the test formats and reduce test anxiety.

Time Limitations.   Students may need more time to answer individual questions due to the time needed for mental translation and response formulation. Students from other cultures do not necessarily operate under the same conception of time as do European Americans. Some students may need a time extension or should be given untimed tests.

Rapport.   When testers and students do not share the same language or dialect, the success of the testing may be reduced. Students may not freely verbalize if they are shy or wary of the testing situation. Students who ostensibly share the primary language with the test administrator may not have in common certain dialectic features, with reduced understanding as a result. Rapport may also suffer if students are defensive about teachers' negative stereotypes or if students resent the testing situation itself.

Cultural Differences.   Students from some cultural groups may not feel comfortable making eye contact with a test administrator. The student may be unfamiliar with the test format. Cultures that discourage individuals from displaying knowledge may not be quick to answer questions and may be reluctant to guess unless they are certain they are accurate. They may be embarrassed to volunteer a response or receive positive feedback about their performance (Cloud, Genesee, & Hamayan, 2000).

Problematic Test Content

For the most part, language placement tests are well suited to assess language. Other tests, however, particularly achievement tests, may have translation problems or bias that affect the performance of English learners.

Equivalent First and Second Language Versions.   Translating an English language achievement test into another language or vice versa to create equivalent vocabulary items may cause some lack of correspondence in the frequency of the items. For example, *belfry* in English is a much less frequently understood term than its Spanish counterpart, *campanario.* The translation of a test is a hybrid belonging to neither culture. Additionally, even the most obvious test items may be difficult or impossible if the items have not been experienced by the child in either language (Sattler, 1974).

Linguistic Bias. Linguistic bias can take several forms. *Geographic bias* happens when test items feature terms used in particular geographic regions but that are not universally shared. *Dialectical bias* occurs when a student is tested using expressions relevant to certain dialect speakers that are not known to others. *Language-specific bias* is created when a test developed for use with one language is used with another language. For example, a test that measures a student's ability to use appropriate thanking behavior in English may demonstrate linguistic bias because the "thank-you" routines in another culture may occur under very different circumstances and require different behaviors. Instead of testing purely linguistic knowledge, such a test is actually biased toward those students whose first language has similar routines.

Cultural Bias. Tests may be inappropriate not only because the language provides a dubious cue for students but also because the content may represent overt or subtle bias. The values of the dominant culture appearing in test items may be understood differently or not at all by EL students.

Cultural content appearing in tests may provide difficulty for students without that cultural background. Many students never experience common European American food items such as bacon; common sports in the United States may be unfamiliar; musical instruments may be mysterious to students; even nursery rhymes and children's stories may refer only to one culture; and so on.

In addition, students may be naive about the process of testing and not recognize that tests perform a gatekeeping function. Deyhle (1987) found that students at the Red Canyon School (a pseudonym) on the Navajo Reservation did not perform well on standardized tests largely because they did not attribute importance to the test process. Students in grade 2 became very excited when taking tests but the test-taking behavior showed "inappropriate" shouting out and frequent sharing of answers among students.

Class Bias. Test content may represent a class bias; for example, the term *shallots* appeared on a nationally administered standardized achievement test, but only students whose families consume gourmet foods may be familiar with the term.

Content Bias. Even mathematics, a domain that many believe to be language free, has been shown to cause difficulties because language proficiency plays a relatively more important role than previously suspected (Kintsch & Greeno, 1985). (See Chapter 5 for examples.)

Interpretation of Test Results

One last caution in the assessment of English learners is to understand the emphasis of the test: Is it on language proficiency or on content knowledge? When testing content, educators should select or devise tasks on which EL students can achieve, regardless of their language proficiency. When scoring the test, teachers must evaluate students' responses to distinguish responses that are conceptually correct but may contain language problems from those that are conceptually incorrect. The box on page 194 offers attributes for the appropriate assessment of English learners.

Attributes of an Appropriate Assessment Plan for English Learners

1. Both content knowledge and language proficiency are tested.
2. Students' content knowledge and abilities in the native language as well as in English are assessed.
3. Various techniques are used to measure content knowledge and skills (e.g., portfolios, observations, anecdotal records, interviews, checklists, exhibits, students' self-appraisals, writing samples, dramatic renditions, and criterion-referenced tests).
4. The teacher is aware of the purpose of the assessment (e.g., whether the test is intended to measure verbal or writing skills, language proficiency, or content knowledge).
5. Students' backgrounds, including their educational experiences and parents' literacy, are taken into account.
6. Context is added to assessment tasks in the following ways:
   - Incorporates familiar classroom material as a stimulus, such as brief quotations, charts, graphics, cartoons, and works of art
   - Includes questions for small group discussion and individual writing
   - Mirrors learning processes with which students are familiar, such as the writing process and reading conferencing activities
7. Administration procedures match classroom instructional practices (e.g., cooperative small groups, individual conferences, and assessment in the language of instruction).
8. Extra time is given to complete or respond to assessment tasks.
9. Other accommodations are made, such as simplifying directions in English and/or paraphrasing in the student's native language, as well as permitting students to use dictionaries or word lists.

Source: Adapted from August and Pease-Alvarez (1996) and Navarrete and Gustke (1996).

Technical Concepts

A good test has three qualities: validity, reliability, and practicality. A test must test what it purports to test (valid), be dependable and consistent (reliable), and applicable to the situation (practical).

Validity

A test is *valid* if it measures what it claims to be measuring. If a test measures the ability to read English, then it should test that ability. A test has *content* validity if it samples the content that it claims to test in some representative way. For example, if a decision is made that a reading test should include proficiency in reading for inference or reading for vocabulary, then a test of reading would include tests of inference and vocabulary. *Empirical* validity is a measure of how effectively a test relates to some other known measure. One kind of empirical validity is *predictive*, or how well the test correlates with subsequent success or performance. A second type of empirical validity is *concurrent*, or how well the test correlates with another measure used at the same time. Teachers often apply this concept of concurrent validity when they grade examinations. Intuitively, they expect the better students to receive better scores. This is a check for concurrent validity between the examination and the students' daily performance.

Reliability

A test is *reliable* if it yields predictably similar scores when it is taken again. Although many variables can affect a student's test score—such as error introduced by fatigue, hunger, or poor lighting—these variables usually do not introduce very large deviations in students' scores. A student who scores 90 percent on a teacher-made test probably has scored 45 on one half of the test and 45 on the other half, regardless whether the halves are divided by odd/even items or first/last sequence. These are common ways of checking for reliability within the test itself within the test itself.

Practicality

A test may be valid and reliable but may cost too much to administer either in time or in money. A highly usable test should be relatively easy to administer and score. When a portfolio is kept to document student progress, issues of practicality still emerge. The portfolio should be easy to maintain, accessible to students, and scored with a rubric agreed on by teachers and students.

Many of the assessment practices and issues touched on in this chapter are further discussed in "An Examination of Assessment of Limited English Proficient Students" (Zehler, Hopstock, Fleischman, & Greniuk, 1994, online at http://www.ncbe.gwu.edu/miscpubs/siac/lepasses.htm). In addition, a classic article is DeGeorge's "Assessment and Placement of Language Minority Students: Procedures for Mainstreaming" (1987–1988, online at http://www.ncbe.gwu.edu/ncbepubs/classics/focus/03mainstream.htm).

Regardless of how valid, reliable, and practical a test may be, if it serves only the teachers' and the institution's goals, the students' language progress may not be promoted. Testing must instead be an integral part of a learning environment that encourages students to seek meaning and use a second language as a means to fulfill personal and academic goals.

CHAPTER

8 The Nature of Culture and Cultures in Contact

Unlike my grandmother, the teacher did not have pretty brown skin and a colorful dress. She wasn't plump and friendly. Her clothes were of one color and drab. Her pale and skinny form made me worry that she was very ill. . . . The teacher's odor took some getting used to also. Later I learned from the girls this smell was something she wore called perfume. The classroom . . . was terribly huge and smelled of medicine like the village clinic I feared so much. Those florescent light tubes made an eerie drone. Our confinement to rows of desks was another unnatural demand made on our active little bodies. . . . We all went home for lunch since we lived a short walk from the school. It took coaxing, and sometimes bribing, to get me to return and complete the remainder of the school day.

—Suina, 1985, writing his impressions upon entering school at age 6

The narrative of this Pueblo youth illustrates two cultural systems in contact. Neither is right or wrong, good or bad, superior or inferior. Suina was experiencing a natural human reaction that occurs when a person moves into a new cultural situation—culture shock. He had grown up in an environment that had subtly, through every part of his life, taught him appropriate ways of behavior—for example, how people looked (their color, their size, their dress, their ways of interacting) and how space was structured (the size of rooms, the types of lighting, the arrangement of furniture). His culture had taught him what was important and valuable. The culture Suina grew up in totally enveloped him and gave him a way to understand life. It provided him with a frame of reference through which he could make sense of the world.

Culture is so pervasive that often people perceive other cultures as strange and foreign without realizing that their own culture may be equally mystifying to others. Schools, as institutions of learning and socialization, are representatives of a particular culture. Culture, though largely invisible, influences instruction, policy, and learning in schools (see Figure I.1). Members of the educational community accept the organization, teaching/learning styles, and curriculum of the schools as natural and right. And the schools *are* natural and right for members of the community that created them. As children of nondominant cultures enter the schools, however, they may find the organization, teaching/learning styles, and curriculum to be alien, incomprehensible, and exclusionary.

As an initial step in learning about the complexity of culture and how the culture embodied within the school affects diverse students, the following sections examine the nature of culture and issues that occur when cultures come into contact. A knowledge of the deeper elements of culture—beyond superficial aspects such as food, clothing, holidays, and celebrations—can give teachers a crosscultural perspective that allows them to educate students to the greatest extent possible. These deeper elements include values, belief systems, family structures and child-rearing practices, language and nonverbal communication, expectations, gender roles, biases—all the fundamentals of life that affect learning.

The Nature of Culture

Does a fish understand water? Do people understand their own culture? Teachers are responsible to help pass on cultural knowledge through the schooling process. Can teachers (masters of the culture of schooling) step outside this culture long enough to see how it operates and to understand its effects on culturally diverse students? A way to begin is to examine what culture is, how culture affects perception, how geography affects culture, what differences occur naturally within cultural groups, and how cultures provide congruence.

Definitions of Culture

The term *culture* is used in many ways. It can refer to activities such as art, drama, and ballet or to items such as pop music, mass-media entertainment, and comic books. It can be used for distinctive groups in society—adolescents and their culture. It can be used as a general term for a society—the "French culture." Such uses do not, however, define what a culture is. As a field of study, culture is conceptualized in various ways (see Table 8.1). The definitions in Table 8.1 have common factors but vary in emphasis. The following definition of culture combines the ideas in Table 8.1:

> Culture is the explicit and implicit patterns for living, the dynamic system of commonly-agreed-upon symbols and meanings, knowledge, belief, art, morals, law, customs, behaviors, traditions and/or habits that are shared and make up the total way of life of a people, as negotiated by individuals in the process of constructing a personal identity.

The important idea is that culture involves both observable behaviors and intangibles such as beliefs and values, rhythms, rules, and roles. The concept of culture has evolved over the last 50 years away from the idea of culture as an invisible, patterning force to that of culture as an active tension between the "social short-

TABLE 8.1   Definitions of Culture

Definition	Source
The explicit and implicit patterns of behaviors, symbols, and ideas that constitute the distinctive achievements of human groups.	Kroeber & Kluckhohn (1952)
The sum total of a way of life of a people; patterns experienced by individuals as normal ways of acting, feeling, and being.	Hall (1959)
Patterns for living . . . the individual's role in the unending kaleidoscope of life situations of every kind and the rules and models for attitude and conduct in them.	Brooks (1968)
That complex whole which includes knowledge, belief, art, morals, law, and custom, and any other capabilities acquired by humans as members of society.	Tylor (in Pearson, 1974)
A dynamic system of symbols and meanings that involves an ongoing, dialectic process where past experience influences meaning, that in turn affects future experience, that in turn affects subsequent meaning, and so on.	Robinson (1985)
The means by which a community communicates . . . a commonly agreed upon set of meanings in interactions with one another.	Steele (1990)
Partial solutions to previous problems that humans create in joint mediated activity; the social inheritance embodied in artifacts and material constituents of culture as well as in practices and ideal symbolic forms; semi-organized hodgepodge of human inheritance. Culture is exteriorized mind and mind is interiorized culture.	Cole (1998)
Culture is a social symbolic construct, the product of self and other perceptions. . . . Cultural imagination or public consciousness is formed by centuries of discourses of various genres: maps and censuses, works of literature and other artistic productions, as well as by certain public discourse in the press and other media. Culture is . . . an interpersonal process of meaning construction.	Kramsch (1998)
Frames carried by each individual (nationality, gender, ethnicity, religion) that are internalized, individuated, and emerge in interactions.	Smith, Paige, & Steglitz (1998)

cuts" that make consensual society possible and the contributions and construction that each individual creates while living in society. Culture is not only the filter through which people see the world but it is also the raw dough from which each person fashions a life that is individual and satisfying.

Key Concepts about Culture

Despite the evolving definitions of culture, theorists agree on a few central ideas (see Damen, 1998). These concepts will be summarized here and will be treated with more depth in this chapter. First, culture is universal. Everyone in the world belongs to one or more cultures. Second, culture simplifies living. Social behaviors and customs offer structures to daily life that avoid interpersonal difficulties and endless negotiation about each detail of living. Third, cultural patterns are so familiar that members of a culture find it difficult to accept that other ways can be right. As cultural patterns are learned or acquired through observation and language, seldom are alternatives given. Fourth, cultures change over time, so learning about culture (one's own or others) is a lifelong pursuit.

Unfortunately, teachers—who, with parents, are the prime acculturators of society—often have little training as to the key role of culture in teaching and learning. Too often, culture is incorporated into classroom activities in superficial ways—as a group of artifacts (baskets, masks, distinctive clothing), or celebrations of holidays (Cinco de Mayo, Martin Luther King Jr. Day), or a laundry list of traits and facts (Asians are quiet; Hispanics are family oriented; Arabs are Moslem). Teachers who have a deeper view of culture and cultural processes are able to use their understanding to move beyond the superficial and to recognize that people live in characteristic ways. They understand that the observable manifestations of culture are but one aspect of the cultural web—the intricate pattern that weaves and binds a people together. Knowing that culture provides the lens through which people view the world, teachers can look at the "what" of a culture—the artifacts, celebrations, traits, and facts—and ask "why."

Perceptions of Culture

All cultures provide templates for the rituals of daily interaction: the way food is served, the way children are spoken to, the way people's needs are met. Some human needs are so fundamental that they are provided for in all cultures. Thus, all cultures share some universal characteristics. The manner in which these needs are met differs across cultures, and within a culture no two individuals view the world in exactly the same way. Each may exhibit very different personalities and behaviors, and may vary in their beliefs and values. What their culture does for them is provide them with an internalized way to organize and interpret experience. The interpretation is individual.

Cultural Universalism.   All human beings create culture. Members of a particular culture tend to believe that their own ways are the best. Culture influences how and what people see, hear, and feel, and how people and events are evaluated. Each group responds in its own way to meet humanity's basic needs: food, shelter, clothing, family organization, religion, government, social organization, defense, arts and crafts, knowledge acquisition, and survival skills.

Cultural influences help unify a society by providing a common base of communication and common social customs. The patterns that dominate a society form the *macroculture* of that society. For example, in the United States a variety of cultures co-exist, but the Anglo-European tradition has largely determined the social values and formal institutions. Individuals who grow up within a macroculture and never leave it may assume that many of its values are universal. When encountering cultures of radically different beliefs, they may be unable or unwilling to recognize that alternative beliefs and behaviors are legitimate.

Cultural Relativism.   The fact that each culture possesses its own particular traditions, values, and ideals means that the culture of a society provides judgments that make any action right or wrong for its members. Actions may only be judged in relation to the cultural setting in which they occur. This point of view has been called *cultural relativism.* Attempting to impose "international" standards on diverse peoples with different cultural traditions causes problems. This means that some cardinal values held by teachers in the United States are not cultural universals—for example, the value that academic activities should be based on competition or that children are expected to work on their own. Whole systems of instruction in the schools of the United States are based on these cultural values of competition and individualization (spelling contests, computer assisted instruction, independent study projects). Students who come from cooperative, group-conforming cultures where it is permissible and even desirable to work together and where it is abhorrent to display knowledge individually may find themselves negatively evaluated because of their different value systems, not because of any academic shortcomings.

Physical Geography and Its Effects on Culture and Learning

A social group must develop the knowledge, ideas, and skills that it needs to survive in the kind of environment the group inhabits. The geographical environment or physical habitat challenges the group to adapt to or modify the world to meet its needs. When the Native Americans were the sole inhabitants of the North American continent, a wide variety of cultures existed, a necessary response to the variety in the environment. The Iroquois were a village people who lived surrounded by tall wooden palisades. The Chumash, in contrast, lived a leisurely seashore existence on the California coast where fishing was plentiful and the climate moderate. Still a third group, the Plains Indians, were a nomadic people who followed the bison. Each group's culture was adapted for success in these environments.

Classrooms constitute physical environments. These environments have an associated culture. In a room in which the desks are in straight lines facing forward, participants are enculturated to listen as individuals and to respond when spoken to by the teacher. What a contrast this must be for a young Pueblo child whose learning takes place largely in the communal courtyards outside comfortable adobe dwellings and who is taught the traditional recipes by a mother or grandmother, or the secrets of tribal lore in an underground *kiva* by the men of the village. The physical environments in which learning takes place vary widely from one culture to another.

Intragroup Differences

Even among individuals from the same general cultural background, there are intragroup differences that affect their world view. In her study of students of Mexican descent, Matute-Bianchi (1991) described the differences between successful Mexican immigrant students and unsuccessful nonimmigrant Chicano students at a California high school. A range of identities and behaviors were identified that were associated with varying patterns of school performance. Most of the students could be placed in five major categories: (1) recent Mexican immigrants, (2) Mexican oriented, (3) Mexican American, (4) Chicano, and (5) Cholo.

The recent immigrants had arrived within the last three to five years and still referred to Mexico as home. They dressed differently from the rest of the student body, and their clothing was considered unstylish by other groups. Most of these students were monolingual in Spanish, with varying levels of English proficiency. Within the group, students used various differences to distinguish among themselves (e.g., rural versus urban, upper class versus working class, *mestizo* versus *indio*).

The second group of students had lived most of their lives in the United States but still maintained a strong identity as Mexicanos. Their parents were Mexican-born, and there was often considerable interaction with family members still in Mexico. These students tended to be bilingual.

The Mexican American students were almost always U.S.-born English speakers. Many were Mexican in last name only, were strongly acculturated, and did not manifest any overt cultural symbols. Often they did not speak Spanish well and preferred to use English.

The fourth group, the Chicanos, were usually the second generation of their family in the United States. They were among the most alienated Mexican-descent students in the school. They called themselves "homeboys" or "homegirls," in contrast to the academic achievers, whom they called "schoolboys" or "schoolgirls." They sometimes displayed an attitude of apathy toward or outright defiance of the school culture. Even though they declared a desire to do well in school, according to Matute-Bianchi's interviews, they frequently disrupted class or were absent.

The last group, Cholo, were frequently identified as gang members by other students. Even though some exhibited obvious stylistic cultural symbols (particular kinds of pants, shirts, shoes, and ways of walking), many were not necessarily gang-affiliated.

Each of these groups can be considered a *microculture* within the larger microculture of people of Mexican descent living within the United States.

In this case, social identification and language usage, as well as dress, were the markers of the distinct microcultures. In some cases, generational experiences cause intragroup differences. The first generation of Japanese came to the United States starting about 1900 and were, for the most part, young men who became agricultural laborers or skilled craftsmen. They often referred to themselves as *issei* or first-generation immigrants to the United States. The industrious labor of this generation was often seen as a threat by European Americans, and these immigrants were often the target of discrimination. Discrimination peaked after the attack on Pearl Harbor, when *issei* were divested of their property and removed to relocation camps. Their children, the *nisei* generation (born in the United States), bore the responsibility of reassimilating into the macroculture after World War II. This generation is often considered to have a very low ethnic profile, perhaps as a response to the treatment given to their parents (Leathers, 1967).

As immigrants enter American life, they make conscious or unconscious choices about which aspects of their culture to preserve and which to modify. These decisions are a response to cultural contact.

Cultural Contact

We cannot know all things about all cultures, but it is possible to understand what happens when cultures come into contact with one another and how this contact can affect schooling. When cultures meet, they affect one another: Cultures can be swallowed up (*assimilation*); one culture may adapt to a second (*acculturation*); both may adapt to each other (*accommodation*); or they may coexist (*pluralism* or *biculturalism*). When an individual comes in contact with another culture, there are characteristic responses, usually stages, an individual goes through in adapting to the new situation. Contact between cultures is often not a benign process. It may be fraught with issues of prejudice, discrimination, and misunderstandings. Means of mediation or resolution must be found to alleviate cultural conflict, particularly in classrooms.

Concepts of Cultural Contact

The 1980s witnessed an unprecedented flow of immigrants and refugees into the United States. Many of them were from countries in Central America undergoing revolutions. About 300,000 to 400,000 Salvadorans immigrated to the United States between 1979 and 1983; almost one million Guatemalans became refugees as a result of war in that country, many settling in the United States. After the bloody overthrow of Somoza's dictatorship, over 200,000 Nicaraguans left their country, 30,000 of whom settled in Miami. At the turn of the twenty-first century, the situation of huge numbers of immigrants from selected countries has abated, but the pressure on U.S. society to accept large numbers of immigrants has not lessened.

One of the impacts of this immigration is that many school districts not only have students speaking three or more languages in a single classroom but they also have students who speak the same non-English language but who come from different cultures. School officials have found, for example, that many immigrants from Central America do not follow the same pattern of school performance as Mexican American students. These demographic issues pose a number of questions about cultures in contact. Are there characteristic differences in the patterns of adaptation to schooling among individuals from various cultures? Can we understand how to increase the school success of all students by studying the process of cultural contact?

Cultures in general and individuals specifically respond in certain ways to contact with another culture. This contact can result in assimilation, acculturation, accommodation, pluralism, or biculturalism. Each of these concepts will be explored in relation to the classroom.

Assimilation. Assimilation is a process in which members of an ethnic group are absorbed into the dominant culture, losing their culture in the process (deculturalization). This is done without regard to the ramifications for ethnic community life or the cultural identity of individuals. For assimilation to be complete, there must be both cultural and structural assimilation (Gordon, 1964). *Cultural assimilation* is the process by which individuals adopt the behaviors, values, beliefs, and lifestyle of the dominant culture. *Structural assimilation* is participation in the social, political, and economic institutions and organizations of mainstream society. It is structural assimilation that has been problematic for many. Gordon (1964) found that only limited structural assimilation occurred for groups other than white Protestant immigrants from northern and western Europe.

Individuals may make a choice concerning their degree of cultural assimilation. However, the dominant society determines the extent of structural assimilation. These two related but differing concepts have important consequences in classrooms. Teachers may be striving to have students assimilate (see the Point/Counterpoint on page 204), but may be blind to the fact that some of their students will not succeed because of attitudes and structures of the dominant society.

Acculturation. Acculturation means adapting effectively to the mainstream culture. This concept should be distinguished from *enculturation,* the process through which individuals learn the patterns of their own culture. To acculturate is to adapt to a second culture without necessarily giving up one's first culture. It is an additive process in which, while individuals adapt to the mainstream culture, their right to participate in their own heritage is preserved (Finnan, 1987). Some researchers have emphasized the importance of acculturation for success in school. For example, Schumann (1978a) claims that the greater the level of acculturation in a particular individual, the greater the second language learning will be for that individual.

Assimilation, not acculturation, was the aim of many immigrants who sought to become part of the "melting pot." More recently, minority groups and their advocates have begun to assert that minority ethnic groups have a right, if not a responsibility, to maintain valued elements of their ethnic cultures (Kopan, 1974).

Point/Counterpoint

What is the teacher's role in the instruction of culturally diverse students?
Schools have traditionally been society's melting pot, the place in which the children of immigrants are inculcated with the basics of U.S. culture and cultural values. Teachers were the front-line workers in the struggle to enculturate newcomers. Is this the best role for teachers to play in the education of culturally diverse students?

Point: **Teachers are "assimilators."**
Teachers who see themselves as agents of assimilation tend to promote the melting pot as a model for their students. This entails the belief that nonmainstream students should change their cultural patterns to match those of the society at large, and should seek success in mainstream terms. Students whose beliefs and behaviors do not mirror those of successful mainstream students may be seen as lacking in ability, prior knowledge, motivation, or communication skills. In applying a single frame of reference to denote success, such teachers may not realize that standard measures of achievement and aptitude have traditionally been most appropriate for European American, middle-class groups, as have instructional content and strategies. The past experiences, knowledge, and learning styles of ethnically different students may not be fully recognized and valued, either by the teacher or by mainstream peers. Lack of respect and esteem from teacher and peers may lead to feelings of rejection and lowered expectations, a recipe for reduced academic success (see Bennett, 1990).

Counterpoint: **Teachers are "accommodators."**
Teachers who can accommodate instruction to facilitate learning for nonmainstream students help to widen the doors of opportunity for classroom learning and academic success. When students feel respected by teachers for who they are, regardless of their cultural, ethnic, or socioeconomic background, they can maintain throughout their school years the natural excitement and love of learning that is characteristic of children just entering school. Some students respond better to cooperation than to competition; some are motivated by peer approval, external rewards, or the chance to perform before others. Whatever the background, prior knowledge, motivation, or communication skills each student brings, the teacher who has a variety of teaching techniques, activities, and themes can inspire positive learning within all students. Teachers may need to spend additional moments with nonmainstream students to teach those responses, behaviors, and language skills that are often assumed to be present in students from homes that represent mainstream, middle-class European America. Flexibility (Ramírez, 1991) and the ability and desire to innovate, if necessary, to meet the learning needs of culturally diverse students is a characteristic of accommodating teachers. These teachers realize that nontraditional schooling may be a key to unlocking achievement in the nontraditional student.

The pluralist position is that coexistence of multicultural traditions within a single society provides a variety of alternatives that enrich life in the United States.

Schools are the primary places in which children of various cultures learn about the mainstream culture. Sometimes culture is taught explicitly as a part of the ELD curriculum (Seelye, 1984). According to Cortés (1993):

> Acculturation . . . should be a primary goal of education. Schools have an obligation to help students acculturate because additive acculturation contributes to individual empowerment and expanded life choices. But schools should not seek subtractive assimilation, which can lead to personal and cultural disempowerment by eroding students' multicultural abilities to function effectively both within the mainstream and within their own ethnic milieus. School-fostered acculturation is empowering—"adducation." School-fostered assimilation is disempowering—"subtractucation." Although assimilation is acceptable, it should be regarded as a student's choice and not as something for the school to impose. In our increasingly multicultural society, even traditional additive acculturation is not the only acculturation goal. Education for the twenty-first century should embrace what I call "multiculturation," the blending of *multiple* and *acculturation*. (p. 4)

Accommodation. Accommodation is a two-way process: Members of the mainstream culture change in adapting to a minority culture, the members of which in turn accept some cultural change as they adapt to the mainstream. Thus, accommodation is a mutual process. To make accommodation a viable alternative in schools, teachers need to demonstrate that they are receptive to learning from the diverse cultures in their midst, and they need to also teach majority students the value of "interethnic reciprocal learning" (Gibson, 1991b).

Philips (1972) gives examples of ways in which non-Native American teachers can adapt schooling to accommodate the culture of Native American students.

> Conspicuous in Indian classes is the absence of the ubiquitous "show and tell" or "sharing," through which students learn to get up in front of the class, standing where the teacher stands, and presenting, as the teacher might, a monologue relating an experience or describing a treasured object that is supposed to be of interest to the rest of the class. When asked whether this activity was used in the classroom, one teacher explained that she had previously used it, but so few children ever volunteered to "share" that she finally discontinued it. . . . While in non-Indian classes students are given opportunities to ask the teacher questions in front of the class, and do so, Indian students are given fewer opportunities for this because when they do have the opportunity, they don't use it. Rather, the teacher of Indians allows more periods in which she is available for individual students to approach her alone and ask their questions where no one else can hear them. (pp. 382–383)

Pluralism. Pluralism is the condition in which members of diverse cultural groups have equal opportunities for success, in which cultural similarities and differences are valued, and in which students are provided cultural alternatives

(BEOutreach, 1993). But does pluralism endanger society, as cultural purists have charged, by heightening ethnic group identity, leading to separatism and intergroup antagonism? Although some separatism is unavoidable, in order for society to survive, all groups must conform to some set of common, necessary norms. A dynamic relationship between ethnic groups is inevitable. In a healthy society, these groups may sometimes clash in the process of coexistence, but the strength of the society is founded on a basic willingness to work together to resolve conflicts. According to Bennett (1990), schools can evince *integrated pluralism* (actively trying to foster interaction among different groups) or *pluralistic coexistence* (different racial or ethnic groups informally resegregate). Integration creates the conditions for cultural pluralism. Merely mixing formerly isolated ethnic groups does not go far enough, because groups rapidly "unmix" and resegregate.

Biculturalism.   Biculturalism is the state of being able to function successfully in two cultures. Everyone is to some extent bicultural. For example, the medical student who attends class in the morning and accompanies practitioners in hospital rounds in the afternoon dwells in two distinct cultures every day. Every pluralistic society (take, for example, life in New York City) contains individuals who become a part of more than one culture. At a minimum level, everyone who works outside the home functions daily in two cultures—personal (home) and professional (work). For some individuals, the distance between the cultures of work and home are almost indistinguishable, while for others the distance is great. For example, Native American children sent to Bureau of Indian Affairs boarding schools often experienced great difficulties in adjusting to the disparate cultures of home and school.

What is it like to be bicultural in the United States? Bicultural people are sometimes viewed with distrust. The suspicion toward Japanese Americans during World War II, and the resulting internment is an example of this. Parents may also be threatened by their bicultural children. Appalachian families who moved to large cities to obtain work often pressured their children to maintain an agrarian, preindustrial lifestyle, a culture that is in many ways inconsistent with urban environments (Pasternak, 1994).

The process of becoming bicultural is not without stress, especially for students who are expected to internalize dissimilar, perhaps conflicting values. Darder (1991) defines biculturalism in the following manner:

> a process wherein individuals learn to function in two distinct sociocultural environments: their primary culture, and that of the dominant mainstream culture of the society in which they live. It represents the process by which bicultural human beings mediate between the dominant discourse of educational institutions and the realities they must face as members of subordinate cultures. (pp. 48–49)

Madrid (1991) describes the experience of having been raised in an isolated mountain village in New Mexico and ultimately becoming a member of the faculty at Dartmouth College. As he grew older and his schooling moved him into an increasingly European American environment, the daily challenge of living in two worlds with conflicting values resulted in his internalizing and embracing his own complex consciousness.

Cultural Congruence

Cultures are more than the mere sum of their traits. There is a wholeness about cultures, an integration of the various responses to human needs. "A culture, like an individual, is a more or less consistent pattern of thought and action" (Benedict, 1934, p. 42). In classrooms, cultural content takes two forms. The first form is the explicit teaching of culture by examining external features of a culture, such as art and artifacts. For example, a teacher who travels to Japan may return laden with kimonos and chopsticks, hoping these objects will document Japanese culture. There is a danger here: Cultures cannot be understood only by assembling a collection of cultural artifacts; rather, the living patterns and the values of the culture must be examined.

The second form of cultural content is harder to detect: the actual contact of cultures that occurs daily in U.S. schools. In this contact, the congruence or lack thereof between mainstream and minority cultures has lasting effects on students. Students from families whose cultural values are similar to those of the European American culture may be relatively advantaged in schools. (See Overachievement in Chapter 6.) In contrast, African American students learn at home to project their personalities and call attention to their individual attributes (Gay, 1975). Such actions are not generally accepted by the school culture, often leading to poor academic performance by African American children and increased disciplinary action by teachers with the intent of discouraging physical displays of individuality.

Teachers, who have the responsibility to educate students from diverse cultures, find it relatively easy to help students whose values, beliefs, and behaviors are congruent with U.S. schooling but find it perhaps painful to work with others. The teacher who can find a common ground with diverse students will promote their further education. Relationships between individuals or groups of differing cultures are built through commitment, a tolerance for diversity, and a willingness to communicate. The teacher acting as intercultural educator accepts and promotes cultural content in the classroom as a valid and vital component of the instructional process, and helps students to achieve within the cultural context of the school.

Stages of Individual Cultural Contact

Experiencing a second culture causes emotional ups and downs. Reactions to a new culture vary, but there are distinct stages in the process of experiencing a different culture (Brown, 2000). The stages are characterized by typical emotions and behaviors beginning with elation or excitement, moving to anxiety or disorientation, and culminating in some degree of adjustment (Levine & Adelman, 1982). These same emotional stages can occur for students. The intensity will vary depending on the degree of similarity between home and school culture, the individual child, and the teacher.

Euphoria. Euphoria may result from the excitement of experiencing new customs, foods, and sights. This may be a "honeymoon" period in which the newcomer is fascinated and stimulated by experiencing a new culture.

Culture Shock. Culture shock may follow euphoria as cultural differences begin to intrude. The newcomer is increasingly aware of being different and may be disoriented by cultural cues that result in frustration. Deprivation of the familiar may cause a loss of self-esteem. Depression, anger, or withdrawal may result. The severity of this shock may vary as a function of the personality of the individual, the emotional support available, and the perceived or actual differences between the two cultures.

Adaptation. Adaptation to a new culture may take several months to several years. Some initial adjustment takes place when everyday activities such as housing and shopping are no longer a problem. Long-term adjustment may take several forms. Ideally, the newcomer accepts some degree of routine in the new culture with habits, customs, and characteristics borrowed from the host culture. This results in a feeling of comfort with friends and associates and the newcomer feels capable of negotiating most new and different situations. On the other hand, individuals who do not adjust as well may feel lonely and frustrated. A loss of self-confidence may result. Certain aspects of the new culture may be actively rejected. Eventually, successful adaptation results in newcomers finding value and significance in the differences and similarities between cultures and in being able to actively express themselves and to create a full range of meaning in the situation.

In the classroom, some students may show culture shock as withdrawal, depression, or anger. Mental fatigue may result from continually straining to comprehend the new culture. Individuals may need time to process personal and emotional as well as academic experiences. Great care must be taken that the teacher does not belittle or reject a student who is experiencing culture shock.

Dynamics of Prejudice

One factor that inhibits cultural adaptation is prejudice. Although prejudice can include favorable feelings, it is generally used in a negative sense. Allport (1954) defined ethnic prejudice as follows:

> Ethnic prejudice is an antipathy based on a faulty and inflexible generalization. It may be felt or expressed. It may be directed toward a group as a whole, or toward an individual because he is a member of that group. (p. 10)

Prejudice takes various forms: excessive pride in one's own ethnic heritage, country, or culture so that others are viewed negatively; ethnocentrism where the world revolves around oneself and one's own culture; a prejudice against members of a certain racial group; and stereotypes that label all or most members of a group. All humans are prejudiced to some degree, but it is when people act on those prejudices that discriminatory practices and inequalities result.

Allport (1954) offers several explanations for the phenomenon of prejudice. First, an historical explanation suggests that people may become prejudiced as an outcome of the history of relations between groups of people; for example, European Americans may be prejudiced against African Americans because of the history of slavery. A sociocultural explanation is that the pressures of urban life have caused people to depersonalize and discriminate against minorities. A third explanation is that all groups discriminate against nonmembers and that such discrimination is a part of the psychology of humans. Another explanation is that people learn prejudice from others around them. A psychodynamic explanation is that people are prejudiced because prejudice acts as a release from personal frustration. Yet another explanation is that prejudice is an outcome of people's perception of the world; some people view others as repulsive, annoying, or threatening. A last explanation is that members of cultures may view the traits of other cultures in terms of their own values and view alternative behaviors negatively.

A simpler, more global explanation for prejudice is that it is based on fear—fear of the unknown, fear of engulfment by foreigners, or fear of contamination. Allport observes that much of the human tendency to separate into groups may be due to a need for ease. Eating, visiting, even mating are easier when they are done with one's own kind. People find congeniality and pride in distinct ethnic group identity. This impulse for separatism, however, may readily lead to misunderstanding of other groups.

A closer look at various forms of prejudice, such as racism and stereotyping, as well as resulting discriminatory practices, can lead to an understanding of these issues. Teachers can then be in a position to adopt educational methods that are most likely to reduce prejudice.

Racism.   Racism is the view that a person's race determines psychological and cultural traits—and, moreover, that one race is superior to another. Racism is a process that categorizes people according to observable traits and then uses these to infer personality, behavioral, or mental traits. For example, one nineteenth-century justification for slavery was that African Americans lacked initiative, were not as intelligent as European Americans, and therefore had to be taken care of. Racism can also be cultural when one believes that the traditions, beliefs, language, artifacts, music, and art of other cultures are inferior. On the basis of such beliefs, racists justify discriminating against or scapegoating other groups. Weinberg (1990) points out that racism is "a system of privilege and penalty," in which people are rewarded or punished by simply belonging to a particular group regardless of their merits or faults. More importantly, goods and services as well as respect is distributed in accordance with such judgments of unequal worth.

Racism is often expressed in hate crimes, which are public expressions of hostility directed at a specific group or individuals. These may take the form of harassment (scrawling graffiti on people's homes; pelting houses with eggs; burning crosses on lawns; verbally taunting children; sending hate-filled emails to individuals or groups; carving swastikas into public textbooks, school desks, or other property; etc.) or, at the extreme, assaults and murder directed toward minorities (Díaz-Rico, 1999). At present, data show that 60 percent of hate crimes are directed toward African Americans. *Youth at the Edge,* a report from the Southern Poverty Law Center (1999), describes a new underclass of disenchanted youth in the United States susceptible to hate groups. Perhaps due to feelings of frustration at social and economic forces they cannot control, those who are marginally employed and poorly educated often seek out scapegoats to harass. Too often, the targets are immigrants, particularly those of color. The availability of information on the Internet has unfortunately encouraged a resurgence of hate groups worldwide. Over 250 Internet sites are available that foment White supremacy and other forms of racial hatred. Schools are often prime sites in which hate crimes are committed. This fact underscores the urgency of educators' efforts to understand and combat racism.

Stereotypes.   Stereotypes often result from racist beliefs. A stereotype is a preconceived and oversimplified generalization about a particular ethnic or religious group, race, or gender. The danger of stereotyping is that people are not considered as individuals but are categorized with all other members of a group (Anti-Defamation League of B'nai B'rith, 1986). One might believe that a racial group has a global trait (e.g., Asians are "overambitious overachievers"), and subsequently all Asians one meets are judged in this stereotypic way. Conversely, an individual may judge an entire group on the basis of an experience with a single individual. A stereotype may be favorable or unfavorable; but, whether it is positive or negative, the results are negative: The perspective of an entire group of people is distorted.

Teaching against Racism.   Racism and stereotyping are difficult to combat because this type of prejudice is irrational. Furthermore, many teachers feel that teaching about values and beliefs is not a part of the curriculum. They have been reluctant to address these subjects, as well as topics such as racism, prejudice, and discrimination. To work effectively with diverse student populations, however, teachers can open the dialogue and help students understand the effect that racist ideas and behaviors have on all people. Even students who voice racist beliefs or act in a prejudiced manner may not be deeply prejudiced and may benefit from an attempt to reduce ethnic group stereotypes. An ideal outcome of discussions of racial and cultural heritage would be that students would feel an ethnic pride in their own background without becoming ethnocentric and believing that their group was superior to others.

School curriculum can be used to help students be aware of the existence and impact of racism. Science and health teachers can debunk myths surrounding the concept of race. Content area teachers can help students develop skills in detecting bias. Positive interracial attitudes can be fostered whenever students have an opportunity to work together. Students and teachers alike must raise awareness of racism in the attempt to achieve racial equality and justice. Bennett, in the book *Comprehensive Multicultural Education* (1990), offers a checklist (pp. 352–354) that students can use to recognize examples of racism. Such a list can be used as the springboard for discussion. Other antiracist activities and discussion topics include the following:

- Recognize racist history and its impact on oppressors and victims.
- Understand the origins of racism and why people hold racial prejudices and stereotypes.
- Be able to identify racist images in the language and illustrations of books, films, television, news media, and advertising.
- Be able to identify current examples of racism in the immediate community and society as a whole.
- Identify specific ways of combating racism.
- Examine personal attitudes, experiences, and behaviors concerning racism. (Bennett, 1990, p. 78)

Programs to Combat Racism.   The Southern Poverty Law Center has a National Campaign for Tolerance, a new initiative co-chaired by Rosa Parks and Morris Dees. Its goal is to enlist five million people to participate in tolerance initiatives and related activities in their local communities. The center will send individuals who sign on to the campaign a Citizen's Action Kit containing tools for fighting hate and intolerance. A website, tolerance.org, serves as a national resource of teachers, parents, and students seeking to promote tolerance. The Southern Poverty Law Center is available at http://www.splcenter.org.

Institutional Racism.   Institutional racism consists of "those laws, customs, and practices which systematically reflect and produce racial inequalities in American society" (Jones, 1981). An individual may not personally be a racist, but may work in an institution in which policies and practices effectively discriminate against a group of people as a class. Classroom teaching that aims at detecting and reducing racism may be a futile exercise when the institution itself—the school—promotes racism through its policies and practices. For example, many testing practices in schools are ethnocentric and racist because some students are stigmatized and labeled while others are not. The European American culture represented in these tests makes it difficult for members of certain other racial and ethnic groups to identify with the test content. A second example of institutionalized racism is the shortage of minority group teachers in classrooms where children are predominately of minority background. Is this the fault of the European American teacher who is employed in this classroom? Probably not. The nature of the institution of schooling itself has made it difficult for minorities to attain the education and certification needed for employment as a teacher.

Classism.   In the United States, racism is compounded with classism, the distaste of the middle and upper classes for the lifestyles and perceived values of the lower classes. Although this classism is often directed against linguistic and cultural minorities—a typical poor person in the American imagination is urban, Black, and young, either a single teen mother or her issue—portraying poverty that way makes it easier to stigmatize the poor (Henwood, 1997). In fact, as Henwood points out, although a larger percentage of minorities live in poverty, there are far more poor European Americans in the United States than there are poor minorities. In 1993, the poverty rate for non-Hispanic Whites was 9.9 percent. Therefore, almost half (48.1 percent) of the poor are non-Hispanic Whites.

Classism has engendered its own stereotype against poor European Americans—for example, the stereotyped White indigent who is called, among other things, "White trash" (Wray & Newitz, 1997). The distaste for "White trash" on the part of the U.S. middle class is compounded in part by ignorance and frustration. According to Wray and Newitz, "Americans love to hate the poor.... In a country as steeped in the myth of classlessness, we are often at a loss to explain or understand poverty. The white trash stereotype serves as a useful way of blaming the poor for being poor" (p. 1). Often, middle-class teachers view the poor as unwilling or unable to devote resources to schooling. Ogbu (1978) postulates that indigenous minorities may be unable to accept the belief in the power of education to elevate individuals to middle-class status. Poor Whites may bear the brunt of a "caste-like" status in the United States as much as do linguistic and cultural minorities.

Discrimination.   Discrimination refers to actions that serve to limit the social, political, or economic opportunities of particular groups. Discriminatory practices tend to legitimize the unequal distribution of power and resources between groups defined by such factors as race, language, culture, gender, and/or social class. There may be no intent to discriminate on the part of an institution such as a school; however, interactions with minority students may reflect unquestioned assumptions about the abilities or participation of these students. Blatant discrimination, in which differential education for minorities is legally sanctioned, may be a thing of the past, but discrimination persists. *De facto* segregation continues; most students of color are still found in substandard schools. Students of color tend to receive a curriculum that is watered down and at a lower level than that received by European American students. Schools with a high percentage of minority enrollment tend to employ faculty who have less experience and academic preparation. Teachers who do not share the ethnic background of their students may not communicate well with their students or may tend to avoid interaction, including eye and physical contact (Ortiz, 1988). Teachers may communicate low expectations to minority students. The "hidden curriculum" of tracking and differential treatment results in schools that perpetuate the structural inequities of society. Thus, school becomes a continuation of the discrimination experienced by minorities in other institutions in society (Grant & Sleeter, 1986).

In the past, those in power often used physical force to exclude people and to discriminate. Those who did not go along were physically punished: Children were separated from their parents and their own group and were punished for speaking their language or adhering to their own cultural or ethnic customs. With the spread of literacy, there is a trend away from the use of physical force and toward the use of shame and guilt. The school plays a part in this process. The values, norms, and ideology of those in power are taught in the school. Skutnabb-Kangas (1981, 1993) calls this symbolic-structural violence. Direct punishment is replaced by self-punishment and the group discriminated against internalizes the shame associated with rule breaking. The emotional and intellectual bonds of internalized injustice make the situation of minorities more difficult. Schooling, too often, helps to keep minority children powerless—socially, economically, politically—and perpetuates the powerlessness of parents.

School programs in which children are separated from their own group are examples of structural discrimination. Students are not taught enough of their own language and culture to be able to appreciate it and are made to feel ashamed of their parents and origins. The message is that the native language is only useful as a temporary instrument in learning the dominant language. Majority students, on the other hand, are seldom taught enough about the minority culture to achieve appreciation. Skutnabb-Kangas (1981) cites a variety of examples of discrimination that has taken place against minority students in Swedish and Norwegian schools. These examples demonstrate the internalization of shame.

> The headmaster said, "You have a name which is difficult for us Swedes to pronounce. Can't we change it? . . . And besides, perhaps some nasty person will make fun of your name." "Well, I suppose I'd better change it," I thought. (p. 316)

> I love my parents and I respect them but what they are and everything they know count for nothing. . . . Like lots of Turkish children here, they know lots about farming and farm animals, . . . but when is a Turkish child given the task at school of describing the cultivation of vines? (p. 317)

> Sometimes the teacher asks us to sit together in pairs and then no one wants to sit with me. Even when the teacher says someone has got to sit with me, still no one wants to. (p. 317)

> The longer all this went on, the more urgent and deep the pressure to conform. I began to avoid my brothers and sisters. . . . I refused to go shopping with my mother and when we had a Christmas party at school, I simply told my parents they weren't to come. (p. 318)

Strategies for Conflict Resolution

Students experiencing cultural conflict may meet racism and anti-immigration sentiments from others in their environment. Subtle incidents occur every day across campuses in the United States. Graffiti is the most visual evidence: Obscene wall messages foster hatred against ethnic, racial, and religious groups. Verbal abuse, threats, and physical violence, motivated by negative feelings and opinions, are all too common. The scope of these incidents together with the increasing involvement of young adults (see Bodinger-deUriarte, 1991) is a disturbing trend on today's campuses. Schools are crucial to the resolution to hate crime because the young are perpetrators and the schools are staging grounds. Policies, curriculum, and antiracism programs are needed to prevent and control hate crimes.

Even well-intended educators have found that censoring racially and ethnically incendiary speech is problematic (Siegel, 1993). The University of Wisconsin at Madison instituted a hate speech code on September 1, 1989, in an attempt to reduce the frequency of racist epithets and hate crimes on campus. The Wisconsin American Civil Liberties Union brought suit against the University of Wisconsin, arguing that the speech codes were unconstitutional. Minority students on campus filed many claims, charging students and student groups with incidences of hate speech. In the end, the university rescinded the speech code and, in its place, prohibited only epithets that "would tend to evoke an immediate violent response" (p. 46). The irony was that the hate speech code could not have prohibited or punished any of the series of racial hate incidents that led to its inception. U.S. courts have upheld the notion that U.S. citizens have the right to free speech, even speech which denigrates others. Rather than prohibiting public speech that exhibits racial or ethnic prejudice, schools must find ways to alter the school climate or work directly with individuals to increase interethnic harmony.

> I am sensitive to cultural barriers that exist among educators. These barriers are created by lack of communication between people coming from different backgrounds and cultures. We don't discuss cultural conflicts openly. We have learned that conflicts are negative and produce racial disharmony when, in fact, the opposite is true—Latina elementary teacher. (The Institute for Education in Transformation, 1992)

In general, research suggests that substantive changes in attitudes, behaviors, and achievement occur only when the entire school environment changes to demonstrate a multicultural atmosphere. Parents are welcomed in the school; counselors, teachers, and other staff utilize culturally compatible practices; and programs are instituted that permit interactions among students of different backgrounds. Appropriate programs are needed to prepare the communities and schools that anticipate large numbers of minority students. Students must learn to understand cultures different from their own. A culturally receptive host school may preclude these minority students from internalizing negativity about their culture and customs. Cooperative learning groups and programs that allow interaction among students of diverse backgrounds usually result in fewer incidents of name calling and ethnic slurs as well as in improved academic achievement (Nieto, 2000).

It is not easy for students to maintain pride in cultures that represent minority points of view if these cultures suffer low status in the majority culture. Students feel conflict in this pride if their culture is devalued. Many students face the burden of having either to deny or lose their culture if they want to succeed or to keep it and fail (Nieto, 2000). In many cases, bilingual programs are responsible for helping students to value their home language and culture. When the languages and cultures of students are highly evident in their schools and teachers refer to them explicitly, they gain status. Schools that convey the message that all cultures are of value—by displaying explicit welcome signs in many languages, by attempts to involve parents, by a deliberate curriculum of inclusion, and by using affirmative action to promote hiring of a diverse faculty—help to maintain an atmosphere that reduces interethnic conflict.

Educational programs that are effective in reducing prejudice, according to Allport (1954), have the following characteristics:

- Lead to a sense of equality in social status
- Occur in ordinary purposeful pursuits
- Avoid artificiality
- Enjoy the sanction of the community in which they occur
- Involve participants who regard themselves as part of a team

Johnson and Johnson (1979, 1994, 1995) have emphasized the usefulness of cooperative, heterogeneous grouping in the classroom in the resolution of classroom conflict. Explicit training for elementary students in negotiation and mediation procedures has proven effective in managing conflict, especially when such programs focus on safely expressing feelings, taking the perspective of the other, and providing the rationale for diverse points of view (Johnson, Johnson, Dudley, & Acikgoz, 1994). Especially critical is the role of a mediator in establishing and maintaining a balance of power between two parties in a dispute, protecting the weaker party from intimidation, and assuring that both parties have a stake in the process and the outcome of mediation (Umbreit, 1991). In contrast, those programs that teach about "group differences," involve exhortation or mere verbal learning, or are designed directly for "prejudice reduction" are usually not effective.

Should interethnic conflict occur, techniques exist for problem solving. Katz and Lawyer (1993), in their book *Conflict Resolution: Building Bridges,* offer means of understanding and resolving conflicts. Many authorities, particularly in schools, attempt to handle conflict by punitive and suppressive measures or, at the other extreme, by "counseling" individuals without administering consequences for irresponsible or inflammatory acts. By understanding the source of conflicts and teaching various parties to value productive dialogue that includes compromise, collaboration, and accommodation to diverse views, conflicts can be resolved in a manner that forges positive cooperation and communication.

There is much that teachers can do to resolve conflicts in the classroom. First, teachers can talk to students privately, encouraging the sharing of perceptions on volatile issues and communicating expectations that students will be able to resolve their differences. In this way, teachers can intervene in the early stages of conflicts to defuse the problem. If problems escalate to the point of confrontation, allowing students to vent feelings as a group and setting aside a brief period of verbal expression can provide an outlet for frustration. A teacher must resolve to be calm in the face of verbalized anger and hostility, and violence or personal attacks should not be tolerated. Teachers seeking information about conflict resolution at the school or societal level may wish to explore professional references in this area. TESOLers for

Social Responsibility (TSR) is a caucus within the organization Teachers of English to Speakers of Other Languages, Inc., that brings teachers together who are actively engaged in integrating language teaching with social responsibility, world citizenship, and an awareness of global issues such as peace, human rights, and the environment. More information is available at http://tesol.org.

One should not assume that cultural contact entails cultural conflict. Perhaps the best ways to prevent conflict is to include a variety of cultural content and make sure the school recognizes and values cultural diversity. If conflict does occur, however, there are means to prevent its escalation. Teachers should be aware of conflict resolution techniques before they are actually needed.

This chapter has emphasized the profound influence of culture on people's perceptions, feelings, and actions, and the variety of ways in which individuals experience contact with other cultures. Let us revisit briefly Joe Suina, the Pueblo youth whose contact with school created cultural conflict for him. How could the school have been more accommodating? Ideally, Suina's teacher would be a Pueblo Indian and would share his culture. Classrooms in a Pueblo school would resemble the home, with intimate spaces and furniture designed for student comfort. If these conditions are not feasible, a non-Pueblo teacher would accommodate to the ways of the students in the same way that students are expected to accommodate to the school. Actually, students of any culture would appreciate schools that were more comfortable and less institutional, wouldn't they?

9 Cultural Diversity in the United States

Before I came to America I had dreams of life here. I thought about tall Anglos, big buildings, and houses with lawns. I was surprised when I arrived to see so many kinds of people—Black people, Asians. I found people from Korea and Cambodia and Mexico. In California I found not just America, I found the world.

—Mexican immigrant student (Olsen, 1988)

They still come—a medical student from India who remains in Knoxville to set up a practice; a Danish *au pair* worker who meets a U.S. college student and extends her green card; a Vietnamese grandmother who follows her daughter who followed her teenage sons; a Salvadoran resistance fighter who seeks political asylum; a Mexican lawyer who sets up an import-export practice in Tijuana and San Diego; Romanian orphans brought to the United States through an adoption service; a Hong Kong capitalist who settles his family in San José while he commutes by jet to maintain his businesses. The immigration that has enriched the United States shows little sign of abating.

Each successive wave of immigration has had unique characteristics and a distinct impact on U.S. society. Whether attracted to the United States or forced here from their native country, immigrants have brought with them cultural, political, religious, and economic values, along with multiple tongues and various skills. The laws and policies of the United States have, in turn, accepted, constrained, and rejected these people. For many, these laws exist to be circumvented. Whether legally or illegally residing in the United States, immigrants contribute material aspects of their culture (crafts, foods, technology) as well as nonmaterial aspects (family values, spiritual beliefs, medical practices). During the process of settlement, these immigrants require social services to help them adapt to their new environment.

The extent of immigration and the policies that shape it have been controversial issues since the founding of this country. This great experiment—the United States of America—has required the innovation, fabrication, and synthesis of whole new patterns of existence. Those who have participated in this great cultural amalgamation have been themselves transformed. This transformation has not ended and will not end in the foreseeable future. Not only do we need to live with it, but we also have the unique opportunity to enjoy and value it.

Historical Perspectives

The North American continent has hosted people from all over the world. Diverse ethnic groups have arrived on both coasts and have caused continuous intermingling and confrontation with indigenous populations and among themselves. In what was to become the United States, these contacts began when the Europeans arrived in the original 13 colonies and met the many cultures of the Native American Indians. Later, the colonists imported African slaves who brought with them the various cultures of West Africa. Then, as settlers moved toward the interior, they encountered different native groups in the plains and pueblos. In the mid-nineteenth century, English-speaking Americans expanded into the Southwest, home to Native Americans as well as the Spanish-speaking heirs of land grants dating back to the sixteenth century. Finally, in the nineteenth and twentieth centuries, immigrant groups from all over the world poured into the United States, coming into contact with the descendants of all earlier groups.

From this contact came the expectation that these many cultures would merge into a homogeneous, shared national culture. The idea that the United States was a melting pot nation generated pressure on newcomers to conform in thought and behavior—if this were not possible, pressure for the children of these newcomers to assimilate. For some, assimilation was easier than for others; language, clothing, and other forms of distinction were easy to erase. For others, however, discarding traditions was not so easy. The Hassidic Jews, the Amish, the Hopi, the Navajo—those clinging to religious rites, lifestyles, or property without choosing to compromise—resisted assimilation pressures (Rubel & Kupferer, 1973). These groups and others have created a more modern metaphor, that of the salad bowl—a mix in which the individual ingredients are not melted but, rather, retain their flavor and texture. Another powerful metaphor is that of the kaleidoscope, in which the shifting patterns of culture, language, and race combine and recombine ceaselessly, yet are bound together by an idea: that in the United States, diverse peoples are held together through common ideals. The contributions of the ethnic cultures to the United States cannot be underestimated, yet the picture is not uniformly sunny. Dark and sordid episodes of conflict among, and discrimination against, various groups cloud the history of this nation. Minorities have systematically been denied opportunities and rights accorded the more privileged. Those groups that are least similar to the original Anglo-European immigrants have suffered exploitation and, in some cases, linguistic, racial, or cultural genocide. Despite the hardships that many have endured, ethnic groups in this country have become inseparable threads in the cultural tapestry of the United States.

Contributions

The North American continent had a myriad of indigenous cultures characterized by high levels of civilization before the European invasion began. These civilizations were obliterated, or they accommodated the arrival of new cultures through the creation of a hybrid New World. The result has been a broad mix of lifestyles and contributions of both artifacts and patterns that reflect life in contemporary North America. For the most part, European invaders attempted to replicate the life they had lived in the Old World, and those who were not a part of this main stream of culture had the choice of assimilating or leading a separate existence. Assimilation was never intended for everyone. Those who could not assimilate were largely left alone to carry on their linguistic and cultural traditions. Many contributions of nonmainstream peoples remained just beneath the surface of the American dream—in some cases, *too* far beneath to influence the main paths of culture. For example, the spiritual heritage of the Native Americans—the deep and abiding respect for nature—has scarcely the impact on the dominant culture that may be necessary for the survival of the flora and fauna of the continent.

In many ways, the indigenous civilizations of precolonial North America were more highly developed than European cultures. The cities and roads of the Aztec culture astounded the European conquerors. The agricultural systems featured advanced forms of irrigation with the cultivation of foods that were unknown to the old world. Some of these foods (potatos, corn, peanuts, and other grains) were later to provide 60 percent of Europe's diet and were responsible for the greatest explosion of population since the Neolithic age (Feagin & Feagin, 1993). Other substances (cocoa, tobacco, coca) were to provide Europeans with exhilarating addictions in the centuries to come. Medicinal products from the Americas revolutionized the treatment of disease in Europe and still fascinate pharmacologists with as yet untapped treasures. The political systems of native peoples ranged from the religious theocracies in Mexico, sources for advanced astronomical and mathematical achievement unparalleled in the world of that day, to the democratic councils of the Algonquin, Iroquois, and other nations that were much admired by Franklin and Jefferson (Hardt, 1992).

African American culture has evolved from an African base that survived despite harshly limiting circumstances: Slaves could bring little or none of the material aspects of African culture with them. The aspects that survived did so in the hearts and minds of those who were forcibly carried to the new world. The present-day legacies of the African past are evident not only in the dance, music, literature, and religion of the contemporary African American but also in the sheer power of the patterns of everyday life and language that were strong enough to survive despite centuries of oppression. Ironically, that genre of music most associated with the United States—jazz—is permeated with African American influence. One could argue that the music of America would not exist in its current form without this influence. Even today, the endlessly mutating forms of African American culture constitute an ongoing avant-garde (Criston, 1993), aspects of which are alternately embraced and denigrated by the wider society (some say, appropriated and abused by White performers and producers—see Dyson, 1996). Despite substantial discrimination, a long line of African American writers, such as James Weldon Johnson, Claude McKay, Richard Wright, Ralph Ellison, James Baldwin, Imamu Baraka (Le Roi Jones), Maya Angelou, Toni Morrison, and Langston Hughes, have enriched U.S. literature and have inspired a new generation of poets, writers, and rapsters. The religion of Black America has been a source of sustenance to African Americans since the arrival of the first slaves and has played a major role in fomenting protest for social justice. The nonviolent civil disobedience movement from the mid-1950s to the 1970s had religious underpinnings with prominent minister-leaders such as the Reverend Martin Luther King, Jr.

African Americans have made substantial contributions to science. In the years preceding 1900, more than 1,000 patents were awarded to African American inventors, despite the fact the slaves were barred from applying for patents. For example, Jo Anderson, a slave in the Cyrus McCormick household, was the co-inventor of the McCormick reaper. A slave of Jefferson Davis, president of the Confederate States of America, invented a boat propeller but was unable to patent the device. In the twentieth century, major scientists were active in such fields as aviation, electrical, mechanical, and construction engineering, rocketry, and many others (Carlson, 1970). African Americans who have contributed in social science and philosophy are W. E. B. DuBois, Marcus Garvey, Elijah Mohammed, Frederick Douglass, E. Franklin Frazier, Oliver C. Cox, and Malcolm X (Cherry, 1970).

The story of Ernest E. Just illustrates the difficulties faced by African American scientists in their ascent to prominence. Just, a marine biologist, rose to become vice-president of the American Society of Zoologists, but was once refused admittance to Rockefeller Institute. Although Just authored over 60 scholarly papers and was a leading authority on egg fertilization, artificial parthenogenesis, and cell division, he was never appointed to a White university and became embittered by the lack of professional recognition and research funding. By contrast, George Washington Carver never aspired to take his place alongside White scientists in their well-equipped, well-financed research facilities but was content to work in his small laboratory in Tuskegee (Carlson, 1970).

Hispanic contributions have also been significant. Hispanic influence in North America predates the landing of the Pilgrims at Plymouth Rock. Hispanic settlers in the Southwest helped to lay the foundations for the agricultural, mining, and cattle industries on which early city and state economies were built (Hispanic Concerns Study Committee, 1987). This influence continues today. With the outpouring of Cubans during the 1960s, Miami was transformed, becoming a vibrant international and bicultural metropolis. New York and its environs contain more Puerto Ricans than the island of Puerto Rico. Los Angeles is now the second largest Latin American city in the world. Although Hispanics living in the United States can trace their roots to several different countries, a common denominator of Hispanic culture in the United States includes language, religious beliefs and practices, holidays, and life patterns. Values shared among Hispanics include the importance of interdependence and cooperation of the immediate and extended family and the importance of emotional relationships. As the mainstream culture comes into more contact with the Hispanic culture, it is beginning to recognize the importance of these family values.

In politics, Hispanic Americans have influenced urban life and education. The political impetus behind bilingual education stems from the culmination of Cuban immigrant pressure in Florida and the Chicano power movement of the 1960s. A lasting contribution of this bilingual legislation may be current attempts to preserve the "small incidence" languages of Native Americans and Micronesia, linguistic resources that are endangered. Thus, Hispanic leadership has helped to preserve cultural resources in unforeseen ways. In literature and the other arts, Hispanic Americans have made significant contributions. An impressive folk tradition of Spanish songs and ballads has maintained a musical current containing the history, joys, and sorrows of the Mexican American, Puerto Rico, and Cuban experience. Spanish radio and television stations and newspapers have played a major role in sustaining the language and reinforcing the values of Spanish America. Spanish words have enriched the minds and tongues of North Americans. Fiction and poetry, in both languages, affirm the Hispanic heritage and identity. Puerto Rican and Mexican American theater has dramatized the struggles for a voice. The public art of Mexico is a centuries-old tradition with the colorful *steles* of the Aztecs and Mayans vibrating through time and reappearing in the murals of the barrios and the public art of cities throughout the Southwest. Art, to the Hispanic, is a breath of culture and artists, like intellectuals, are esteemed as the cultural leaders. The culinary contributions of Hispanics are legion, and include enchiladas from Mexico, black beans from Cuba, *mangú* from the Dominican Republic, and *pasteles* from Puerto Rico.

Contributions of the Pacific Rim peoples to the United States will be of increasing importance in the twenty-first century. The economic power of Asian capital stems not only from Japanese post–World War II efforts, but also from the Chinese diaspora that has provided capital for economic investment in much of Southeast Asia, Indonesia, Australia, and California. Although Chinese and Japanese immigration to western America was severely curtailed throughout the history of the United States, by sheer force of numbers and by the volume of the international trade, Asian economic and cultural influences on the United States have been consistent. The cultures of Asia, characterized by unparalleled continuity from ancient times to the present, have contributed to Western culture in innumerable ways. The U.S. fascination with Asian cultures has included the martial arts, Eastern spiritual philosophies, fireworks, acupuncture, Oriental food and decor, and gardening. The chief stumbling block toward greater acceptance of Asian influences in the United States is the perceived linguistic barrier. The fact that more Asians speak English than the reverse closes the doors to a deeper knowledge of Asian cultures for many Americans. Perhaps the current generation of high school students will begin to bridge this gap; Japanese is now taught in 454 U.S. schools (according to the University of Minnesota's Center for Advanced Research on Language Acquisition, which provides information on locations in North America where students can study specific less commonly taught languages).

Exploitation

The contributions of minorities to the cultural mainstream have not consistently been valued. On the contrary, many peoples in the cultural mix have been exploited. Their labor, their art, their votes have been used and abused without adequate compensation.

From the beginning, the European settlers exploited others. Many indentured servants worked at low wages for years to repay their passage to the New World. Native Americans brought food to the starving colonists, and, in return, saw their fertile coastal land taken away. The westward movement features many a sordid tale of killing and robbery on the part of the European settlers (Eckert, 1992). On the West Coast, Spanish missionaries also colonized the natives with somewhat more pious motives and a similar result. The Hispanic settlers in the West were, in turn, exploited when European Americans desired hegemony. Although superior firearms still carried the day, legal manipulations carried out in the English language systematically disenfranchised Hispanic settlers and caused them to lose their property and water rights on a vast scale. Chinese settlers who were permitted into the West during the nineteenth century found that their labor was valued only in the meanest way and the jobs available constituted "woman's work" such as laundry and cooking. And the story of exploitation of Africans brought to the New World is a tale of tears mixed with genocide and forced miscegenation.

In many cases, this exploitation continues to this day as the underclass of America, whether white, brown, or black, is inadequately paid and undereducated, without health benefits or adequate housing. Temporary jobs without benefits are the hallmark of the crueler, harsher world of the twenty-first century as economic and political forces polarize society.

The most difficult piece of the puzzle is the challenge of population growth. Creating jobs for a burgeoning population that will provide the financial means for the purchase of health care, education, housing, and an adequate diet is the issue. The growth of the population of the United States is so uneven, with European Americans having the lowest birth and immigration rate, that the challenge can almost be redefined as that of providing adequate employment for minorities. Demographic pressures will not abate during this new century. The population in 2050 is projected to consist largely of Third World peoples. The challenge is evident. Wrongs from the past cannot be righted, but present and future citizens can avoid those wrongs by understanding exploitative measures and working to disable them.

Demography

By the year 2010, one of every three Americans will be either African American, Hispanic American, or Asian American. This represents a dramatic change from the image of America throughout its history: In the past, when Americans have looked in the mirror, they have seen a largely European American reflection. Immigration, together with differing birth rates among various populations, is responsible for this demographic shift. Along with the change in racial and ethnic composition has come a dramatic change in the languages spoken in the United States and the languages spoken in U.S. schools.

The changing demographics have impacted society in many ways. Whether this impact is seen as positive or negative depends on one's point of view; certainly the trends are mixed. Some economists have balanced the cost-benefit ratio for immigration and found that immigrants contribute considerably to the national economy by filling low-wage jobs that help keep domestic industry competitive, by spurring investment and job creation, by revitalizing once decaying communities, and by paying billions annually in taxes. Unfortunately, the money generated from taxes that is paid to the federal government is not returned to those areas of the country most affected by immigration. Communities with large immigrant populations tend to spend local dollars in disproportionate amounts on schools, hospitals, and social services needed by new citizens (Shuit & McConnell, 1992). The resultant stress on these services raises the visibility of ethnic and/or racial diversity on the part of residents who may view newcomers negatively.

The Changing Face of America

The U.S. population is undergoing a shift from a predominately European American population to one that is substantially non-White. In 1980, 74 percent of the population consisted of European Americans; 14.5 percent African American; 8 percent Hispanic; and 3 percent other (including Asians, Pacific Islanders, Native Americans, and all others). In 2000, the profile changed, with a decrease in the European American population by 10 percent and an increase in other groups: 17 percent for Hispanics, 16 percent for African Americans, and 3 percent for all others. "Minorities" became the majority in California as of the year 2000, as U.S. Census Bureau estimates enumerated Whites as 49.9 percent of the state's 33.1 million residents. Latinos follow at 31.6 percent; Asians, 11.4 percent; Blacks, 6.7 percent; and American Indians, less than 1 percent (Nelson & O'Reilly, 2000). In the year 2040, the projected ethnic composition of the United States will be 59 percent European American, 12.4 percent African American, 18 percent Hispanic, and 10.3 percent Asian, Pacific Islanders, Native Americans, and all others (González, 1990).

From these figures, it is clear that the increase in Hispanics plays a large role in the demographic shift. This group comprises several components. In 1999, of the 31.7 million Hispanic origin residents, 65.2 percent were Mexican American; 14.3 percent Central and South American; 9.6 percent Puerto Rican; 4.3 percent Cuban; and 6.6 percent other Hispanic (Ramírez, 2000). This population is largely urban. The ancestors of today's Hispanics, between the years 1542 and 1777, created 200 new cities throughout North and South America, and 92 percent of Hispanics still live in cities today. Of the 50 metropolitan areas with the largest Hispanic population, 10 have populations greater than 100,000 (in order from the most numerous to the least: Los Angeles–Long Beach; New York; Miami–Hialeah; Chicago; Houston; San Antonio; San Bernardino–Riverside, CA; San Diego; Anaheim–Santa Ana, CA;

Did You Know?

There are approximately 2.4 million American Indians in the United States (almost 1 percent of the population). The largest tribe, the Cherokee, has a population of about 308,000. Oklahoma and California have the largest Native American populations. About 39 percent of the American Indian population are under 20 years of age. About 80 percent live in extended-family households. The high school graduation rate for American Indians is the lowest of any ethnic group: 34 percent of Indians over age 25 never graduated from high school, although 9 percent have B.A. degrees and 3 percent have graduate or professional degrees.

Source: U.S. Census Bureau (1995).

El Paso) (U.S. Census Bureau, 1995). The Hispanic subgroups are found in distinct geographic areas, with Mexican Americans in the Southwest, Puerto Ricans in the Northeast, and Cubans in Florida.

The U.S. Asian population in 1980 was 3.4 million; this grew to 6.9 million in 1990, a 100 percent increase. The population of Chinese Americans has doubled, the number of Hmong people has increased by 1,600 percent, Cambodians and Bangladeshis by 800 percent, Pakistanis by over 400 percent, and Japanese Americans by only 21 percent. Pacific Islander populations increased by 41 percent in the decade 1980–1990. Asian immigration is largely to the South and West. Of the 22 largest cities where "minorities" became "majorities," 7 are in California (Bovee, 1991).

In fact, California is experiencing the initial wave of immigration that will soon impact the entire United States. California is the nation's most racially diverse state with a greater percent of Asian and Latino residents than any other state and the second highest number of African Americans and Native Americans of any state. The state's Asian population is ten times as large as that of any other state, with varied geographic distribution: Cambodians and Hmong in the Central Valley, and Chinese Americans largely in urban areas such as San Francisco. The state's already sizable Latino population is expected to grow to 15 million in 2020, almost double the current level. These demographics trends will gradually expand to other states (U.S. Bureau of Census, 1999).

The Impact of America's Changing Population

In the changing demographics in the United States, two minority groups—immigrants and economically disadvantaged minorities within the country—face similar challenges. Both immigrants and indigenous minorities must adjust to the demands of modern technological societies and must redefine their cultural self-identity. Economic and educational achievement are not equally accessible to these minorities. A key difficulty for many minorities is that of poverty. One-third (33.1

percent) of African Americans and 30.1 percent of Hispanic Americans live in poverty. Worse, Blacks and Hispanics are even more likely not to be simply poor, but to be extremely poor—with incomes under half the poverty level of Whites. In fact, at 16.1 percent, the share of the Black population that is extremely poor is over four times that of non-Hispanic White (3.7 percent) and well above that of Hispanics (10.5 percent) (Henwood, 1997). Poverty is associated with a host of difficulties, such as underemployment, homelessness, educational deprivation, single-parent homes, and other types of instability. However, not all poverty can be linked to these difficulties; some minorities continue in poverty because of social and political factors in the country at large, such as racism and discrimination.

Poverty hits minority children particularly hard. According to a report of the Children's Defense Fund (2000), 20 percent of all children (13.5 million) in the United States live in poverty; 5.8 million live in extreme poverty, in a household with an income of less then $6,500 for a family of three. In 1998, 19.7 percent of America's children—3.7 million children—went to bed hungry. There are 850,000 homeless children and youth. Compounded with poverty are poor health, poor child care, and child abuse. Children in low-income communities get sick more often from preventable acute and infectious illnesses, such as measles, conjunctivitis, and ear infections, and are more likely to suffer from chronic medical conditions, such as asthma and diabetes. African American infants continue to die at twice the rate as White infants. Only 42 percent of low-income children between ages 3 and 5 are in prekindergarten programs, compared with 65 percent of higher-income children; 5 million children are left home alone after school. African American and Native American children are overrepresented at twice their proportion in the general population in reports of child abuse and neglect.

Poverty plays a large role in the education of America's youth. It impacts the ability of the family to devote resources to educational effort. This situation, coupled with social and political factors that mitigate against minority children in schools, stack the deck against minority student success. Demographic trends ensure that this will be a continuing problem in the United States. More than two-thirds (67.7 percent) of the Hispanic population are under 35 years of age, compared with a little more than half (53.2 percent) of the non-Hispanic population. Mean family size for Hispanic families is 3.30 persons, compared with 3.20 for non-Hispanic Whites (U.S. Bureau of Census, 1995). The average Hispanic female is well within childbearing age and Hispanic children constitute the largest growing school population. Thus, the educational achievement of Hispanic children is of particular concern.

The economy of the United States in the future will rest more on Asian and Hispanic workers than at present. As a consequence, the education of these populations will become increasingly important. Consider that in 1996, 36 percent of students enrolled in public elementary and secondary schools were minorities—an increase of 12 percent from 1976, largely due to the growth in the Hispanic population (National Center for Education Statistics, 1999). Of these minorities, 82 percent of Asian Americans 25 years or older have a high school diploma and 42 percent have bachelor degrees (Hooper & Bennett, 1998). In contrast, 27.8 percent of Hispanics 25 years of age and older had less than a ninth-grade education. Only 56.1 percent have high school diplomas and 10.9 percent college degrees. Compare these figures to those of non-Hispanic Whites, 87.7 percent of whom have high school diplomas and over a quarter (27.7 percent) of whom have college degrees (Ramírez, 2000) and the extent of the issue becomes clearer.

Large city school populations are overwhelmingly minority—for example, Miami, 71 percent; Philadelphia, 73 percent; and Baltimore, 80 percent (Kellogg, 1988). Hispanic students, in particular, typically live in racially isolated neighborhoods and are more likely to attend segregated schools than are African American students. Orum (1986) found that more than one-fourth of Hispanic students attended schools with minority enrollments of 90 to 100 percent. Minority children are overrepresented in compensatory programs in schools. Poor African Americans are 3.5 times more likely to be identified as mentally retarded than their European American counterparts and constitute 28 percent of total enrollment in special education, while they make up only 12 percent of public school enrollments (University of Texas at Austin, 1991).

Thus, nearly a half-century after *Brown* v. *Board of Education,* a student who is Black, Latino, or Native American remains much less likely to succeed in school. A major factor is a disparity of resources—the richest school districts spend 56 percent more per student than do the poorest; schools with large numbers of poor children tend to have fewer books and supplies and teachers with less training and experience (Children's Defense Fund, 2000).

The conclusion is inescapable: The educational system of the United States has been fundamentally weak in serving the fastest-growing school-age populations. Today's minority students are entering school with significantly different social and economic backgrounds from those of previous student populations, and thus require educators to modify their teaching approaches to ensure that these students have access to the American dream (Hyland, 1989).

Many minority students come to school with home languages other than English. According to the 1990 census, one American in seven, 32 million, speaks a language other than English at home. Seventeen million of these speak Spanish, the most used language in the nation after English. French, German, Italian, and Chinese follow with between one million and two million speakers each. More than three million Americans speak East Asian languages, double the number in 1980. Nearly one-third of these said they speak English poorly or not at all (Waggoner, 1992). In California alone, about 25 percent of California's 5.9 million students (or 36 percent of the approximately 4.1 million English learners in the United States in 1999) were catagorized as English learners (California Department of Education, 2001).

How is the impact of these large numbers of students with English learning needs felt in schools? Districts find themselves scrambling for teachers and staff with second language competencies and/or for those knowledgeable about language, culture, and academic development for English learners; for primary language as well as appropriate English language materials; and for ways of working with and involving parents.

Immigration and Migration

The United States has historically been a nation of immigrants, but the nature and causes of immigration have changed over time. The earliest settlers to the east coast of North America came from England and Holland, while those to the south and west came mainly from Spain. In the early eighteenth century, these settlers were joined by involuntary immigrants from Africa. Subsequent waves of immigrants came from Scotland, Ireland, and Germany, and later from central and eastern Europe. Immigration from the Pacific Rim countries was constrained by severe immigration restrictions until the last decades of the twentieth century. However, imperialistic policies of the United States, primarily the conquest of the Philippines, Puerto Rico, Hawaii, and the Pacific Islands, caused large influxes of these populations throughout the twentieth century. The wars in Southeast Asia and Central America throughout the 1970s and 1980s led to increased immigration from these areas.

Immigrants have come to the United States for a variety of reasons. The earliest immigration was prompted by the desire for adventure and economic gain in a new world combined with the desire to flee religious and political persecution. These factors provided both attractive forces ("pull") and expulsive forces ("push"). Later, U.S. foreign policy created connections with populations abroad that pulled certain groups to the United States. For example, the conquest of the Philippines at the turn of the century eventually resulted in large Philippine immigration to the United States. Immigration laws have responded to both push and pull factors throughout the nineteenth and twentieth centuries, at times curtailing immigration from specific regions, and at other times allowing increased immigration. Both immigrants and natives of the United States have historically been restless populations. Much of the history of the United States consists of the migration of groups from one part of the country to another.

Causes of Immigration

Migration is an international phenomenon. Throughout the world, populations are dislocated by wars, famine, civil strife, economic changes, persecution, and other factors. The United States has been a magnet for immigrants seeking greater opportunity and economic stability. The social upheavals and overpopulation that characterized nineteenth-century Europe and Asia brought more than 14 million immigrants to the United States in the 40-year period between 1860 and 1900. A century later, this phenomenon can be witnessed along the border between the United States and Mexico. Politics and religion as well as economics provide reasons for emigration. U.S. domestic and foreign policies affect the way in which groups of foreigners are accepted. Changes in immigration policy, such as amnesty, affect the number of immigrants who enter the country each year.

Economic Factors in Immigration. The great disparity in the standard of living attainable in the United States compared to that of many underdeveloped countries makes immigration attractive. Self-advancement is uppermost in the minds of many immigrants and acts as a strong incentive despite the economic exploitation often extended to immigrants (lower wages, exclusion from desirable jobs). Immigrants may bring with them unique skills. On the whole, however, the economy of the United States does not have an unlimited capacity to employ immigrants in specialized niches.

Immigration policy has corresponded with the cycles of boom and bust in the U.S. economy; the Chinese Exclusion Act in 1882 stopped immigration from China to America because of the concern that Chinese labor would flood the market and leave no jobs for Americans. The labor shortage in the western United States resulting from excluding the Chinese had the effect of welcoming Japanese immigrants who were good farm laborers. Later, during the Depression of the 1930s, with a vast labor surplus in the United States, the U.S. Congress severely restricted Philippine immigration, and policies were initiated to "repatriate" Mexicans back across the border. When World War II transformed the labor surplus of the 1930s into a severe worker shortage, the United States and Mexico established the Bracero Program, a bilateral agreement allowing Mexicans to cross the border and work on U.S. farms and railroads. The border was virtually left open during the war years (Wollenberg, 1989). Despite the economic attractiveness of the United States, however, most newcomers to this society experience a period of economic hardship.

Political Factors in Immigration.   Political factors, such as repression, civil war, and change in government, create a "push" for emigration from foreign countries, while political factors within the United States create a climate of acceptance for some political refugees and not for others. After the Vietnam War, many refugees were displaced in Southeast Asia: Some sense of responsibility for their plight caused the U.S. government to accept many of these people into the United States. For example, Cambodians who cooperated with the U.S. military immigrated to the United States in waves: first, a group including 6,300 Khmer in 1975; second, 10,000 Cambodians in 1979; and third, 60,000 Cambodians between 1980 and 1982 (Gillett, 1989a). The decade of the 1980s was likewise one of political instability and civil war in many Central American countries, resulting in massive civilian casualties. In El Salvador, for example, 1,000 civilians were killed each month by death squads comprising both paramilitary right-wing groups and guerrillas. Such instabilities caused the displacement of 600,000 Salvadorans who live as refugees outside their country (Gillett, 1989b). Through the Deferred Enforced Departure program of the U.S. government, nearly 200,000 Salvadoran immigrants have been given the right to live and work legally in the United States.

Other populations, such as Haitians claiming political persecution, have been turned away from U.S. borders. In a similar fashion, women fleeing from abusive husbands in male-dominated cultures have been refused immigration rights with the argument that these are personal rather than political issues. In the case of the Haitians, U.S. policy did not consider them to be victims of political repression, but rather of economics—a fine distinction, in many cases, and here one might suspect that racial issues in the United States make it more difficult for them to immigrate.

In the case of the abused women, women's rights activists argue that wife abuse is indeed a political issue. In both cases, however, it becomes clear that the issue of what constitutes political grounds for asylum is clouded by confounding factors.

In sum, people are pushed to the United States because of political instability or political policies unfavorable to them in their home countries. Political conditions within the United States affect whether immigrants are accepted or denied.

U.S. Foreign Policy.   As the United States grew as a capitalist nation, economic forces had a great influence on U.S. foreign policy. In the early growth of commercial capitalism from 1600 to 1865, the settlers were a source of labor; Africans were enslaved to provide plantation labor, and poor Europeans such as Irish Catholics were recruited abroad for low-wage jobs in transportation and construction. U.S. foreign policy supported unfettered international sea trade to ensure a steady source of imported labor. In the phase of industrial capitalism (1865–1920), U.S. treaties with Europe and intervention in European affairs (World War I) maintained the labor supply until the 1924 Immigration Act. U.S. imperialist policies in Asia (conquest of the Philippines and Hawaii) ensured a supply of raw materials and a home for U.S. military bases in the Pacific but immigration policy denied access to the United States for the majority of Asians. As U.S. capitalism advanced to multinationalist capitalism (1920–1990), U.S. foreign policy encouraged industries to employ cheap labor abroad. Immigration was restricted from Asia and Europe and immigrants from Puerto Rico and Mexico fulfilled the domestic need for low-wage labor. The U.S. opposition to communist Cuba resulted in the acceptance of large numbers of Cuba's upper and middle classes in the 1960s. U.S. intervention in Asia caused an influx of Asian immigrants in the 1970s and 1980s. In the 1990s, special provisions were made for refugees caused by natural disasters in Central America (5,000 of the 55,000 diversity slots were earmarked for this purpose). These foreign policies, largely driven by capitalism, have been closely connected with U.S. immigration policies.

Religious Factors in Immigration.   Many of the early English settlers in North America came to the New World to found colonies in which they would be free to establish their form of religious domination. Later, Irish Catholics left Ireland in droves because their lands were taken by Protestants. Many eastern European Jews, forced to emigrate because of anti-Semitic pogroms in the nineteenth century, came to the United States in great numbers. Unfortunately, during the 1930s and 1940s, Jews persecuted by Nazism were not free to emigrate or were not accepted as immigrants abroad, and were killed. Under the communist regime in the former USSR, Russian Jews were allowed to emigrate in small numbers and were accepted into the United States. For the most part, however, today's immigration policies permit refugees to be accepted for political rather than religious reasons.

Family Unification.   The risks associated with travel to the New World have made immigration a male-dominated activity since the early settlement of North America. In some cases, such as that of the Chinese in the nineteenth century, immigration laws permitted only young men to enter. Initial Japanese immigration, which was not restricted as severely as Chinese, involved predominantly young men between the ages of 20 and 40. Similarly, today's Mexican immigrant population consists largely of young men who have come to the United States to work and send money home. Once settled, these immigrants seek to bring family members. Family unification is a primary motivation for many applications to the U.S. Immigration and Naturalization Service (INS).

Migration

Americans have always been restless. Historically, crowding and the promise of greater economic freedom were reasons for moving west. The Gold Rush attracted, for the most part, English-speaking European Americans from the eastern United States, but other minority groups and foreign immigrants were also drawn to the search for instant wealth. Miners from Mexico, Peru, and Chile increased California's Latino population; Greeks, Portuguese, Russians, Poles, Armenians, and Italians flocked to the San Francisco Bay area. During the Depression, many of these populations migrated once again to California's central valley to find work as farm laborers (Wollenberg, 1989). With the rise of cities, rural populations saw economic advancement in urban environments. Many African Americans migrated to northern cities after World War I to escape prejudice and discrimination. Now, many immigrants are sponsored by special interest groups such as churches and civic organizations that invite them to reside in the local community. Once here, however, some groups find conditions too foreign to their former lives and eventually migrate to another part of the United States. For example, a group of Hmong families sponsored by Lutheran charities spent two years in the severe winter climate of the Minneapolis area before resettling in California. Hispanics, on the other hand, are migrating from cities in the Southwest, New York, and Miami toward destinations in the Midwest and middle South (Wilson, 1984).

Immigration Laws and Policies

Economic cycles in the United States have affected immigration policies, liberalizing them when workers were needed and restricting immigration when jobs were scarce. These restrictive immigration policies were often justified with overtly racist arguments. Asian immigration was targeted for specific quotas. The first Asian population that was specifically excluded was the Chinese (the Chinese Exclusion Act of 1882), but the growth of Japanese immigration as a result of this quota prompted Congress to extend the concept of Chinese exclusion to Japan (1908) and the rest of Asia. The immigration laws of the 1920s (the National Origins Acts of 1924 and 1929) banned most Asian immigration and established quotas that favored northwestern European immigrants. The quota system did not apply to Mexico and the rest of the Western Hemisphere; nor did the immigration laws affect the Philippines, which was a U.S. territory. In 1943, Congress symbolically ended the Asian exclusion policy by granting the United States' wartime ally,

China, a token quota of 100 immigrants per year. The Philippines and Japan received similar tiny quotas after the war.

A great change in immigration policy came as a result of a comprehensive reform of the immigration law in 1965. Congress abolished the old quota system and set up a new preference system emphasizing family ties and occupation. A third category has also been included—the Diversity Immigrant category in which 55,000 immigrant visas can be awarded each fiscal year to permit immigration opportunities for persons from countries other than the principal sources of current immigration to the United States. For fiscal year 2000, the limit for family-sponsored preference immigrants is 294,601 and the limit for employment-based preference immigrants is 142,299. There is a per-country limit for these preference immigrants set at 7 percent of the total annual family-sponsored and employment-based preference limits (i.e., 30,583 for the year 2000). However, certain countries are "oversubscribed" and hopeful immigrants are on long waiting lists, some extending to as many as 12 years (China-mainland born, India, Mexico, and the Philippines) (United States Department of State, 2000).

Legal Status. Many immigrants are *documented*—legal residents who have entered the United States officially and live under the protection of legal immigration status. Some of these are officially designated *refugees* with transitional support services and assistance provided by the U.S. government. Most immigrants from Cambodia, Laos, Vietnam, and Thailand have been granted refugee status. *Undocumented* immigrants are residents without any documentation, who live in fear of being identified and deported. Many Central American immigrants are undocumented, and applications for refugee status or political asylum are seldom granted. Because these immigrants have come since 1986, they are not eligible for amnesty under the provisions of the 1986 immigration law.

Being in the United States illegally brings increased instability, fear, and insecurity to school-age children because they and their families are living without the protection, social services, and assistance available to most immigrants. With the passage of the Immigration Reform and Control Act, however, undocumented children are legally entitled to public education. Often they and their families are unclear about this right, and school staff and authorities sometimes worsen the situation by illegally asking for immigration papers when children are being registered (Olsen, 1988).

Resources Available to Immigrants. The Emergency Immigrant Education Program (EIEP) (Improving America's School Act, Title VII, Part C) provides assistance to school districts whose enrollment is impacted by immigrants. Newcomer immigrant students meet the eligibility requirements for participation in the EIEP if they were born outside of the United States and its territories, and if they have been enrolled in kindergarten through grade 12 for less than three full academic years in any U.S. school. School districts and county offices of education qualify for EIEP funding if they have an enrollment of at least 500 eligible immigrant pupils and/or if the enrollment of eligible immigrant pupils represents at least 3 percent of the total enrollment. For the 2000–2001 school year, 347 California educational agencies qualified for participation, indicating the heavy impact of immigration on that state.

How far have we come? The Puritans brought to New England a religion based on a monochromatic world view. They outlawed Christmas and disapproved of celebration. The United States of America has struggled with this severe cultural reductionism since its founding. As the beauty and celebratory spirit of many other world cultures have been imported to this continent, the people of the United States have opened up to accept the beauty and brilliant hues that immigrants have brought. As more and more diverse groups settle and resettle throughout the continent, customs and traditions mingle to create an ever-new mix. The salad bowl, the kaleidoscope—these are metaphors for diversity in taste, in pattern, and in lifestyle. The American portrait is still being painted, in ever brighter hues.

10 Manifestations of Culture

Learning about Students

"Teacher," Maria said to me as the students went out for recess. "Yes, Maria?"
I smiled at this lively Venezuelan student and we launched into conversation.
The contents of this talk are now lost from me, but not the actions. For as we
talked, we slowly moved, she forward, me backward until I was jammed up
against the chalkboard. And there I remained for the rest of the conversation,
feeling more and more agitated. She was simply too close.

This incident and thousands of others, which may be unpredictable,
puzzling, uncomfortable, or even threatening, occur in situations in which
cultural groups come into contact. Because I knew the differing cultural norms
from which Maria and I were operating—the fact that the requirement for
space between interlocutors is greater for me as a North American than for her
as a South American—I did not ascribe any negative or aggressive tendencies
to her. But knowing the norm did not lessen my anxiety. What it afforded me
was the knowledge that we were behaving differently and that such differences
were normal for our respective groups.

—K.W.

Knowledge about various cultural norms is critical in multicultural situations. Teachers should not expect that they will be fully knowledgeable about every cultural nuance, nor should they be; but there are general patterns of behavior within which all human societies operate. An understanding of the patterns will help teachers understand the worlds of their students and help guide students to an understanding of the cultural norms of school life. Culture influences every aspect of school life (see Figure I.1); as a domain of learning, culture can be a specific area of study within the curriculum.

This chapter first outlines those general areas of culture that teachers, in their role as educators, will find most useful. Techniques are then offered that can be used to learn about students' cultures. Teachers can in turn use this new knowledge about students' cultures to design appropriate classroom organizational procedures and can use culturally responsive teaching behaviors.

The Classroom Teacher as Intercultural Educator

Teachers with a strong interest in intercultural communication and a sense of compassion for the difficulties faced by culturally diverse students are often successful in promoting the academic success of English learners. However, many prospective teachers initially are unaware of their own cultural values, and how these values engender behaviors that may be at odds with the home cultures of students. Those who are willing to engage in self-assessment activities are often richly rewarded with an understanding and appreciation of the origins and characteristics of the values underlying their professional and personal lives. The goal of such assessment is to enable prospective teachers to sustain intercultural contact, foster culturally responsive and responsible pedagogy, and develop the skills of advocacy for, and appreciation of, English learners.

Middle-class European American teachers, however well intentioned, often enter teacher education with racial, ethnic, and class prejudices. Reid (1992) captures the ubiquity of these prejudices:

> We are all caught up on the continuum of racism. The only viable position is an antiracist one which acknowledges the ideological influences and recognises that everyone in one way or another is involved in discriminatory structures, and needs to take a stand against racism to dismantle both racist structures and racist attitudes. (p. 16)

For the most part, racist beliefs are unexamined and earnestly denied by the population of prospective teachers. Endemic to modern American society are stereotypical beliefs about cultural and linguistic disadvantage, cultural mismatch, and lack of positive parental values as a cause of low achievement on the part of minority students. Chávez, O'Donnell, and Gallegos (1995) document that undergraduate teacher education students enter multicultural education with attitudes and beliefs that largely reflect the status quo. Research suggests that changes in the belief systems and attitudes of college students can be accomplished by participation in a multicultural course, but that the change has little lasting effect (Grant & Secada, 1990). Such educated youths usually think of racism in terms of the overt behaviors of individuals that can be readily identified and labeled, and a person who does not behave in these identified ways is not considered a racist. Most European American students deny their own racism (Scheurich, 1993). Research indicates that deliberate attempts to confront students with evidence of the ubiquitous nature of racism fails to change the view that racism is the set of isolated acts of prejudiced individuals, rather than a social practice embedded in institutions within the dominant culture (Chávez et al., 1995). Prospective teachers may resist engagement on issues of social equity and multicultural education, and be reluctant to reexamine political beliefs, gender issues, or race/class prejudice. Without such engagement, however, they may not modify subsequent teaching behavior or catalyze transformative change. Only those who take responsibility for their own growth will permit self-change and personal development in ways that lead to mature emotional and cognitive progress.

Bennett and Bennett's (1996) developmental model of intercultural sensitivity postulates that intercultural educators move from a position of *ethnocentrism* (in which one's own culture is the prism through which all other cultures are judged) to *ethnorelativity* (in which one is able to see other cultures on their own terms) as they become more able to accept the existence of alternative patterns for the organization of reality, and integrate these alternatives into a flexible repertoire of intercultural communication options. This frees the individual from the ethnocentric need to deny, defend against, or minimize the differences of others.

Visualizing the growth toward engagement in social change in the form of a continuum is not to suggest that growth in the capacity to become both aware and effective in overcoming ethnocentrism and racism is a linear process. On the contrary; each person confronts monumental social edifices that invest the status quo with authority and that invisibly support acquiescence. The little-understood relationship between belief and actualization and the subtle rewards for maintaining the status quo too often undermine the dedication toward achieving successful intercultural communication (Díaz-Rico, 1998).

Three strands comprise the skills and responsibilities of an intercultural educator. The first is the growth of an *understanding of cultural diversity;* the second is an *engagement in the struggle for equity;* and the third is the *commitment to promote educational achievement for all students* (see Figure 10.1). Each of these strands has three subcomponents. With this preparation, teachers can use intercultural communication effectively in the classroom.

FIGURE 10.1   **The Skills and Responsibilities of the Intercultural Educator**

Understand Diversity
Recognize the role of culture and language in learning
Explore the self: How the primary culture has socialized us
Identify the dimensions of how students can differ

Struggle for Equity
Detect unfair privilege
Combat prejudice in ourselves and others
Fight for fairness and equal opportunity

Promote Achievement
Work with culturally supported facilitating or limiting attitudes and abilities
Sustain high expectations for all students
Marshal parental and community support for schooling

Source: Díaz-Rico (2000).

What Teachers Need to Learn about Their Students

Any learning that takes place is built on previous learning. Students have learned the basic patterns of living in the context of their families. They have learned the verbal and nonverbal behaviors appropriate for their gender and age and have observed their family members in various occupations and activities. The family has taught them about love, and relations between friends, kin, and community members. They have observed community members cooperating to learn in a variety of methods and modes. Their families have given them a feeling for music and art, and have shown them what is beautiful and what is not. Finally, they have learned to use language in the context of their homes and communities. They have learned when questions can be asked and when silence is required. They have used language to learn to share feelings and knowledge and beliefs. Indeed, they are native speakers of the home language by the age of 5, and can express their needs and delights.

The culture that students bring from the home is the foundation for their learning. All cultures provide an adequate pattern of living for their members. Therefore, no children are "culturally deprived." Certain communities may exist in relative poverty; that is, they are not equipped with middle-class resources. Poverty, however, should not be equated with cultural deprivation. Every community's culture incorporates vast experience in and knowledge about successful living. Teachers can utilize this cultural knowledge to organize students' learning in schools.

In-depth background on the culture and history of all minority groups in the United States is clearly beyond the scope of this book. However, all cultures share general features. These features will be discussed here along with ways in which insightful teachers can use this general knowledge in their classrooms.

Values, Beliefs, and Practices

Values are "what people regard as good or bad, beautiful or ugly, clean or dirty . . . right or wrong, kind or cruel, just or unjust, and appropriate or inappropriate" (Lustig, 1988). Values come to the fore when cultures organize systems to govern their members and regulate and manage social life. Values are particularly important to people when they educate their young, because education is a primary means of transmitting cultural knowledge. Parents in minority communities are often vitally interested in their children's education even though they may not be highly visible at school functions.

Values cannot be seen, heard, or tasted but are manifest in social customs, in rituals and ceremonies, in vital areas of life such as health, religion, and law, and in ways of working and playing. All the influences that contribute to the cultural profile of the family and community affect the students' reaction to classroom practices. Students whose home culture is consistent with the beliefs and practices of the school are generally more successful in school. However, teachers concerned about advancing the success of all their students make every effort to understand that various cultures organize the general facets of individual and community behavior in radically different ways—ways that, on the surface, may not seem compatible to school practices and beliefs. To understand these differences is to be able to mediate for the students by helping them bridge relevant differences between the home and school cultures.

Social Customs and Mores. Social customs and mores dictate very different ways of living daily life. These customs are paced and structured by deep habits of using time and space. *Time* is organized in culturally specific ways:

> Adela, a Mexican American first-grade girl, arrived at school about 20 minutes late every day. Her teacher was at first irritated and gradually exasperated. In a parent conference, Adela's mother explained that braiding her daughter's hair each morning was an important time for the two of them to be together. This family time presented a value conflict with the school's time norm.

Other conflicts may arise when teachers demand abrupt endings to activities in which children are deeply engaged or when events are scheduled in a strict sequence. In fact, schools in the United States are often paced very strictly by clock time, whereas family life in various cultures is not regulated in the same manner. Some students may resent the imposition of an arbitrary beginning and ending to the natural flow of an activity. Moreover, teachers often equate speed of performance with intelligence, and standardized tests are often a test of rapidity. Many teachers find themselves in the role of "time mediator"—helping the class to adhere to the school's time schedule while working with individual students to help them meet their learning needs within the time allotted.

Within the dimension of time, teachers can consider these facets:

- How students have been taught to make use of their time
- How students deal with punctuality in their cultures
- What kinds of activities students perform quickly, and which they do not

How Late Is Rude?

Psychologist Robert Levine studied the time habits in 31 different countries and found, as one might expect, that every culture keeps time somewhat differently. He asked a sampling of Brazilians just how early someone would have to show up for a party to be considered really rude. The answer was 44 minutes. In the United States, on the other hand, the answer was 26 minutes. The guest at a party in the United States who rings the doorbell half an hour ahead of schedule risks being treated as a social outcast.

Source: Ehrenhalt (2000).

Space is another aspect of cultural experience. Personal space varies: In some cultures, individuals touch each other frequently and maintain high degrees of physical contact; in other cultures, touch and proximity cause feelings of tension and embarrassment. A cultural sense of space influences the rooms and buildings in which people feel comfortable. Large cavernous classrooms may be overwhelming to students whose family activities are carried out in intimate spaces. The organization of the space in the classroom sends messages to students: how free they are to move about the classroom, how much of the classroom they "own," how the desks are arranged. Both the expectations of the students and the needs of the teacher can be negotiated to provide a classroom setting in which space is shared.

Teachers can be sensitive to the following aspects of space:

- What personal distance students use in interacting with other students and with adults
- How the culture determines the space allotted to boys and girls
- How the spatial organization of the home compares to that of the school

Other *symbolic systems* include overt indicators of meaning, such as dress and personal appearance. For example, a third-grade girl wearing makeup is communicating a message that some teachers may find inappropriate because to the teacher wearing makeup symbolizes premature sexuality. Other symbolic systems are intrinsic, such as beliefs about natural phenomena, luck and fate, vocational expectations, and so forth. For example, a new teacher noticed during a strong earthquake that the Mexican American students seemed much less perturbed than their European American peers. In succeeding days, several of the European American children were referred to the school counselor because of anxiety, but the Mexican American children showed no signs of this anxiety. The principal attributed this difference to the Mexican Americans' cultural belief that nature is powerful and that humans must accept this power. In contrast, European American culture views nature as something to be conquered; when natural forces are greater than human control, anxiety results. Thus, behavior during earthquakes is a result of a symbolic system that is consonant with the culture.

Some facets to consider in understanding symbolic systems include the following:

- How dress differs for age, gender, and social class
- What clothing and accessories are considered acceptable
- What behavior is called for during natural phenomena such as rain, lightning, thunder, earthquakes, and fire

Rites, Rituals, and Ceremonies.   Each culture incorporates expectations of the proper means to carry out formal events. Formal events can be holidays and/or holy days in which particular ceremonies are incorporated. People celebrate births, marriages, and deaths with specific rites and rituals. Schools themselves have ceremonies. For example, the school culture of the United States mandates that assemblies begin with formal markers such as the Pledge of Allegiance, a flag salute, or a greeting from the principal. Rituals in some elementary classrooms in the United States are also relatively formal. For example, students must line up, come in quietly, take their seats, and wait for the teacher. Hmong students from Laos are accustomed to a different type of formality in the classroom. In Laos, when it is time for recess or lunch break, students rise and stand by their seats, waiting for permission to leave the room. When passing the teacher, students clasp their hands in front of their faces in a ritual of respect. Few students dare to raise their hands to ask questions when a teacher is lecturing (Bliatout, Downing, Lewis, & Yang, 1988).

Rituals are also involved in parent conferences. Greeting and welcome behaviors, for example, vary across cultures. The sensitive teacher understands how parents expect to be greeted and incorporates some of these behaviors in the exchange.

In considering how rituals affect the classroom, teachers should think about the following:

- What rituals students use to show respect
- What celebrations students observe and for what reason (political, seasonal, religious)
- How and where parents expect to be greeted when visiting the classroom

Work and Leisure Systems. Crosscultural variation in work and leisure activities is one of the most frequently discussed value differences. Many members of mainstream U.S. culture value work over play; that is, one's status is directly related

Christmas Light in Los Angeles

As Christmas dawns, a variety of cultures celebrate the holiday season with rituals that illuminate the winter darkness. Families from Mexico and Central America host the *posada,* a candlelit procession that reenacts the biblical story of Joseph and Mary's search for lodging before the birth of Jesus. Iranian families attend a *shabeyalda,* a concert of traditional Iranian music and poetry that celebrates the winter solstice. Filipinos celebrate the days leading up to Christmas with *Simbang Gabi,* a traditional novena of masses that began in the seventeenth century as an outdoor service held before dawn to accommodate fieldworkers and fishermen who spent their nights at sea. Although New England Puritans outlawed Christmas as a pagan festival in the eighteenth century, the Yule season serves many cultures as a mythic observance of "light over darkness, faith over despair."

Source: Watanabe and Ramírez (1999).

to one's productivity, salary, or job description. Play is often used in ways that reinforce this status. For example, executives conduct business informally on the golf course, co-workers form bowling leagues, and alumni enjoy "tailgate" parties before attending football games. Young people, particularly those in the middle class, are trained to use specific tools of play, and their time is structured to attain skills (organized sports, music lessons). In contrast, other cultures do not afford children any structured time to play but, instead, expect children to engage in adult-type labor at work or in the home. In still other cultures, such as that of the Hopi Nation in Arizona, children's play time is relatively unstructured, and parents do not interfere with play. Cultures also vary in the typical work and play activities expected of girls and boys. All these values have obvious influence on the ways children work and play at school (Schultz & Theophano, 1987).

In work and play groups, the orientation may be *individual* or *group*. The United States is widely regarded as a society in which the individual is paramount. This individualism often pits students against one another for achievement. In Japan, by contrast, individuals compete fiercely for admission to prestigious universities, but accompanying this is a sense that one must establish oneself within a group. Competition in the Japanese classroom is not realized in the same way as in U.S. schools; being singled out for attention or praise by teachers may result in embarrassment (Furey, 1986). American Indian children who come from group-directed cultures may enjoy competing against one another in teams but not as individuals (Philips, 1972).

Teachers can learn about work and play, individual and group orientation by considering the following:

- What types of work students are expected to perform and at what age, in the home and the community
- The purpose of play
- Whether individual work is private or shared
- The extent to which students are expected to work together

Health and Medicine.   Health and medicine practices involve deep-seated beliefs because the stakes are high: life and death. Each culture has certain beliefs about sickness and health, beliefs that influence the interaction in health care settings. Students may have problems—war trauma, culture shock, poverty, addiction, family violence, crime—with solutions that are culturally acceptable. When students come to school with health issues, teachers need to react in culturally compatible ways. Miscommunication and noncooperation can result when teachers and the family view health and disease differently (Witte, 1991). For example, community health practices, such as the Cambodian tradition of coining (in which a coin is dipped in oil and then rubbed on a sick person's back, chest, and neck), can be misinterpreted by school officials who, seeing marks on the child, swiftly call Child Protective Services.

Teachers and other school personnel can use the following questions to help inform them of beliefs about health:

- Who or what causes illness and who or what is responsible for curing illness?
- What practices exist regarding personal hygiene?
- If a student were involved in an accident at school, would any of the common first aid practices be unacceptable? (Saville-Troike, 1978)

Institutional Influences: Economic, Legal, Political, and Religious. The institutions that support and govern family and community life have an influence on behavior and beliefs. The economic institutions of the United States are largely dual: small business enterprises and large corporate/government agencies. Small businesses reward and channel the initiative to those who come to the United States with capital to invest, but generally pay low wages to low-skilled workers. Professional workers in the larger corporate and governmental agencies (education, utilities, medicine, law) must pay dues to enter whether by passing elaborate licensing and examination processes or by achieving a close fit to the corporate culture. These institutions influence daily life in the United States by means of a complex web of law, custom, and regulation that provides the economic and legal infrastructure of the dominant culture. These institutions can be affected through formal political processes or via more informal means such as selective purchasing and retail participation (boycotts, consumption of ethnic products, etc.).

Interwoven into this rich cultural/economic/political/legal texture are religious beliefs and practices. In the United States, religious practices are heavily embedded but formally bounded: Witness the controversy over Christmas trees in schools, but the almost universal cultural and economic necessity for increased consumer spending at the close of the calendar year. Religious beliefs underlie other cultures even more fundamentally. Immigrants with Confucian religious and philosophical beliefs subscribe to values that mandate a highly ordered society and family through the maintenance of proper social relationships. In Islamic traditions, the Koran prescribes proper social relationships and roles for members of society. When immigrants with these religious beliefs encounter the largely secular U.S. institutions, the result may be that customs and cultural patterns are challenged, fade away, or cause conflict within the family (Chung, 1989).

Teachers may want to consider the following issues about institutional influences in the home and community culture:

- What jobs/income are available in the community and to whom?
- What role does the law play in community life, and what relationships exist with legal authorities (police, immigration officials)?
- Who dominates the political processes in the community?
- What aspects of religion should not be discussed in school and what behavior should not be required?

Educational Systems. Educational systems in the past were designed to pass on cultural knowledge and traditions, much the same learning that parents taught their children. However, in the increasingly complex and technologically changing society of the United States, schools have shifted their emphasis to teaching unforeseen kinds of content: "a change from a stable pattern of cultural transmission to the teaching of what the parents never knew" (Singleton, 1973, p. 279). This shift affects all students but is particularly troublesome for children whose parents teach them in different ways than the school does. Students come to school already steeped in the learning practices of their own family and community. They come with expectations about learning and generally expect that they will continue to learn in school. Many of the organizational and teaching practices of the school may not support the type of learning to which students are accustomed.

For immigrant children with previous schooling, experience in U.S. classrooms may engender severe conflicts. For example, Polynesian students coming from the South Pacific may have experienced classroom learning as a relatively passive activity. They expect teachers to give explicit instruction about what to learn and how to learn it, and homework to be checked daily with careful scrutiny. When these students arrive in the United States and encounter teachers who value creativity and student-centered learning, they may appear passive as they wait to be told what to do (Funaki & Burnett, 1993). Indochinese students expect to listen, watch, and imitate. They may be reluctant to ask questions or volunteer answers and may be embarrassed to ask for the teacher's help or reluctant to participate in individual demonstrations of a skill or project (Armour, Knudson, & Meeks, 1981). Teachers who can accommodate to these students' proclivities can gradually introduce student-centered practices while supporting an initial dependence on the teacher's direction.

Teachers who seek to understand the value of education within the community can examine the following questions:

- What methods for teaching and learning are used in the home (e.g., modeling and imitation, didactic stories and proverbs, direct verbal instruction)?
- What role does language play in learning and teaching?
- How are children expected to interact with teachers (observe only, ask questions, volunteer)?
- How many years are children expected to attend school?

Roles and Status

Cultures differ in the roles people play in society and the status that is accorded to these roles. For example, in the Vietnamese culture, profoundly influenced by Confucianism, authority figures are ranked in the following manner: The father ranks below the teacher, who ranks only below the king (Chung, 1989). Such a high status is not accorded to teachers in U.S. society, where, instead, medical doctors enjoy this type of prestige. Such factors as gender, social class, age, occupation, and educational level influence the manner in which status is accorded to various roles. Students' perceptions about the roles possible for them in their culture affect their school performance.

Gender. Gender is related to social roles in a similar way in many cultures. Anthropologists have found men to be in control of political and military matters in all known cultures. Young boys tend to be more physically and verbally aggressive and to seek dominance more than girls do. Traditionally, women have had the primary responsibility for child-rearing, with associated tasks, manners, and responsibilities. Immigrants to the United States often come from cultures in which men and women have rigid and highly differentiated gender roles. The gender equality that is an ostensible goal in classrooms in the United States may be difficult for students of these cultures. For example, parents may spend much time correcting their sons' homework while ascribing little importance to their daughters' schoolwork.

To assess the roles played by males and females in various cultures, teachers may consider the following:

- What tasks are performed by boys, what tasks by girls?
- When, where, and how may girls and boys interact?
- What expectations do parents and students hold for boys' and girls' achievement, and how does this differ by subject?

Social Class. Social class stratification differs across cultures. Cultures that are rigidly stratified, such as India's caste system, differ from cultures that are not as rigid or in some cases, border on the anarchic, such as continuously war-torn countries. The belief that education can enhance economic status is widespread in the dominant culture in the United States, but individuals in other cultures may not have similar beliefs. For example, immigrants to St. Croix from West Indian islands to the south (Antigua, Trinidad, St. Lucia, Nevis) appeared to view schooling as instrumental to their future success and were willing to work hard and abide by the rules. In contrast, young men born in St. Croix appeared to perceive education as an instrument of oppression and a threat to their identity. The native-born males believed that they could achieve prestigious government positions on the basis of their family connections, not through educational success (Gibson, 1991a).

In general, individuals and families who are in the upper socioeconomic status levels are able to exert power by sitting on college, university, and local school boards and, in this way, determining who receives benefits and rewards through schooling. However, middle-class values are those that are generally incorporated in the culture of schooling. The social class values that children learn in their homes largely influence not only their belief in schooling but also their routines and habits in the classroom.

Teachers can observe closely the following social class differences that may affect students' behavior:

- What type of home environment do students have—the amount and quality of material possessions, housing, consumer goods, and diet?
- What power do parents have to obtain information about the school or to influence educational choices?
- What resources are available in the home to augment school assignments?

Age.   Age interacts with culture, socioeconomic status, gender, and other factors to influence an individual's behavior and attitudes. In Puerto Rico, for example, breakfast food varies depending on age: Children may eat creamed cereal, whereas adults drink strong coffee and eat bread. In contrast, in the United States, both adults and children may eat cereal for breakfast. In various cultures, expectations about appropriate activities for children and the purpose for those activities differ. Middle-class European Americans expect children to spend much of their time playing and attending school rather than performing tasks similar to those of adults. Cree American Indian children, on the other hand, are expected from an early age to learn adult roles, including contributing food to the family. Parents may criticize schools for involving children in tasks that are not related to their future participation in Cree society (Sindell, 1988).

Cultures also differ in their criteria for moving through the various (culturally defined) life cycle changes. An important stage in any culture is the move into adulthood, but the age at which this occurs and the criteria necessary for attaining adulthood vary according to what *adulthood* means in a particular culture. For example, in a culture in which the duty of the male adult is to show prowess in war, entry into adulthood involves long-term preparation and is therefore delayed. In contrast, in cultures where adulthood includes the privilege of dancing in representation of masked gods, adulthood is awarded at a younger age (Benedict, 1934).

Teachers can begin to understand how age is a factor in students' interaction by considering the following:

- What activities and roles are expected of individuals at different life stages?
- What activities and behaviors are appropriate—or forbidden—for children of various ages?
- What criteria define the various stages or periods in the life cycle?

Occupation.   Occupation, in the United States, very often determines income, which in turn is a chief determinant of prestige in the culture. Other cultures, however, may attribute prestige to those with inherited status or to those who have a religious function in the culture. Prestige is one factor in occupational choices. Other factors can include cultural acceptance of the occupation, educational requirements, gender, and attainability. Students thus may not see all occupations as desirable for them or even available to them and may have mixed views about the role education plays in their future occupation. Some cultural groups in the United States are engaged in a voluntary way of life that does not require public schooling (e.g., the Amish). Other groups may not be adequately rewarded in the United States for school success but expect to be rewarded elsewhere (e.g., children of diplomats and short-term residents who expect to return to their home country). Still another group may be involuntarily incorporated into the U. S. society and relegated to menial occupations and ways of life that do not reward and require school success (e.g., Chicanos in the Southwest). As a reaction they may not apply academic effort (Ogbu & Matute-Bianchi, 1986).

Teachers may wish to ask students their views of occupations and work. The following information may be relevant:

- What kinds of work are considered prestigious or desirable?
- What assumptions exist about the attainability of specific occupations?
- What role does education play in achieving occupational goals?

Educational Level.   Educational level, for many individuals, is a factor of the job desired, the importance parents ascribe to education, and the investment in education that the culture values. The son of blue-collar workers may not value a college education because his parents, who have not attained such an education, have nevertheless prospered. The daughter of a college professor may find her parent's workload too demanding and desire a less stressful occupation. The educational opportunity available in the United States may appeal to immigrants from other cultures who may not desire to have their children remain in the United States to establish occupations. For example, parents who are residents of Hong Kong will often sacrifice to send their children abroad to the United States, Great Britain, or Canada to be educated, yet desire for them to return to Hong Kong to carry on family business or tradition. For these parents, the educational level attainable in Western countries may serve solely an instrumental (goal attainment) function and not an affiliative (social-relation) purpose.

In working with diverse students, teachers will want to know:

- What educational level the student, family, and community desire for the student
- What degree of assimilation to the dominant culture (and to English) is expected and desired

Family Socialization: The Structure of Daily Life

The family unit is a complex web that influences and shapes the individual. Family relationships make up an intricate network of affiliations that contribute to the child's learning and adjustment. School socialization must build on, rather than replace, that of the family because the family has helped to create the child's personality and habits—in effect, helped develop identity itself. In the home, a child is named and thus learns about names and forms of address. The child is taken care of and thus learns how people are cared for. The child interacts with parents and thus learns roles for children and adults. The child is fed and thus learns what to enjoy and what to abhor.

Naming Practices and Forms of Address.   Naming practices and forms of address differ across cultures. The custom in the United States is to have a first (or given), a middle, and a last (or family) name. On lists, the first and last names are often reversed in order to organize or "alphabetize" the names. In Vietnam, names also consist of three parts, in the following order: family name, middle name, and given name. The names are always given in this order and cannot be reversed because doing so would denote a different person—Nguyên Van Hai is different from Hai Van Nguyên. Similarly, Puerto Ricans generally use three names: a given name, followed by the father's surname and then the mother's surname. If one last name must be used, it is generally the father's surname. Thus, Esther Reyes Mimosa can be listed as Esther Reyes. If the first name is composed of two given names (Hector Luis), both are used. This person may have a brother who is Hector José; for either to be called simply Hector would be a loss of identity.

In addressing people, practices also vary considerably. Vietnamese are never known by their family names, but are always called by their given names. These given names can be preceded by a title—Mr., Mrs., or Dr. In contrast, Koreans can be addressed with Mr., Mrs., or Dr. before their family names. Teachers should avoid using given names when addressing adults, as these are used for addressing those who are younger, who are very close friends, or who are of lower status (California State Department of Education, 1992).

In many cultures adults are referred to by their function rather than their name. In Hmong, *xib fwb* means "teacher," and Hmong children may use the English term "teacher" in the classroom rather than a title plus surname ("Mrs. Jasko"). Middle-class European American teachers may consider this to be rude rather than realizing this is a cultural difference.

Educators often change and mispronounce the names of immigrants. A sensitive teacher strives not only to understand the use and order of names but also to pronounce them correctly.

Child-Rearing Practices.   Child-rearing practices have wide implications for schools. Factors such as who takes care of children, how much supervision they receive, how much freedom they have, who speaks to them and how often, and what they are expected to do affect their behavior on entering schools. Many of the misunderstandings that occur between teachers and students arise because of differing expectations about behavior, and these differing expectations stem from early, ingrained child-rearing practices. In Hmong society, for example, family values are placed above individual concerns. Children spend the majority of every day in close physical proximity to their parents. Parents carry and touch their children more than is common in Western cultures (Bliatout et al., 1988). In contrast, students from Korean American backgrounds may be accustomed to an authoritarian discipline style in the home. These parents often seek to influence their children's behavior by expecting reciprocity for the sacrifices made for them. Decision-making strategies reward conformity and obedience, and teachers are expected to reinforce this. An egalitarian classroom atmosphere may create conflicts for Korean American students between the pressures they experience in their families and the school environment (California State Department of Education, 1992). Several excellent sources that describe child-rearing practices in various cultures are currently available from the California Department of Education. In addition, a rich description of child-rearing practices among Mexican immigrant families can be found in *Crossing Cultural Borders* (Delgado-Gaitan & Trueba, 1991).

Parental Involvement.   Parental involvement in the school is influenced by cultural beliefs. The U.S. system was developed from small, relatively homogeneous local schools with considerable community and parental control. The pattern of community and parental involvement continues today with school boards, PTAs, and parent volunteers in the schools. This pattern is not universal outside the United States. For example, in traditional Cambodia, village families who sent their children to schools in cities had no means of involving themselves in the school (Ouk, Huffman, & Lewis, 1988).

In cultures where teachers are accorded high status, parents may consider it improper to discuss educational matters or bring up issues that concern their children. Other factors that make parental involvement difficult are school procedures such as restrictive scheduling for parent conferences and notification to parents that siblings are not welcome at school for conferences and other events. These procedures tend to divide families and exclude parents. School staffs can involve the community by talking with parents and community liaisons to work out procedures that are compatible with cultural practices.

Food Preferences.   Food preferences are an important consideration in schools as the numbers of school-provided breakfasts and lunches increase. Further, as more courses in health and nutrition are mandated, teachers who are knowledgeable about students' dietary practices can incorporate their students' background knowledge into instruction. Besides knowing in general what foods are eaten, in what order, and how often, teachers will want to find out about students' favorite foods, taboo foods, and typical foods.

Besides customs of what and when to eat, eating habits vary widely across cultures, and "good" manners at the table in some cultures are inappropriate or rude in others. For example, Indochinese consider burping, lip smacking, and soup slurping to be common behaviors during meals, even complimentary to hosts. Teachers who eat lunch with their students can use the opportunity to learn about students' habits, rather than blindly insisting on culturally specific table habits. If, however, a student's habits alienate peers, the teacher may need to discuss appropriate manners.

Humanities and the Arts

In many cultures, crafts performed at home—such as food preparation, sewing and weaving, carpentry, home building and decoration, religious and ritual artistry for holy days, holidays, and entertaining—are an important part of the culture that is transmitted within the home. Parents also provide an important means of access to the humanities, and visual and performing arts of their cultures. Often, if immigrants are to gain an appreciation of the great works of art, architecture, music, and dance that have been achieved by their native culture, it is the classroom teacher who must provide this experience and awareness by drawing on the resources of the community and then sharing these with all the members of the classroom.

Culturally Influenced Learning Styles

Learning styles can be defined as individual preferences for processing information. Information is perceived or gathered; it is stored or attached to the memory base; and it is then used for making decisions and taking action. Culture appears to influence each part of this process by providing a set of rules that guide the way individuals select strategies and approach learning (Shade & New, 1993). For example, students who live in a farming community may have sensitive and subtle knowledge about weather patterns, knowledge that is essential to the economic survival of their family. This type of knowledge may predispose students to value learning in the classroom that helps them better understand natural processes like climate. These students may prefer kinesthetic learning activities that build on the same kind of learning that has made it possible for them to sense subtleties of weather. In a similar manner, Chicano children from traditional families who are encouraged to view themselves as an integral part of the family may prefer social learning activities. For more discussion of learning strategies and cognitive styles, see Chapter 2.

Learning Modalities. Students can acquire knowledge via several distinct means: visualizing, viewing the written word, listening, and acting. These modalities are often combined in culturally specific ways. The Navajo child is taught by first observing and listening, then taking over parts of the task in cooperation with and under the supervision of an adult. In this way, the child gradually learns all the requisite skills. Finally, the child tests himself or herself privately—failure is not seen by others, whereas success is brought back and shared. The use of speech in this learning process is minimal (Phillips, 1978). In contrast, acting and performing are the focus of learning for many African American children. Children observe other individuals to determine appropriate behavior and to appreciate the performance of others. In this case, observing and listening culminates in an individual's performance before others (Heath, 1983b). Reading and writing may be primary learning modes for other cultures. Traditionally educated Asian students equate the printed page with learning and appear to need the reinforcement of reading and writing to learn. Observing students learning from one another in a natural, unstructured setting can inform teachers of students' preferred ways of learning. This knowledge can be transferred to the classroom teaching and learning situation.

Culturally Supported Facilitating or Limiting Attitudes and Abilities. A skilled intercultural educator recognizes that each culture supports distinct attitudes, values, and abilities. These may facilitate or limit the learning situation in U.S. public schools. For example, the cultures of Japan, China, and Korea, which promote high academic achievement, may foster facilitating behaviors, such as the ability to listen and follow directions, attitudes favoring education, respect for teachers and authorities, attitudes toward discipline as guidance, and high achievement motivation. However, other culturally supported traits may hinder adjustment to the U.S. school—for instance, lack of experience in participating in discussions; little experience with independent thinking; strong values to conformity, which inhibits divergent thinking; and distinct sex-role differentiation, with males more dominant.

Similarly, African American family and cultural values that encourage independent action, self-sufficiency, and imagination and humor may facilitate adjustment to the classroom, but dialect speakers with limited experiences with various types of standard English patterns may be hindered. The Mexican American cultural values that encourage cooperation, affectionate and demonstrative parental relationships, children assuming mature social responsibilities such as child care and translating family matters from English to Spanish, and eagerness to try out new ideas may facilitate classroom success. On the other hand, such attitudes as depreciating education after high school, especially for women; explicit sex-role stereotyping favoring limited vocational roles for women; emphasis of family over achievement and life goals of children; and dislike of competition may go against classroom practices and hinder classroom success (Clark, 1983).

Cooperation versus Competition. Cultures also differ in their emphasis on cooperation over competition. Traditional U.S. classrooms mirror middle-class European American values of competition: Students are expected to "do their own work"; rewarded publicly through star charts, posted grades, and academic honors; and admonished to do their individual "best." In the Cree American Indian culture, however, children are raised in a cooperative atmosphere, with siblings, parents, and other kin sharing food as well as labor (Sindell, 1988). In the Mexican American culture, interdependence is a strength; one has a commitment to others, and all decisions are made together. Those who are successful have a responsibility to others to help them succeed. A classroom structured to maximize learning through cooperation can help students extend their cultural predilection for interdependence. This interdependence does not devalue the uniqueness of the individual. The Mexican culture values *individualismo*, the affirmation of one's intrinsic worth and uniqueness aside from any successful actions or grand position in society (deUnamuno, 1925). A workable synthesis of this individualism/ interdependence would come from classroom activities that are carried out as a group but that affirm the unique gifts of each individual student.

Use of Language

In learning a second language, students (and teachers) often focus on the form. Frequently ignored are the ways in which that second language is used. The culture that underlies each language prescribes distinct patterns and conventions about when, where, and how to use the language (see Labov, 1972). Heath (1983b) noted that children in "Trackton," an isolated African American community in the South, were encouraged to use spontaneous verbal play, rich with metaphor, simile, and allusion. In contrast, the children of "Roadville," a lower middle-class European American community in the South, used language in more restricted ways, perhaps because of habits encouraged by a fundamentalist religious culture. Heath contrasts language usage in these two cultures: verbal and nonverbal communication (the "said" and the "unsaid"), the use of silence, discourse styles; the nature of questions, and the use of oral versus written genres.

Social Functions. Using language to satisfy material needs, control the behavior of others, get along with others, express one's personality, find out about the world, create an imaginative world, or communicate information seems to be universal among languages. How these social functions are accomplished, however, varies greatly among cultures. For example, when accidentally bumping some one, Americans, Japanese, Koreans, and Filipinos would say "excuse me" or "pardon me." The Chinese, however, would give an apologetic look. Within a family, Hispanics often do not say "thank you" for acts of service, whereas European American children are taught to say "thank you" for any such act, especially to a family member.

Verbal and Nonverbal Expression.   Verbal and nonverbal means are used to communicate a language function. Educators are oriented toward verbal means of expression and are less likely to accord importance to the "silent language." However, more than 65 percent of the social meaning of a typical two-person exchange is carried by nonverbal cues (Birdwhistell, 1974). *Kinesic* behavior—including facial expressions, body movements, postures, and gestures—can enhance a message or constitute a message in itself. For example, a gesture such as the expressive Gallic shrug of the shoulders can communicate emotions (disillusionment, frustration, and disbelief) far beyond the capacity of verbal language. *Physical appearance* is an important dimension of the nonverbal code during initial encounters. *Paralanguage*—the nonverbal elements of the voice—is an important aspect of speech that can affirm or belie a verbal message. *Proxemics,* the communication of interpersonal distance, varies widely across cultures. Last, but not least, *olfactics*—the study of interpersonal communication via smell—may constitute a factor that is powerful yet often overlooked.

The Role of Silence.   People throughout the world employ silence in communicating. Silence can in fact speak loudly and eloquently. The silence of a parent in front of a guilty child is more powerful than any ranting or raving. As with other language uses, however, silence differs dramatically across cultures. In the United States, silence is interpreted as expressing embarrassment, regret, obligation, criticism, or sorrow (Wayne in Ishii & Bruneau, 1991). In Asian cultures, silence is a token of respect. Particularly in the presence of the elderly, being quiet honors their wisdom and expertise. Silence can also be a marker of personal power. In Eastern cultures, women view their silent role as a symbol of control and self-respect. In many Native American cultures silence is used to create and communicate rapport in ways that language cannot.

> Edgar, a Paiute youth from Reno, Nevada, had an agonizing decision to make. At the age of 18, he had graduated from the Indian Youth Training Program in Tucson, Arizona, and was free to return home to live. Living at home would possibly jeopardize the hard-won habits of diligence and self-control that he had learned away from the home community, in which he had been arrested for juvenile delinquency. As the counselor in Edgar's group home, I knew he could possibly benefit by talking over his decision. After school, I entered his room and sat on the

chair by his bed, indicating that I was available to help him talk through his dilemma. One half hour of total silence elapsed. After thirty minutes he began to speak. Silence rather than language had achieved the rapport I sought. (L.D-R.)

In a research project that took place in several Ogala Sioux classrooms, a central factor was the withdrawal of the Sioux students. Teachers were faced with unexpectedly intense, sometimes embarrassingly long periods of silence. They cajoled, commanded, badgered, and pleaded with students, with an inevitable monosyllabic or nonverbal response. Yet outside the classroom children were noisy, bold, and insatiably curious. Closer observation revealed a student-developed and -controlled silence, a tactic on the part of whole groups of children to shut the teacher out and defend against the teacher-student learning exchange. The lack of verbal responses from students frustrated teachers. When teachers redefined the silence as an intercultural opportunity, they were able to create conditions of change. The solution? The teachers involved themselves in the daily life of the community and reduced the isolation of the school from the values of the community. They went so far as to locate classrooms in community buildings. In a differing context, students were more willing participants (Dumont, 1972).

The Role and Nature of Questions.   The role of silence in the language acquisition classroom may extend to intercultural differences in asking and answering questions. In middle-class European American culture, children are exposed early on to their parents' questioning. While taking a walk, for example, a mother will ask, "See the squirrel?" and, later, "Is that a squirrel? Where did that squirrel go?" It is obvious to both parent and child that the adult knows the answer to these questions. The questions are asked to stimulate conversation and to train children to focus attention and display knowledge. In the Inuit culture, on the other hand, adults do not question children or call their attention to objects and events in order to name them (Crago, 1993).

Responses to questioning differ across cultures. Students from non-Western cultures may be reluctant to attempt an answer to a question if they do not feel they can answer absolutely correctly. For Korean students, for example, to put forth a mistaken answer would be a personal embarrassment and a personal affront to the teacher (California State Department of Education, 1992). Students do not share the European American value of answering questions to the best of their ability regardless of whether that "best" answer is absolutely correct or not, nor will students from many Eastern countries speak up when they do not understand or ask questions solely to demonstrate intelligence.

Discourse Styles.   Cultures may differ in ways that influence conversations: the way conversations open and close, the way people take turns, the way messages are repaired to make them understandable, and the way in which parts of the text are set aside. Those who have traveled to a foreign country recognize that a small interaction such as answering the telephone may have widely varying sequences across cultures. Sometimes callers may give immediate self-identification, sometimes not. Sometimes politeness is accorded the caller automatically; sometimes greetings are followed with "how are you?" sequences. Deviations from these routines may be cause to terminate a conversation in the earliest stages. These differences in discourse are stressful for second language learners. Multiply this stress by the long hours children spend in school, and it is no wonder that English learners may feel subjected to prolonged pressure.

Discourse in the classroom can be organized in ways that involve children positively, in ways that are culturally compatible. A group of Hawaiian children, with the help of an encouraging and participating adult, produced group discourse that was co-narrated, complex, lively, imaginative, and well connected. Group work featured 20-minute discussions of text in which the teacher and students mutually participated in overlapping, volunteered speech and in joint narration (Au & Jordan, 1981). In contrast, Navajo children in a discussion group patterned their discourse after the adults of their culture. Each Navajo student spoke for an extended period with a fully expressed statement, and other students waited courteously until a clear end was communicated. Then another took a similar turn. In both communities, children tended to connect discourse with peers rather than the teacher functioning as a central "switchboard." If the teacher acted as a central director, students might respond with silence and eventual resentfulness (Tharp, 1989a).

How Students Tell You They Don't Understand

Arabic (men): *Mish fahem*
Arabic (women): *Mish fahmeh*
Armenian: *Yes chem huskenur*
Chinese (Cantonese): *Ngoh m-ming*
Chinese (Mandarin): *Wo bu dung*
Persian: *Man ne'me fah'man*
Japanese: *Wakarimasen*
Korean: *Juh-neun eehae-haji mot haget-seum-nida*
Russian: *Ya nye ponimayu*
Spanish: *No comprendo*
Vietnamese: *Toi khong hieu*
Yiddish: *Ikh veys nikht*

In addition to ways to say "I don't understand" in 230 languages, J. Runner's webpage has translations in many languages for the following phrases: *Hello, How are you?, Welcome, Goodbye, Please, Thank you, What is your name?, My name is . . . , Do you speak English?, Yes,* and *No.* There is also a link to Internet Language Resources; see http://www.elite.net/~runner/jennifers/understa.htm.

Source: Runner (2000).

Oral versus Written Language.   Orality is the foundation of languages. Written expression is a later development. In fact, of the thousands of reported languages in use, only 78 have a written literature (Edmonson, 1971). Research has suggested that acquiring literacy involves more than learning to read and write. Thinking patterns, perception, cultural values, communication style, and social organization can be affected by literacy (Goody, 1968; Ong, 1982; Scribner & Cole, 1978). In studying oral societies, researchers have noted that the structure and content of messages tend to be narrative, situational, oriented toward activity or deeds, and lacking in detail. In contrast, the style of literacy is conceptual rather than situational. Words are separate from the social context of deeds and events, and ideas can be extracted from narratives. In an oral society, learning takes place in groups because narration must have an audience. This contrasts to a literate society in which reading and writing can be solitary experiences. Separation from the group appears to be one of the burdens of literacy. In an oral society, much reliance is placed on memory, as this is the principal means of preserving practices and traditions (Ong, 1982).

Hmong immigrants in the United States demonstrate the comparative disadvantage of an individual from an oral culture when expected to perform in a literate environment. When registering children in school, Hmong parents are required to know such details as children's birthdates, ages, and immunization dates—facts that are not normally maintained by these families—whereas the knowledge that they have about their children's abilities, strengths, and skills is seldom tapped. In the abstract, categorical world of school, detached from situation and nature, Hmong individuals may become frustrated. The very concept of independent study is alien to this culture because learning had always occurred in community groups. Learning in groups of strangers and doing homework, a solitary endeavor, may run counter to traditional group practices and may distance children from their families. As Hmong children become literate and engage in independent study, parents may become disturbed over the loss of centrality and power in their children's lives. This may produce family tension (Shuter, 1991).

Students from literate cultures whose alphabets radically differ from the Roman alphabet may experience delays in acquiring written English. Some writing systems represent a direct sound-symbol correspondence; Khmer, for example, is far more regular and phonetic than the English writing system. Other writing systems, such as Korean and Japanese, which incorporate Chinese ideographs, have an even more indirect sound-symbol correspondence than does English. Vietnamese students have an advantage over Cambodian, Laotian, and Chinese students in studying English because Vietnamese writing uses the Roman alphabet with the addition of diacritical marks to represent different tonal values. The California State Department of Education *Handbooks for Teaching Students from Diverse Cultures* (*Cantonese-Speaking Students* [1989a]; *Japanese-Speaking Students* [1987]; *Korean-American Students* [1992]; *Pilipino-Speaking Students* [1986]; *Portuguese-Speaking Students* [1989b]; and *Vietnamese-Speaking Students* [1994]) are designed to help school personnel understand and work with these second language students. For ordering information, see http://www.cde.ca.gov/cdepress, then click on "catalog."

Understanding in general how culture affects education can enable teachers to adapt instruction to bridge the home/school gap for English learners. Teachers need to pursue specific information about the cultures of their students by means of two distinct learning routes. One approach is to research the students' cultures through reading, viewing films, and using other media that present cultural information. A second approach is to interact directly with students' cultures by attending community meetings, making home visits, getting to know parents or spokespersons in the community, and inviting such people to the classroom. Recent techniques borrowed from anthropology can be used to investigate culture more closely.

How Teachers Can Learn about Their Students

Schools are organized to expect certain processes: ways of thinking, communicating, and participating. When children possess the repertoires on which school depends, they are predisposed to succeed in the school environment. When cultures provide a different set of social and psychological practices, teachers and students may become mutually frustrated. Teachers who understand the culture of their students can introduce changes in the classroom to make practices more compatible with students' styles. The study of culture is important because this information can help to understand how groups of students are similar in their reaction to schooling. The need to educate individual students does not decline in importance but, rather, is heightened through a deeper understanding of individuals within their cultural context. With this cultural knowledge, classroom routines can be organized to encourage more effective learning, and information about the students' cultures can be incorporated into the content of instruction.

One method, ethnographic study, has proved useful in learning about the ways that students' cultural experiences in the home and community compare with the culture of the schools. Ethnography is an inquiry process that seeks to provide cultural explanations for behavior and attitudes. Culture is described from the insider's point of view, as the classroom teacher becomes not only an observer of the students' cultures but also an active participant (Erickson, 1977; Mehan, 1981; Robinson, 1985). Parents and community members, as well as students, become sources for the gradual growth of understanding on the part of the teacher.

Techniques

Ethnography involves gathering data in order to understand two distinct cultures: the culture of the students' communities and the culture of the classroom. To understand the home and community environment, teachers may participate in community life, interview community members, and visit the student's home. To understand the school culture, teachers may observe in a variety of classrooms, be observed by visitors in their own classroom, audio- and videotape classroom inter-action, and interview other teachers and administrators. However, before engaging in the study of students' cultures, teachers can engage in self-assessment activities that will provide them with a beginning understanding and appreciation of their own origins and values.

Self-Study. Self-study is a powerful tool for understanding culture. One can start a culture inquiry by investigating one's personal name, by asking oneself, "Where did I get my name? Who am I named for? In which culture did the name originate? What does the name mean?" A self-examination of one's favorite cultural customs—such as holiday traditions, home decor, and favorite recipes—is also suggested. More difficult self-examination questions treat the mainstream U.S. values of individual freedom, self-reliance, competition, individualism, and the value of hard work. One might ask oneself, "If someone in authority tells me to do something, do I move quickly or slowly? If someone says, 'Do you need any help?' do I usually say, 'No, thanks. I can do it myself'? Am I comfortable promoting

Cultural Self-Study: Self-Exploration Questions

Describe yourself as a preschool child. Were you compliant, curious, adventure-some, goody-goody, physically active, nature loving? Have you observed your parents with other children? Do they encourage open-ended exploration, or would they prefer children to play quietly with approved toys? Do they encourage initiative?

What was the knowledge environment like in your home? What type of reading did your father/mother do? Was there a time when the members of the family had discussions about current events or ideas/issues? How much dissent was tolerated from parental viewpoints? Were children encouraged to question the status quo? What was it like to learn to talk/think in your family?

What kind of grade-school pupil were you? What is your best memory from elementary school? What was your favorite teacher like? Were you an avid reader? How would you characterize your cognitive style and learning style preferences? Was the school you attended ethnically diverse? What about your secondary school experience? Did you have a diverse group of friends in high school?

What is your ethnic group? What symbols or traditions did you participate in that derived from this group? What do you like about your ethnic identity? Is there a time now when your group celebrates its traditions together? What was the neighborhood/community like in which you grew up?

What was your experience with ethnic diversity? What were your first images of race or color? Was there at time in your life when you sought out diverse contacts to expand your experience?

What contact do you have now with people of very dissimilar racial/ethnic backgrounds? How would you characterize your desire to learn more? Given your learning style preferences, how would you go about this?

myself (for example, talking about my achievements in a performance review)? Do I prefer to work by myself or on a team? Do I prefer to associate with high achievers, and avoid spending much time with people who do not work hard?" These and other introspective questions help pinpoint one's own cultural attitudes. Without a firm knowledge of one's own beliefs and behaviors, it is difficult to contrast the cultural behaviors of others. However, the process is challenging and ongoing. It is hard to observe one's own culture!

Observations.   Observations of other cultures must be carried out, ideally, with the perspective that one is seeing the culture for the first time from the point of view of a complete outsider. Nunan (1993) calls this the use of an "estrangement device"—for example, pretending one is an alien from Mars and watching without preconceived ideas. Of course, when observing interactions and behaviors in another culture, one always uses the frame of reference supplied by one's own culture. When observing a religious ceremony in a local church, for example, one would feel a sense of strangeness and discomfort in not knowing quite how to react in comparison with behavior in one's own church. This is the essence of observation/participation.

Observers need to be descriptive and objective and make explicit their own attitudes and values in order to overcome hidden sources of bias. This requires training. However, the classroom teacher can begin to observe and participate in the students' culture, making field notes after participating and perhaps summing up the insights gained in an ongoing diary that can be shared with colleagues in shared inquiry. Such observation can document children's use of language within the community, etiquettes of speaking, listening, writing, greeting, getting or giving information, values, and aspirations, norms of communication—in short, data about the categories of culture described in this chapter. When analyzing the culture of the classroom, one might look at classroom management and routines; affective factors (students' attitudes toward activities, teachers' attitudes toward students); classroom talk in general; and nonverbal behaviors and communication. In addition to the raw data of behavior, the thoughts and intentions of the participants can also be documented.

Interviews.   Interviews can be divided into two types: structured and unstructured. Structured interviews have a set of questions predetermined to gain specific kinds of information. Unstructured interviews are more like conversations in that they can range over a wide variety of topics, many of which the interviewer would not necessarily have anticipated. As an outsider learning about a new culture, the classroom teacher would be better served initially with an unstructured interview, beginning with general questions and being guided in follow-up questions by the interviewee's responses. The result of the initial interview may in turn provide a structure for learning more about the culture during a second interview or conversation. A very readable book about ethnography and interviewing is *The Professional Stranger: An Informal Introduction to Ethnography* (Agar, 1980).

Home Visits.   Home visits are one of the best ways teachers can learn what is familiar and important to their students. The home visit can be a "social call" or a brief report on the student's progress that enhances rapport with students and parents. Scheduling an appointment ahead of time is a courtesy that some cultures may require and provides a means for one to ascertain if home visits are welcome. Dress should be professional. The visit should be short (20 to 30 minutes) and the conversation positive, especially about the student's schoolwork. Viewing the child in the context of the home provides a look at the parent/child interaction, the resources of the home, and the child's role in the family. One teacher announces to the class at the beginning of the year that she is available on Friday nights to be invited to dinner. Knowing in advance that their invitation is welcomed, parents and children are proud to act as hosts.

Sources

As literate individuals, teachers can use printed, electronic, and video materials, books, and magazines to learn about other cultures. However, the richest source of information is local—the life of the community. Students, parents, and community members can provide insights about values, attitudes, and habits.

Students.   Students generally provide teachers with their initial contact with other cultures. Through observations, one-on-one interaction, and group participatory processes, teachers gain understanding about various individuals and their cultural repertoire. Teachers who are good listeners offer students time for shared conversations by lingering after school or opening the classroom during lunchtime. Teachers may find it useful to ask students to map their own neighborhood. This is a source of knowledge from the students' perspectives about the boundaries of the neighborhood and surrounding areas.

Parents.   Parents can be sources of information in much the same way as their children. Rather than one or two formal conferences, PTA open house events, and gala performances, the school may encourage parent participation by opening the library once a week after school. This offers a predictable time in which parents and teachers may casually meet and chat. Parents can also be the source for information that can form the basis for classroom writing. Using the Language Experience Approach, teachers can ask students to interview their parents about common topics such as work, interests, and family history. In this way students and parents together can supply knowledge about community life. Although it may be more difficult to involve working parents, the work that they perform can be a source about the knowledge and expertise in the community.

Community Members.   Community members are an equally rich source of cultural knowledge. Much can be learned about a community by walking or driving through it, stopping to make a purchase in local stores and markets. One teacher who was hesitant about visiting a particular area in a large city arranged to walk through the neighborhood with a doctor whose office was located there. Other teachers may ask older students to act as "tour guides." During these visits, the people of the neighborhood can be sources of knowledge about housing, places where children and teenagers play, places where adults gather, and sources of food, furniture, and services.

Through community representatives, teachers can begin to know about important living patterns of a community. A respected elder can provide information about the family and which members constitute a family. A community leader may be able to contrast the community political system with the city or state system. A religious leader can explain the importance of religion in community life. Teachers can attend local ceremonies and activities to learn more about community dynamics.

The Internet.   Websites proliferate that can introduce the curious to other cultures. Webcrawler programs assist the user to explore content using keyword prompts.

How Teachers Can Use What They Learn about Their Students (Culturally Responsive Pedagogy)

> The selection of a particular teaching method reflects cultural values more than it argues for the superiority of the method. Cultures succeed in educating those they choose to educate, and whom they choose to educate also reflects a cultural bias. . . . Nothing about the educational process is absolute. Every component reflects a cultural choice, conscious or unconscious, about whom to educate, how, when, in what subjects, for what purpose, and in what manner. (Andersen & Powell, 1988, pp. 210–211)

Culture is embedded in the life of the school. Teachers are cultural transmitters. The way they teach is a product of their own culture and the way that their culture taught them to learn. For some children, the culture of the school may be so

Learning about Cultures: Indian Culture via the Internet

IndusVillage.com is a comprehensive and interactive Internet site that makes cultural content available for the growing Indian population in the United States and Canada. A writing team comprised of 45 urban journalists provides information, services, entertainment, arts and culture, and ecommerce updates to Indians who no longer live in India but who still seek a connection to their native country. Registered users can also utilize features such as Village MatchMaker, a customized dating service, and Your Village, wherein users can create personal websites for family and friends.

Source: M. (2000).

different from the culture of the home that they have difficulty learning in the context and manner provided by the school. However, it is not enough simply to explain children's differential school success as a cultural mismatch between home and school. What happens in a classroom can be influenced by teachers whose behavior and values bridge any gap between home and school for the benefit of the students.

Teachers who understand students' cultures can design instruction to meet children's learning needs. They invite students to learn by welcoming them, making them feel that they belong, and presenting learning as a task at which they can succeed. Barriers are often erected between students of culturally diverse communities and the school because teachers and students do not share the same perceptions of what is acceptable behavior and what is relevant learning. Teaching styles, interaction patterns, classroom organization, curriculum, and involvement with parents and the community are factors that are within the teacher's power to adapt. The result is culturally compatible teaching.

Teaching Styles (Cultural Orientation)

Becoming an active member of a classroom learning community requires specific cultural knowledge and the ability to use that knowledge appropriately in specific contexts. Students from a nonmainstream culture are acquiring a second culture in school. The contrast between the patterns acquired at home and those demanded by the school may create behavioral conflicts that require selective change and adjustment (Trueba, 1989). Teachers raised in a mainstream culture have elements of that culture embedded in their personal teaching approach. Some of these elements may need to be modified to meet the needs of students from other cultures. As a beginning step, teachers can examine six teaching styles that have been identified by Fischer and Fischer (1979), along with their possible effect on students from a variety of cultural backgrounds (see Figure 10.2).

Even in monocultural classrooms, the teacher's style is more in accordance with some students than with others. Flexibility becomes a key in reaching more students. In a multicultural classroom, this flexibility is even more crucial. With knowledge of various teaching styles, teachers can examine their own style, observe students' reactions to that style, ask questions about a teacher's expected role and style in the community, and modify their style as necessary.

Teacher/Student Interactions

The teacher/student relationship is culturally mandated in general ways, although individual relationships vary. Teacher/student interaction may derive from parent/child relationships or from values transmitted by the parent toward teachers and schooling. Students who immigrate may bring with them varying teacher/student interactions. For example, in some cultures, learning takes place in an absolutely quiet classroom where the teacher is in complete control and authority is never questioned. In other cultures, students talk among themselves and move

FIGURE 10.2   **Teaching Styles and Impact on Cultural Diversity**

Task-Oriented Teacher
- Requires specific performance from students and expects them to be independent of the social environment when working.
- Appeals to students who have field-independent learning styles but may be difficult for those from group-oriented cultures.

Cooperative Planner
- Involves students in setting objectives and choosing activities.
- Appeals to students who are more comfortable taking responsibility for their own learning.

Emotionally Exciting Teacher
- Embues learning with excitement and high energy.
- Some students respond to this sense of excitement, whereas others may be overstimulated and unable to complete tasks.

Child-Centered Teacher
- Structures learning activities in which students can pursue their own interests.
- Difficult for students from cultures that center around adults and their needs.

Subject-Centered Teacher
- Believes in "covering" the curriculum and may feel little ownership of the content.
- Relevance of the curriculum may not always be clear to students.

Learning-Centered Teacher
- Displays equal concern for the students and for the subject to be learned and focuses on the individual student's ability.
- Can be highly successful when cultural learning patterns are taken into consideration.

Source: Adapted from Fischer and Fischer (1979).

freely about the classroom. Attitudes toward authority, teacher/student relationships, and teacher expectation of student achievement vary widely. Yet the heart of the educational process is in the interaction between teacher and student. This determines the quality of education the student receives.

Power and Authority.   Most students expect power and authority to be vested in the teacher, and teachers expect respect from students. Respect is communicated verbally and nonverbally and is vulnerable to cultural misunderstanding. In the United States, respect is shown to teachers by looking at them, but in some cultures looking at the teacher is a sign of disrespect. Moreover, students are expected to raise their hands in North American classrooms if they wish to ask or answer a question. Vietnamese culture, on the other hand, does not have a way for students to signal a desire to talk to a teacher; students speak only after the teacher has spoken to them (Andersen & Powell, 1991). In general, one must not conclude that a particular behavior is disrespectful; it may be that the child has learned different customs for communicating with those in authority.

Teacher/Student Relationships. The relationships that are possible between teachers and students also show cultural influences. In some parts of the world, it is acceptable to call a teacher by the first name, indicating that relations between teachers and students are warm, close, and informal. Others may be wary of a teacher's motives and take a long time to share a feeling of rapport. The role of teachers in multicultural classrooms is to make explicit their understandings of the teacher/student relationship, to elicit from students their respective expectations, and to build a mutually satisfying classroom community.

Teachers' Expectations. Expectations for student achievement are also a feature of student/teacher interactions. Students of whom much is expected are given more frequent cues and prompts to respond, are asked more and harder questions, are given a longer time to respond, are encouraged to provide more elaborate answers, and are interrupted less often (Good & Brophy, 1984). Teachers tend to be encouraging toward students for whom they have high expectations. They smile at these students more often and show greater warmth through nonverbal responses such as leaning toward the students and nodding their head as students speak (Woolfolk & Brooks, 1985). Some teachers expect more from Asian Americans than from other minorities because of the "model minority" myth. Acting toward students on the basis of these stereotypes is a form of racism, which is detrimental to all.

Classroom Organization

The typical organization of U.S. classrooms is that of a teacher-leader who gives assignments or demonstrates to the students who act as audience. Teacher presentations are usually followed by some form of individual study. Learning is then assessed through recitation, quizzes, or some other performance. Small group work, individual projects, or paired learning require distinct participation structures, ways of behaving and speaking. Learning how to behave in these settings may require explicit cultural adaptation. Many students new to U.S. classrooms have never before taken part in group problem solving, story retelling, or class discussion. Such activities entail social as well as linguistic challenges. Teachers can help students by providing clear instructions and ample models, by calling on more self-confident students first, and by assigning self-conscious students minor roles at first in order not to embarrass them.

The explicit cultural knowledge needed to function well in a classroom is evident when students first encounter school, in preschool or kindergarten. Heath (1983b) describes children from two distinct communities as they play in preschool. Children from one community were able to comply with teachers' rules for various activity centers (block building, reading, playing with puzzles). They had learned in their homes to play only certain kinds of games in certain areas and to put their toys away when finished. Children from a different community did not confine toys to specific areas but, instead, were creative and improvised new and flexible functions for the toys, often mixing items from different parts of the room. A puzzle piece that looked like a shovel, for example, was taken outside to the sandbox. The preschool teacher, in despair, could only remind them, "Put the puzzle pieces back where they belong." As Heath points out:

> [These] children . . . were accustomed to playing with toys outdoors almost all of the time and they insisted on taking the school's "indoor toys" outside; at home, almost all their toys stayed outside, under the porch, or wherever they were left when play ended. Moreover, at home, they were accustomed to using toys for purposes they created, not necessarily those which the toy manufacturer had envisioned. (p. 275)

Thus, the cultural difference in the home created differences in the school that teachers used to validate their perceptions about which students were better behaved and which students were more academically capable than others.

Curriculum

Many aspects of the school curriculum are highly abstract and contain themes and activities for which many minority students have little referent. Some teachers, rather than finding ways in which students can become familiar with academically challenging content, are quick to devise alternative activities of lower academic worth. Research on Alaska Native Education suggests a number of abuses perpetrated in the name of "being sensitive to children's cultural backgrounds." Teachers often exempt Alaska Native students from standards applicable to other students. For example, they assign an essay on "Coming to the City from the Village" as a substitute for a research paper. They justify the lack of challenging courses with comments such as, "Well, they are going home to live in their village. What do they need algebra for anyway?" Too many lessons are created featuring stereotypic content (kayaks and caribou) that demonstrate a shallow cultural relevance (Kleinfeld, 1988).

Teachers who lack a solid foundation of cultural knowledge are often guilty of trivializing the cultural content of the curriculum. The sole cultural reference may be to holidays or food, or they may have "ethnic" bulletin boards only during certain times of the year (Black History Month). Books about children of color are read only on special occasions and units about different cultures are taught once and never mentioned again. People from cultures outside the United States are only shown in "traditional" dress and rural settings or, if they are people of color, are always shown as poor. Native Americans may be represented as from the past. Moreover, students' cultures are misrepresented if pictures and books about Mexico, for example, are used to teach about Mexican Americans or books about Africa are used to teach about African Americans (Derman-Sparks & Anti-Bias Curriculum Task Force, 1988).

In her article "Educating Teachers for Cultural and Linguistic Diversity: A Model for All Teachers," Parla (1994) discusses issues related to the multicultural classroom and includes information on cultural sensitivity, linguistic diversity, and teaching strategies that can help teachers grow in their understanding of cultural issues and translate that understanding into classroom practice. The article can be found at http://www.ncbe.gwu.edu/miscpubs/nysabe/vol9/model.htm.

The following checklist can help teachers assess the extent to which ethnic, linguistic, and gender biases exist in the curriculum:

- What groups are represented in texts, discussion, and bulletin board displays? Are certain groups invisible?
- Are the roles of minorities and women presented in a separate manner from other content—isolated or treated as a distinct topic?
- Are minorities (and women) treated in a positive, diversified manner or stereotyped into traditional or rigid roles?
- Are the problems faced by minorities presented in a realistic fashion, with a problem-solving orientation?
- Is the language used in the materials inclusive or are biased terms used such as masculine forms (mankind, mailman)?
- Does the curriculum foster appreciation of cultural diversity?
- Are experiences and activities, other than those common to middle class/ European American culture, included?

Parental Involvement in Cultural Mediation

Parent and community involvement supports, encourages, and provides opportunities for parents and educators to work together in educating students. Parents need to become involved in different settings and different levels of the educational process. Parents help teachers to establish a genuine respect for their children and the strengths that they bring to the classroom. They can work with their own children at home or serve on school committees. Collaborative involvement in school restructuring includes parent and community members who help to set goals and allocate resources.

Parents play an important role as "brokers" or go-betweens who can mediate between the school and home to solve cultural problems and create effective home/school relations (Arvizu, 1992). One Chinese American parent successfully intervened in a school situation to the benefit of her daughter and her classmates:

> After my daughter was teased by her peers because of her Chinese name, I gave a presentation to her class on the origin of Chinese names, the naming of children in China, and Chinese calligraphy. My daughter has had no more problems about her name. What is more, she no longer complains about her unusual name, and she is proud of her cultural heritage. (Yao, 1988)

It is important that parents not be used in a compensatory manner or given the message that they need to work to bring students "up" to the level of an idealized norm. This approach often makes parents feel that they are the cause of their children's failure in school. Attributing students' lack of success to parental failure does not recognize that the school itself may be the culprit by failing to meet students' needs.

Whether parents are willing to come to school is largely dependent on their attitude toward school, a result in part of the parents' own school experiences. This attitude is also a result of the extent to which they are made welcome to the schools. "Invitational barriers" can exclude parents as well as students. On the other hand, teachers who are willing to reach out to parents and actively solicit information from them about their children and their hopes for their children's schooling are rewarded with a richer understanding of students' potential. Ways to involve parents as cultural mediators include the following (Banks, 1993):

- Establish an explicit open-door policy so parents will know they are welcome.
- Send written information home about classroom assignments and goals and encourage parents to reply.
- Call parents periodically when things are going well and let them know when they can call.
- Suggest specific ways parents can help in assignments.
- Get to know the community by visiting the community, letting parents know when you are available to visit homes or talk at some other location.
- Arrange several parent conferences a year and let parents talk about their child's achievement.
- Solicit parents' views on education by a simple questionnaire, telephone interviews, or student/parent interviews.

Parents and older siblings can be encouraged to work with preschool and school-age children in a variety of activities. Rather than recommending that parents speak English more at home (speaking broken English may severely limit the quality and quantity of verbal interaction between parents and children), teachers can encourage parents to verbalize with children in ways that build underlying cognitive skills. Parents can sit with the child and look at a book, pointing to pictures and asking questions; they can read a few lines and let the child fill in the rest, or let the child retell a familiar story. Children can listen to adults discuss something or observe reading and writing in the primary language. Schools can assist communities with implementing literacy or cultural classes or producing a community primary language newspaper. The school can also educate students and parents on the benefits of learning the home language of the parents and can find ways to make dual-language proficiency a means of gaining prestige at school (Ouk, Huffman, & Lewis, 1988).

This chapter has emphasized the important role that teachers can play in learning about their communities and cultures, and in reducing the cultural shock between home and school by working actively toward the creation of culturally compatible instruction. The best way for a teacher to understand culture is first to understand himself or herself, and the extent to which U.S. mainstream cultural values are explicitly or implicitly enforced during instruction. A teacher who understands his or her own teaching and learning styles can then ask to what extent each student is similar or dissimilar. This goes a long way toward understanding individual differences. Then, the teacher may use direct personal observation of social behavior to construct an image of students' cultures from the perspective of the members of those cultures. This understanding can then be used to organize classroom activities in ways that are comfortable and promote learning. Thus, an understanding of cultural diversity leads to engagement in the struggle for equity, and then to a commitment to promoting educational achievement for all students. In a multicultural classroom, there may be no single best way for teachers to teach or for students to learn. A variety of activities—ones that appeal to different students in turn—may be the most effective approach. The observation cycle continues as teachers watch students to see *which* approaches meet *whose* needs. The key for the intercultural educator is to be sensitive, flexible, and open.

The Role of Educators in Language Planning and Policy

The teacher had a new student who came from Ethiopia and spoke no English. She could not speak the student's language . . . but rather than allowing him to languish, she chose to allow him to teach the class enough of his native language so that they could all communicate a little bit. . . . The children got excited about discovering a new language. This led to the teacher doing a unit on Africa complete with a wall-size relief mural of the entire continent. The end result was that the Ethiopian student was treated as a valued part of the class. He was able to contribute the richness of his culture while learning about his new home.

—Freeman & Freeman, 1992

Teachers have a significant influence over the daily lives of students in their classroom. They can actively create a climate of warmth and acceptance for English learners, supporting the home language while fostering the growth of a second language. Conversely, they can allow policies of the school to benefit only the language majority students by accepting the exclusive use of the dominant language, and permitting majority language students to gain advantage at the expense of those students who speak minority languages. This day-to-day influence and reaction of teachers amounts to a *de facto* language policy.

Language policies determine the organization and management of schooling (see Figure I.1). Such factors as class size, allocation of classrooms, availability of primary language instruction, availability of support services for English learners, and funds for curricular materials are determined by policies that are made by decisions at the federal, state, local, or school level. The question of *who makes policy* and *who influences policy* is important. Can teachers influence language policy and planning on a scale larger than their single classroom—on a schoolwide level, on a districtwide level, on the level of a community as a whole, on a statewide or national basis? Or are decisions of language planning and policy too remote from the daily life of classrooms for teachers to be influential?

Language planning has been defined by Rubin (1976) as "the study of solutions to language problems by authorized government organizations" (p. 403). Robinson (1988) echoes the idea that language planning is a governmental activity. "Language planning is official, government-level activity concerning the selection and promotion of a unified administrative language or languages. It represents a coherent effort by individuals, groups, or organizations to influence language use or development" (p. 1). The central idea of language planning is that actions and decisions are deliberate: The term *language planning* suggests "an organized pursuit of solution to language problems typically at the national level" (Fishman, 1973, pp. 23–24). An example of a government language decision is the Voting Rights Act of 1975, which mandates that bilingual ballots be provided in areas in which over 5 percent of the population is non-English speaking. In many countries of the world, such decisions regarding native languages are top down, stemming from the highest levels of government. In the United States, language decisions are made at many levels, depending on the jurisdiction of the government agencies involved. Therefore, it is important to examine language planning and policy decisions at many levels.

Planning and policies can be formal and official or informal, such as efforts exerted to create and manipulate attitudes toward languages and language variations (Corson, 1990). Both formal and informal policies have an impact on second language teaching. Like it or not, teachers work under conditions that are highly affected by social and political conditions. Language planning is performed on a daily basis by classroom teachers. Ideally, such daily decisions are performed within a context of support for exemplary instructional practices. If this is not the case, classroom teachers' efforts are undermined or undone by other forces.

A Critical Approach to Language Planning and Policy

Several sociologists and social philosophers who study language and society have urged a wider perspective on the social tensions that underlie arguments about educational language usage. A critical perspective, one that looks at broad social issues of dual language proficiency and language policy, has developed from the work of five theorists in particular: James Tollefson, Michel Foucault, Norman Fairclough, Pierre Bourdieu, and Jim Cummins.

Tollefson: Power and Inequality in Language Education

Tollefson (1995) has brought together the work of many researchers who have examined the social policies and practices that lead to inequity for nonnative language speakers. By raising issues of language equity in various international contexts, Tollefson has expanded the often-narrow perspective of national language advocates and laid the foundation for a worldwide vision of language equity issues.

He contrasts two distinct directions taken by the study of the sociology of language: the *descriptive* and the *evaluative* (Tollefson, 1991). A descriptive approach seeks to understand the relationship of language behavior and social participation. Sociologists who use this approach examine such linguistic phenomena as *diglossia* (why low-status versus high-status language is used in various contexts); *code shifting* (why bilingual speakers choose one language over another in social contexts); *relations of dominance* (how language is used to establish and maintain social position); and *register shifts* (how the formality/informality of language shapes rules and norms of interaction).

An evaluative approach, on the other hand, looks at such language policy issues as efforts to *standardize or purify language,* attempts to *preserve or revive endangered languages,* and movements to *establish national languages* or *legislate language usage.* It is clear from the separate domains of inquiry that those who study language descriptively focus on language as it is actually used, and those who take an evaluative perspective have an agenda of shaping or changing language behavior.

Many of the issues underlying descriptive versus evaluative approaches pivot around one's view of language diversity. Language diversity can be seen as a *problem,* as a *right,* or as a *resource* (Galina, 1997; Ruiz, 1984). The view that dual language proficiency is a problem that must be remedied is, at best, socially and economically shortsighted and, at worst, the foundation for linguistic genocide (defined by Skutnabb-Kangas, 1993, as "systematic extermination of a minority language"). The position that language diversity is a right has been the basis for the court cases and congressional mandates that have created bilingual education; however, these movements have probably been successful because of the emphasis on transitional efforts, with bilingual education seen as a right that expires when a student makes the shift into English.

The idea that language diversity is a resource—particularly economic, but also social and personal—is a difficult proposition for many U.S. Americans who believe that investing in human cultural and linguistic resources is not essential. The persistent trade deficit incurred by the United States has been caused in large part because people in other countries use English to market goods successfully in the United States, whereas the number of U.S. Americans who are sufficiently fluent in two or more languages to reciprocate is nowhere adequate. Instead of a successful dual language educational system, many schools in the United States allow a young child's primary language to wither and die and then fail to create foreign language proficiency within a three-year high school program. Dual language proficiency is too often the privilege of the elite, who can afford private tutors and foreign travel.

In contrast, many in the working class maintain conversational proficiency in the primary language but do not attain a high level of cognitive/academic proficiency either in the primary language or in English. The work of Tollefson and his colleagues (see Pennycook, 1994; Skutnabb-Kangas, 2000) have documented that fights for language equity have profound ramifications for social as well as economic policy on a worldwide basis.

Tollefson's work in providing a larger context for viewing the struggles of minority language speakers is useful in policy settings in which an economic argument is made for English-only schooling (that English-only schooling furthers economic success for EL students). Ironically, this is not the case. Dual language proficiency—attaining advanced skills in more than one language—will be the source of employment advancement for most job seekers in the coming global economy.

Foucault: The Power of Discursive Practices

Foucault, a twentieth-century social historian, traced the spread of power relations in the modern world—relations that are sustained by means of networks shaped largely by language practices. In several important treatises, Foucault outlined the links between power and language. He documented ways in which authorities have used language to repress, dominate, and disempower social groups in favor of social norms that are favorable to those in power; yet conversely, certain social groups have appropriated or acquired language practices that mimic those in power and thus have shaped power to their own ends. Foucault (1979, 1980) emphasized that the struggle for power is "a struggle for the control of discourses" (Corson, 1999, p. 15). In this same vein, Gramsci (1971) conceptualized social power as hegemonic; that is, people are influenced to follow invisible norms and forms of cultural power, even when it is not to their advantage to do so. Thus, the forms of power that benefit the dominant class influence and shape the behavior of subordinated classes, sometimes to their detriment.

Foucault's contribution to the study of language policy, although indirect, is profound. He has shown that language is not neutral; discursive practices are inseparable from the workings of power, and, in fact, are the direct vehicle for the circulation of power. Power, however, is neutral; it can be a creative force for the internalization of power for those who use discourse masterfully, as well as a destructive force that excludes those without effective language practices.

Fairclough: Critical Language Analysis

Although Foucault laid the foundation for the study of the role of language in the workings of power, Fairclough (1989, 1997) offers a structured means to analyze linguistic features of discourse in order to discover the power messages that are conveyed. Fairclough conceives of discourse as a nested set of boxes: first, the text itself that constitutes the message; second, the institutional influence on the message; and third, the social/cultural influence on the message. Any text, whether spoken or written, has features at these three levels. These levels comprise the power that the message carries. Fairclough's Critical Language Analysis (CLA) offers tools to tease out the hidden messages of power in a discourse.

The first, or innermost box, describes the features of the text. In order to read the message "between the lines," one might ask of any text, "What is the style of writing? What level of vocabulary is employed? What is assumed that the reader knows? What features of gendered language are noticeable? Who is responsible for the actions, opinions, or stance taken in the text? Where did the text originate? What interaction generated it? What is said? What is unsaid, but implied? What is the tone of the message?"

The second box, or middle layer of analysis, probes the institutional influence on the text. In order to interpret this influence, one might ask, "What social group or agency (a school, television, schooling, friendship, etc.) supplied the context for the message? What was the institutional origin of the message? Who supplied the platform, the paper, the computer or word processor, or the microphone? Who stands to benefit from the message? How was the text influenced by an institution?"

The third box, or outermost layer of analysis, is the level of sociocultural context. In order to explain the influence this context has on the message, one might ask, "What sociocultural factors came into play (accompanied the text)? How did society's attitudes/treatment of age, gender, culture influence the text?" Or one might speculate, "How might the text have been different had its origin been a person of different culture, gender, or age?"

Fairclough's critical language analysis can be used to examine any item of discourse. For example, suppose CLA is used to scrutinize a parent newsletter sent home from an elementary school to Spanish-speaking parents. The intent of the newsletter is to explain to parents how to help their child with homework. At the level of text, the newsletter appears to be a word-for-word translation of the reverse side of the newsletter, a letter to English-speaking parents. The text seems to have been written on a word processor, in dual columns like a newspaper. There are no illustrations—merely a page full of text. The content has 10 paragraphs, each explaining a different feature of "homework tips." At the institutional level, the parent newsletter is a part of a "School Open House" packet distributed with about six other papers, some of which are in Spanish and some of which are not. The text of the newsletter was written by an assistant principal and translated by an aide. At the sociocultural level, the text assumes that the parents welcome the advice of the school authorities, and that the parents' role is to help the students complete the assignments sent home by the teachers. There is no mention of a role for parents as collaborating with the teacher to determine the worth or value of the assignments.

In contrast, another teacher works with students to write a "Homework Help" manual. The manual is a six-page "little book" composed by students themselves in cooperative groups. Each group decides on a title for their book and students draw on the cover a scene of a student doing school work at home. Each group brainstorms about the book's content. Will this include recommendations of a special place to study at home? Will it mention adequate lighting? Will it discuss how to deal with the distractions of television or of siblings? Will it advise students how to solicit help from parents? Will it advise parents how to communicate to teachers the comparative worth of different types of assignments? Will the book be in dual languages? Each group adds the ideas that the members choose. When the books are ready, the teacher asks each student to take the book home, discuss it with the family, and then come back to class with feedback about whether the suggestions are apt.

Examined with the analytical tools of CLA, one sees a very different product from the parent newsletter previously described. At the level of text, this effort is an individual product each student is proud to show at home, with personalized artwork, student-generated ideas, and student-generated language that is understandable to family members. At the institutional level, both the existing habits of the family and the needs of the school are respected, and communication between home and school are built into the project. At the sociocultural level, the student is positioned as a consultant on the family's habits and values, and the family is positioned as a valued partner in teaching and learning.

Thus, CLA, a structured means of creating awareness of hidden levels of language, can be used to examine assumptions and practices that lie beneath schooling practices. This awareness operates unconsciously but smoothly in skilled power players, but is useful as a conscious tool for those who could benefit from an increased understanding of power, particularly as it operates at the institutional and sociocultural levels. As an analytic tool, it is simple yet easy enough to teach to children as they become aware of what is said—and unsaid—in discourse.

Bourdieu: Language as Social Capital

The French anthropologist Bourdieu has worked to create awareness of the importance of language as cultural capital—that is, as a part of the social "goods" that people accumulate and deploy to assert power and social class advantage. In a capitalist society, those who are born with capital have the advantage of being able to use that capital to amass further capital, whereas those born without capital must work harder to overcome the lack of such capital. Bourdieu includes *social capital* as a major form of cultural capital. The most common form of social capital generated for children in most middle-class families includes providing transportation to public libraries, buying additional school-related materials, visiting museums, providing music or art lessons, traveling, supervising homework, hiring tutors, attending school functions, and even moving into the best school districts (Chang, 2000). Those who are native speakers of a language with high social status receive their language skills as a part of their social capital, the advantage that their family maintains in society; conversely, those born into a language with lower social status have a stigmatized language inheritance to overcome as they move forward in life.

Bourdieu (1977) emphasizes that schools act as agents of an economic system to reproduce the existing distribution of capital. Schools permit the "haves" (those already possessing cultural capital) to succeed at the expense of the "have-nots," those who are comparatively lacking in the linguistic skills, prior knowledge, or other social resources to succeed. This recognition of the importance of schools in the functioning of society emphasizes the key role that education plays in the determination of social success, and permits further understanding of the challenges faced by those whose language skills are not deemed of social importance.

The unique contribution of Bourdieu is his recognition that language, and other intangible social factors, are assets, just as are physical resources. Moreover, in a capitalist society, capital itself is an attractive force that shapes behavior and attitudes. In this same vein, one must recognize that in the classroom of a capitalist society, a teacher's predilection is to be attracted toward social capital—to those children who already appear to be successful—and to shun those who appear to lack this attraction. One might also deduce that a teacher's attention, admiration, and reinforcement are therefore aspects of a teacher's social capital, which he or she can deploy at will. Bourdieu has placed schooling, with its behaviors and practices, squarely in the center of the surrounding economic reality, with policies that act as currency—currency that functions every bit as powerfully as does "hard cash."

Cummins: Language Policies as Emancipatory

Cummins (1996) clearly delineates educational practices that function as collaborative relations of power, and sets these against counterpractices that are coercive in nature. Cummins cautions that children who enter schools in which diversity is *not* affirmed soon grasp that their "difference" is not honored, but, rather, is suspect. If students are not encouraged to think critically, to reflect, and to solve problems, then they are being submitted to a "transmission model" of pedagogy. The result of relations that communicate a sense of reduced worth is underachievement. The result of pressuring students to conform, or participate in schooling practices that are unfair or discriminatory, is that students lose their identity as human beings: They are subjected to what Cummins (1989) calls "identity eradication." To counteract this devaluation of students, teachers' and students' roles must be redefined.

Cummins thus takes a critical pedagogy stance, in line with Paulo Freire's (1985) call for a liberating education of "transforming action," in which teachers are dedicated to social change. Unfortunately, many teachers are unaware of the power practices that either help students to develop or hinder them from developing a sense of control over their own lives with confidence and motivation to succeed academically. They are equally unaware of the ways in which spoken and unspoken language can circulate messages of dominance or subordination—features of institutional racism and disempowerment. Cummins's work, together with the work of other critical pedagogists, highlights the need for structural changes within schools that support positive attitudes, strong personal and social identities on the part of English learners, and academic success.

To summarize the contributions of the critical language theorists, power relations hidden within language issues are a characteristic of societies around the world. The tools of the social language critic work to clarify and reveal the covert power relations that language enables. Language is a chief vehicle for deploying power, whether constructively or destructively. The power potential of any message, verbal or nonverbal, can be systematically analyzed. Language is a kind of social asset, and schools are agencies in which language is used to benefit or to detract from the accrual of social wealth. Schooling practices can empower or dis-empower, depending on the language and cultural policies within the school.

Planning and Policy: The Classroom

A policy that promotes dual language proficiency as a local, state, or national resource begins in the classroom, with teachers who carefully plan and carry out equitable, empowering educational practices. Teachers *can* influence language planning and policy, and those who are experts on the education of English learners *should* be influential. If teachers do not influence planning and policy, decisions will be made by others: by the force of popular opinion, by politicians, by bureaucrats, by demagogues. Teacher influence will not be felt, however, by wishing or hoping. Teachers need to examine closely the possibilities that exist for influence on policy and planning, and then work hard to make this influence a reality. This influence can be wielded in different ways in various social and political arenas: by monitoring procedures and curriculum within the classroom itself, at the school level, and at the level of the local school district; by engendering support within the community; by working within state commissions and professional organizations; and by lobbying for federal policies that benefit English learners.

Educational Equity in Everyday Practices

Equitable educational practices require discipline and vigilant self-observation on the part of the classroom teacher (Tollefson, 1991). Practicing gender, socioeconomic, racial, and cultural equity requires that males and females from minority and majority races and cultures, whether rich or poor, receive equal opportunity to participate, such as being given equally difficult questions to answer during class discussion, along with adequate verbal and nonverbal support. Cultural equity requires teachers to accept students' personalization of instruction; to use multicultural examples to illustrate points of instruction; to listen carefully to the stories and voices of the students from various cultures; and to tie together home and school for the benefit of the students. Issues of socioeconomic equity arise, for example, when assignments for at-home projects are evaluated more highly when they incorporate a wealth of resources that some families can provide and others cannot. Teachers must endeavor to extend the rich, close relationship of mentor and protégé to all students. Referrals to special education, on the one hand, and to gifted or enriched instruction, on the other, should not favor or target students of one gender, race, or culture unfairly. (If school site or district criteria result in *de facto* lack of equity in these areas, teachers may need to ask for a review of the criteria.) Practicing "everyday equity" ensures the possibility of equal opportunity for all. The following classroom policies promote inclusion for students:

- Teachers value the experiences of culturally different children.
- The primary language is seen as a worthy subject for instruction and as a means by which students can acquire knowledge.
- Classroom strategies guarantee boys and girls equal access to the teacher's attention.

The Social Environment

Students come to school for social as well as academic reasons. In observing instruction, students who are socially successful, for a variety of reasons, are often assigned a "halo effect" that makes them also appear more academically successful (Lotan & Benton, 1989). Cohen has demonstrated that an equitable social environment is furthered when cooperative grouping explicitly treats the status differences among students in the classroom (Cohen, DeAvila, Navarrete, & Lotan, 1988; Cohen, Lotan, & Catanzarite, 1990).

School practices in noncurricular areas, such as discipline, and in extracurricular activities, such as school clubs, should be nondiscriminatory. These activities provide ways in which the school climate can foster or retard students' multicultural competence (Bennett, 1986). If the school climate is accepting of the linguistic and cultural identities of students, these identities will develop in ways that are consonant with an academic environment. If not, a resistance culture may develop that rejects schooling, with outcomes such as high dropout rates and high incidences of school vandalism. The formal and the hidden curriculum of a school need to be consistent with one another so that they support diversity and achievement. The social climate of the school can be one of acceptance for all students in the following ways:

- Culturally and linguistically diverse students are grouped heterogeneously.
- Children and staff learn about the cultural practices of the families represented in the school.
- Students can win prestige positions in extracurricular activities regardless of their ethnic or cultural background.
- Dress codes do not discriminate against some subcultures while allowing others to dress as they wish.
- School staff (e.g., office personnel) are equally courteous to all students and visitors.

The Policies Embodied in Teachers' Plans

Teachers can be explicit about issues of equity and multicultural inclusion in planning yearly units and daily lessons. Teachers are responsible for obtaining materials that are nonbiased and promote positive role models from a variety of ethnic groups, and for designing and planning instruction that makes success possible for all students (see Díaz-Rico, 1993). This responsibility cannot be transferred to other decision-making bodies. Materials are readily available that describe multicultural education (see Bennett, 1990; Harris, 1997; Nieto, 2000); it is each teacher's responsibility to make these approaches real for students. Teachers can plan for culturally and linguistically fair instruction in the following ways:

- Students' interests and backgrounds are taken into consideration when planning instruction.
- Materials depict individuals of both genders and of various races and cultures in ways that suggest success.
- Materials for bilingual and multicultural instruction receive an equitable share of budgeted resources.
- Daily plans include adequate time for development of primary language skills.

Policy at the School Level

An exemplary teacher's greatest contribution at the school site may be the positive outcomes evident throughout the school as that teacher's students provide leadership, goodwill, and academic models for other students. However, a school site can be the setting for scores of such students when school personnel take explicit roles in school site decision making.

Collaboration with Colleagues

Schools can benefit greatly when teachers work together. Sharing resources, working together to plan instruction, and teaching with each other add insights and vitality to a job that is often isolating. However, not all teachers at a school seek collaboration, and some may wish to work alone. Regardless, it is vital that personal relations be established and maintained with all colleagues at a school site to ensure that the staff not be polarized along lines of cultural, linguistic, or philosophical differences. Decisions that are often made collaboratively are the following:

- Extra-duty assignments are adjusted for teachers who must translate letters sent home to parents or develop primary language materials.
- Assistance is available for teachers whose classes are affected by students who may be making a transition out of primary language instruction.
- Primary language materials and other materials are freely shared among professional staff.
- Primary language instructors are socially integrated with mainstream staff.

School-Site Leadership

School authorities, particularly principals, can support ELD and bilingual instruction in many ways. Often, principals are the leading advocates for funding increases at the district level. Principals can work with teachers to configure classes and class sizes to the benefit of English learners. Appointing a lead or mentor teacher can help new teachers to adjust to and meet the needs of EL students. Lead teachers may be able to develop professional presentations that showcase student abilities or program features. Districtwide principals' meetings or school board meetings may be venues where these presentations can be seen and heard. By communicating to others about students' abilities as well as innovative program structures for English learners, principals begin to develop a climate of acceptance for linguistic and cultural diversity. This can be accomplished in the following ways:

- Marking policies are monitored to ensure that all students have equal opportunity to receive high grades.
- Staff members with expertise in English language development or primary language instruction are given time to be of assistance to other teachers.
- Teachers with English language development or primary language assignments are given an equal share of mentoring and supervisory assistance.
- Leaders in the school set an example of respect and encouragement for diverse language abilities and cultures within the school.

The Academic Ambiance of the School

Schools that are noted for academic excellence attract community attention because of the success of their students and alumni. Academic competitions outside of schools are one way in which certain schools garner academic laurels and gain the reputation for an academic ambiance. Although spelling bees are traditional competitive events, too often these promote decontextualized skills. Academic decathlons, by contrast, are team efforts in which dedicated teachers can involve students from many ability levels. The better examples of this type of competition tend to promote problem solving rather than simple recall skills. Competitions that require inventive thinking are also available, and the fact that these are less language-dependent may be more attractive to English learners. Schools can foster an academic ambiance in a variety of ways:

- Teachers who sponsor academically oriented extracurricular activities are given extra pay as are athletic coaches.
- Funds are available for students to travel to intellectual competitions.
- Individuals from diverse cultural and linguistic backgrounds are actively solicited for teams that compete for academic awards.
- Some intellectual activities such as contests are held in the primary language.

Involving Parents

Encouraging parents to participate in school activities is vital. The extra step of sending parents letters, reports, and notices in their home language helps to build rapport and extend a welcome to the school. These language policies constitute the daily message that home languages are important and valued. Parents can receive the message that they are valued in many ways:

- Representative parent committees can advise and consent on practices that involve culturally and linguistically diverse students.
- Parents can use the school library to check out books with their children.
- School facilities can be made available for meetings of community groups.

Policy in Local School Districts

The policies of the local school districts are shaped by the values of the community. This may create frustration for teachers who feel that educational decisions are not in the hands of educators. On the other hand, teachers who take responsibility for helping to shape the community's beliefs and values may find that their leadership as teachers is very welcome.

Professional Growth and Service

Serving on district curriculum adoption committees is a way in which teachers can share and contribute their expertise. Teacher-led presentations to other teachers, staff, or community members are also important contributions. Many opportunities exist for such service. Service clubs such as Rotary and Kiwanis provide opportunities for speakers: What better way to reach the business leaders of the community with current information about multicultural and linguistic issues? These activities deliver the message that teachers are knowledgeable and interested in the community at large. Consider the following ideas for teacher involvement:

- Teachers' opinions are consulted for materials purchased by school district and community libraries.
- Teachers perform staff training for others.
- Teachers can participate in leadership training for English language development programs.

The School Board

Teachers are very much aware that school policies are determined by the beliefs of school board members as well as by legal precedents set by state and federal laws and court decisions. Part of the advocacy position suggested by Cazden (1986) is the need for teachers of English learners to espouse and support appropriate programs for EL students before local boards. Federal regulations for schools receiving funds available from the federal government under Title VII (the Bilingual Education Act) mandate that school districts organize and maintain parent advisory groups at the school site level. Such parent groups can be effective in marshaling support for programs designed for language minority groups. School board policies can be influenced in positive ways:

- Policy committees can place policies before the school board in a timely manner, with clear, concise, well-researched presentations.
- Frequent attendance at school board meetings sends the message that the meetings are monitored by friends of language minority issues.

Community Support for English Learners

A supportive community offers a home for linguistic and cultural diversity. This support takes many forms: affirming variety in neighbors' lifestyles, patronizing minority businesses, fund-raising for college scholarships for English learners, and providing community services that are user-friendly for all.

The Public Forum

Communities accept other languages being spoken in the community if there is little fear of economic or political encroachment by immigrants. The following case study illustrates one community's reaction to linguistic diversity:

> Monterey Park, a California community with a large number of Chinese immigrants, was designated an all-American city because of its apparent racial harmony. The Fall 1986 edition of the community activities publication featured articles on the Monterey Park golf course, senior citizens' center, and other local services and included a page written in Chinese to summarize the contents of the issue. Even as this issue was in press, however, a city council meeting in June of that year passed resolutions endorsing legislation to make English the official language of the United States (Roy, 1990). Dicker (1992) describes the following incident. Barry Hatch, a Monterey Park city council member and supporter of the state proposal making English the official language, led a fight to halt the use of public funds for the purchase of Chinese language books for the city's library. Viewing these books as solely benefiting the Chinese community overlooks the fact that the Chinese population has as much right to be supported by the government as any other group. Furthermore, such a view does not recognize the possibility that English-speaking Americans studying Chinese might benefit from these books. In this case, the linguistic chauvinism of a community leader determined local language policy in a *de facto* manner.

Policies of community agencies such as the library can be influenced by the following teacher-led activities:

- Librarians can file teachers' lesson plans in the library and make specific materials accessible to students.
- Bilingual teachers can justify to librarians the need for primary language materials.
- Schools can encourage parents to make better use of community resources such as libraries.

Community Organizations

Service organizations are often run by community leaders who set the tone for the community and who are a source of employment for workers. Business leaders sometimes have strong ideas about education. They usually enjoy dialogue with professional educators and seek to be updated on current beliefs and practices. It is in this dialogue that professional educators need to present the foundation for current pedagogy The leaders of community organizations want to help schools to improve so that their children and their workers will be productive. Obtaining this help is easier when requests are concrete and the justification is strong.

Opposing Racism

In the teachers' lounge, at the post office, and at social gatherings, people express opinions about others' behavior. Often these opinions serve to test the waters, to find out who else holds similar opinions. Remarks that are derogatory to individuals on the basis of race, language, or culture do not further liberty and justice for all. One minority teacher responded to such comments by widening her eyes and saying, "Why, it surprises me to hear a person like you express that kind of opinion." In this way she affirms the person while refusing to accept the derogatory sentiment. Letters to the editor of the local paper are sometimes sources of misinformation or expressed prejudice. Literate people need to protest to the editor of newspapers that publish overtly racist letters and should write letters to rebut such opinions. Teachers as well as other staff members can oppose racism in several ways:

- Teachers can refuse to use materials that contain derogatory images toward certain races and cultures.
- Majority group members can promote the appreciation of minority cultures.
- The school can feature minority languages and cultures in school shows, written communications, and displays.

State Commissions and Professional Organizations

Outside the immediate community, a larger community awaits. Statewide commissions organized by the office of the governor or state boards of education are opportunities for teachers to be involved in writing statewide curricula, adopting textbooks, and serving on advisory boards. Professional organizations at the state and national levels have state counterparts. Joining TESOL (Teachers of English to Speakers of Other Languages) or NABE (National Association for Bilingual Education) puts educators in contact with language development specialists nationally and internationally. These organizations' publications carry news from state affiliates, and newsletters from the state organizations carry news of local associations. If there is no local organization, why not start one?

The Voice of the Expert

Attending district or regional professional conferences is a beginning step toward developing one's own expertise on linguistic and cultural issues and teaching practices. Successful teachers may be able to join with colleagues to develop school-level or district-level presentations about some area of instruction. Reading articles in professional magazines and journals helps to develop particular expertise, as does advanced university coursework. Some journals and publishers solicit publications from teachers. This is one way to share successful classroom practices.

Professional Leadership Roles

A career is developed over a lifetime. Expertise in particular areas continues to grow, along with teaching experience. One can envision a more just and equitable society thirty years from now as today's new teachers reap the harvest of the support for linguistic and cultural diversity that they have promoted. Who acts as a leader in the teaching profession is a direct function of who has the energy to devote to policy issues outside the classroom. Those who are willing to take responsibility within professional organizations by serving on committees, drafting proposals, attending meetings, calling members, stuffing envelopes, and other activities are those who can be called on to serve in leadership positions. It is particularly important for mentors and other experienced teachers to invite beginning teachers to professional meetings so the organizations can benefit from fresh energy. In this way, new teachers can form relationships with peers outside their school site.

Legislation and Public Opinion

State and national legislators are responsive to popular opinion as expressed by letters of support and phone calls on controversial issues. Bilingual education and language issues often arouse strong emotions, perhaps because language itself is so closely connected to the soul of a person or because language policies affect the criteria set for success in the employment vital to economic survival and success in the United States (Heath, 1983a). It is important for legislators to hear from professionals in the field to balance the effect of those who perceive that language and cultural diversity is a threat. The debate that takes place within a legislature brings to public attention the issues involved in any complex area of public life, and allows a public forum for criticizing government policies (Jewell, 1976). The strong backing of professional organizations supports legislators who have the courage to promote dual language education. Public policy can be supported in the following ways:

- Organizations can send subscriptions to professional magazines to legislative libraries.
- Teachers and parents can organize letter-writing campaigns and visit legislators personally to convey interest in language minority issues.

Influencing Federal Policies

In countries where more than one language is spoken, rarely do these languages share an equal social status. Speakers of the dominant language are those who make social policy, including language policy. These policies can range from support for the subordinate language, through benign neglect, to overt language suppression. Decisions are primarily made on political and economic grounds and reflect the values of those in political power (Bratt Paulston, 1992). In general, language situations within a country are symptoms of social and cultural conditions. In the history of the United States, decisions about subordinate languages were sometimes supportive and sometimes repressive. For example, early schooling in German for German immigrants was common until the onset of World War I, when aggressive policy decisions eradicated non-English languages from the public school (Hakuta, 1986). Japanese-language schools were closed down during World War II, and Hispanics were commonly punished for using Spanish in the schools until the 1960s. This pendulum swing from support to suppression defines the extremes of U.S. second language policy. In times of plenty, the attitude toward immigrant languages has been benign neglect. Americans tend to rely on social pressure to enforce the English-only dominance of society. In times of stress, explicit attempts are made to suppress other languages. The current English-only movement (see Chapter 6) is just such an attempt.

English-only groups are particularly incensed by state services in foreign languages, such as drivers' tests, welfare applications, school notices, and state university financial aid forms (Crawford, 1992). Bilingual education funds are the particular target of their lobbying efforts. The success of this movement in California is particularly ironic because Spanish was widely used in early California, and the first California state constitution was written in both English and Spanish (Roy, 1990). Language planning and policy has been influenced by economic and social climates ranging from supportive to repressive; on the whole, teachers have traditionally made little effort to exert any influence within the sphere of these forces. Teachers, however, particularly through their professional organizations, have an increasingly important role to play in public debate.

Federal Funds for Innovation

With the passage of the Goals 2000 reform legislation in 1994, federal funds became available to design innovative programs that provide success for all students.

Numerous schools have restructured using dual language and other enrichment models that actively engage English learners and mainstream students (see McLeod, 1996). Teachers can work with district grant specialists to write successful grant proposals. Notices about competitions for funds and special programs are usually available from state and county offices of education. Individuals who have competed successfully for such funds may be willing to offer workshops for others to increase the general expertise in such areas.

Federal Legislation

Programs such as Title VII (the Bilingual Education Act) originate in Congress. Periodically, such programs must be reauthorized and legislation introduced that continues or modifies them. At such intervals, public opinion plays a large role in determining the continuation of programs that benefit English learners. When bills are introduced that commit federal funds on a large scale to minorities, conservative forces within Congress often target these programs for extinction. At these times, lobbying efforts are needed to communicate the demand for these programs. Cards and letters to congressional representatives may be requested by professional organizations. This is a chance for teachers to use the literacy they advocate.

The National Spirit

A national spirit is created in part by individuals who voice their opinions freely. A national magazine, for example, offers a platform to writers whose opinions can be influential. These magazines are responsive to consumer forces. Writing letters to national magazines on a regular basis helps editors sense the opinions of their readers. Teachers need to exercise their writing skills frequently and at length in order to participate in national arguments that are rehearsed in the media.

Controversial actions and media figures also shape the national spirit. When demagogues arise who voice reactionary or incendiary viewpoints, the population at large must take steps to defuse their voices. Letters to national networks voicing an opposition and distaste for antiminority or racist viewpoints, for example, are necessary in order that these media do not glorify controversial figures and give them undue voice. The United States operates on a system of checks and balances. Those who oppose racism or bigotry must speak up and must speak as loudly as the voices of separation and intolerance. Often, teachers of English learners must become advocates for their concerns until the voices of the minority community become skilled enough to speak for themselves and powerful enough to be heard. Teachers who share the culture and language of the minority community have a natural function as community leaders.

In a nation consisting of over 280 million people, the majority of whom share English as the language of daily interchange, the language skills and rights of minorities are a fragile resource. In times of economic hardship, the majority often turns on the minorities, looking for scapegoats. In times of exterior threats, such as in the national crisis of a world war, differences are forgotten and the efforts of all citizens, including minorities, are needed to achieve victory. Unfortunately, too often in the past, the call for national unity has resulted in segregation, repression, or expulsion of minority groups.

Social and political forces on a national scale may seem overwhelming. Indeed, as much as individualism is a part of the national mythology of the United States, the individual is important only when backed by hundreds of thousands of supporters or hundreds of thousands of dollars. To attain national influence, teachers need to achieve the leadership of large professional organizations and use this leadership wisely to effect constructive change in the education of English learners. This constructive change is possible at every level, from the national to the local, by the use of appropriate professional activities.

At the level of the classroom, language planning and policy mean creating an educational and social climate that makes school a place where all students are comfortable, where all students meet success in learning. The days are past when the failure of large numbers of EL students could be blamed on the students' personal shortcomings or supposed deficiencies in family backgrounds. When students fail to learn, schools and teachers have failed.

If teachers are willing to step outside the confines of the classroom to help students be successful, then it is time to learn how to influence policy on a larger scale. The belief that teachers have no role in language planning and language politics is a denial of professional responsibility, an abdication of authority. A teacher who believes in the potential for success of English learners is in a strong position to fight for the recognition of their rights and the allocation of resources that make educational success possible.

CHAPTER

12 English Learners and Special Education

Srinivasa Ramanujan was born in 1887 in Erode, India, a town in southern India. Nothing is known of his early schooling. At the age of 15, he obtained a copy of Carr's Synopsis of Elementary Results in Pure and Applied Mathematics, *a collection of 6,000 mathematical theorems. By himself, he verified the results of the 6,000 theorems and began to develop his own. He obtained a scholarship to the University of Madras, but lost it because he was wholly devoted to mathematics. Through private correspondence with a leading mathematician of the time, he obtained a position as a visiting scholar at Cambridge, where his inventive powers astounded his peers. He published brilliant papers in English and European journals, and became the first Indian elected to the Royal Society of London. He died at the age of 33 from tuberculosis he contracted in London. Generally unknown to the world at large, he is recognized by mathematicians as one of the most phenomenal geniuses of all time.*

Because India was under the British rule, Ramanujan would have been an English language learner. If he would have been in an American school, would his teacher have referred him to education designated for the gifted/talented?

English learners, as any other cross-section of today's learners, may need special education services. Often, mainstream classroom teachers find themselves responsible for teaching students with special education needs who also need to acquire English. A consultation model introduces constructive ways for teachers of English learners and other certified personnel to collaborate in order to meet the needs of such special learners.

Given the rapid demographic changes that have occurred in schools, communities, and workplaces, a major concern in the field of special education and rehabilitation today is the provision of effective services to multilingual/multicultural diverse populations.... Children and youth of these diverse groups will form a major part of the future workforce in this country. Therefore, the services provided in schools as well as in rehabilitation play an important role in strengthening this workforce for our society. (Chang, 2000)

This chapter includes such topics as identifying English learners with special instructional needs, teaming with resource or special education teachers, teaching strategies for inclusion, and alternative assessments for student performance in the mainstream classroom. The emphasis will be on students with a need for additional instructional mediation, because those students' needs tend to surface in an obvious way. However, similar principles—if not strategies—can be applied to EL students who are gifted and talented.

Researchers who have looked at the special education services available to EL students (e.g., Baca & Cervantes, 1984; Figueroa, 1993; González, 1994) have called this domain "bilingual special education." This tends to connote that services for these students are rendered in the primary language, which may not be the case. Because teachers who are knowledgeable in crosscultural, language, and academic development (CLAD) teaching strategies often deal with the education of exceptional English learners, the education of these students is an important part of the academic preparation of CLAD teachers.

Both special education and special education/English learner interface have come under attack from those who criticize the current models of service delivery. Sleeter (1986) is concerned that the process be examined that labels certain kinds of students as "handicapped" without a critical look at the social and cultural conditions that leave some students unable to profit by regular schooling. Stainback and Stainback (1984) advocate that special education and regular education be merged and that all students receive individualized education. Others (Artiles & Trent, 1994; Bernstein, 1989; Figueroa, Fradd, & Correa, 1989) have addressed the over- or underrepresentation of culturally and linguistically diverse students in special education. Few believe, however, that the current special education system, including the treatment of English learners within that system, will undergo vast systemic reform in the near future, despite contemporary calls for reform.

In their call for a restructuring of bilingual special education, Baca and Valenzuela (1994) offer three primary goals: (1) classrooms should conform to the needs of students rather than students conforming to the classroom; (2) efforts should be made to increase the academic performance of culturally and linguistically diverse special education students; and (3) teachers should be actively involved throughout the assessment process, with assessment-based curricular adaptations becoming a part of the preferral intervention process and a diagnostic teaching model put in place instead of a remedial approach. These goals provide a direction for the efforts to augment and improve the overall delivery of education to English learners. But first, who are these learners? What educational and policy issues does their education raise?

Scenarios and Issues

The issues surrounding learning and second language acquisition are complex. The needs of many students can be addressed only with the aid of careful diagnostic work and documentation of student progress. However, many cases involve similar situations and evoke consistent fundamental questions.

Who Are English Learners with Special Needs?

Because of the complexity of the issues that underlie special educational services for English learners, both personal and academic, it is helpful to personalize these issues with cases drawn from the field. Each scenario does not represent any student in particular, but a composite created from similar circumstances.

Elisa's Memory

Elisa is in third grade and her teacher, Stephanie Robinson, is wondering if Elisa has a memory problem. She did not attend kindergarten, and in first grade the instruction was primarily in Spanish. In second grade, the only class taught in English was social studies. Now that she is being asked to learn to read in English, she doesn't seem to remember words that she has read before. When she reads aloud orally, she can decode most new words adequately, but acts as if each word is new each time—there is little sense of recognition or increase in comprehension when she reencounters a word. Mrs. Robinson is just about to make a referral to special education. Does she have adequate grounds for referral?

Losing ESL after Referral

Alsumana comes from a family that recently emigrated from Papua New Guinea. His mainstream classroom teacher has successfully made a case for referral to testing, but Ron Patton, his pull-out ESL teacher, is not supportive of this referral, because in the past, when a student is placed into a special education environment, that student has lost access to ESL services. Because, in Ron's opinion, success in school ultimately depends on the child's acquisition of English, he would like to ensure that English learners are not deprived of any other services that would help them. How can he still be involved if Alsumana is placed in special education?

Conflict over Testing

Mrs. Espinoza, the fourth-grade classroom teacher, is struggling with Luke. Luke's parents emigrated from Romania and settled in a rural area in the school district. Luke attends school only reluctantly and says that he would rather be working with his father outdoors. Mrs. Espinoza insists his poor performance in school is due to his family situation and his attitude toward schooling, and not a learning disability. The school social worker, however, has advocated all year for Luke to be referred for a special education evaluation. During this time, he has made little academic progress. Should he be referred to special education?

Gangs and Threats

New arrivals are "fresh meat" for the gangs in the area around Bud Kaylor's elementary school. Bud has taught ELD and fifth grade at his school for six years, and although he finds rewards in the challenges of an urban school, he sees the fear and threats that students experience outside the school environment as detrimental to their learning. Although he currently has several students who are bright and eager to learn, they are tense and frightened when they come to school and soon seem to take on a hard, brittle irritability that makes them "tough" in the eyes of their peers. One student, José Luis, seems overcome by fear in the school setting and never speaks a word. Bud feels that psychological counseling could be a way to deal with the social and emotional problems José Luis seems to be experiencing—this seems to be an unacknowledged part of their language acquisition period. Should he refer José Luis for help?

Pressure for Early Exit

Ginny Yang received a request from the parents of Mei-Hua Wang, a student placed in a primary-Mandarin-language classroom, asking the school to place Mei-Hua in an English-only classroom, where she would receive no primary-language support. Ginny has observed that Mei-Hua is a very slow reader who would benefit from more time learning to read in Chinese before being exposed to reading in English. Rather than supporting the transfer to the English-only program, should Ginny refer Mei-Hua for testing to ascertain if she is learning disabled?

Sonia Doesn't Read

Sonia is a native Spanish speaker whose parents are from the Dominican Republic. She did not attend school until the second grade, and now she is in the fifth grade. She was taught reading as soon as possible in Spanish, but now that she does not have access to Spanish reading instruction, she is falling behind. She attends a resource program in reading, but the resource teacher sees that the problems that show up in English (poor oral language, limited vocabulary development, difficulties with writing, and poor comprehension) limit her progress. Because she is so far behind the others in the class in reading, her teacher thinks it is unfair to the other students that she could potentially take up so much time to instruct. Should she be referred to special education?

Tran the Troubled

Tran is a new student in the fourth grade. His family lives a fairly isolated life in a community of Vietnam refugees, but his parents want Tran to grow up speaking English, so they speak to his sister and him in English. However, because they work, they leave Tran for long periods with his grandmother, who only speaks Vietnamese. Tran acts like a dual personality. In class, his performance is uneven; he does not volunteer and does not complete work, yet he seeks constant attention and approval from his teacher. On the playground, his teacher sees in him a quick intelligence that comes out when he interacts with the other boys.

The teacher is unsure of how to handle Tran; he may have a learning disability, but his school problems may be due to extreme cultural differences between home and school. Does she have adequate grounds for referral for psychological testing?

Issues Underlying the Scenarios

Each of these scenarios reflects a particular aspect of the relationship among three distinct domains: learning, second language acquisition, and special education services in the schools. Table 12.1 outlines the relationships between the scenarios and underlying issues.

TABLE 12.1   Scenarios and Issues in Special Educational Services for EL Students

Scenario	Issues
Elisa's Memory. Does Elisa, a third-grade student who demonstrates low English reading skills, have a memory problem connected with a learning disability?	At what point is a learning problem considered a language acquisition delay and not a learning disability?
Losing ESL after Referral. Will Alsumana, a recent immigrant, be deprived of ELD services if he is placed in special education?	Should ESL services be available to special education students?
Conflict over Testing. Does Luke's poor performance in school indicate a learning disability or is it due to his low academic motivation?	What role do family attitudes and values play in the issue of special education referral?
Gangs and Threats. Should his teacher refer José Luis to psychological counseling to deal with his social and emotional problems in an urban school?	What is the role of psychological counseling in second language acquisition?
Pressure for Early Exit. Should Mei-Hua, a slow learner, learn to read in Chinese before being exposed to reading in English, or should she be referred for testing as learning disabled?	Is an English-only program the best program for an English language learner with potential learning disabilities?
Sonia Doesn't Read. Should Sonia, a fifth-grader with limited prior schooling experience and low English skills, be referred to special education?	What is the role of special education for immigrant students with little prior literacy experience?
Tran the Troubled. Tran's quick intelligence shines on the playground but not in the classroom. Is he learning disabled?	What role does cultural difference play in a case in which a student has classroom learning problems?

The scenarios and the issues surrounding the education of English learners center on two basic questions: How can these students' language acquisition, cultural adjustment, and emotional/motivational difficulties be distinguished from learning problems? How can these issues best be addressed? The special education/English learner issues are complex, yet a central dilemma focuses the essential debate: How can a school district avoid inappropriate referrals and placements, yet ensure access for English learners who are learning disabled? The ELD/special education interface brings with it a set of collaboration issues. What is the role of the ELD specialist in referral, assessment, and subsequent services to students who may be placed in special education? In general, what is the relationship between second language acquisition and cultural issues in the ELD classroom, and a school's services and policies for special education?

Principles for the Education of EL/Special Education Students

Several basic assumptions characterize fair and effective processes for determining the educational services appropriate for the English learner who may be experiencing learning difficulties. These assumptions engender principles that may be used to guide initial identification and early intervention, diagnostic evaluation and testing, and, if necessary, placement in a special education learning environment. The principles address five domains: the responsibility of students for learning, students' need for self-knowledge, goals for instruction, relationship of educational services to mainstream instruction, and the need for informed decision making. Table 12.2 presents each of these five domains and its accompanying principle.

Identification, Referral, and Early Intervention

Classroom teachers, along with parents and other school-site personnel, are responsible for identifying English learners with special instructional needs. When a classroom teacher initially identifies a student who may need additional mediation, a phase of intensive focus begins that may, or may not, result in a placement in special education.

The Referral Process: The Role of the ELD Specialist

The School Screen Team, School Site Assessment Council, or otherwise-named entity is a school-site committee that bears responsibility for receiving and acting on an initial referral by the classroom teacher for a student who is in need of additional mediation in learning. The team not only reviews the classroom teacher's specific concerns about the student but also makes suggestions for modifying the learning environment for the student within the regular classroom and provides guidance, training, and assistance in implementing interventions that may prove

TABLE 12.2   Principles for the Education of English-Learning
Special Education Students

Domain	Principle
Responsibility of students for learning	English learners need to become self-responsible, active students who know how to learn. They need linguistic and nonlinguistic strategies, including metalinguistic and metacognitive strategies that may be generalizable across learning contexts.
Students' need for self-knowledge	Students need to understand their own learning styles and preferences, as well as discover their intrapersonal strengths and weaknesses in a variety of areas, including both linguistic and nonlinguistic (logical-mathematical, musical, and spatial) domains.
Goals for instruction	Students need meaningful and relevant language and academic goals that promote effective communication and learning, in social as well as academic domains.
Relationship of educational services to mainstream instruction	Any education setting must provide educational content and approaches that facilitate students' abilities to make smooth transitions to mainstream instruction.
Need for informed decision making	Educational decisions concerning English learners should involve ELD specialists, parents, and other professionals in collaborative, informed judgments that are based on a thorough, fair assessment of the child's language acquisition stage, culture, and individual needs and talents.

Source: Adapted from Wallach and Miller (1988).

helpful in educating the student in question. This process of gathering data and implementing changes in the educational environment for the student before testing is called the period of *initial intervention.*

The school ELD or bilingual specialist, as a member of the team, may be asked to fill out a data sheet containing test data, school history, language preferences, and other information about the student. Thus, this person plays an important role in investigating the following aspects of the English learner's case:

1. *Background experience and previous school settings.* Although an English learner may display learning difficulties for the first time at any point during schooling, it is equally likely that the student has had a previous history of difficulty. In this case, contacting a previous teacher and checking records from previously attended schools can provide important background information. A file containing a history of special education services is not routinely transferred with a student unless specifically requested by the receiving school personnel.

2. *Response to the classroom environment.* A question to ask concerns the following: Does the student seem uncomfortable or unaccustomed to a classroom environment? A history of previous schooling may uncover evidence of little or no prior schooling.

3. *Cultural and linguistic background.* The Home Language Survey given upon entering a school should properly identify the home language. If the home culture of the English learner is new to the classroom teacher, it may be useful to perform an ethnographic study of the home culture (see Chapter 10).

4. *Level of acculturation.* It may be useful to contact parents to determine the degree of acculturative stress that the family of the student is experiencing; for example, recent immigrants from rural, non-Western societies may experience more stress when immigrating to an urban area than immigrants from Westernized urban backgrounds. One might observe the student interacting with other students, staff, and parents in the home, school, and community to identify differences in behavior, language use, and confidence.

5. *Sociolinguistic development.* Do students or their families need help with basic interpersonal communication skills? Is there a need for language development interventions such as the services of an interpreter, or primary language development such as adult L1 literacy programs for parents?

6. *Learning styles.* Observation of the student across a variety of academic tasks and content areas may show the need for curricular interventions that provide instructional variety.

7. *Physical health.* The school nurse may provide or obtain a health record and developmental history, as well as a record of vision and hearing examinations and determination of overall physical health and diet.

Academic and Learning Problems That EL Students May Experience

English learners and students with learning disabilities may experience similar difficulties. This creates a challenge to determine whether a learning impairment is due to the students' language acquisition process or due to an underlying learning disability that warrants a special education placement. Gopaul-McNicol and Thomas-Presswood (1998) note the following possible characteristics of EL students that may overlap with those of students with learning disabilities:

1. *Discrepancies between verbal and nonverbal learning.* Exposure to enriching and meaningful linguistic experiences and activities may have been limited in the student's culture; however, the student may have skills in nonlinguistic domains.

2. *Perceptual disorders.* If an EL student's home language is not alphabetic, there may be difficulty with alphabetic letters. If a student was not literate in L1, there may be difficulty with sound-symbol relationships.

3. *Language disorders.* A student may experience difficulty processing language, following directions, and understanding complex language.

4. *Metacognitive deficits.* English learners without CALP may process information slowly. If from a nonliterate background, the student may lack preliteracy behaviors and strategies, such as regulatory mechanisms (planning, evaluating, monitoring, and remediating difficulties), or not know when to ask for help.

5. *Memory difficulties.* There may be a lack of transfer between the first and second language, or limited information retention in the second language.

6. *Motor disorders.* Cultural differences and lack of previous education can influence motor performance such as graphomotor (pencil) skills.

7. *Social-emotional functioning.* English learners may experience academic frustration and low self-esteem. This may lead to self-defeating behaviors such as learned helplessness. Limited second language skills may influence social skills, friendships, and teacher/student relationships.

8. *Difficulty attending and focusing.* English learners may exhibit behavior such as distractibility, short attention span, impulsivity, or a high motor level (e.g., finger tapping, excessive talking, fidgeting, or inability to remain seated). These may stem from cognitive "overload" when immersed in a second language for a long period of time.

9. *Culture/language shock.* Culture shock may result in uneven performance, not volunteering, not completing work, or seeking constant attention and approval from the teacher. The emotional reactions to long-term acculturation stress may lead to withdrawal, anger, or a pervasive sense of sadness.

10. *Reading dysfunctions.* English learners may exhibit a variety of reading problems, ranging from low skills to low interest. These include the following: slow rate of oral or silent reading (using excessive lip movement or vocalization in silent reading); short perceptual span (reading word by word rather than in phrases); reading without expression; mispronunciation of words (lack of word attack skills, or random substitutions); omission, insertion, or substitutions of words and letters in oral reading; excessive physical movement when reading (squirming); reversals or repetition of words or groups of words in oral reading; lack of comprehension; inability to state the main idea or topic or to remember what has been read; failure to reread or summarize; lack of skill in using information tools such as table of contents; and lack of interest in reading in or out of school.

11. *Written expression skill deficits.* Writing may present an additional area of difficulty for EL students, at the level of grammar and usage or at the level of content. Teachers often judge writing as "good" if it shows the following characteristics:

variety in sentence patterns; variety in vocabulary (choosing correct words and using synonyms); coherent structure in paragraphs and themes; control over usage, such as punctuation, capitalization, and spelling; and the ability to detect and correct one's own errors. In addition, students are expected (depending on the grade level) to make summaries and paraphrases from notes taken in class; to write descriptions and reports of happenings or procedures from class or from the world outside of school; to explore these happenings with the tools of critical thinking (hypotheses, comparison/contrast, classification, cause and effect, qualitative analyses, and sequential analyses); and to express personal views (feelings, preferences, opinions, and judgments). In all these areas, students are expected to be motivated to write on demand.

Similarities between Ethnic Language Variations and Learning Disability Symptoms

A systematic analysis among three sets of language users (standard American English speakers, English learners, and students with disabilities) reveals similarities in abilities and dysfunctions between English learners and students who are learning disabled. This overlap in language characteristics highlights the difficulty in identifying an English learner as possibly learning disabled. Table 12.3 illustrates the three sets of language abilities and disabilities according to five language components: pragmatics, prosody, phonology, syntax, and semantics.

Early Intervention

The School Screen Team works with the classroom teacher to design intervention strategies that address the EL student's language acquisition, language development, and acculturation needs. These strategies help to sort out with greater confidence which learning and behavior problems are caused by a possible handicapping problem and which problems may be due to acculturation and language acquisition needs. By documenting the student's performance and response to the initial interventions suggested by the School Screen Team, preliminary judgments can be made about the student's needs for further intervention and/or formal referral to testing.

A key to the diagnosis of language-related disorders is the presence of similar patterns in both the primary and the second languages. Poor oral language/vocabulary development, difficulties with writing, and poor comprehension in both languages often indicate learning disabilities.

The classroom teacher adopts an experimental attitude, implementing strategies over a period of one or two weeks and documenting the effect these innovations have on the student in question. Hanson (1989) recommends a variety of interventions. First, *altered teaching patterns* may change the student's response to instruction. These include breaking down tasks into smaller increments or shorter assignments; using aids, such as graphic organizers, audiotapes of materials, word banks, flash cards, pictures, teacher-prepared outlines, study guides, charts, and

TABLE 12.3   Similarity in Language Abilities and Disabilities among Standard American English Speakers, English Learners, and Students with Learning Disabilities

Component of Oral Language	Definition	Standard American English Speakers	English Learners	Learning-Disabled Students
Pragmatics	The ability to use and manipulate language (including nonverbal language) in a given context	Children are expected to know how to use language in a social context and to behave nonverbally with language.	Children use non-verbal language in a way that they learn from their native culture (e.g., eye contact).	LD children may have difficulties with social rules in communicative exchanges (e.g., turn-taking, reading social cues).
Prosody	An understanding of the correct use of rhythm, intonation, and stress patterns of a language	Children are expected to have developed the ability to understand and use different intonation to convey information.	L1 may influence the intonation curves of sentences.	Neurologically damaged or language-impaired children may have prosodic difficulties such as ambiguous intonation.
Phonology	The speech sounds that constitute spoken language and the pronunciation rules	Children are expected to produce and comprehend phonemes normally.	L2 speakers may have difficulty with certain L2 phonemes that are not present in their L1.	LD children may have difficulty articulating or differentiating language sounds.
Syntax	How words are formed and organized to produce meaningful phrases and sentences	Children are expected to use words appropriately in a sentence to convey meaning.	L2 speakers may have difficulty with articles, word order in sentences, noun-verb agreement, negation, and verb tenses.	LD children may have difficulty in sentence-level comprehension or understanding verb aspects such as mood.
Semantics	The meaning of words and sentences	Children are expected to use words that mean what they want to say.	English learners may have difficulties with connotation and denotation of words, as well as understanding *be* verbs.	LD children might have difficulty understanding multiple meanings of words or figurative language.

Source: S. Gopaul-McNicol and T. Thomas-Presswood, *Working with Linguistically and Culturally Different Children* (Boston: Allyn and Bacon, 1998). Reprinted by permission.

graphs; previewing, repeating, and reviewing or reteaching; using behavior contracts; employing varied learning modalities (visual, auditory, kinesthetic, multisensory); providing for variety in learning strategies; giving frequent feedback and verbal or nonverbal reinforcement; and reducing the reading level of material, or using high-interest/low-reading-level content materials.

Use of varied learning structures may be of benefit. Peers sharing the same primary language as the student, English-speaking peer tutors, cross-grade tutors, bilingual parent volunteers, senior citizens or other volunteers, graduate students who speak the same language, instructional aides, one-on-one teacher time with the classroom teacher, group work, or individualized instruction may prove useful. *Clarification or modification of classroom procedures and rules* may be necessary, such as modifying the student's schedule or school day. *Altered means of assessment* may alter student success, including exams with word banks, reduced amounts of material on exams, increased amounts of drawing and labeling, visual/picture exams or reports, use of interactive journals, portfolio assessment rather than exams, use of audiotaped tests, teaching test-taking skills, allowing more time to complete assignments/tests, and use of nonverbal assessments. The *physical environment may need modification* by having the student change seats, use a study carrel, or sit next to a peer buddy or with a cooperative learning group.

Several checklists that assist in the initial intervention process are offered by Aladjem (2000, online at http://www.ncbe.gwu.edu/classroom/voices/aladjem.pdf).

Roles for ELD Teachers during the Process of Determining Eligibility for Additional Services

The ELD teacher may play a variety of roles during the process of determining a student's eligibility for additional services. These include organizer, instructor, investigator, mentor to student, and colleague.

1. *Organizer.* In addition to following through with paperwork relating to the referral to the School Screen Team, the ELD teacher helps organize student records, records of interventions attempted and the relative success thereof, records of parent contact, and records of contact with other community agencies.

2. *Instructor.* The ELD teacher knows how to adapt learning environments to greater diversity in students' learning styles, how to devise initial intervention strategies, and how to use curriculum-based assessment to document student achievement.

3. *Investigator.* The ELD teacher may accomplish preliminary testing, study students' culture and language, interview parents, and investigate appropriate tests and interventions.

4. *Mentor to students.* As an advocate for students, the ELD teacher may get to know the student and family, suggest a testing environment compatible with the student's culture, and prepare the student for the evaluation process.

5. *Colleague.* The ELD teacher is a helpful colleague, sharing with colleagues his or her expertise about L2 acquisition effects, potential crosscultural misunderstandings, and possible effects of racism or discrimination on English learners and families. He or she collaborates to resolve conflicts, helps to work with translators, and draws on community members for information, additional resources, and parental support. In particular, parents should be an intimate part of the early intervention. This collaboration will be discussed later in this chapter.

Testing for Special Education

The School Screen Team, after reviewing the evidence provided by the classroom teacher and analysis of the early intervention accommodations, will approve or deny the request for special education testing. If approved, such testing will take place only after parental approval has been secured in writing. A school psychologist or equivalent licensed professional evaluator performs the testing. Figueroa (1989) and the American Psychological Association, Office of Ethnic and Minority Affairs (1991) offer guidelines for the testing of ethnic, linguistic, and culturally diverse populations. The box below offers some fundamentals that must be in place to ensure the validity of such testing.

The Descriptive Assessment Process

The process of evaluating English learners for possible placement in a special education classroom involves attention to linguistic and cultural factors that may impede the school success of the student. Jitendra and Rohena-Díaz (1996) use the term *descriptive assessment*. Once an English learner or a student from a non-U.S.-

Assumptions in Psychological Testing

1. The person administering testing is licensed and certified, and has adequate training concerning the following:
   - Administration, scoring, and interpretation of the test
   - Pitfalls and limitations of a particular test
   - Capability to establish rapport and understand the nonverbal language and cultural beliefs/practices of the person being tested
   - Oral ability in the language of the person or provision made for a trained interpreter
2. Instruments chosen for assessment have norms that represent the population group of the individual being tested.
3. The person being tested understands the words used and can operate from a worldview that understands what is expected from the testing situation.
4. Standardized tests are the preferred assessment and unassisted performance is the best format. (A mediated [assisted] assessment is valid only with school district approval.) The person being tested is compared to peers and placement is made based on results of the test, which is assumed to predict future performance
5. Behavior sampled is an adequate measure of the individual's abilities.

Some caveats preceeding the preceding assumptions:

1. Inadequately trained translators may impede evaluation. Translators must have good vocabulary and comprehension skills, have good mastery of idioms of both languages, and be aware of dialectical differences within languages. They must be able to paraphrase effectively, and have an understanding of child development and educational terminology. Moreover, the interpreter should be bound by the same ethical constraints as the assessor: maintain confidentiality and impartiality, respect feelings and beliefs of the individual, and respect the role of other professionals.

2. Translated tests may not be equivalent to their English forms in areas such as content validity and the amount of verbalization that can be expected from different cultures. Even having discrete norms for different languages may not provide norms for different cultures.

3. Many individuals do not have testing experience or experience with test materials, such as blocks or puzzles. Conversely, what they do have expertise in may not be measured in the test. The individual's learning style or problem-solving strategies can be culturally bound.

4. Individuals who have the following characteristics will do well on tests. These are consistent with the dominant U.S. American mainstream culture and may not be present, or may be present to a limited degree, in an individual from another culture:
   - Monochronic orientation: Focus on one task at a time
   - Passive style in interacting: Restrictive range of body expressiveness
   - Close proximity: Can tolerate small interpersonal space
   - Minimal physical touching
   - Frequent and sustained eye contact
   - Flexibility in response to male or female examiner
   - Individual orientation: Motivated to perform well in testing situation
   - Understanding of verbal and nonverbal aspects of majority culture
   - Internal locus of control: Taking responsibility for one's own success
   - Field-independent cognitive style: Can perceive details apart from the whole
   - Reflective, methodological, analytical cognitive style

5. Ethnic or immigrant minorities may underutilize special services, such as counseling. It may be hard for immigrant families to see the value in such services, to pay for these services, or to understand which services they have a right to demand from the schools. They may be in an undocumented status and not want to draw attention to family members' problems. They may lack the transportation to avail themselves of referrals to community agencies.

Source: Adapted from Gopaul-McNicol and Thomas-Presswood (1998).

mainstream cultural background is referred for a special education evaluation, a psychologist uses the descriptive assessment process in three phases. The first phase is descriptive analysis, in which an oral monologue, an oral dialogue, and observation of the student in class are used together to ascertain if the student has a communicative proficiency problem. If this is the case, the assessment may end, and the student may be referred to a speech/language therapist for additional mediation in language development. Alternatively, the student may be referred for additional mediation in language development *and* the evaluation process may continue, indicating that the student has a communicative proficiency problem as well as other problems.

If the student does not have a communicative proficiency problem, but there is evidence of some other learning problem, the second phase, explanatory analysis, begins; the assessor examines extrinsic factors, such as cultural or ethnic background or level of acculturation, that determine if normal language acquisition or crosscultural phenomena can account for the student's learning difficulties. If these factors do not account for the described difficulties, the examination continues to phase three, assessment for the presence of intrinsic factors, such as a learning disability. This three-phase evaluation process helps to ensure that linguistic and cultural differences receive thoughtful consideration in the overall picture of the student's academic progress.

Parental Support for Evaluation

During the evaluation process, the classroom teacher who keeps the parents informed about the process reaps the benefit of knowing that parents understand the need for professional assessment and support the student's need for additional mediation of learning. Parent conferences play an important part in engendering parental support. One experienced teacher keeps three portfolio folders available that have been prepared in advance for use during parent conferences. One folder displays average work for the grade level (all names have been removed from such work samples); one folder displays superior work; and a third folder contains work samples that are below grade level. Parents can compare their child's work with these samples to gain a context for achievement at that grade level. If the child's performance is not at grade level, the parents may more readily support the provision of additional help for that child.

Collaboration among ELD Teachers and Special Educators

Organizing a collaborative program requires cooperation among professionals who are concerned for the welfare of the student. Teachers can play a variety of collaborative and consultative roles within school contexts, using a variety of problem-solving strategies to design successful ways to create student success.

Definition and Principles of Collaboration

Collaboration is "a style for direct interaction between at least two coequal parties voluntarily engaged in shared decision making as they work toward a common goal" (Friend & Cook, 1996, p. 6). This definition pinpoints several necessary principles: professionals must treat one another as equals; collaboration is voluntary; a goal is shared (that of finding the most effective classroom setting for the student under consideration); and responsibility for participation, decision making, and resources, as well as accountability for outcomes, are shared. These principles are predicated on a collegial working environment of mutual respect and trust.

Collaboration among Professionals during the Testing Phase

English language development services, whether delivered by the classroom teacher or by an ELD resource teacher, should continue during the period of evaluation and testing, which may take several months. The ELD teacher, as ever, plays the role of advocate for the student's best interests. During the time period in which descriptive assessment takes place, the student should not be placed in a special education classroom under such auspices as "diagnostic" or "temporary" placement. Once students are placed in a special education setting, it is more difficult to have them return to a mainstream classroom where they may have missed needed curriculum.

Working with an Interpreter

Teachers who do not share a primary language with the student under consideration may benefit from collaborative relations with an interpreter. It is important that instructional aides who are hired as teaching assistants not be automatically pressed into service as translators or interpreters. Interpretation is a professional service that should be provided by trained and certified personnel. The box on page 300 gives guidelines for successful cooperative relations with interpreters.

Relationship of Continued ELD with Other Services

English language development services are a continuing resource for students throughout the initial intervention, testing, and recommendation phase of special education referral. An ELD teacher may work with the student directly, continuing to implement early intervention strategies, or help the student indirectly by working with other teachers, parents, and peers. Direct services may include tutoring or testing the child in the curricular material used in the classroom or charting daily measures of the child's performance to see if skills are being mastered. Indirect services may include consulting with other teachers on instructional interventions; devising tests based on the classroom curriculum, and giving instruction on how to develop and use them; showing how to take daily measures of a child's academic

How to Work with an Interpreter

1. Meet regularly with the interpreter in order to facilitate communication, particularly before meeting with a student or parent.
2. Encourage the interpreter to chat with the client before the interview to become aware of the educational level and attitudes toward schooling and to determine the appropriate depth and type of communication.
3. Speak simply, avoiding technical terms, abbreviations, professional jargon, idioms, and slang.
4. Encourage the interpreter to translate the client's own words as much as possible to give a sense of the client's concepts, emotional state, and other important information. Encourage the interpreter to refrain from inserting his or her own ideas or interpretations, or from omitting information.
5. During the interaction, look at and speak directly to the client. Listen to clients and watch their nonverbal, affective response by observing facial expressions, voice intonations, and body movements.
6. Be patient. An interpreted interview takes longer.

Source: Adapted from Randall-David (1989).

and social behavior; helping to implement reinforcement contingencies for behavior management in the classroom; establishing parent groups for discussion of and help with issues of concern; training older peers, parent volunteers, and teacher aides to work with younger children as tutors; and offering in-service workshops for teachers that focus on special interest areas such as curriculum-based assessments, cultural understanding, and language acquisition issues (West & Idol, 1990). If possible, the ELD teacher may prove to be an asset to help English learners with socioemotional adjustment problems as well as language acquisition efforts. One ELD teacher worked with the school counselor to hold "magic circle" discussions about issues the students were facing—including bouncing from school to school and having parents who do not speak English.

If the evaluation process results in the recommendation of special education services, ELD teachers are an important part of the process of writing the student's individual educational plan (IEP). Collaboration among ELD and special educators, parents, and the student is vital to the drafting and approval of an IEP that will result in academic success. The plan for continued participation of the referring teacher (when appropriate), the plan for ELD services, and the plan for assessing completion of the IEP's goals and objectives are a part of the total document and must be approved by collaborating parties before finalized.

Teaching Strategies for the ELD Special Learner

Modified instruction can be organized to accommodate differing instructional needs within the classroom and foster learning across academic content areas.

Inclusion is a term that is often used to describe the provision of instruction within the conventional/mainstream classroom for students with special needs and/or talents. Although this term has been primarily associated with the education of exceptional students, the term has also been used for the varying degrees of inclusion of English learners as well as of special education EL students in the mainstream classroom (Garcia, 1995). The use of this term should not, however, be interpreted as encouraging an indiscriminate overlap of the instruction recommended for English learners and that of special education students.

Inclusion as an Instructional Model

The term *inclusion* in this chapter will denote the inclusion of a student who is an English learner with special education needs in a mainstream classroom. The instructional day of such a student is planned so that the context of the mainstream classroom furnishes a rich, nonrestrictive setting for content instruction and language development activities. The three components of an exemplary program for English learners—comprehensible instruction in the content areas using primary language and SDAIE, language arts instruction in English, and heritage (primary) language maintenance/development—should be included in an inclusion program. Inclusion demands an ongoing effort to make the "included" student "as dynamically a part of the class as any student that is perceived as routinely belonging to that class" (Garcia, 1995, p. 2).

Overall, teaching for inclusion features the use of teaching practices that showcase the strong points of learners and support the areas in which they may struggle. A high degree of interactivity between teacher and student actively engages students and permits teachers ample opportunity to discover which methods and activities correspond to student success. Teachers who are advocates for students search continuously for ways to show that students are successful, and then share these successes with collaborating professionals in order to build a shared repertoire of successful strategies for the student.

The task for the teacher becomes more complex as the increasingly varied needs of students—mainstream (non-EL/non-special education), EL, EL/special education, and non-EL/special education—are mixed in the same classroom. Such complexity would argue that an inclusion classroom be equipped with additional educational resources, such as teaching assistants, lower student/teacher ratio, and augmented budget for instructional materials. The chief resource in any classroom, however, is the breadth and variety of instructional strategies upon which the experienced teacher can draw. The following sections suggest multiple strategies in the areas of listening skills, reading, and writing.

Adapting Listening Tasks

Teachers may use certain techniques to teach listening skills. These have been grouped in Table 12.4 into the three phases of the listening process (Before Listening, During Listening, After Listening).

TABLE 12.4   **Strategies for Additional Mediation for Included Students According to the Listening Process**

Phase	Strategies
Before Listening	■ Directly instruct listening strategies. ■ Arrange information in short, logical, well-organized segments. ■ Preview ways to pay attention. ■ Preview the content with questions that require critical thinking. ■ Establish a listening goal for the lesson. ■ Provide prompts that the information about to be presented is important enough to remember or write down.
During Listening	■ Actively involve students in rehearsing, summarizing, and taking notes. ■ Use purposeful, curriculum-related listening activities. ■ Act as a model of listening behavior and use peer models. ■ Teach students to attend to teacher cues and nonverbal signs that denote important information. ■ Use verbal, pictorial, or written prelistening organizers to cue students to important information. ■ Teach students to self-monitor their listening behavior, using self-questioning techniques and visual imagery while listening.
After Listening	■ Discuss content. Use teacher questions and prompts to cue student response (e.g., "Tell me more"). ■ Integrate other language arts and content activities with listening as a follow up.

Source: Adapted from Mandlebaum and Wilson (1989).

Adapting Reading Tasks

Teachers may use the techniques shown in Table 12.5 to adapt reading assignments for inclusion students. These follow the three-part division of the reading process (Before Reading, During Reading, and After Reading, alternatively named Into, Through, and Beyond).

Adapting Writing Tasks

Writing is used in two main ways in classrooms: to capture and demonstrate content knowledge (taking notes, writing answers on assignments or tests, etc.) and to express creative purposes. If the acquisition of content knowledge is the goal, students can often use a variety of alternatives to writing that avoid large amounts of

TABLE 12.5   Strategies for Additional Mediation for Included Students According to the Reading

Phase	Strategies
Before/Into Reading	■ Preview reading materials to assist students with establishing purpose, activating prior knowledge, budgeting time, and focusing attention. ■ Explain how new content to be learned relates to content previously learned. ■ Create vocabulary lists and teach these words before the lesson to ensure that students understand the vocabulary words rather than just recognize them. ■ Ensure that readability levels of the textbooks and trade books used in class are commensurate with the student's language level. ■ Locate lower-reading-level supplements in the same topic so that tasks can be adapted to be multilevel and multimaterial. ■ Rewrite material (or solicit staff or volunteers to do so) to simplify the reading level, or provide chapter outlines or summaries. ■ Tape text reading or have it read orally to a student. Consider the use of peers, volunteers, and/or paraprofessionals in this process.
During/Through Reading	■ Highlight key words, phrases, and concepts with outlines or study guides. ■ Reduce extraneous noise. ■ Utilize visual aids (e.g., charts and graphs) to supplement reading tasks.
After/Beyond Reading	■ When discussing stories, paraphrase material to clarify content. ■ Encourage feedback from students to check for understanding. ■ Reteach vocabulary so students can use the words rather than just recognize them. ■ Provide page numbers where specific answers can be found in a reading comprehension/content assignment. ■ Use brief individual conferences with students to verify comprehension.

Source: Adapted from Smith, Polloway, Patton, and Dowdy (1995).

written work (both in class and homework). In general, Smith, Polloway, Patton, and Dowdy (1995) suggest that teachers of students with special needs in inclusive settings change the response mode to oral when appropriate. To achieve comprehension checks, teachers can allow students to circle or choose responses, or tape-record answers, rather than to write them. If students must respond in writing, they may need additional time. If the lesson plan incorporates writing as the way students demonstrate comprehension, teachers who evaluate the *content* rather than the *form* of writing do not dwell on surface mistakes unnecessarily. For the purpose of checking comprehension, it is more important to respond to errors (those that show factual misunderstanding) rather than mistakes of grammar or usage. In a similar focus on content rather than on rote learning, some teachers provide a written outline of key content from lecture notes to reduce the amount of board copying.

When encouraging writing for purposes of self-expression, instruction should follow a well-defined writing process, with provision for generating ideas, drafting, and peer editing. Rather than pressuring individual students to produce their own work, teachers may allow group written responses via projects or reports, with the understanding that each member take equal turns in writing. Displaying a word bank on a classroom wall with commonly used words that native speakers would already know helps English learners to spell common words. Using a portfolio is a valuable way to trace improvement in writing. Students can use a stamp that indicates "first draft" to distinguish drafts from polished, or recopied, versions; this helps to honor rough drafts as well as completed writing. The sustained focus on process rather than product in writing helps students overcome a sense of impatience or shame when their writing is untidy.

When writing, students should be able to select the most comfortable method of writing (i.e., cursive or manuscript). For the purpose of improving handwriting, a calligraphy center may be available where students can go to practice elegant forms of handwriting, with correct models available of cursive styles. This should be an optional activity.

Assessing Student Performance in the Mainstream Classroom

A key feature of instruction for inclusion is continuous student assessment. Ongoing assessment accomplishes three purposes: it evaluates the curriculum using immediate, measurable results; it diagnoses which instructional tasks and strategies are responsible for student success; and it provides a basis to communicate this success to the student, parents, and collaborating team members. A variety of means are available to assess the success of the student in response to the curriculum, instructional strategies, and psychosocial aspects of the inclusion environment, and to judge if the inclusion placement of the student is appropriate.

Methods of Assessing the Success of Included Students

Direct observation, teacher interview, and analysis of student products are three ways to assess the success of included students. *Direct observation,* by the teacher or by a collaborating team member, can evaluate if the student has opportunities to speak in class, has enough academic engaged time and time to complete assigned tasks, and is receiving teacher feedback that communicates high expectations and immediate contingencies for completion or noncompletion of work, correct responding, or misbehavior. Team members who *interview* one another formally or informally can share aspects of student progress, such as response to specific strategies and activities or areas of specific skill strength or weakness. *Analysis of student products* can help team members determine which instructional activities have been successful and which may need to be modified. Keeping parents informed as full participating members of the collaborating team ensures that they know what they can do at home to assist their child. Persistence and positive feedback in this effort helps parents stay motivated and engaged. It is important to note that these assessment activities should be detailed to the greatest extent possible when the IEP is approved so that all members of the collaborating team are aware of their roles and responsibilities.

Using the Results of Assessment

For students who need a significantly modified curriculum, the issue of assigning grades should be addressed before the IEP is approved. The grading system that is used for included students in a mainstream classroom should not differ significantly from that used for other students. Alternative grading systems for students with learning disabilities are appropriate as long as the school district ensures that the grading practices and policies are not discriminatory. For example, if a student will be assessed using a portfolio evaluation process, then this option must be made available to all students. The IEP for the included student may stipulate what kinds of work samples will be gathered in the portfolio and what criteria will be used to assign a letter grade to the work. Teachers working together in the classroom collaborate to establish guidelines for achievement and assign grades. The grading process may include teachers' writing descriptive comments that offer examples of student performance or of certain instructional approaches or strategies that have proven successful, or observations about students' learning styles, skills, effort, and attitude.

Teaching English learners in United States classrooms is a challenge on a scale without precedent in modern education. As the social and economic stakes are raised, students who fail to reach their potential represent a loss to society as a whole. Each student—including those with special needs, whether for additional mediation or acceleration of instruction—is a treasure box, with his or her individual and specific talents, cultural background, and life experiences locked inside. Opening this treasure chest and releasing these talents to the world is an educational adventure of the highest order. The teacher with crosscultural, language, and academic development training holds the key.

BIBLIOGRAPHY

Ada, A. (1989). Los libros mágicos. *California Tomorrow*, pp. 42–44.

Adamson, H. (1993). *Academic competence*. New York: Longman.

Addison, A. (1988, November). Comprehensible textbooks in science for the nonnative English-speaker: Evidence from discourse analysis. *The CATESOL Journal, 1* (1), 49–66.`

Adger, C. (2000). School/community partnerships to support language minority student success. *CREDE Research Brief #5*. Santa Cruz, CA: Center for Research on Education, Diversity and Excellence. Online at http://www.crede.ucsc.edu.

Af Trampe, P. (1994). Monitor theory: Application and ethics. In R. Barasch & C. James (Eds.), *Beyond the monitor model*. Boston: Heinle and Heinle.

Agar, M. (1980). *The professional stranger: An informal introduction to ethnography*. Orlando, FL: Academic Press.

Aladjem, P. (2000). *A suggested guide to the special education pre-referral process for bilingual learners*. Washington, DC: National Clearinghouse for Bilingual Education. Online at http://www.ncbe.gwu.edu/classroom/voices/aladjem.pdf.

Alderson, J., Krahnke, K., & Stansfield, C. (Eds.). (1987). *Reviews of English language proficiency tests*. Washington, DC: Teachers of English to Speakers of Other Languages.

Allen, E., & Valette, R. (1977). *Classroom techniques: Foreign languages and English as a second language*. San Diego, CA: Harcourt Brace Jovanovich.

Allport, G. (1954). *The nature of prejudice*. Garden City, NY: Doubleday Anchor.

American Heritage Dictionary. (1992). Boston: Houghton Mifflin.

American Psychological Association, Office of Ethnic Minority Affairs. (1991). *Guidelines for providers of psychological services to ethnic, linguistic, and culturally diverse populations*. Washington, DC: Author.

Amery, H. (1979). *The first thousand words: A picture word book*. London: Usborne.

Amery, H., & Milá, R. (1979). *The first thousand words in Spanish*. London: Usborne.

Amselle, J. (1999). Dual immersion delays English. *American Language Review, 3* (5), 8.

Andersen, J., & Powell, R. (1988). Cultural influences on educational processes. In L. Samovar & R. Porter (Eds.), *Intercultural communication: A reader* (5th ed.). Belmont, CA: Wadsworth.

Andersen, J., & Powell, R. (1991). Intercultural communication and the classroom. In L. Samovar & R. Porter (Eds.), *Intercultural communication: A reader* (6th ed.). Belmont, CA: Wadsworth.

Anstrom, K. (1996). Federal policy, legislation, and education reform: The promise and the challenge for language minority students. *NCBE Resource Collection Series No. 5*. Washington, DC: NCBE. Online at http://www.ncbe.gwu.edu/ncbepubs/resource/fedpol.htm.

Anstrom, K. (1998a). Preparing secondary education teachers to work with English language learners: English language arts. *NCBE Resource Collection Series, No. 10*. Washington, DC: National Clearinghouse for Bilingual Education. Online at http://www.ncbe.gwu.edu/ncbepubs/resource/ells/language.htm.

Anstrom, K. (1998b). Preparing secondary education teachers to work with English language learners: Science. *NCBE Resource Collection Series, No. 11*. Washington, DC: National Clearinghouse for Bilingual Education. Online at http://www.ncbe.gwu.edu/ncbepubs/resource/ells/language.htm.

Anstrom, K. (1999a). Preparing secondary education teachers to work with English language learners: Social studies. *NCBE Resource Collection Series, No. 12*. Washington, DC: National Clearinghouse for Bilingual Education. Online at http://www.ncbe.gwu.edu/ncbepubs/resource/ells/social.htm.

Anstrom, K. (1999b). Preparing secondary education teachers to work with English language learners: Mathematics. *NCBE Resource Collection Series, No. 13*. Washington, DC: National Clearinghouse for Bilingual Education. Online at http://www.ncbe.gwu.edu/ncbepubs/resource/ells/math.htm.

Anti-Defamation League of B'nai B'rith. (1986). *A world of difference*. New York: Author.

Arias, I. (1996). Proxemics in the ESL classroom. *English Teaching Forum, 34*, 1, 32. Online at http://exchanges.state.gov/forum/vols/vol34/no1/032.htm.

Armour, M., Knudson, P., & Meeks, J. (1981). *The Indochinese: New Americans.* Provo, UT: Brigham Young University Language Research Center.

Artiles, A. J., & Trent, S. C. (1994). Overrepresentation of minority students in special education: A continuing debate. *The Journal of Special Education, 27* (4), 410–437.

Arvizu, S. (1992). Home-school linkages: A cross-cultural approach to parent participation. In M. Saravia-Shore & S. Arvizu (Eds.), *Cross-cultural literacy: Ethnographies of communication in multiethnic classrooms.* New York: Garland.

Asher, J. (1982). *Learning another language through actions: The complete teachers' guidebook.* Los Gatos, CA: Sky Oaks.

Asher, J., & García, R. (1969). The optimal age to learn a foreign language. *Modern Language Journal, 8,* 334–341.

Association for Supervision and Curriculum Development (ASCD). (1987). *Building an indivisible nation: Bilingual education in context.* Alexandria, VA: Author.

Au, K., & Jordan, C. (1981). Teaching reading to Hawaiian children: Finding a culturally appropriate solution. In H. Trueba, G. Guthrie, & K. Au (Eds.), *Culture and the bilingual classroom: Studies in classroom ethnography.* Rowley, MA: Newbury House.

August, D., & Pease-Alvarez, L. (1996). *Attributes of effective programs and classrooms serving English language learners.* Santa Cruz, CA: Center for Research on Cultural Diversity and Second Language Learning.

Baca, L., & Cervantes, H. T. (1984). *The bilingual special education interface.* Columbus, OH: Merrill.

Baca, L., & Valenzuela (1994). *Reconstructing the bilingual special education interface.* National Clearinghouse for Bilingual Education Program Information Guide Series, 20. Washington, DC: National Clearinghouse for Bilingual Education.

Baker, C. (1993). *Foundations of bilingual education and bilingualism.* Clevedon, England: Multilingual Matters.

Baker, K. (1987). Comment on Willig's "A meta analysis of selected studies of bilingual education." *Review of Educational Research, 57* (3), 351–362.

Banks, C. (1993). Parents and teachers: Partners in school reform. In J. Banks & C. Banks (Eds.), *Multicultural education: Issues and perspectives.* Boston: Allyn and Bacon.

Barnitz, J. (1985). *Reading development of nonnative speakers of English.* Center for Applied Linguistics. Orlando, FL: Harcourt, Brace, Jovanovich.

Barrett, J. (1978). *Cloudy with a chance of meatballs.* New York: Scholastic Books.

Benedict, R. (1934). *Patterns of culture.* New York: New American Library.

Bennett, C. (1986). *Comprehensive multicultural education: Theory and practice.* Boston: Allyn and Bacon.

Bennett, C. (1990). *Comprehensive multicultural education: Theory and practice* (2nd ed.). Boston: Allyn and Bacon.

Bennett, M. J., & Bennett, J. (1996). *A developmental model of intercultural sensitivity: Language classroom applications.* Presentation, annual meeting, Teachers of English to Speakers of Other Languages, Chicago.

BEOutreach (1993, March). A glossary for diversity. *BEOutreach, 4* (1), 2.

Berman, P., Minicucci, C., McLaughlin, B., Nelson, B., & Woodworth, K. (1995). *School reform and student diversity: Case studies of exemplary practices for LEP students.* Emeryville, CA: Institute for Policy Analysis and Research. Online at http://www.ncbe.gwu.edu/miscpubs/schoolreform/ipar.htm.

Bermúdez, A., & Márquez, J. (1996). An examination of a four-way collaborative to increase parental involvement in the schools. *The Journal of Educational Issues of Language Minority Students, 16.* Online at http://www.ncbe.gwu.edu/miscpubs/jeilms/vol16/jeilms1601.htm.

Bernstein, D. K. (1989). Assessing children with limited English proficiency: Current perspectives. *Topics in Language Disorders, 9,* 15–20.

Bilingual Education Act, Pub. L. No. (90–247), 81 Stat. 816 (1968).

Bilingual Education Act, Pub. L. No. (93–380), 88 Stat. 503 (1974).

Bilingual Education Act, Pub. L. No. (95–561), 92 Stat. 2268 (1978).

Bilingual Education Act, Pub. L. No. (98–511), 98 Stat. 2370 (1984).

Bilingual Education Act, Pub. L. No. (100–297), 102 Stat. 279 (1988).

Bilingual Education Act, Pub. L. No. (103–382), (1994).

Birdwhistell, R. (1974). The language of the body: The natural environment of words. In A. Silverstein (Ed.), *Human communication: Theoretical explorations.* Hillsdale, NJ: Erlbaum.

Bliatout, B., Downing, B., Lewis, J., & Yang, D. (1988). *Handbook for teaching Hmong-speaking students.* Folsom, CA: Folsom Cordova Unified School District, Southeast Asia Community Resource Center.

Bodinger-deUriarte, C. (1991, December). The rise of hate crime on school campuses. *Research Bulletin, Phi Delta Kappa, No. 10.*

Bolinger, D., & Sears, D. (1981). *Aspects of language* (3rd ed.). New York: Harcourt Brace Jovanovich.

Bourdieu, P. (1977). *Reproduction in society, education, and culture* (with J. Passeron). Los Angeles: Sage.

Bovee, T. (1991, September 18). San Bernardino, Ontario gain ethnic majorities. *San Bernardino County Sun*, p. A8.

Bransford, J., & Baca, L. (1984). Bilingual special education: Issues in policy development and implementation. In L. Baca & H. Cervantes (Eds.), *The bilingual special education interface.* St. Louis, MO: Times Mirror/Mosby.

Bratt Paulston, C. (1992). *Sociolinguistic perspectives on bilingual education.* Clevedon, England: Multilingual Matters.

Brinton, D., Snow, M., & Wesche, M. (1989). *Content-based second language instruction.* New York: Newbury House.

Brooks, N. (1968). *Language and language learning: Theory and practice.* New York: Harcourt Brace Jovanovich.

Brown, D. (1987). *Principles of language learning and teaching* (2nd ed.). Englewood Cliffs, NJ: Prentice-Hall.

Brown, D. (2000). *Principles of language learning and teaching* (4th ed.). Englewood Cliffs, NJ: Prentice-Hall.

Brown, G., & Yule, G. (1983). *Discourse analysis.* Cambridge: Cambridge University Press.

Brown, R. (1973). *A first language: The early stages.* Cambridge, MA: Harvard University Press.

Buchanan, K., & Helman, M. (1997). Reforming mathematics instruction for ESL literacy students. *ERIC Digest.* Online at http://www.cal.org/ericcll/digest/buchan01.html.

Buckmaster, R. (2000, June 22–28). First and second languages do battle for the classroom. *(Manchester) Guardian Weekly: Learning English* supplement, p. 3.

Bunting, E. (1988). *How many days to America?* New York: Clarion.

Burkart, G., & Sheppard, K. (2001). *Content-ESL across the USA.* Retrieved April 28, 2001, from the World Wide Web: http://www.ncbe.gwu.edu/miscpubs/cal/contentesl/.

Bye, M. (1975). *Reading in math and cognitive development.* Unpublished manuscript. (ERIC Document Reproduction Service ED 124 926).

Caine, R., & Caine, G. (1994). *Making connections: Teaching and the human brain.* Menlo Park, CA: Addison Wesley.

Calderón, M., Tinajero, J., & Hertz-Lazarowitz, R. (1990, spring). Adapting cooperative integrated reading and composition to meet the needs of bilingual students. *Journal of Educational Issues of Language Minority Students, 10,* special issue, 79–106.

California State Department of Education. (1984). *Individual learning programs for limited-English-proficient students.* Sacramento: Author.

California Department of Education. (1986). *Handbook for teaching Pilipino-speaking students.* Sacramento: Author.

California Department of Education. (1987). *Handbook for teaching Japanese-speaking students.* Sacramento: Author.

California Department of Education. (1989a). *Handbook for teaching Cantonese-speaking students.* Sacramento: Author.

California Department of Education. (1989b). *Handbook for teaching Portuguese-speaking students.* Sacramento: Author.

California State Department of Education. (1992). *Handbook for teaching Korean-American students.* Sacramento: Author.

California Department of Education. (1994). *Handbook for teaching Vietnamese-speaking students.* Sacramento: Author.

California Department of Education. (1998a). *Reading Instruction Competence Assessment (RICA).* Sacramento: Author. Online at http://www.ctc.ca.gov/profserv/examinfo/ricaexam.html.

California Department of Education. (1998b). *Challenge standards for students' success, physical education.* Sacramento: Author. Online at http://www.cde.ca.gov/challenge/pe.html

California Department of Education (1998c). *Challenge standards for students' success, visual and performing arts.* Sacramento, CA: Author. Online at http://www.cde.ca.gov/challenge/vpa.html.

California Department of Education. (1999a). *English language development standards.* Sacramento: Author. Online at http://www.cde.ca.gov/statetests/eld/eld_grd_span.pdf

California Department of Education. (1999b). *Reading/language arts framework for California public schools.* Sacramento: Author. Online at http://www.cde.ca.gov/cdepress/lang_arts.pdf.

California State Code of Regulations. (1998). *Title 5, Division 1, Chapter 11: English Language Learner Education. Subchapter 4. English Language Learner Education.* Online at http://www.cde.ca.gov/prop227.html.

California State Department of Education. (2000). *Foreign language framework.* Sacramento: Author.

California Department of Education. (2001). *Resources for English learners.* Online at http://www.cde.ca.gov/el.

Canale, M. (1983). From communicative competence to communicative language pedagogy. In J. Richards & R. Schmidt (Eds.), *Language and communication.* New York: Longman.

Canfield, J., & Wells, H. C. (1976). *100 ways to enhance self-concept in the classroom.* Englewood Cliffs, NJ: Prentice-Hall.

Carlson, L. (1970). The Negro in science. In J. Roucek & T. Kiernan (Eds.), *The Negro impact on Western civilization.* New York: Philosophical Library.

Cartagena, J. (1991). English only in the 1980s: A product of myths, phobias, and bias. In S. Benesch (Ed.), *ESL in America: Myths and possibilities.* Portsmouth, NH: Boynton/Cook.

Casteñada v. Pickard, 648 F.2d 989 (5th Cir. 1981).

CATESOL (1998). CATESOL *position statement on literacy instruction for English language learners, grades K–12.* Online at http://www.catesol.org/literacy.html.

Cazden, C. (1986). ESL teachers as language advocates for children. In P. Rigg & V. Allen (Eds.), *When they don't all speak English.* Urbana, IL: National Council of Teachers of English.

Cazden, C. (1988). *Classroom discourse.* Portsmouth, NH: Heinemann.

Celce-Murcia, M., & Goodwin, J. (1991). Teaching pronunciation. In M. Celce-Murcia (Ed.), *Teaching English as a second or foreign language* (2nd ed.). New York: Newbury House.

Center for Research on Education, Diversity, and Excellence. (1999). *Five standards for effective pedagogy.* Santa Cruz, CA: Author. Online at http://www.crede.ucsc.edu/Standards/standards.html.

Chambers, J., & Parrish, T. (1992). *Meeting the challenge of diversity: An evaluation of programs for pupils with limited proficiency in English: Vol. 4. Cost of programs and services for LEP students.* Berkeley, CA: BW Associates.

Chamot, A., & O'Malley, J. (1987, June). The Cognitive Academic Language Learning Approach: A bridge to the mainstream. *TESOL Quarterly, 21* (2), 227–249.

Chamot, A., & O'Malley, J. M. (1994). *The CALLA handbook: Implementing the cognitive academic language learning approach.* Reading, MA: Addison-Wesley.

Chandler, D. (2001). *Semiotics for beginners.* Retrieved April 28, 2001, from the World Wide Web: http://www.aber.ac.uk/media/Documents/S4B/semiotic.html.

Chang, J-M. (2000). *Asian American children in special education: Need for multidimensional collaboration.* Online at http://www.dol.gov/dol/odep/public/media/reports/diverse/chang.htm.

Charles, C. (1983). *Elementary classroom management.* New York: Longman.

Chávez, R., O'Donnell, J., & Gallegos, R. (1995). *Multiculturalism in the pedagogy of the "everyday": Students' perspective on dilemmas in a multicultural education course.* Presentation, annual meeting, American Educational Research Association, San Francisco.

Cheng, L. (1987). English communicative competence of language minority children: Assessment and treatment of language "impaired" preschoolers. In H. Trueba (Ed.), *Success or failure? Learning and the language minority student.* Boston: Heinle and Heinle.

Cherry, F. (1970). Black American contributions to Western civilization in philosophy and social science. In J. Roucek & T. Kiernan (Eds.), *The Negro impact on Western civilization.* New York: Philosophical Library.

Chesterfield, R., & Chesterfield, K. (1985). Natural order in children's use of second language learning strategies. *Applied Linguistics, 6,* 45–59.

Cheung, O., & Solomon, L. (1991). *Summary of state practices concerning the assessment of and the data collection about limited English proficient (LEP) students.* Washington, DC: Council of Chief State School Officers.

Children's Defense Fund. (2000). *Booming economy leaves millions of children behind: 12.1 million children still living in poverty.* Washington, DC: Author. Online at http://www.childrensdefense.org/release000926.htm.

Chin, B. (1996). *Call to join the literacy compact.* Urbana, IL: National Council of Teachers of English. Online at http://www.ncte.org/standards/compacts.html.

Chomsky, N. (1959). Review of B. F. Skinner "Verbal Behavior." *Language, 35,* 26–58.

Christian, D., & Genesee, F. (Eds.). (2001). *Bilingual education.* Alexandria, VA: Teachers of English to Speakers of Other Languages.

Christie, J., Enz, B., & Vukelich, C. (Eds.). (1997) *Teaching language and literacy.* New York: Longman.

Chung, H. (1989). Working with Vietnamese high school students. Available from New Faces of Liberty/SFSC, P.O. Box 5646, San Francisco, CA 94101.

Civil Rights Act, Pub. L. No. (88–352), 78 Stat. (1964).

Clark, B. (1983). *Growing up gifted: Developing the potential of children at home and at school* (2nd ed.). Columbus, OH: Merrill.

Cloud, N., Genesee, F., & Hamayan, E. (2000). *Dual language instruction.* Boston: Heinle and Heinle.

Cohen, A. (1991). Second language testing. In M. Celce-Murcia (Ed.), *Teaching English as a second or foreign language* (2nd ed.). New York: Newbury House.

Cohen, E., DeAvila, E., Navarette, C., & Lotan, R. (1988). *Finding out/descubrimiento implementation manual.* Stanford, CA: Stanford University Program for Complex Instruction.

Cohen, E., Lotan, R., & Catanzarite, L. (1990). Treating status problems in the cooperative classroom. In S. Sharon (Ed.), *Cooperative learning: Theory and research.* New York: Praeger.

Cohen, R. (1969). Conceptual styles, cultural conflict, and nonverbal tests of intelligence. *American Anthropologist, 71,* 828–856.

Cole, M. (1998). *Cultural psychology: Can it help us think about diversity?* Presentation, annual meeting, American Educational Research Association, San Diego.

College Composition and Communication. (1974). *Students' rights of language.* Urbana, IL: National Council of Teachers of English.

College Entrance Examination Board. (1999). Scholastic assessment test score averages, by race/ethnicity: 1986–87 to 1997–98, Table 134. *College Entrance Examination Board: National report on college-bound seniors 1998.* Online at http://nces.ed.gov/pubs2000/Digest99/d99t134.html.

Collie, J., & Slater, S. (1987). *Literature in the language classroom.* Cambridge: Cambridge University Press.

Collier, V. (1987). Age and rate of acquisition of second language for academic purposes. *TESOL Quarterly, 21* (4), 617–641.

Collier, V. P. (1995). Acquiring a second language for school. *Directions in Language & Education,* National Clearinghouse for Bilingual Education, 1 (4). Online at http://www.ncbe.gwu.edu/ncbepubs/directions/04.htm.

Corder, S. (1978). Language-learner language. In J. Richards (Ed.), *Understanding second and foreign language learning: Issues and approaches.* Rowley, MA: Newbury House.

Corson, D. (1990). *Language policy across the curriculum.* Clevedon, England: Multilingual Matters.

Corson, D. (1999). *Language policy in schools: A resource for teachers and administrators.* Mahwah, NJ: Erlbaum.

Cortés, C. (1993). Acculturation, assimilation, and "adducation." *BEOutreach, 4* (1), 3–5.

Counihan, G. (1998) What type of student are you? *The Internet TESL Journal, 4* (9). Online at http://www.aitech.ac.jp/~iteslj/Lessons/Counihan-TypeOfStudent.html.

Crago, M. (1993). Communicative interaction and second language acquisition: An Inuit example. *TESOL Quarterly, 26* (3), 487–506.

Crandall, J. (Ed.). (1987). *ESL through content-area instruction: Mathematics, science, social studies.* Englewood Cliffs, NJ: Regents/Prentice-Hall.

Crandall, J., Dale, T., Rhodes, N., & Spanos, G. (1987). *English skills for algebra.* Englewood Cliffs, NJ: Regents/Prentice-Hall.

Crawford, J. (1992). *Hold your tongue: Bilingualism and the politics of "English only."* Reading, MA: Addison-Wesley.

Crawford, J. (1997). *Best evidence: Research foundations of the Bilingual Education Act.* Washington, DC: National Clearinghouse for Bilingual Education. Online at http://www.ncbe.gwu.edu/ncbepubs/reports/bestevidence/.

Crawford, J. (1999). *Bilingual education: History, politics, theory, and practice* (4th ed.). Los Angeles: Bilingual Educational Services.

Crawford, L. (1993). *Language and literacy learning in multicultural classrooms.* Boston: Allyn and Bacon.

Criston, L. (1993, May 23). Has he stepped out of the shadow? *Los Angeles Times Calendar,* pp. 6, 70, 72.

Crookall, D., & Oxford, R. (1991). Dealing with anxiety: Some practical activities for language learners and teacher trainees. In E. Horwitz & D. Young (Eds.), *Language anxiety: From theory and research to classroom implications.* Englewood Cliffs, NJ: Prentice-Hall.

Cummins, J. (1976). The influence of bilingualism on cognitive growth: A synthesis of research findings and explanatory hypothesis. *Working Papers on Bilingualism, 9,* 1–43.

Cummins, J. (1979a). Cognitive/academic language proficiency, linguistic interdependence, the optimum age question and some other matters. *Working Papers on Bilingualism, 19,* 121–129.

Cummins, J. (1979b). Linguistic interdependence and the educational development of bilingual children. *Review of Educational Research, 49* (2), 222–251.

Cummins, J. (1980). The cross-lingual dimensions of language proficiency: Implications for bilingual education and the optimal age issue. *TESOL Quarterly, 14* (2), 175–187.

Cummins, J. (1981a). Age on arrival and immigrant second language learning in Canada: A reassessment. *Applied Linguistics 2* (2), 132–149.

Cummins, J. (1981b). The role of primary language development in promoting educational success for language minority students. In *Schooling and language minority students: A theoretical framework.* Sacramento: California State Department of Education.

Cummins, J. (1984). *Bilingualism and special education: Issues in assessment and pedagogy.* San Diego: College-Hill.

Cummins, J. (1986). Empowering minority students: A framework for intervention. *Harvard Educational Review, 56* (1), 18–36.

Cummins, J. (1989). *Empowering minority students.* Sacramento: Association for Bilingual Education.

Cummins, J. (1996). *Negotiating identities: Education for empowerment in a diverse society.* Los Angeles: California Association for Bilingual Education.

Curran, C. (1982). Community language learning. In R. Blair (Ed.), *Innovative approaches to language teaching.* Rowley, MA: Newbury House.

Dale, T., & Cuevas, G. (1987). Integrating language and mathematics learning. In J. Crandall (Ed.), *ESL through content-area instruction: Mathematics, science, social studies.* Englewood Cliffs, NJ: Regents/Prentice-Hall.

Dale, T., & Cuevas, G. (1992). Integrating mathematics and language learning. In P. Richard-Amato & M. Snow (Eds.), *The multicultural classroom.* White Plains, NY: Longman.

Dalton, S., & Sison, J. (1995). *Enacting instructional conversation with Spanish-speaking students in middle school mathematics.* (Research Report 12). Santa Cruz, CA: National Center for Research on Cultural Diversity and Second Language Learning. Online at http://www.ncbe.gwu.edu/miscpubs/ncrcdsll/rr12/index.htm.

Damen, L. (1998). Closing the language and culture gap: An intercultural-communication perspective. In D. L. Lange, C. A. Klee, R. M. Paige, & Y. A. Yershova (Eds.), *Culture as the core: Interdisciplinary perspectives on culture teaching and learning in the language curriculum* (pp. 33–51). Minneapolis: Center for Advanced Research on Language Acquisition, University of Minnesota.

Darder, A. (1991). *Culture and power in the classroom.* New York: Bergen and Garvey.

DeÁvila, E., Duncan, S., & Navarrete, C. (1992). *Finding out/descubrimiento.* Compton, CA: Santillana.

DeGeorge, G. (1987–1988, Winter). Assessment and placement of language minority students: Procedures for mainstreaming. *NCBE Occasional Papers #3.* Online at http://www.ncbe.gwu.edu/ncbepubs/classics/focus/03mainstream.htm.

Delgado-Gaitan, C., & Trueba, H. (1991). *Crossing cultural borders: Education for immigrant families in America.* London: Falmer Press.

dePaola, T. (1981). *Now one foot, now the other.* New York: G. P. Putnam's Sons.

Derman-Sparks, L., & Anti-Bias Curriculum Task Force. (1988). *Anti-bias curriculum: Tools for empowering young children.* Washington, DC: National Association for the Education of Young Children.

deUnamuno, M. (1925). *Essays and soliloquies.* New York: Knopf.

Deyhle, D. (1987). Learning failure: Tests as gatekeepers and the culturally different child. In H. Trueba (Ed.), *Success or failure? Learning and the language minority student.* Boston: Heinle and Heinle.

Díaz, R. (1983). Thought and two languages: The impact of bilingualism on cognitive development. *Review of Research in Education, 10,* 23–34.

Díaz-Rico, L. (1991). Increasing oral English in the university classroom: Strengthening the voice of the multinational student. *Fine Points.* San Bernardino: California State University, San Bernardino, Office of Faculty Development.

Díaz-Rico, L. (1993). From monocultural to multicultural teaching in an inner-city middle school. In A. Woolfolk (Ed.), *Readings and cases in educational psychology.* Boston: Allyn and Bacon.

Díaz-Rico, L. T. (1998). Towards a just society: Recalibrating multicultural teachers. In R. Chávez Chávez & J. O'Donnell (Eds.), *Speaking the unpleasant: The politics of (non)engagement in the multicultural terrain* Albany: SUNY Press.

Díaz-Rico, L. T. (1999, April). *Intercultural communication: Superglue for a (dis) United States.* Presentation, Annual Conference, California Teachers of English to Speakers of Other Languages, Reno, NV.

Díaz-Rico, L. T. (2000). Intercultural communication in teacher education: The knowledge base for CLAD teacher credential programs. *CATESOL Journal, 12* (1), 145–161.

Díaz-Rico, L., & Weed, K. (1995). *The crosscultural, language, and academic development handbook.* Boston: Allyn and Bacon.

Dicker, S. (1992). Societal views of bilingualism and language learning. TESOL: *Applied Linguistics Interest Section Newsletter, 14* (1), 1, 4.

Doggett, G. (1986). *Eight approaches to language teaching.* Washington, DC: Center for Applied Linguistics/ERIC Clearinghouse on Languages and Linguistics.

Doyle, W. (1983). Academic work. *Review of Educational Research, 53,* 287–312.

Dresser, N. (1993). *Our own stories: Cross-cultural communication practice.* White Plains, NY: Longman.

Dryfoos, J. (1998). *Safe passage: Making it through adolescence in a risky society.* New York: Oxford University Press.

Dudley-Marling, C., & Searle, D. (1991). *When students have time to talk.* Portsmouth, NH: Heinemann.

Dulay, H., Burt, M., & Krashen, S. (1982). *Language two.* New York: Oxford University Press.

Dumont, R. (1972). Learning English and how to be silent: Studies in Sioux and Cherokee classrooms. In C. Cazden, V. John, & D. Hymes (Eds.), *Functions of language in the classroom.* New York: Teachers College Press.

Duncan, S., & DeAvila, E. (1979). Bilingualism and cognition: Some recent findings. *NABE Journal, 4* (1), 15–50.

Dunlop, I. (1994). The true and the new. In R. Barasch & C. James (Eds.), *Beyond the Monitor Model.* Boston: Heinle and Heinle.

Durkin, D. (1995). *Language issues: Readings for teachers.* White Plains, NY: Longman.

Dwyer, J. (1991). Talking in class. In J. Dwyer (Ed.), *A sea of talk.* Portsmouth, NH: Heinemann.

Dyson, M. E. (1996). *Between God and gangsta rap: Bearing witness to black culture.* New York and Oxford: Oxford University Press.

Echevarria, J., Vogt, M. E., & Short, D. (2000). *Making content comprehensible for English language learners: The SIOP model.* Boston: Allyn and Bacon.

Eckert, A. (1992). *Sorrow in our heart.* New York: Bantam.

Edelsky, C. (1991). *With literacy and justice for all: Rethinking the social in language and education.* London: Falmer Press.

Edelsky, C., Altwerger, B., & Flores, B. (1991). *Whole language: What's the difference?* Portsmouth, NH: Heinemann.

Edmonson, M., (1971). *Lore: An introduction to the science of fiction.* New York: Holt, Rinehart and Winston.

Ehrenhalt, A. (2000, July 25). Airlines slam the door on normal behavior. *USA Today,* p. 15A.

Ekman, P., & Friesen, W. (1971). Constants across cultures in the face and emotion. *Journal of Personality and Social Psychology, 17* (2), 124–129.

Ellis, R. (1986). *Understanding second language acquisition.* Oxford: Oxford University Press.

Ellis, R. (1988). *Classroom second language development.* New York: Prentice-Hall.

Ellis, R. (1994). Variability and the natural order hypothesis. In R. Barasch & C. James (Eds.), *Beyond the Monitor Model.* Boston: Heinle and Heinle.

English First. (1999). 23 states have made English official (20 State laws still in effect). Springfield, VA: Author. Online at http://www.englishfirst.org/efstates.htm.

Enright, D., & McCloskey, M. (1988). *Integrating English: Developing English language and literacy in the multilingual classroom.* Reading, MA: Addison-Wesley.

Equal Educational Opportunities Act of 1974, Pub. L. No. (93–380), 88 Stat. 514 (1974).

ERIC Digest. (1991). *Semiotics and the English language arts.* Online at http://www.ed.gov/databases/ERIC_Digests/ed409557.html.

ERIC Digest. (1997). *Whole language and adult education.* Online at http://www.ed.gov/databases/ERIC_Digests/ed409557.html.

ERIC Digest. (1999). *What is balanced reading instruction?* Online at http://www.indiana.edu/~eric_rec/ieo/digests/d144.html.

Erickson, F. (1977). Some approaches to inquiry in school-community ethnography. *Anthropology and Education Quarterly, 8* (2): 58–69.

Erickson, F., & Mohatt, G. (1982). Cultural organization of participant structures in two classrooms of Indian students. In G. Spindler (Ed.), *Doing the ethnography of schooling: Educational anthropology in action.* New York: Holt, Rinehart and Winston.

Escalante, J., & Dirman, J. (1990). The Jaime Escalante math program. *Journal of Negro Education, 59* (3), 407–423.

Evaluation Assistance Center—East. (1990, November). *State minimum competency testing practices.* Washington, DC: Georgetown University.

Fairclough, N. (1989). *Language and power.* London and New York: Longman.

Fairclough, N. (1997). *Critical discourse analysis: The critical study of language.* Reading, MA: Addison-Wesley.

Faltis, C. (1993). Critical issues in the use of sheltered content instruction in high school bilingual programs. *Peabody Journal of Education, 69* (1), 136–151.

Feagin, J., & Feagin, C. (1993). *Racial and ethnic relations* (4th ed.). Englewood Cliffs, NJ: Prentice-Hall.

Feng, J. (1994). Asian-American children: What teachers should know. *ERIC Digest.* Champaign, IL: Clearinghouse on Elementary and Early Childhood Education. Online at http://ericps.ed.uiuc.edu/eece/pubs.

Ferguson, C. (1975). Toward a characterization of English foreigner talk. *Anthropological Linguistics, 17* (1), 1–14.

Figueroa, R. A. (1989). Psychological testing of linguistic minority students: Knowledge gaps and regulations. *Exceptional Children, 56* (2), 145–152.

Figueroa, R. A. (1993). The reconstruction of bilingual special education. *Focus on Diversity, 3* (3), 2–3.

Figueroa, R., Fradd, S. II., & Correa, V. I. (1989). Bilingual special education and this issue. *Exceptional Children, 56,* 174–178.

Finnan, C. (1987). The influence of the ethnic community on the adjustment of Vietnamese refugees. In G. & L. Spindler (Eds.), *Interpretive ethnography of education: At home and abroad.* Hillsdale, NJ: Erlbaum.

Fischer, B., & Fischer, L. (1979, January). Styles in teaching and learning. *Educational Leadership, 36* (4), 245–251.

Fishman, J. (1973). Language modernization and planning in comparison with other types of national modernization and planning. *Language in Society, 2* (1), 23–42.

Flood, J., Lapp, D., Tinajero, J., & Hurley, S. (1997). Literacy instruction for students acquiring English: Moving beyond the immersion debate. *The Reading Teacher,* 356–358.

Flores, B., Garcia, E., González, S., Hidalgo, G., Kaczmarek, K., & Romero, T. (1985). *Bilingual instructional strategies.* Chandler, AZ: Exito.

Folse, K. S. (1996). *Discussion starters.* Ann Arbor: University of Michigan Press.

Foucault, M. (1979). *Discipline and punish: The birth of the prison.* New York: Vintage Books.

Foucault, M. (1980). *Power/knowledge: Selected interviews and other writings 1971–1977.* New York: Pantheon Books.

Fox, B. (1987). *Discourse structure and anaphora.* Cambridge: Cambridge University Press.

Freeman, Y., & Freeman, D. (1992). *Whole language for second language learners.* Portsmouth, NH: Heinemann.

Freeman, Y., & Freeman, D. (1998). *ESL/EFL teaching: Principles for practice.* Portsmouth, NH: Heinemann.

Freire, P. (1985). *The politics of education* (D. Macedo, translator). New York: Bergin & Garvey.

Friedlander, M. (1991, fall). *The newcomer program: Helping immigrant students succeed in U.S. schools.* Washington, DC: National Clearinghouse for Bilingual Education.

Friend, M., & Cook, L. (1996). *Interactions: Collaboration skills for school professionals.* White Plains, NY: Longman.

From the Classroom. (1991). *Teachers seek a fair and meaningful assessment process to measure LEP students' progress.* Fountain Valley, CA: Teacher Designed Learning, 2 (1), 1, 3.

Fromkin, V., & Rodman, R. (1993). *An introduction to language* (5th ed.). New York: Holt, Rinehart and Winston.

Funaki, I., & Burnett, K. (1993). *When educational systems collide: Teaching and learning with Polynesian students.* Presentation, annual conference, Association of Teacher Educators, Los Angeles.

Furey, P. (1986). A framework for cross-cultural analysis of teaching methods. In P. Byrd (Ed.), *Teaching across cultures in the university ESL program.* Washington, DC: National Association of Foreign Student Advisors.

Galambos, S., & Goldin-Meadow, S. (1990). The effects of learning two languages on metalinguistic development. *Cognition, 34,* 1–56.

Galina, R. (1997). Language wars: The ideological dimensions of the debates on bilingual education. *Bilingual Research Journal, 21* (2 & 3). Online at http://brj.asu.edu/archives/23v21/articles/art5.html#issues.

García, B. A. (1995). *Inclusion as an instructional model for LEP students.* Technical Assistance Paper, No. 019–ESOL-95, Florida Department of Education, 1–3.

Gardner, H. (1983). *Frames of mind: The theory of multiple intelligences.* New York: Basic Books.

Gardner, R., & Lambert, W. (1972). *Attitudes and motivation in second language learning.* Rowley, MA: Newbury House.

Gass, S. (2000). *Interaction in classroom discourse.* Presentation, annual conference, Teachers of English to Speakers of Other Languages, Vancouver, Canada.

Gatbonton, E., & Segalowitz, N. (1988). Creative automatization: Principles for promoting fluency within a communicative framework. *TESOL Quarterly, 22* (3), 473–492.

Gattegno, C. (1982). Much language and little vocabulary. In R. Blair (Ed.), *Innovative approaches to language teaching.* Rowley, MA: Newbury House.

Gay, G. (1975, October). Cultural differences important in education of Black children. *Momentum*, 30–32.

Genesee, F. (Ed.). (1999). *Program alternatives for linguistically diverse students*. Santa Cruz, CA: Center for Research on Education, Diversity and Excellence. Online at http://www.cal.org/crede/pubs/edpractice/Epr1.pdf.

Giacchino-Baker, R. (1992). *Recent Mexican immigrant students' opinions of their use and acquisition of English as a second language in an "English-only" American high school: A qualitative study*. Unpublished doctoral dissertation, Claremont Graduate School, Claremont, CA.

Gibson, M. (1987). Punjabi immigrants in an American high school. In G. & L. Spindler (Eds.), *Interpretive ethnography of education: At home and abroad*. Hillsdale, NJ: Erlbaum.

Gibson, M. (1991a). Ethnicity, gender and social class: The school adaptation patterns of West Indian youths. In M. Gibson & J. Ogbu (Eds.), *Minority status and schooling. A comparative study of immigrant and involuntary minorities*. New York: Garland.

Gibson, M. (1991b). Minorities and schooling: Some implications. In M. Gibson & J. Ogbu (Eds.), *Minority status and schooling. A comparative study of immigrant and involuntary minorities*. New York: Garland.

Gillett, P. (1989a). *Cambodian refugees: An introduction to their history and culture*. Available from New Faces of Liberty/SFSC, P.O. Box 5646, San Francisco, CA 94101.

Gillett, P. (1989b). *El Salvador: A country in crisis*. Available from New Faces of Liberty/SFSC, P.O. Box 5646, San Francisco, CA 94101.

Giroux, H. (1983). Theories of reproduction and resistance in the new sociology of education: A critical appraisal. *Harvard Educational Review, 53*, 257–293.

Givens, D. (2000). *Nonverbal dictionary of gestures, signs and body language cues*. Online at http://members.aol.com/nonverbal2/diction1.htm.

Glaser, S., & Brown, C. (1993). *Portfolios and beyond: Collaborative assessment in reading and writing*. Norwood, MA: Christopher-Gordon.

Glick, E. (1988, August 8). English-only: New handicap in world trade. *Los Angeles Times*.

Goals 2000: Educate America Act Pub. L. No. (103–227), (1994).

Goldenberg, C. (1991). *Instructional conversations and their classroom application*. Educational Practice Report 2. Santa Cruz, CA: National Center for Research on Cultural Diversity and Second Language Learning. Online at http://www.ncbe.gwu.edu/miscpubs/ncrcdsll/epr2/.

Goldenberg, M. (1999). *SUAVE Online*. Online at http://www.csusm.edu/SUAVE/index.htm.

Gómez v. Illinois State Board of Education, 811 F. 2d 1030 (7th Cir. 1987).

González, R. (1990). When minority becomes majority: The changing face of English classrooms. *English Journal, 79* (1), 16–23.

González, V. (1994). Bilingual special voices. *NABE News, 17* (6), 19–22.

Good, T., & Brophy, J. (1984). *Looking in classrooms* (3rd ed.). New York: Harper and Row.

Goodman, K. (1986). *What's whole in whole language*. Portsmouth, NH: Heinemann.

Goody, J. (1968). *Literacy in traditional societies*. Cambridge: Cambridge University Press.

Gopaul-McNicol, S., & Thomas-Presswood, T. (1998). *Working with linguistically and culturally different children*. Boston: Allyn and Bacon.

Gordon, M. (1964). *Assimilation in American life*. New York: Oxford University Press.

Gottlieb, M. (1995). Nurturing student learning through portfolios. *TESOL Journal, 5* (1), 12–14.

Grabe, W., & Kaplan, R. (1990). Writing in a second language: Contrastive rhetoric. In D. Johnson & D. Roen (Eds.), *Richness in writing: Empowering ESL students*. New York: Longman.

Graham, C. (1978a). *Jazz chants*. New York: Oxford University Press.

Graham, C. (1978b). *Jazz chants for children*. New York: Oxford University Press.

Graham, C. (1986). *Small talk*. New York: Oxford University Press.

Graham, C. (1988). *Jazz chant fairy tales*. New York: Oxford University Press.

Graham, C. (1992). *Singing, chanting, telling tales*. Englewood Cliffs, NJ: Regents/Prentice-Hall.

Gramsci, A. (1971). *Selections from the prison notebooks of Antonio Gramsci* (Trans. & Ed. by Q. Hoare & G. N. Smith). New York: International Publishers.

Grant, C. A., & Secada, W. G. (1990). Preparing teachers for diversity. In W. R. Houston (Ed.), *Handbook of research on teacher education* (pp. 403–422). New York: Macmillan.

Grant, C. A., & Sleeter, C. (1986). *After the school bell rings*. Philadelphia: Falmer.

Grasha, A. F. (1990). Using traditional versus naturalistic approaches to assess learning styles in college teaching. *Journal on Excellence in College Teaching, 1*, 23–38.

Greenbaum, S., & Quirk, R. (1990). *A student's grammar of the English language*. Harlow, England: Longman.

Grossen, B. (1997). *30 years of research: What we now know about how childern learn to read.* Santa Cruz, CA: Center for the Future of Teaching and Learning (ED 415 492).

Groves, M. (2000, January 26). Vast majority of state's schools lag in new index. *Los Angeles Times*, pp. 1, 14.

Guiora, A., Beit-Hallami, B., Brannon, R., Dull, C., & Schovel, T. (1972). The effects of experimentally induced changes in ego states on pronunciation ability in second language: An exploratory study. *Comprehensive Psychiatry, 13*, 421–428.

Gunderson, L. (1991). *ESL literacy instruction: A guidebook to theory and practice.* Englewood Cliffs, NJ: Regents/Prentice-Hall.

Hakuta, K. (1986). *Mirror of language.* New York: Basic Books.

Hakuta, K., Butler, Y. G., & Witt, D. (2000). *How long does it take English learners to attain proficiency?* Santa Barbara: University of California Linguistic Minority Research Institute Policy Report 2000–1.

Hall, E. (1959). *The silent language.* New York: Anchor Books.

Halliday, M. (1975). *Learning how to mean: Explorations in the development of language.* London: Edward Arnold.

Halliday, M. (1978). *Language as a social semiotic.* Baltimore, MD: University Park Press.

Halliday, M., & Hasan, R. (1976). *Cohesion in English.* London: Longman.

Hamayan, E. (1994). Language development of low-literacy students. In F. Genesee (Ed.), *Educating second language children.* Cambridge: Cambridge University Press.

Hancock, C. (1994). Alternative assessment and second language study: What and why? *ERIC Digest.* Online at http://www.cal.org/ericcll/digest/hancoc01.html.

Hanson, M. J. (1989). *Early intervention* (pp. 104–106). Austin, TX: Pro-Ed.

Hanson-Smith, E. (1997). *Technology in the classroom: Practice and promise in the 21st century.* Alexandria, VA: TESOL. Online at http://www.tesol.edu/pubs/profpapers/techclass.html.

Hardt, U. (1992, spring). Teaching multicultural understanding. *Oregon English Journal XIV, 1*, 3–5.

Harel, Y. (1992). Teacher talk in the cooperative learning classroom. In C. Kessler (Ed.), *Cooperative language learning.* Englewood Cliffs, NJ: Prentice-Hall.

Harkness, S. (1971). Cultural variation in mother's language. *Word, 27*, 495–498.

Harris, V. (1997). *Teaching multicultural literature in grades K–8.* Norwood, MA: Christopher-Gordon.

Hart, L. (1975). *How the brain works: A new understanding of human learning, emotion, and thinking.* New York: Basic Books.

Hart, L. (1983). *Human brain, human learning.* New York: Longman.

Hatch, E. (1992). *Discourse and language education.* Cambridge: Cambridge University Press.

Hayes, C. (1998). *Literacy con cariño: A story of migrant children's success.* Portsmouth, NH: Heinemann.

Heath, S. (1983a). Language policies. *Society, 20* (4), 56–63.

Heath, S. (1983b). *Ways with words.* Cambridge: Cambridge University Press.

Henwood, D. (1997). Trash-o-nomics. In M. Wray, M. Newitz, & A. Newitz, (Eds.), *White trash: Race and class in America* (pp. 177–191). New York and London: Routledge.

Hernández, R. (1993, November 9). Use of terms "Anglo" and "Hispanic" is justifiable. *The San Bernardino County Sun*, p. A9.

Hernández-Chávez, E. (1984). The inadequacy of English immersion as an educational approach for language minority students. *Studies on immersion education: A collection for U.S. educators.* Sacramento: California State Department of Education.

Hispanic Concerns Study Committee. (1987). *Hispanic concerns study committee report.* Available from National Education Association, 1201 Sixteenth Street, N.W., Washington, DC 20036.

Hispanic Dropout Project. (1998). *No more excuses: The final report of the Hispanic Dropout Project.* Washington, DC: U.S. Department of Education, Office of the Under Secretary. Online at http://www.ncbe.gwu.edu/miscpubs/hdp/final.htm.

Holt, D., Chips, B., & Wallace, D. (1992, summer). *Cooperative learning in the secondary school: Maximizing language acquisition, academic development, and social development.* Washington, DC: National Clearinghouse for Bilingual Education.

Hooper, L., & Bennett, C. (1998). Current population reports: Asian and Pacific Islanders. Washington, DC: U.S. Bureau of Census. Online at http://www.census.gov/population/www/socdem/race/api.html.

Hornsby, D. (1991). *Understanding whole language.* Workshop presentation, Riverside, CA.

Horwitz, E., Horwitz, M., & Cope, J. (1991). Foreign language classroom anxiety. In E. Horwitz & D.

Young (Eds.), *Language anxiety: From theory and research to classroom implications*. Englewood Cliffs, NJ: Prentice-Hall.

H.R. 123: English Language Empowerment Act of 1996.

Hruska-Riechmann, S., & Grasha, A. F. (1982). The Grasha-Riechmann Student Learning Scales: Research findings and applications. In J. Keefe (Ed.), *Student learning styles and brain behavior*. Reston, VA: NASSP.

Hudelson, S. (1994). Literacy development of second language children. In F. Genesee (Ed.), *Educating second language children*. Cambridge, England: Cambridge University Press.

Hyland, C. (1989, summer). What we know about the fastest growing minority poulation: Hispanic Americans. *Educational Horizons, 67* (4), 131–135.

Hymes, D. (1961). The ethnography of speaking. In T. Gladwin & W. Sturtevant (Eds.), *Anthropology and human behavior*. Washington, DC: Anthropological Society of Washington.

Hymes, D. (1972). On communicative competence. In J. Pride & J. Holmes (Eds.), *Sociolinguistics*. Harmondsworth, UK: Penguin.

Igoa, C. (1995). *The inner world of the immigrant child*. New York: St. Martin's Press.

Idaho Migrant Council v. Board of Education, 647 F. 2d 69 (9th Cir. 1981).

Improving America's Schools Act (IASA). 1994 (P.L. 103–382).

Institute for Education in Transformation. (1992). *Voices from the inside: A report on schooling from inside the classroom*. Available from the Institute for Education in Transformation at The Claremont Graduate School, 121 East Tenth Street, Claremont, CA 91711–6160.

International Reading Association & National Council of Teachers of English. (1996). *Standards for the English language arts*. Newark, DE & Urbana, IL: Authors.

Ishii, S., & Bruneau, T. (1991). Silence and silences in cross-cultural perspective: Japan and the United States. In L. Samovar & R. Porter (Eds.), *Intercultural communication: A reader* (6th ed.). Belmont, CA: Wadsworth.

Jasmine, J. (1993). *Portfolios and other assessments*. Huntington Beach, CA: Teacher Created Materials.

Jensen Learning Corporation. (2001.). *Brain based learning: Truth or deception*. Retrieved April 28, 2001, from the World Wide Web: http://jlcbrain.com/truth.html.

Jewell, M. (1976). Formal institutional studies and language. In W. O'Barr & J. O'Barr (Eds.), *Language and politics*. The Hague: Mouton.

Jitendra, A. K., & Rohena-Díaz, E. (1996). Language assessment of students who are linguistically diverse: Why a discrete approach is not the answer. *School Psychology Review, 25* (1), 40–56.

Johnson, D. W., & Johnson, R. T. (1979). Conflict in the classroom: Controversy and learning. *Review of Educational Research, 49* (1), 51–70.

Johnson, D. W., & Johnson, R. T. (1994). Constructive conflict in the schools. *Journal of Social Issues, 50* (1), 117–137.

Johnson, D. W., & Johnson, R. T. (1995). Why violence prevention programs don't work—And what does. *Educational Leadership, 52* (5), 63–68.

Johnson, D. W., Johnson, R. T., Dudley, B., & Acikgoz, K. (1994). Effects of conflict resolution training on elementary school students. *The Journal of Social Psychology, 134* (6), 803–817.

Johnston, J., & Johnston, M. (1990). *Content points*. Reading, MA: Addison-Wesley.

Jones, J. (1981). The concept of racism and its changing reality. In B. Bowser & R. Hunt (Eds.), *Impacts of racism on White Americans*. Beverly Hills, CA: Sage.

Joos, M. (1967). *The five clocks*. New York: Harcourt, Brace and World.

Jussim, L. (1986). Self-fullfilling prophecies: A theoretical and integrative review. *Psychological Review, 93* (4), 429–445.

Kagan, S. (1986). Cooperative learning and sociocultural factors in schooling. *Beyond language: Social and cultural factors in schooling language minority students*. Los Angeles, CA: Evaluation, Dissemination and Assessment Center, California State University, Los Angeles.

Kagan, S. (1989). *Cooperative learning: Resources for teachers*. San Juan Capistrano, CA: Resources for Teachers.

Kang, H-W., Kuehn, P., & Herrell, A. (1996). The Hmong literacy project: Parents working to preserve the past and ensure the future. *The Journal of Educational Issues of Language Minority Students, 16*. Online at http://www.ncbe.gwu.edu/miscpubs/jeilms/vol16/jeilms1602.htm.

Kaplan, R. (1967). Contrastive rhetoric and the teaching of composition. *TESOL Quarterly, 1* (4), 10–16.

Katz, N., & Lawyer, J. (1993). *Conflict resolution: Building bridges*. Thousand Oaks, CA: Corwin.

Keefe, M. W. (1987). *Learning style theory and practice*. Reston, VA: National Association of Secondary School Principals.

Kessler, C., & Quinn, M. (1980). Positive effects of bilingualism on science problem-solving abilities. In J. Alatis (Ed.), *Current issues in bilingual education.* Washington, DC: Georgetown University Press.

Kessler, C., & Quinn, M. (1987). ESL and science learning. In J. Crandall (Ed.), *ESL through content-area instruction: Mathematics, science, social studies.* Englewood Cliffs, NJ: Regents/Prentice-Hall.

Kessler, C., Quinn, M., & Fathman, A. (1992). Science and cooperative learning for LEP students. In C. Kessler (Ed.), *Cooperative language learning.* Englewood Cliffs, NJ: Regents/Prentice-Hall.

Keyes v. School District Number One, Denver, Colorado, 576 F. Supp. 1503 (D. Colo. 1983).

Khisty, L. L. (1993). A naturalistic look at language factors in mathematics teaching in bilingual classrooms. *Third National Research Symposium on Limited English Proficient Student Issues.* Online at http://www.ncbe.gwu.edu/ncbe pubs/symposia/third/khisty.htm.

Kinsella, K. (1992). How can we move from comprehensible input to active learning strategies in content-based instruction? The *CATESOL Journal, 5* (1), 127–132.

Kintsch, W., & Greeno, J. (1985). Understanding and solving word arithmetic problems. *Psychological Review, 92* (I), 109–129.

Kitzhaber, A., Sloat, C., Kilba, E., Love, G., Aly, L., & Snyder, J. (1970). Language/Rhetoric VI. In A. Kitzhaber (Ed.), *The Oregon curriculum: A sequential program in English.* New York: Holt, Rinehart and Winston.

Kleinfeld, J. (1988, June). Letter to the editor. *Harvard Education Letter, 4* (3).

Koch, A., & Terrell, T. (1991). Affective reactions of foreign language students to natural approach activities and teaching techniques. In E. Horwitz & D. Young (Eds.), *Language anxiety: From theory and research to classroom implications.* Englewood Cliffs, NJ: Prentice-Hall.

Kopan, A. (1974). Melting pot: Myth or reality? In E. Epps (Ed.), *Cultural pluralism.* Berkeley, CA: McCutchan.

Koryrev, J. R. (1998). *Talk it up! Oral communication for the real world.* Boston: Houghton Mifflin.

Koryrev, J. R., & Baker, M. (2000). *Talk it through! Integrating listening, speaking, and pronunciation.* Boston: Houghton Mifflin.

Kramsch, C. (1998). Teaching language across the cultural faultline. In D. L. Lange, C. A. Klee, R. M. Paige, & Y. A. Yershova (Eds.), *Culture as the core: Interdisciplinary perspectives on culture teaching and learning in the language curriculum* (pp. 15–31). Minneapolis: Center for Advanced Research on Language Acquisition, University of Minnesota.

Krashen, S. (1980). The theoretical and practical relevance of simple codes in second language acquisition. In R. Scarcella & S. Krashen (Eds.), *Research in second language acquisition.* Rowley, MA: Newbury House.

Krashen, S. (1981). *Second language acquisition and second language learning.* Oxford: Pergamon.

Krashen, S. (1982). *Principles and practice in second language acquisition.* Oxford: Pergamon.

Krashen, S. (1985). *The input hypothesis: Issues and implications.* New York: Longman.

Krashen, S., Long, M., & Scarcella, R. (1979). Age, rate, and eventual attainment in second language acquisition. *TESOL Quarterly, 13* (4), 573–582.

Krashen, S., & Terrell, T. (1983). *The natural approach: Language acquisition in the classroom.* Oxford: Pergamon.

Kroeber, A., & Kluckhohn, C. (1952). *Culture: A critical review of concepts and definition.* Cambridge, MA: The Peabody Museum of American Archaeology & Ethnology, Harvard University, Vol. XLVII, No. 1.

Kroll, B. (1991). Teaching writing in the ESL context. In M. Celce-Murcia (Ed.), *Teaching English as a second or foreign language* (2nd ed.). New York: Newbury House.

Labov, W. (1969). *The study of nonstandard English.* Urbana, IL: National Council of Teachers of English.

Labov, W. (1972). *Sociolinguistic patterns.* Philadelphia: University of Pennsylvania Press.

Lambert, W. (1984). An overview of issues in immersion education. In California Department of Education, *Studies on immersion education.* Sacramento: California Department of Education.

Larsen-Freeman, D., & Long, M. (1991). *Introduction to second language acquisition research.* London: Longman.

Lau v. Nichols, 414 U.S. 563 (1974).

Law, B., & Eckes, M. (2000). *The more-than-just-surviving handbook* (2nd ed.). Winnipeg, Canada: Peguis.

Leathers, N. (1967). *The Japanese in America.* Minneapolis: Lerner Publications.

LeCompte, M. (1981). The Procrustean bed: Public schools, management systems, and minority students. In H. Trueba, G. Guthrie, & K. Au (Eds.), *Culture and the bilingual classroom: Studies in classroom ethnography.* Rowley, MA: Newbury House.

Lee, J. (2000). Success for all? *American Language Review, 4* (2), 22, 24.

LeLoup, J., & Ponterio, R. (2000). *Enhancing authentic language learning experiences through internet tech-*

nology. ERIC Digest. Online at http://www.cal.org/ericcll/digest/0002enhancing.html.

Lenneberg, E. (1967). *Biological foundations of language.* New York: John Wiley and Sons.

Lessow-Hurley, J. (1996). *The foundations of dual language instruction* (2nd ed.). White Plains, NY: Longman.

Levine, D., & Adelman, M. (1982). *Beyond language: Intercultural communication for English as a second language.* Englewood Cliffs, NJ: Prentice-Hall.

Lindholm, K. (1992). Two-way bilingual/immersion education: *Theory, conceptual issues, and pedagogical implications.* In R. Padilla & A. Benavides (Eds.), *Critical perspectives in bilingual education research.* Tucson, AZ: Bilingual Review/Press.

Lockwood, A. T. (2000). *Transforming education for Hispanic youth: Broad recommendations for teachers and program staff.* Washington, DC: National Clearinghouse for Bilingual Education. Online at http://www.ncbe.gwu.edu/ncbepubs/issue/about-atl.htm.

Lockwood, A. T., & Secada, W. G. (1999). *Transforming education for Hispanic youth: Exemplary practices, programs, and schools.* National Clearinghouse for Bilingual Education Resource Collection Series, 12. Washington, DC: National Clearinghouse for Bilingual Education. Online at http://www.ncbe.gwu.edu/ncbepubs/resource/hispanicyouth/hdp.htm.

Los Angeles Unified School District. (1993). *Sheltered instruction teacher handbook: Strategies for teaching LEP students in the elementary grades.* (Publication No. EC-617). Los Angeles: Author.

Lotan, R., & Benton, J. (1989). Finding out about complex instruction: Teaching math and science in heterogeneous classrooms. In N. Davidson, (Ed.), *Cooperative learning in mathematics: A handbook for teachers.* Menlo Park, CA: Addison Wesley.

Lozanov, G. (1982). Suggestology and suggestopedia. In R. Blair (Ed.), *Innovative approaches to language teaching.* Rowley, MA: Newbury House.

Lucas, T., & Wagner, S. (1999). Facilitating secondary English language learners' transition into the mainstream. *TESOL Journal, 8* (4), 6–13.

Lustig, M. (1988). Value differences in intercultural communication. In L. Samovar & R. Porter (Eds.), *Intercultural communication: A reader* (5th ed.). Belmont, CA: Wadsworth.

M., A. (2000, July 7). IndusVillage.com—Fusing ancient culture, modern life. *India Journal, 12* (2), pp. B1, B2.

Madrid, A. (1991). Diversity and its discontents. In L. Samovar & R. Porter (Eds.), *Intercultural communication: A reader* (6th ed.). Belmont, CA: Wadsworth.

Maeroff, G. (1991, December). Assessing alternative assessment. *Phi Delta Kappan, 73* (4), 272–281.

Malavé, L. (1991). Conceptual framework to design a programme intervention for culturally and linguistically different handicapped students. In L. Malavé & G. Duquette (Eds.), *Language, culture and cognition.* Clevedon, England: Multilingual Matters.

Mandlebaum, L. H., & Wilson, R. (1989). Teaching listening skills in the special education classroom. *Academic Therapy, 24,* 451–452.

Marinova-Todd, S., Marshall, D., & Snow, C. (2000). Three misconceptions about age and L2 learning. *TESOL Quarterly, 34* (1), 9–34.

Marton, W. (1994). The antipedagogical aspects of Krashen's theory of second language acquisition. In R. Barasch & C. James (Eds.), *Beyond the Monitor Model.* Boston: Heinle and Heinle.

Mather, J. R. C., & Chiodo, J. J. (1994). A mathematical problem: How do we teach mathematics to LEP elementary students? The *Journal of Educational Issues of Language Minority Students, 13,* 1–12. Online at http://www.ncbe.gwu.edu/miscpubs/jeilms/vol13/math13.htm.

Matute-Bianchi, M. (1991). Situational ethnicity and patterns of school performance among immigrant and nonimmigrant Mexican-descent students. In M. Gibson & J. Ogbu (Eds.), *Minority status and schooling.* New York: Garland.

McCrum, R., Cran, W., & MacNeil, R. (1986). *The story of English.* New York: Elisabeth Sifton Books.

McDermott, R., & Gospodinoff, K. (1981). Social contexts for ethnic borders and school failure. In H. Trueba, G. Guthrie, & K. Au (Eds.), *Culture and the bilingual classroom: Studies in classroom ethnography.* Rowley, MA: Newbury House.

McGovern, A. (1969). *If you sailed on the Mayflower in 1620.* New York: Scholastic.

McKeon, D. (1994). When meeting common standards is uncommonly difficult. *Educational Leadership, 51* (8), 45–49.

McLaughlin, B. (1987). *Theories of second-language learning.* London: Arnold.

McLaughlin, B. (1990). "Conscious" versus "unconscious" learning. *TESOL Quarterly, 24* (4), 617–634.

McLaughlin, B. (1992). *Myths and misconceptions about second language learning: What every teacher needs to unlearn.* Santa Cruz, CA: National Center for Research on Cultural Diversity and Second Language Learning.

McLeod, B. (1995). *School reform and student diversity: Educating students from diverse linguistic and cultural backgrounds.* Santa Cruz, CA: The National Center for Research on Cultural Diversity & Second Language Learning. Online at http://www.ncbe.gwu.edu/miscpubs/ncrcdsll/srsd/.

McLeod, B. (1996). *School reform and student diversity: Exemplary schooling for language minority students.* Washington, DC: National Clearinghouse for Bilingual Education. Online at http://www.ncbe.gwu.edu/ncbepubs/resource/schref.htm.

Mehan, H. (1981). Ethnography of bilingual education. In H. Trueba, G. Guthrie, & K. Au (Eds.), *Culture and the bilingual classroom: Studies in classroom ethnography.* Rowley, MA: Newbury House.

Mehan, H., Hubbard, L., Lintz, A., & Villavueva, I. (1994). *Tracking untracking: The consequences of placing low track students in high track classes.* Santa Cruz, CA: The National Center for Research on Cultural Diversity & Second Language Learning. Online at http://www.ncbe.gwu.edu/miscpubs/ncrcdsll/rr10/index.htm.

Mehrabian, A. (1969). Communication without words. In *Readings in Psychology Today.* Del Mar, CA: CMR Books.

Meyer v. Nebraska, 262 U.S. 390 (1923).

Miller, G. (1985). Nonverbal communication. In V. Clark, P. Eschholz, & A. Rosa (Eds.), *Language: Introductory readings* (4th ed.). New York: St. Martin's Press.

Miller, W. H. (1995). *Alternative assessment techniques for reading and writing.* West Nyack, NJ: The Center for Applied Research in Education.

Minicucci, C., & Olsen, L. (1992, spring). *Programs for secondary limited English proficient students: A California study.* Washington, DC: National Clearinghouse for Bilingual Education.

Molina, R. (2000). Building equitable two-way programs. In N. Cloud, F. Genesee, & E. Hamayan (Eds.), *Dual language instruction* (pp. 11–12). Boston: Heinle and Heinle.

Monroe, S. (1999). Multicultural children's literature: Canon of the future. Reprinted in *Annual editions 99/00: Teaching English as a second language.* Guilford, CO: Dushkin/McGraw-Hill.

Morley, J. (1991a). Listening comprehension in second/foreign language instruction. In M. Celce-Murcia (Ed.), *Teaching English as a second or foreign language* (2nd ed.). New York: Newbury House.

Morley, J. (1991b). The pronunciation component in teaching English to speakers of other languages. *TESOL Quarterly, 25* (3), 481–520.

Moskowitz, G. (1978). *Caring and sharing in the foreign language classroom.* Cambridge, MA: Newbury House.

Moya, S., & O'Malley, M. (1994). A portfolio assessment model for ESL. *The Journal of Educational Issues of Language Minority Students, 13,* 13–36. Online at http://www.ncbe.gwu.edu/miscpubs/jeilms/vol13/portfo13.htm.

Murphy, J. (1991). Oral communication in TESOL: Integrating speaking, listening, and pronunciation. *TESOL Quarterly, 25* (1), 51–76.

Murray, B. (1989). Talking when English is a foreign language. In J. Dwyer (Ed.), *A sea of talk.* Portsmouth, NH: Heinemann.

Nash, P. (1991). ESL and the myth of the model minority. In S. Benesch (Ed.), *ESL in America.* Portsmouth, NH: Boynton/Cook.

National Clearinghouse for Bilingual Education (NCBE). (1995). *How has federal policy for language minority students evolved in the U.S.?* Washington, DC: Author. Online at http://www.ncbe.gwu.edu/askncbe/.

National Clearinghouse for Bilingual Education (NCBE). (1999). *AskNCBE No. 18: Which states have legislative provisions for limited English proficient student instructional programs?* Washington, DC: Author. Online at http://www.ncbe.gwu.edu/askncbe/faqs/18instr.htm.

National Clearinghouse for Bilingual Education (NCBE). (2000). *History, legislation, and policy: Supreme Court cases.* Washington, DC: Author. Online at http://www.ncbe.gwu.edu/library/policy/legislation.htm.

National Council for the Social Studies. (1994). *Expectations for excellence: Curriculum standards for social studies.* Washington, DC: Author.

National Council of Teachers of Mathematics. (2000). *Principles and standards for school mathematics.* Reston, VA: Author.

National Research Council. (1996). *The national science education standards.* Washington, DC: National Academy Press.

Navarrete, C., & Gustke, C. (1996). A *guide to performance assessment for linguistically diverse students.* Albuquerque, NM: EAC West, New Mexico Highlands University. Online at http://www.ncbe.gwu.edu/miscpubs/eacwest/performance/index.htm#contents.

Navarrete, C., Wilde, J., Nelson, C., Martínez, R., & Hargett, G. (1990). *Informal assessment in educa-*

tional evaluation: Implications for bilingual education programs. Washington, DC: National Clearinghouse for Bilingual Education.

Nelson, B. (1996). *Learning English: How school reform fosters language acquisition and development for limited English proficient elementary school students.* Santa Cruz, CA: The National Center for Research on Cultural Diversity & Second Language Learning. Online at http://www.ncbe.gwu.edu/miscpubs/ncrcdsll/epr 16.htm.

Nelson, S. S., & O'Reilly, R. (2000, August 30). Minorities became majority in state, census officials say. *Los Angeles Times,* pp. A1 & A16.

Nieto, S. (2000). *Affirming diversity* (3rd ed.). New York: Longman.

Nummela, R., & Rosengren, T. (1986). What's happening in students' brains may redefine teaching. *Educational Leadership, 43* (8), 49–53.

Nunan, D. (1991). *Language teaching methodology: A textbook for teachers.* New York: Prentice-Hall.

Nunan, D. (1993, April). *Exploring perceptions of the teaching process.* Presentation, annual conference, Teachers of English to Speakers of Other Languages, Atlanta, GA.

Oakes, J. (1985). *Keeping track: How schools structure inequality.* New Haven, CT: Yale University Press.

Oakes, J. (1992). Can tracking research inform practice? Technical, normative, and political considerations. *Educational Researcher, 21* (4), 12–21.

Ochs, E. (1982). Talking to children in Western Samoa. *Language in Society, 11,* 77–104.

O'Connor, T. (1999). *Understanding discrimination against Asian-Americans.* Online at http://faculty.ncwc.edu/toconnor.

Ogbu, J. (1978). *Minority education and caste: The American system in crosscultural perspective.* New York: Academic Press.

Ogbu, J., & Matute-Bianchi, M. (1986). Understanding sociocultural factors: Knowledge, identity, and school adjustment. In *Beyond language: Social and cultural factors in schooling language minority students.* Los Angeles: Evaluation, Dissemination and Assessment Center, California State University, Los Angeles.

Oh, J. (1992). The effects of L2 reading assessment methods on anxiety level. *TESOL Quarterly, 26* (1), 172–176.

Olmedo, I. M. (1993, summer). Junior historians: Doing oral history with ESL and bilingual students. *TESOL Journal, 2* (4), 7–10.

Olsen, L. (1988). *Crossing the schoolhouse border: Immigrant students and the California public schools.* San Francisco: California Tomorrow.

Olsen, L., & Dowell, C. (1989). *Bridges: Promising programs for the education of immigrant children.* San Francisco: California Tomorrow.

Olsen, R. (1992). Cooperative learning and social studies. In C. Kessler (Ed.), *Cooperative language learning.* Englewood Cliffs, NJ: Regents/Prentice-Hall.

Olson, S., & Loucks-Horsley, S. (2000). *Inquiry and the national science education standards.* Washington, DC: National Academy Press.

Omaggio, A. (1986). *Teaching language in context.* Boston: Heinle and Heinle.

O'Malley, J., Chamot, A., Stewner-Manzanares, G., Kupper, L., & Russo, R. (1985a). Learning strategies used by beginning and intermediate ESL students. *Language Learning, 35* (1), 21–40.

O'Malley, J., Chamot, A., Stewner-Manzanares, G., Kupper, L., & Russo, R. (1985b). Learning strategy applications with students of English as a second language. *TESOL Quarterly, 19* (3), 557–584.

O'Malley, J. M., & Pierce, L. V. (1996). *Authentic assessment for English language learners.* Menlo Park, CA: Addison-Wesley.

O'Neil, J. (1990). Link between style, culture proves divisive. *Educational Leadership, 48* (2), 8.

Ong, W. (1982). *Orality and literacy.* London: Methuen.

Orfield, G., Bachmeier, M. D., James, D. R., & Eitle, T. (1997). Deepening segregation in American public schools: A special report from the Harvard Project on School Desegregation. *Equity and Excellence in Education, 30* (2), 5–24.

Ortiz, F. (1988). Hispanic-American children's experiences in classrooms: A comparison between Hispanic and non-Hispanic children. In L. Weis, (Ed.), *Class, race, and gender in American education.* Albany: State University of New York Press.

Orum, L. (1986). *The education of Hispanics: Status and implications.* Washington, DC: National Council of La Raza.

Ouk, M., Huffman, F., & Lewis, J. (1988). *Handbook for teaching Khmer-speaking students.* Sacramento, CA: Spilman Printing.

Ovando, C., & Collier, V. (1998). *Bilingual and ESL classrooms: Teaching in multicultural contexts.* Boston: McGraw-Hill.

Oxford, R. (1990). *Language learning strategies.* New York: Newbury House.

Oyama, S. (1976). A sensitive period for the acquisition of nonnative phonological system. *Journal of Psycholinguistic Research, 5,* 261–284.

Parla, J. (1994). Educating teachers for cultural and linguistic diversity: A model for all teachers. *New York State Association for Bilingual Education Journal, 9,* 1–6. Online at http://www.ncbe.gwu.edu/miscpubs/nysabe/vol9/model.htm.

Pasternak, J. (1994, March 29). Bias blights life outside Appalachia. *Los Angeles Times,* pp. A1 & A16.

Patthey-Chavez, G., Clark, **L.,** & Gallimore, R. (1995). *Creating a community of scholarship with instructional conversations in a transitional bilingual classroom.* Educational Practice Report 15. Santa Cruz, CA: National Center for Research on Cultural. Diversity and Second Language Learning. Online at http://www.ncbe.gwu.edu/miscpubs/ncrcdsll/eprl5.htm.

Payan, R. (1984). Language assessment for bilingual exceptional children. In L. Baca & H. Cervantes (Eds.), *The bilingual special education interface.* St. Louis, MO: Times Mirror/Mosby.

Peal, E., & Lambert, W. (1962). The relation of bilingualism to intelligence. *Psychological Monographs, 76* (546), 1–23.

Pearson, R. (1974). *Introduction to anthropology.* New York: Holt, Rinehart and Winston.

Peck, S. (1992). How can thematic ESL units be used in the elementary classroom? *CATESOL Journal, 5* (1), 133–138.

Peñalosa, F. (1980). *Chicano sociolinguistics, a brief introduction.* Rowley, MA: Newbury House.

Pennington, M., & Richards, J. (1986). Pronunciation revisited. *TESOL Quarterly,* 20 (2), 207–223.

Pennycook, A. (1994). *The cultural politics of English as an international language.* New York and London: Longman.

Peregoy, S. & Boyle, O. (2001). *Reading, writing, and learning in ESL.* (3rd ed.). New York: Longman.

Pérez, B., & Torres-Guzmán, M. (1992). *Learning in two worlds.* New York: Longman.

Philips, S. (1972). Participant structures and communicative competence: Warm Springs children in community and classroom. In C. Cazden, V. John, & D. Hymes (Eds.), *Functions of language in the classroom.* New York: Teachers College Press.

Phillips, J. (1978). College of, by and for Navajo Indians. *Chronicle of Higher Education, 15,* 10–12.

Pinker, S. (1994). *The language instinct.* New York: HarperPerennial.

Pinnell, G. S. (1985) Ways to look at the functions of children's language. In A. Jaggar & M. Smith-Burke (Eds.), *Observing the language learner.* Newark, DE: International Reading Association.

Plyler v. Doe, 457 U.S.202, 102 S. Ct 2382 (1982).

Pooley, R. (1977). The definition and determination of "correct" English. In G. Goshgariian (Ed.), *Exploring language.* Boston: Little, Brown.

Porter, R. (1990). *Forked tongue: The politics of bilingual education.* New York: Basic Books.

Postman, N., & Weingartner, C. (1973). *How to recognize a good school.* Bloomington, IN: Phi Delta Kappan Educational Foundation.

Ramírez, J. (1992, winter/spring). Executive summary, final report: Longitudinal study of structured English immersion strategy, early-exit and late-exit transitional bilingual education programs for language-minority children. *Bilingual Research Journal, 16* (1&2), 1–62.

Ramírez, III, M. (1988). Cognitive styles and cultural democracry in action. In J. Wurzel (Ed.), *Toward multiculturalism: A reader in multicultural education.* Yarmouth, ME: Intercultural Press.

Ramírez, R. (2000). *Hispanic population in the U.S: Population characteristics.* Washington, DC: U.S. Bureau of Census. Online at http://www.census.gov/prod/2000pubs/p20–527.pdf.

Randall-David, E. (1989). *Strategies for working with culturally diverse communities and clients.* Washington, DC: Office of Maternal and Child Health, United States Department of Health and Human Services. Online at http://www.nmchc.org/html/cattoc.htm.

Reid, D. (1992). Linguistic diversity and equality. In P. Pinsent (Ed.), *Language, culture and young children: Developing English in the multi-ethnic nursery and infant school.* London: David Fulton, Publishers.

Reyhner, J. (1992). American Indian bilingual education: The White House conference on Indian education and the tribal college movement. *NABE News, 15* (7), 7,18.

Richard-Amato, P. (1996). *Making it happen* (2nd ed.). White Plains, NY: Longman.

Richard-Amato, P., & Snow, M. (1992) Strategies for content-area teachers. In P. Richard-Amato & M. Snow (Eds.), *The multicultural classroom.* White Plains, NY: Longman.

Richards, J. (1978). *Understanding second and foreign language learning.* Rowley, MA: Newbury House.

Rico, H. (2000). *Programs for English learners: Overview of federal and state requirements.* Sacramento, CA: California Department of Education. Online at http://www.cde.ca.gov/ccpdiv/eng_learn/ccr2000-el/index.htm.

Rios v. Read. 75 Civ. 296 (U.S. District Ct. Ed. NY, 1977).

Rist, R. (1970). Student social class and teacher expectations: The self-fulfilling prophecy in ghetto education. *Harvard Educational Review, 40* (3), 70–110.

Rivers, W., & Temperley, M. (1978). A *practical guide to the teaching of English as a second or foreign language.* New York: Oxford University Press.

Roberts, C. (1995, summer/fall). Bilingual education program models. *Bilingual Research Journal, 19* (3 & 4). Reprinted in Orozco, L. (Ed.). (1998) as *Perspectives: Educating diverse populations.* Bilingual education program models: A framework for understanding (pp. 79–83). Boulder, CO: Coursewise Publishing.

Roberts, P. (1985). Speech communities. In V. Clark, P. Eschholz, & A. Rosa (Eds.), *Language: Introductory readings* (4th ed.). New York: St. Martin's Press.

Robinson, D. (1988). *Language policy and planning.* Washington, DC: Center for Applied Linguistics/ERIC Clearinghouse on Languages and Linguistics.

Robinson, G. (1985). *Crosscultural understanding.* New York: Pergamon Institute of English.

Rodríguez, R., Prieto, A., & Rueda, R. (1984). Issues in bilingual/multicultural special education. *Journal of the National Association for Bilingual Education, 8* (3), 55–65.

Romero, M. (1991). *Integrating English language development with content-area instruction.* Presentation annual meeting, Educational Research Association, Chicago.

Rooks, G. (1990). *Can't stop talking.* New York: Newbury House.

Ross, S. (1993, March 3). Study: Latinos getting short end of the executive stick. *The San Bernardino County Sun,* p. B8.

Roy, A. (1990). The English-only movement. In P. Eschholz, A. Rosa, & V. Clark (Eds.), *Language awareness* (5th ed.). New York: St. Martin's Press.

Rubel, A., & Kupferer, H. (1973). The myth of the melting pot. In T. Weaver (Ed.), *To see ourselves: Anthropology and modern social issues.* Glenview, IL: Scott, Foresman.

Rubin, J. (1976). Language and politics from a sociolinguistic point of view. In W. O'Barr & J. O'Barr (Eds.), *Language and politics.* The Hague: Mouton.

Rueda, R. (1987). Social and communicative aspects of language proficiency in low-achieving language minority students. In H. Trueba (Ed.), *Success or failure? Learning and the language minority student.* New York: Newbury House.

Ruíz, R. (1984). Orientations in language planning. *NABE Journal, 8* (2), 15–34.

Rumelhart, D. (1977). Toward an interactive model of reading. In S. Dornic (Ed.), *Attention and performance.* New York: Academic Press.

Rumelhart, D. (1980). Schemata: The building blocks of cognition. In R. Spiro, B. Bruce, & W. Brewer (Eds.), *Theoretical issues in reading comprehension.* Hillsdale, NJ: Erlbaum.

Runner, J. (2000). *"I don't understand" in over 230 languages.* Online at http://www.elite.net/~runner/jennifers/understa.htm.

Sanchez, F. (1989). *What is primary language instruction?* Hayward, CA: Alameda County Office of Education.

Santillana Publishing Company and San Diego Unified School District. (1992). *Bridge to communication* (rev. ed.). Compton, CA: Authors.

Sasser, L. (1992). Teaching literature to language minority students. In P. Richard-Amato & M. Snow (Eds.), *The multicultural classroom.* White Plains, NY: Longman.

Sattler, J. (1974). *Assessment of children's intelligence.* Philadelphia: W. B. Saunders.

Saville-Troike, M. (1976). *Foundations for teaching English as a second language: Theory and method for multicultural education.* Englewood Cliffs, NJ: Prentice-Hall.

Saville-Troike, M. (1978). A *guide to culture in the classroom.* Rosslyn, VA: National Clearinghouse for Bilingual Education.

Saville-Troike, M. (1984). What really matters in second language learning for academic purposes? *TESOL Quarterly, 18* (2), 199–219.

Scafe, M., & Kontas, G. (1982). Classroom implications of culturally defined organizational patterns in speeches by Native Americans. In F. Barkin, E. Brandt, & J. Orstein-Galicia (Eds.), *Bilingualism and language contact: Spanish, English, and Native American languages.* New York: Teachers College Press.

Scarcella, R. (1990). *Teaching language minority students in the multicultural classroom.* Englewood Cliffs, NJ: Prentice-Hall.

Scheurich, J. (1993). Toward a white discourse on white racism. *Educational Researcher, 22* (8), 5–10.

Schultz, J., & Theophano, J. (1987). Saving place and marking time: Some aspects of the social lives of three-year-old children. In H. Trueba (Ed.), *Success or failure? Learning and the language minority student.* Cambridge, MA: Newbury House.

Schumann, J. (1978a). The acculturation model for seond-language acquisition. In R. Gringas (Ed.), *Second language acquisition and foreign language teaching.* Washington, DC: Center for Applied Linguistics.

Schumann, J. (1978b). Social and psychological factors in second language acquisition. In J. Richards (Ed.), *Understanding second and foreign lan-*

guage learning: Issues and approaches. Rowley, MA: Newbury House.

Schunk, D. (1991). Self-efficacy and academic motivation. *Educational Psychologist, 26,* 207–232.

Scovel, T. (1991). The effect of affect on foreign language learning: A review of the anxiety research. In E. Horwitz & D. Young (Eds.), *Language anxiety: From theory and research to classroom implications.* Englewood Cliffs, NJ: Prentice-Hall.

Scribner, S., & Cole, M. (1978). Literacy without schooling: Testing for intellectual effects. *Harvard Educational Review, 48,* 448–461.

Seelye, H. (1984). *Teaching culture.* Lincolnwood, IL: National Textbook Company.

Selinker, L. (1972). Interlanguage. *IRAL, 10* (3), 209–231.

Selinker, L. (1991). Along the way: Interlanguage systems in second language acquisition. In L. Malavé & G. Duquette (Eds.), *Language, culture and cognition.* Clevedon, England: Multilingual Lingual Matters.

Serna v. Portales Municipal Schools, 499 F. 2d 1147 (10th Cir. 1972).

Shade, B., & New, C. (1993). Cultural influences on learning: Teaching implications. In J. Banks & C. Banks (Eds.), *Multicultural education: Issues and perspectives.* Boston: Allyn and Bacon.

Shafer, R., Staab, C., & Smith, K. (1983). *Language functions and school success.* Glenview, IL: Scott, Foresman.

Shannon, S. (1994). Introduction. In R. Barasch & C. James (Eds.), *Beyond the Monitor Model.* Boston: Heinle and Heinle.

Short, D. (1991, fall). *Integrating language and content instruction: Strategies and techniques.* Washington, DC: National Clearinghouse for Bilingual Education.

Short, D. (1998). Secondary newcomer programs: Helping recent immigrants prepare for school success. *ERIC Digest.* Online at http://www. cal.org/ericcll/digest/short001.html.

Short, D., & Echevarria, J. (1999). The sheltered instruction observation protocol: A tool for teacher-researcher collaboration and professional development. *ERIC Digest.* Online at http://www.cal.org/ericcll/digest/sheltered. html.

Shuit, D., & McConnell, P. (1992, January 6). Calculating the impact of California's immigrants. *Los Angeles Times,* pp. A1 & A19.

Shukoor, A. (1991). What does being bilingual mean to my family and me? *NABE Conference Program.*

Washington, DC: National Association for Bilingual Education.

Shuter, R. (1991). The Hmong of Laos: Orality, communication, and acculturation. In L. Samovar & R. Porter (Eds.), *Intercultural communication: A reader* (6th ed.). Belmont, CA: Wadsworth.

Siccone, F. (1995). *Celebrating diversity: Building self-esteem in today's multicultural classrooms.* Boston: Allyn and Bacon.

Siegel, B. (1993, March 28). Fighting words. *Los Angeles Times Magazine,* pp. 14–16, 18, 20, 44, 46, 48.

Sindell, P. (1988). Some discontinuities in the enculturation of Mistassini Cree children. In J. Wurzel (Ed.), *Toward multiculturalism.* Yarmouth, ME: Intercultural Press.

Singleton, J. (1973). Schooling: Coping with education in a modern society. In T. Weaver (Ed.), *To see ourselves: Anthropology and modern social issues.* Glenview, IL: Scott, Foresman.

Skinner, B. (1957). *Verbal behavior.* New York: Appleton, Century, Crofts.

Skutnabb-Kangas, T. (1981). *Bilingualism or not: The education of minorities* (L. Malmberg & D. Crane, Trans.). Clevedon, England: Multilingual Matters.

Skutnabb-Kangas, T. (1993, February 3). *Linguistic genocide and bilingual education.* Paper presented at the California Association for Bilingual Education, Anaheim, CA.

Skutnabb-Kangas, T. (2000). *Linguistic genocide in education—Or worldwide diversity and human rights?* Mahwah, NJ: Erlbaum.

Slater, J. (2000). *ELD standards.* Presentation, Linguistic Minority Research Institute Conference, Irvine, CA.

Sleeter, C. E. (1986). Learning disabilities: The social construction of a special education category. *Exceptional Children, 53* (1), 46–54.

Sloan, S. (1991). *The complete ESL/EFL cooperative and communicative activity book.* Lincolnwood, IL: National Textbook Company.

Smith, F. (1983). *Essays into literacy.* Portsmouth, NH: Heinemann.

Smith, S. L., Paige, R. M., & Steglitz, I. (1998). Theoretical foundations of intercultural training and applications to the teaching of culture. In D. L. Lange, C. A. Klee, R. M. Paige, & Y. A. Yershova (Eds.), *Culture as the core: Interdisciplinary perspectives on culture teaching and learning in the language curriculum* (pp. 53–91). Minneapolis: Center for Advanced Research on Language Acquisition, University of Minnesota.

Smith, T. E. C., Polloway, E. A., Patton, J. R., & Dowdy, C. A. (1995). *Teaching children with special needs in inclusive settings.* Boston: Allyn and Bacon.

Snow, C., & Hoefnagel-Hoehle, M. (1978). The critical period for language acquisition: Evidence from second language learning. *Child Development, 49,* 1114–1118.

Sobul, D. (1994). *Strategies to meet the goals of SDAIE.* Presentation, annual meeting, California Association for Bilingual Education, San Jose, CA.

Sonbuchner, G. M. (1991). *How to take advantage of your learning styles.* Syracuse, NY: New Readers Press.

Southern Poverty Law Center. (1999). *Youth at the edge.* Montgomery, AL: Author. Online at http://www.splcenter.

Spradley, J. (1972). Foundations of cultural knowledge. In J. Spradley (Ed.), *Culture and cognition.* San Francisco, CA: Chandler.

Stainback, W., & Stainback, S. (1984). A rationale for the merger of special and regular education. *Exceptional Children, 51* (2), 102–111.

Steele, R. (1990). Culture in the foreign language classroom. *Washington Center for Applied Linguistics, ERIC/CLL News Bulletin, 14* (1), 1, 4, 5, 12.

Stergis, R., & Perrin, J. (1997, March 15). Learning strategy instruction in the bilingual/ESL classroom. *NABE News,* pp. 25–28.

Suarez-Orozco, M. (1987). Towards a psychosocial understanding of Hispanic adaptation to American schooling. In H. Trueba (Ed.), *Success or failure? Learning and the language minority student.* Boston: Heinle and Heinle.

Suina, J. (1985)....And then I went to school. *New Mexico Journal of Reading, V* (2).

Sutman, F., Guzmán, A., & Schwartz, W. (1993). Teaching science effectively to limited English proficient students. *ERIC Digest.* Online at http://eric-web.tc.columbia.edu/digests/dig87.html.

Suzuki, B. (1989, November/December). Asian Americans as the "model minority." *Change, 21,* 12–19.

Tannen, D. (1997). *Discourse analysis.* Linguistic Society of America, "Fields of Linguistics." Online at http://www.lsadc.org/web2/fldcont.html.

Tarone, E. (1981). Some thoughts on the notion of communication strategy. *TESOL Quarterly, 15* (3), 285–295.

Teachers of English to Speakers of Other Languages. (1997). *ESL standards for pre-K–12 students.* Alexandria, VA: Author. Online at http://www.tesol.edu/assoc/kl2standards/it/01.ht ml.

Teachers of English to Speakers of Other Languages. (2001). *Scenarios for ESL standards-based assessment.* Alexandria, VA: Author

Terrell, T. (1981). The natural approach in bilingual education. In *Schooling and language minority students: A theoretical framework.* Los Angeles: Evaluation, Dissemination and Assessment Center, California State University, Los Angeles.

Tharp, R. (1989a). Culturally compatible education: A formula for designing effective classrooms. In H. Trueba, G. Spindler, & L. Spindler (Eds.), *What do anthropologists have to say about dropouts?* New York: Falmer Press.

Tharp, R. (1989b, February). Psychocultural variables and constants: Effects on teaching and learning in schools. *American Psychologist, 44* (2), 349–359.

Thomas, E., & Robinson, H. (1972). *Improving reading in every class: A source book for teachers.* Boston: Allyn and Bacon.

Thomas, W., & Collier, V. (1997). *School effectiveness for language minority students.* Alexandria, VA: National Clearinghouse for Bilingual Education. Online at http://www.ncbe.gwu/ncbepubs/resource/effectiveness/thomas-collier97.pdf.

Tikunoff, W., Ward, B., Romero, M., Lucas, T., Katz, A., Van Broekhuisen, L., & Castaneda, L. (1991, April). *Addressing the instructional needs of the limited English proficient student: Results of the exemplary SAIP descriptive study.* Symposium, annual meeting, American Educational Research Association, Chicago.

Tollefson, J. W. (1991). *Planning language, planning inequality.* London: Longman.

Tollefson, J. W. (Ed.). (1995). *Power and inequality in language education.* Cambridge: Cambridge University Press.

Tompkins, G. (1997). *Literacy for the 21st century: A balanced approach.* Upper Saddle River, NJ: Merrill.

Torbert, M., & Schneider, L. (1992). Using low organized games in multicultural physical education. In P. Richard-Amato & M. Snow (Eds.), *The multicultural classroom.* White Plains, NY: Longman.

Tough, J. (1977). *The development of meaning: Talking with some purpose with young children.* London: George Allen and Unwin.

Trueba, H. (1989). *Raising silent voices.* Boston: Heinle and Heinle.

Trueba, H., Cheng, L., & Ima, K. (1993). *Myth or reality: Adaptive strategies of Asian Americans in California.* Washington, DC: Falmer Press.

Tunmer, W., & Nesdale, A. (1985). Phonemic segmentation skill and beginning reading. *Journal of Educational Psychology, 77,* 417–427.

Umbreit, M. S. (1991). Mediation of youth conflict: A multi-system perspective. *Child and Adolescent Social Work, 8* (2), 141–153.

United States Census Bureau. (1995). *Statistical brief: Housing in metropolitan areas—Hispanic origin households.* Washington, DC: Author. Online at http://www.census.gov/apsd/www/statbrief/sb95_4.pdf.

United States Census Bureau (1999). *State and county quick facts.* Washington, DC: Author.

United States Commission on Civil Rights. (1978, August). *Social indicators of equality for minorities and women: Report of the U.S. Commission on Civil Rights.* Washington, DC: Author.

United States Department of Commerce. (1997). *Current population surveys, 1992 and 1995.* Online at http://nces.ed.gov/pubs2000.

United States Department of Commerce. (1999). *Outcomes of education.* Online at http://nces.ed.gov/pubs2000.

United States Department of Education. (1998). *Fall staff survey.* Online at http://nces.ed.gov/pubs 2000.

United States Department of Education. (2000). 1998 high school transcript study. *Digest of Education Statistics 1999.* Online at http://nces.ed.gov/pubs2000/digest99/d99tl41.html.

United States Department of Health, Education, and Welfare. (1970, May 25). *Memorandum to school districts with more than five percent national origin-minority group children.* Washington, DC: Author. Online at http://ed.gov/offices/OCR/ELL/may25.html.

United States Department of Labor. (1999). *College enrollment and work activity of 1998 high school graduates.* Online at http://nces.ed.gov/pubs 2000.

United States Department of State, Bureau of Consular Affairs. (2000). Visa *Bulletin, 8* (23). Washington, DC: Author. Online at http://travel.state.gov/visa_bulletin.html.

United States Immigration and Naturalization Service. (1999). *Annual report: Legal immigration, fiscal year 1998.* Washington, DC: author. Online at http://www.ins.usdoj.gov/graphics/publicaffairs/newsrels/98Legal.pdf.

United States Office for Civil Rights. (1999). *Programs for English language learners.* Washington, DC: Author. Online at http://www.ed.gov/offices/OCR/ELL/.

United States Office for Civil Rights. (1976). Office for Civil Rights guidelines: Task force findings specifying remedies available for eliminating past educational practices ruled unlawful under *Lau v. Nichols.* In J. Alatis & K. Twaddell (Eds.), *English as a second language in bilingual education.* Washington, DC: Teachers of English to Speakers of Other Languages.

United States Senate Committee on Health, Education, Labor, and Pensions. (2000). *Reauthorization of the Elementary and Secondary Education Acts. 2—"Educational Opportunities Act," Summary of Bill as Reported.* Washington, DC: Author. Online at http://www.senate.gov/~labor/legisl/S_2-ESEA/eseasuml/eseasum2/eseasum2.htm.

University of Texas at Austin. (1991, spring). Individuals with Disabilities Education Act challenges educators to improve the education of minority students with disabilities. *The Bilingual Special Education Perspective, 10,* 1–6.

U.S. English. (2000). *Making English the official language.* Washington, DC: Author. Online at http://www.us-english.org/inc/.

Valdés-Fallis, G. (1978). *Code switching and the classroom teacher.* Washington, DC: Center for Applied Linguistics.

Veeder, K., & Tramutt, J. (2000). Strengthening literacy in both languages. In N. Cloud, F. Genesee, & E. Hamayan (Eds.), *Dual language instruction.* Boston: Heinle and Heinle.

Viorst, J. (1981). *If I were in charge of the world and other worries.* New York: Atheneum.

Vygotsky, L. (1978). *Mind in society.* Cambridge, MA: Harvard University Press.

Waggoner, D. (Ed.). (1992). *Numbers and needs, 2* (5). Washington, DC: Author.

Wallach, G. P., & Miller, L. (1988). *Language intervention and academic success.* Boston: Little, Brown.

Walz, J. (1982). *Error correction techniques for the FL classroom.* Washington, DC: Center for Applied Linguistics.

Ward, A. W., & Murray-Ward, M. (1999). *Assessment in the classroom.* Belmont, CA: Wadsworth.

Warschauer, M., Shetzer, H., & Meloni, C. (2000). *Internet for English teaching.* Alexandria, VA: TESOL.

Watanabe, T., & Ramírez, M. (1999, December 25). Southland: A melting pot of diverse Yule rituals. *Los Angeles Times,* pp. B1 & B10.

Weaver, C. (1988). *Reading process and practice.* Portsmouth, NH: Heinemann.

Webster, M., & DeFilippo, J. (1999). *So to speak 1: Integrating listening, speaking, and pronunciation.* Boston: Houghton Mifflin.

Weed, K. (1989). *Oral tradition in a literate society.* Unpublished manuscript.

Weed, K. (1997). The language of art, the art of language. In D. Brinton & P. Master (Eds.), *New ways in content-based instruction.* Alexandria, VA: Teachers of English to Speakers of Other Languages (TESOL).

Weed, K., & Ford, M. (1999). Achieving literacy through multiple meaning systems. In E. Franklin (Ed.),. *Reading and writing in more than one language.* Alexandria, VA: Teachers of English to Speakers of Other Languages (TESOL).

Weed, K., & Sommer, D. (1990). Non- and limited-English speakers in every classroom: How can we help them? Proceedings of the 13th Annual Reading Conference, California State University, San Bernardino.

Weiler, J. (1998). Recent changes in school desegregation. *ERIC Digest. Clearinghouse on Urban Education.* Online at http://eric-web.tc. cohimbia.edu/digests/digl33.html.

Weinberg, M. (1990). *Racism in the United States: A comprehensive classified bibliography.* New York: Greenwood Press.

West, J. F., & Idol, L. (1990). Collaborative consultation in the education of mildly handicapped and at-risk students. *Remedial and Special Education, 11* (1), 22–31.

Westling, D. L., & Koorland, M. A. (1988). *The special educator's handbook.* Boston: Allyn and Bacon.

Whisler, N., & Williams, J. (1990). *Literature and cooperative learning.* Sacramento, CA: Literature Co-op.

Wiese, A. M., & García, E. (1998). The Bilingual Education Act: Language minority students and equal educational opportunity. *Bilingual Research Journal, 22* (1). Online at http://brj.asu.edu/v221/articles/indext.html.

Williams, J. D., & Snipper, G. C. (1990). *Literacy and bilingualism.* White Plains, NY: Longman.

Williams, M. (1981). Observations in Pittsburgh ghetto schools. *Anthropology and Education Quarterly, 12* (3), 211–220.

Wilson, W. (1984). The urban underclass. In L. Dunbar (Ed.), *Minority report.* New York: Pantheon Books.

Witte, K. (1991). The role of culture in health and disease. In L. Samovar & R. Porter (Eds.), *Intercultural communication: A reader* (6th ed.). Belmont, CA: Wadsworth.

Wittrock, M. (1978). The cognitive movement in instruction. *Educational Psychologist, 13,* 15–30.

Wolfram, W. (1991). *Dialects and American English.* Englewood Cliffs, NJ: Prentice-Hall.

Wollenberg, C. (1989). *The new immigrants and California's multiethnic heritage.* Available from New Faces of Liberty/SFSC, P.O. Box 5646, San Francisco, CA 94101.

Wong-Fillmore, L. (1980). Learning a second language: Chinese children in the American classroom. In J. Alatis (Ed.), *Georgetown University round table on languages and linguistics 1980: Current issues in bilingual education.* Washington, DC: Georgetown University Press.

Wong-Fillmore, L. (1985). When does teacher talk work as input? In S. Gass & C. Madden (Eds.), *Input for second language acquisition.* Cambridge, MA: Newbury House.

Wong-Fillmore, L. (with L. Meyer). (1990). The classroom as a social setting for language learning. *Celebrating Diversity Conference,* Oakland, CA.

Woodbury, A. (1997). *Endangered languages.* In Linguistic Society of America, "Fields of Linguistics." Online at http://www.lsadc.org/web2/fldcont.html.

Woolfolk, A. (1998). *Educational psychology* (7th ed.). Englewood Cliffs, NJ: Prentice-Hall.

Woolfolk, A., & Brooks, D. (1985). The influence of teachers' nonverbal behaviors on students' perceptions and performance. *Elementary School Journal, 85,* 514–528.

Worthen, B., & Spandel, V. (1991). Putting the standardized test debate in perspective. *Educational Leadership, 48* (5), 65–69.

Wray, M., & Newitz, A. (1997). *White trash: Race and class in America.* New York and London: Routledge.

Yao, E. (1988). Working effectively with Asian immigrant parents. *Phi Delta Kappan, 70* (3), 223–225.

Yep, L. (1975). *Dragonwings.* New York: Harper and Row.

Yopp, H. K. (1985). Phoneme segmentation ability: A prerequisite for phonics and sight word achievement in beginning reading? In J. Niles & R. Lalik (Eds.), *Issues in literacy: A research perspective* (pp. 330–336). Rochester, NY: National Reading Conference.

Yorio, C. (1980, November). The teacher's attitude toward the student's output in the second language classroom. *CATESOL Occasional Papers,* California Association of Teachers of English to Speakers of Other Languages, pp. 1–8.

Young, M., & Helvie, S. (1996). Parent power: A positive link to school success. *Journal of Educational Issues of Language Minority Students, 16.* Online at http://www.ncbe.gwu.edu/miscpubs/jeilms/vol16/jeilmsl611.htm.

Zehler, A., Hopstock, P., Fleischman, H., & Greniuk, C. (1994). *An examination of assessment of limited English proficient students.* Arlington, VA: Special Issues Analysis Center. Online at http://www.ncbe.gwu.edu/miscpubs/siac/lepasses.htm.

Zelman, N. (1996). *Conversation inspirations: Over 2000 conversation topics.* Battleboro, VT: Pro Lingua Associates.

AUTHOR INDEX

SUBJECT INDEX